Trust Not

WILLIAM G. HANEKE
JANE C. WALKER

Copyright © 2010 William G. Haneke & Jane C. Walker

All rights reserved.

ISBN: 1452810311

ISBN-13: 9781452810317

Library of Congress Control Number: 2010905614

"There are times when a memoir is so honest and straightforward in depicting a traumatic event that it very subtly becomes a heartwarming epic of astonishing survival and stoicism. *Trust Not* is that book. With amazing detail...of extremely dangerous situations that are often stranger than fiction, William G. Haneke (with the help of co-author Jane C. Walker), takes the reader along the coast of the South China Sea on a military tour during the Vietnam War. Haneke took his tour in 1968 as a senior advisor of the Hoa Da District for the South Vietnamese Army.

Trust Not paints a vivid picture of Vietnamese life in 1968 and is historically important for its detailed account of the lesser-understood fringe areas of the conflict involving America, the hampering politics both within the Army and from Washington, and for the revolutionary medical procedures used to save Haneke's life. The book is also informative of the role of a military advisor and the ways in which the military might better serve their needs. As bold as Solzhenitsyn's history of the Gulag in depicting human hardship, the book provides new understanding of the extreme challenges facing soldiers during the Vietnam War.

...*Trust Not* has something for everyone."

Five Stars (out of Five)
– ForeWord Clarion Review

Dedication

This book is dedicated to the doctors, nurses, and hospital staff, who worked endlessly on my survival and rehabilitation from the combat wounds experienced in the Vietnam War.

Thank you, *Cpt. William G. Haneke*

TABLE OF CONTENTS

Foreword ix

1   The Purple Road 1
2   Training of an Officer 13
3   Vietnam 1968 21
4   Major Bennett 39
5   MAT Team 55
6   Hoa Da District Compound 75
7   Cleaning House 89
8   Major Xuan 107
9   Survival of a New Advisor 127
10   The Medics 147
11   Major Dramis 157
12   Learning the Supply Game 165
13   Realities of Combat 181
14   Rebuild 197
15   The Cambodians 209
16   Chess Game of Life 219
17   Fighting Victor Charlie 233
18   Requisition 241
19   The Police Chief 249
20   The Pale Montagnard Woman 257

21	Life's Cruel Detour	267
22	24th Evacuation Hospital	279
23	Visitors	293
24	The Purple Heart	303
25	Japan	313
26	The Scheme	333
27	Homecoming	347
28	Walter Wonderful	363
29	My Purple Moment	383

Epilogue ... 399

Foreword
A Common Bond
By: Cathie Henderson Solomonson

For You, Bill

The reason I stayed away for all those years disappeared when I found you, Bill Haneke, standing in front of the sign-up sheet to help lobby for the Vietnam Women's Memorial.

There you were, resting only slightly on the Canadian crutches, still an imposing hulk of a frame. I heard the vibrant voice first, then I saw the easy smile. Then I saw the cranial defect, the missing digits, the artificial eye.

We played fifty questions—the Vietnam service match game. When were you there? '68…a match. Where were you stationed…? 24th Evac Hosp…a match. Where were you a patient…? 24th Evac…Another match! What ward…? Neurosurgery. What injury…? Multiple wounds. Head… the defining blow… another match.

Then you said the magic word: "Sister… My sister came to visit me," you said. And then I saw her sitting by your bed. Holding your hand, the way I wished I could sit with all of them, but there were dressings to change, IVs to start, trach to suction, shots and baths to give, blood to hang, Stryker frames to turn, burns to clean, fevers to lessen, tube feedings to coax, bags to empty, notes to chart, eyes to close.

There was only ever one sister, an Army recreational services-type stationed in Japan. She hopped a flight as soon as she heard you were hurt. We worried how she would handle sharing our austere living quarters, with the constant visits from medevac choppers and occasional visits by large creeping rats, and peeping Toms.

"My sister," you said… and then, of course I could see you there too, in the bed closest to the nursing station, barely an inch of you showing through all those soaked dressings… wanting to make it so bad… holding so tight to your sister's hand. You told me… still in the vibrant voice… still with the easy smile…

you had seventeen operations since you returned… you had fathered four children you were so proud of… your wife for years had found specks of grit and water buffalo hair in the bed linen when it had finally worked its way out of your skin.

You said you had searched for twenty years for any one of us that had taken care of you…and I had the luck and the honor of being the first one… you asked if you could hug me… and what a great crushing embrace it was… me sobbing softly the whole while… wishing I could line up all of them to feel it too…Kathy, Ginny, Sandy, Sue, Mary Lou, Patty, Nancy, Kay, Maria, and all the corpsmen and docs, too.

How could you know how terrified I had been that the first patient to find me would tell me how much he hated me for not letting him die when he begged me to… When he told me the first time I resuscitated him that he only wanted to live long enough to hear whether his wife had a baby girl or a baby boy. It was close to Christmas Eve Day, the Red Cross Hospital Service worker… Sally Sunshine we called her… gave him the news… then he became so wild… shaking his swollen neck and head back and forth because that was all he could move… each time I covered his trach he would say… Don't let me live. I don't want to go back home like this…

How could I explain… It wasn't just about the oath… It was about the patient I had taken care of at Fort Sam while I was waiting for orders to Nam. He was a Korean War Vet… had been badly wounded many years before, a head injury. Took him eight years to learn to read again… got around San Antonio on an adapted bike and some drunken asshole drove up on the sidewalk and hit him. He was on my ward with one arm and one leg in traction… and he played the harmonica with his free hand… tunes that make my heart dance… and my legs quiver. He was amazing. I thought at the time… I bet the army nurse in the field hospital taking care of him in Korea would have never known that this beautiful spirit of a man in front of me now was the same one lying barely conscious in front of her then… How could I explain all that to the desperate paraplegic in front of me… it was impossible to know what lay ahead. But still I panicked at the thought that he would find me... and possibly indict me for all my piety in consigning him to a life he considered to be a living hell... Accuse me of turning a deaf ear to his most fervent plea. And he may still... But now I know I can face him... because I am more secure with my memory of Bill's thunderous enthusiasm and his enduring sense of humor.

Once I ran into him near the Wall. He was using his wheelchair that day and joked, "Cath, if you stick with me... I can take you places no man has ever taken you before." When I fell for the bait with, "Whatever do you mean?" he said... "I can get us seating in the handicapped area up close to the Wall!" Then we passed by the panel where his name would have been if he had not survived to become the joyous man he is. I can face any Vet now.

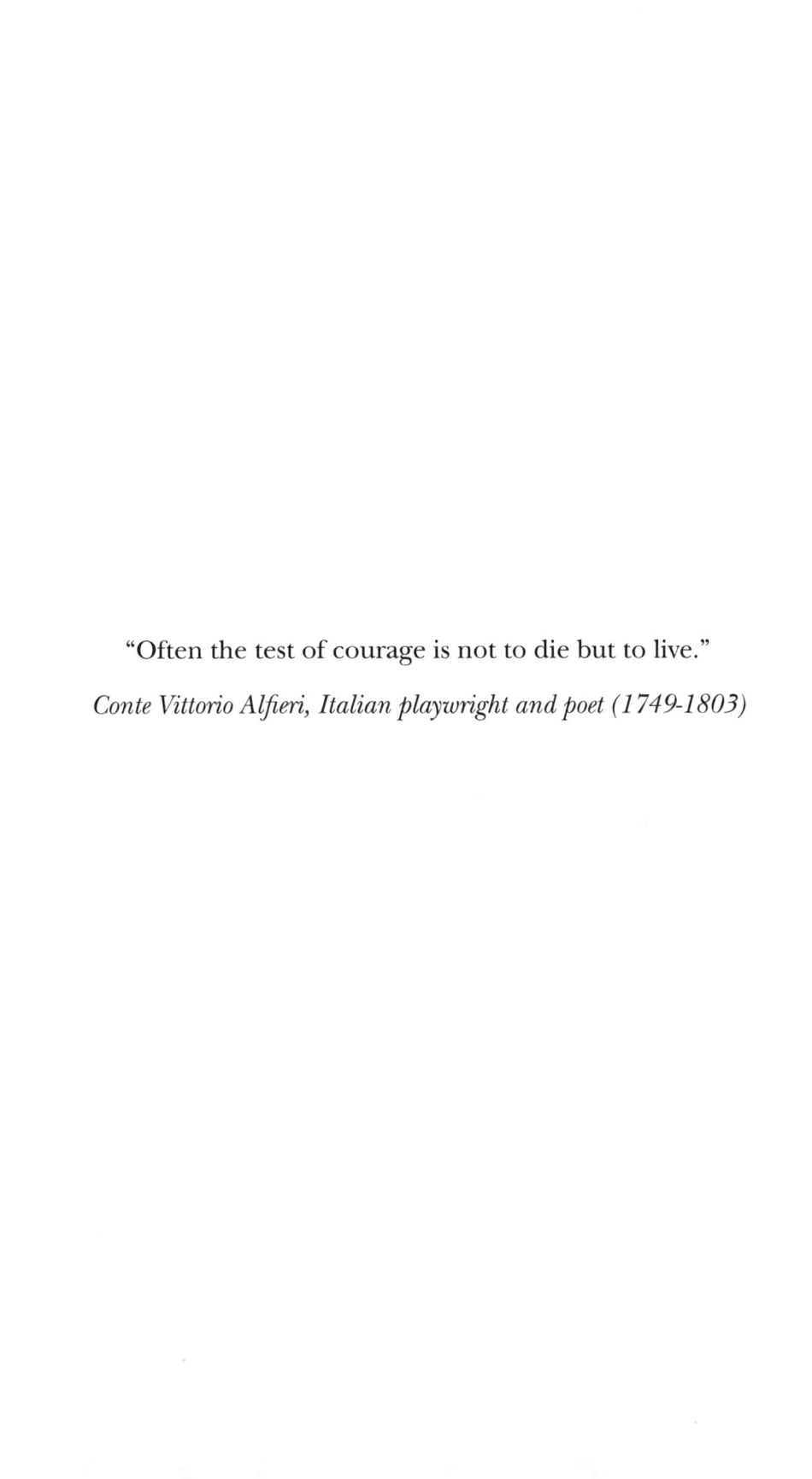

"Often the test of courage is not to die but to live."

Conte Vittorio Alfieri, Italian playwright and poet (1749-1803)

CHAPTER 1
The Purple Road

Contend, O Lord, with those who contend with me; fight against those who fight against me. Take up shield and buckler; arise and come to my aid. Brandish spear and javelin against those who pursue me. Say to my soul, "I am your salvation." May those who seek my life be disgraced and put to shame; may those who plot my ruin be turned back in dismay. May they be like chaff before the wind, with the angel of the Lord pursuing them since they hid their net for me without cause and without cause dug a pit for me, may ruin overtake them by surprise—may the net they hid entangle them, may they fall into the pit, to their ruin. Then my soul will rejoice in the Lord and delight in his salvation.

Psalm 35: 1-10

The oppressive heat and humidity of the Vietnamese day had ebbed just a bit from 125 degrees when I, Captain William G. Haneke, and thirteen other American advisors prepared our evening meal. The date was October 14, 1968. While I swatted off the numerous and omnipresent flies that had ascended on my food, someone poked me from behind. Footsteps scurried off quickly. I hollered, in French, "I'm your real friend and not an evil spirit." Giggles came from behind a twenty-foot-tall cacti on a nearby sand dune. We were an oddity to the Vietnamese children, being six feet tall or more, blond, blue-eyed men, and one African American. The children's petite parents, less than five-feet-six inches, had warned them that the Americans were evil spirits and to stay away from us.

I was not an evil spirit, as depicted in Vietnamese superstitions. I was an American advisor in Vietnam's civil war between the North and the South. I had established, organized, and operated a new advisory team that was part of the American Military Assistance Command Vietnam Advisory Team 37—or MACV 37. MACV was the original command organization the Americans set up when they first started providing assistance to the Vietnamese following the end of World War II. My MACV advisor's mission was to advise and train the local South Vietnamese district chief and his troops on defense, civic action, and medical support for the Hoa Da District people in Binh Thuan Province. We also had a secret mission: to hunt and eliminate specific Vietcong or South Vietnamese Communist political cadres and to set up and maintain a network of agents, which would provide intelligence information about the rival Vietcong. In other words, I was a military advisor, missionary, spy, and hit man.

The common South Vietnamese people did not understand the United States' mission. At the conclusion of the Indo-China War in 1954, the country was split into North Vietnam and South Vietnam. When the division of the countries occurred, the forces going north stripped the machinery and resources out of the factories in the south. What the North Vietnamese failed to realize was the lack of sufficient arable land to produce the food necessary to feed the North Vietnamese people. Instead of trading with South Vietnam, the North Vietnamese invaded them during harvest time and claimed the food, killing the South Vietnamese in the process. This scare tactic was used in the hope of reuniting North and South Vietnam into one nation under Communist domination.

Not wanting to unite, the South Vietnamese government invoked their rights under the Southeast Asian Treaty Organization (SEATO) and asked the signatory United States to send advisors, equipment, and supplies to help them resist North Vietnamese aggression. When American military forces arrived in 1959 to establish an advisory effort, their presence furthered Vietnam's resentment and suspicion of any round-eyed Westerners. The Vietnamese remembered the round-eyed French, who had ruled them for eighty years prior to 1954. The French had taken advantage of the Vietnamese people and their resources. As an officer of the United States Army, I was joining the ranks of those suspicious round-eyes.

I ignored the children and continued to prepare my meal. We advisors used Vietnamese charcoal to cook some tiny, nondescript fish, bamboo shoots, and leftover rice on a primitive grill fashioned from two metal leg splints propped up on five bricks. The final product was doused with *nuoc mam*, a Vietnamese fish sauce. If you could get past the overpowering odor of fermented fish, it didn't taste bad at all.

While polishing off the meal with a Vietnamese fibrous, seedy watermelon and a hunk of local French bread infested with baked black mites (protein, I figured), we discussed the current area intelligence report. Our intelligence officer, Second Lieutenant Carl Zender, informed us that his most reliable intelligence sources had reported increased activity and movement of several larger Main Force Vietcong units into our region. Main Force Vietcong were members of a regular communist military unit serving in South Vietnam.

Increased activity was a typical pattern before the Vietcong launched a major attack against a pre-planned target. I asked Zender if any of his sources had information on potential target sites. He replied that indications pointed to Phan Ri Cua, a town on the South China Sea with a population of about thirty-five thousand people, or the village of Phan Ri Than, which was next to our compound. Hearing this information, I suggested that our advisory team prepare for action.

First Lieutenant Ronald Riley took Master Sergeant Billy Joe Bolling and Sergeant Wesley Amos down to Phan Ri Cua to coordinate the defenses of the Regular Vietnamese Regional Forces company that was spread thinly around the northern and western perimeter of that town. They were to make sure that the platoons guarding the northern side of the perimeter had adequate defensive coverage for the two trails that came into the town from a massive desert sand dune, which spread twenty-eight kilometers from the mountainous jungle. The eastern and southern sides of Phan Ri Cua were of no major concern since, the South China Sea and a fast-flowing river bordered them, respectively.

On his way back to our compound, the slender, reserved Riley needed to check on the defensive perimeter around Phan Ri Cua as well as the three bridges he would be crossing. Like always, strong radio contact with the defending units was essential in case any enemy action developed.

Since the memories were still fresh of our last major defeat, in mid-September, during which a superior Main Force Vietcong unit overran our compound, I decided to take the added precaution of extra scrutiny of our compound internal defenses. Specialist Fourth Class Douglas Thornton coordinated a net of radio contacts while Sergeant Major Raymond Cuthbert, South Vietnamese Major Xuan, and his staff accompanied me around the outside perimeter of the compound. We wanted to make sure that our forces and compound defensive weapons were set up adequately to detect and repel any probes or attacks the Vietcong might try to launch against us during the coming night.

As we walked, Xuan and I noticed that a number of the footlong, rectangular-shaped claymore mines had been removed from their previous locations. These mines allowed a blast field of 140 degrees outward and were essential for our protection. I then recalled that we had removed the mines two days before for another defensive weapons application. We asked Cuthbert, our only African-American advisor, to find and transfer these mines and place them along critical points around the compound walls. He also replaced several trip flares that an enemy probe had set off the night before.

Xuan directed his assistant, First Lieutenant Trung Con, to replenish the grenade and machine gun ammunition supply in the perimeter bunkers, thus finalizing our defense. Satisfied with our precautions, we headed toward our headquarters bunker, where we met with our advisory team commander, Major George Dramis.

Prior to Vietnam, Dramis had eighteen years of military experience in field artillery and civic affairs. Knowing little about combat operations, communications, demolitions, and first aid, Dramis routinely chose me to direct and supervise the advisory team combat operations, defenses, patrols, supply, and ambushes. Dramis, in turn, concentrated on the civic action activities. When Riley and his party returned to the compound just after dark, we shared and compared information with Dramis. We heard incoming radio traffic from several defensive sites during our meeting. Annoyed, Dramis advised Xuan to have his men stop talking on the radio unless they had enemy contact or an emergency. Strict radio silence was ordered.

Around 9:45 P.M., we received a panicked radio message from the Vietnamese company commander, First Lieutenant Ny Tan. He was talking so fast that no one could understand him until Xuan finally calmed him enough to comprehend his distress. On the large sand dune north of Phan Ri Cua, there was enemy movement and sporadic small arms fire aimed toward the town. Xuan requested that I handle this situation for his company commander. Knowing that the Vietcong were trying to probe our defenses to locate our weakest point, I ordered the South Vietnamese troops to cease fire. By not returning the Vietcong's fire, the company would deny the enemy any advantage of knowing their position. I encouraged Tan to keep the Vietcong out of town at all costs and update us on any changes.

A very bad feeling churned in my stomach. I decided to put in the dreaded call for air support through the advisor radio to Phan Thiet Province Headquarters. During the Vietnam War, there were differences between a regular U.S. military unit and an advisory unit. United States military troops rode to the area of operations and had artillery, air, and medical evacuation support readily available. Advisory units lived and worked out of base compounds. They walked to their area of operation and back to the compound. Rarely did the advisory units receive radio-requested artillery, air, or medical evacuation support. Requests were usually granted when the military troops were in need and the advisory unit was in extreme danger. Knowing this and assuming the norm—that it would take an hour to go through five levels of command to get air support approval—I over-exaggerated the intensity of the attack.

Experience in this region had shown me that Vietcong attacks started off slow and rapidly built in strength and intensity. To my amazement, the Phan Thiet Province duty officer informed me that they had released an Air Force AC-47, the old reliable DC-3 model invented in 1935, and it was returning to its base in Phan Rang, about sixty kilometers north of our location. I asked for the plane's call sign and radio frequency. The duty officer said that he would have to change frequencies and talk to the pilot before responding to my requests.

The ensuing five minutes of waiting seemed like eternity. Meanwhile, we received more radio calls from Tan about increased levels of rifle fire and Vietcong attempts to enter two of the approaches to Phan Ri Cua. Finally, when the duty officer came back on our radio, he gave me approval to use the plane, along with the radio frequency and call sign. I thanked him and then switched frequencies to talk to the pilot.

The camouflaged, black-painted AC-47 was nicknamed "Spooky," because it flew only at night, like a ghost, and caused pandemonium from the sky, frightening the superstitious Vietcong. When I called Spooky 62, I told him who I was and my location. The pilot replied that he was currently three kilometers off the coast of Phan Ri Cua.

I told him to fly one circle over the town, kicking out one or more of his parachute flares. These flares burned with an intensity of one million candles, lighting the sky up bright as day. I then stated that, on the plane's second pass, the pilot should fire with one of his 7.62mm mini-guns. He rogered my request and began his pass. I quickly grabbed the Vietnamese radio and informed Tan about what was going on with air support. The still-frantic Tan warned me that the Vietcong were coming in waves to try to gain entry to the town and that the points hit the hardest were the trails we had reinforced a few hours earlier. I handed that radio over to Riley while I returned to the advisor radio to talk to the pilot.

"Jesus Christ! Look at all those black pajamas down there! It looks like someone stuck a stick in a giant ant hill and the angry ants are running all over the place!" the pilot cried out.

The Vietcong force was easy to observe against the desert sand after the two bright flares. A reinforced regiment of three to five thousand soldiers had run all over the sand dunes trying to launch a massive attack just north of town. I realized that our small company would not stand a chance against this larger and better-trained enemy force. I asked the pilot how close he could fire near the houses, and he replied, "Five feet if we fire from above the houses, but that would scare the hell out of the villagers." I assured him better scared than killed or captured, so I ordered him to fire five feet from the houses and work outward toward the largest concentration of the Vietcong forces.

I took the radios outside the bunker, where I heard the ripping sound of the mini-guns and saw the air strike in progress about ten kilometers from our compound. The first three-gun fire volley from the mini-guns looked like a red waterfall coming from the sky. Every tenth bullet had a red-tipped tracer, which accounted for their color. These mini-gun bursts resulted in one bullet striking in every square foot of a hundred-meter square.

The pilot informed me that his firing had slowed the attack as well as killing a large number of Vietcong. He put in a call to his base in Phan Rang to have another AC-47 plane readied to relieve him, as his ammunition supply and fuel were low. I told him to limit his firing passes and use one mini-gun at a time to lengthen his effective time. The pilot agreed and continued to make firing passes after kicking out additional flares.

Riley came over to me and stated that he no longer had radio contact with Tan in Phan Ri Cua. I told him to keep trying.

TRUST *NOT*

It is vitally important to stay in contact when an air strike is in progress. By this time, a second wave of attack had developed. The noise bellowed as rifle and automatic weapon fire punctuated the exploding sounds of mortar rounds and hand grenades. I followed the red and orange tracer rounds coming from the South Vietnamese and the much larger volume of green and purple tracers from the Vietcong.

I ordered Riley to gather up a supply of ammunition and grenades for the company and take Bolling and Amos with him. They were to "drive like hell to Phan Ri Cua to try to reestablish contact with Tan; use your radio to stay in contact; and by all means, keep the Vietcong out of town." To prevent friendly fire, Xuan informed the guards on the three bridges that Riley would be crossing in a jeep.

I received word from the pilot of Spooky 62 that he was out of ammunition but expected to have his relief plane, Spooky 60, on site at any minute. I asked him to brief his replacement on the battlefield situation and drop flares to illuminate the area for him. Just then I received contact on the advisory radio net from the Phan Thiet Province operations officer. He wanted detailed specifics on the battle. I explained that we were under heavy attack from a Vietcong Main Force regiment, and urged him to keep the radio net free. I would contact him when the battle ended and/or we needed medical evacuation assistance. He took the hint and stopped tying up the radio net.

Red tracers fell from the sky, indicating that Spooky 60 had arrived and was actively engaged with the Vietcong. I called and welcomed Spooky 60 and asked if Spooky 62 was still in radio contact for a situation report. Fortunately he was still there and proceeded with his report. He noted that many Vietcong had entered the town and taken refuge inside a number of the houses and buildings while our South Vietnamese troops withdrew to more secure locations. There appeared to be a large number of Vietcong bodies clustered in various locations between the first sand dune and the two contested entrances into the town. Beyond the light from the flares, he could faintly see a mass of

Vietcong assembling along the second sand dune to begin another attack. Before heading back to his base, he requested a third AC-47 be scrambled.

The pilot for Spooky 60 asked if we wanted him to shoot into and around the closely packed houses where the Vietcong had taken refuge. I replied that this was a big negative since we did not want to cause any unnecessary civilian casualties. He complied and continued to illuminate the area and fire upon the Vietcong in the desert sand at the edge of town.

Shortly thereafter, I received a radio call from Riley telling me that he had arrived in Phan Ri Cua. They had left their jeep in the middle of town and were running in the direction of the enemy action, trying to find Tan and his troops. He mentioned that the houses were all closed up tight and no one appeared to be moving about.

Fifteen more minutes passed before Riley called in with good news. He had found Tan. As the pilot had reported, Tan's troops had been forced to withdraw when the Vietcong penetrated the town. Their radio had been knocked out after taking hits from Vietcong bullets. Despite the heavy fire, only three of his men received minor flesh wounds, which Bolling treated. Riley and Amos had distributed a new supply of ammunition to the troops and had remained with the Vietnamese company to give them advice and support.

Spooky 63 arrived on station within a half hour and aided Spooky 60 in hosing down the appointed areas in the sand dunes north and west of town. Spooky 60 reported that this was like shooting ducks in a gallery since they caught the majority of the Vietcong regiment in the open desert with no place to hide. He noted that many of the enemy were running southwest trying to get out of the killing zone with stilled bodies lying all over the dunes.

Both planes remained on station for another hour and a half firing at the newly discovered Vietcong targets until their ammunition and fuel supplies ran low. Spooky 60 told me that their replacement had been diverted to support an American military unit that was experiencing a heavy attack elsewhere in our II Corps area. However, he assured me that he'd do his best to get another plane dispatched soon since we were still under an extreme attack. At 3:00 A.M., the departure of both planes effectively ended our period of illumination.

For two hours, sporadic rifle fire came from the enemy. Riley reported hearing all kinds of movement and highly agitated yelling from the Vietnamese, but Tan insisted that the noise came from the Vietcong. Around 5:00 A.M., radio contact came in from our old friend, Spooky 60, who had refueled and rearmed so that he could return to assist us. He stated that two "jet jockeys" (pilots) flying F-100 Super Sabers would be joining him.

After Spooky 60 kicked out his first flare, he remarked that the Vietcong had cleared out the remaining bodies that had littered the desert. A few Vietcong limped slowly across the desert toward the mountains. They made the fatal mistake of firing at Spooky 60. He, in turn, fired a few bursts at them, permanently ending their journey.

Dawn was breaking when the F-100 Super Sabers arrived on the scene carrying a load of 250-pound bombs. Spooky 60 had remained around Phan Ri Cua, occasionally shooting at newly discovered Vietcong who were trying to escape to their mountain base camp. One jet jockey asked me who had put the new road in overnight between the Phan Ri Cua sand dunes to the base of the mountains.

I asked, "What road?" He told me to go to the edge of town and I would see it. I jumped into my jeep and headed to Phan Ri Cua.

The sun was up when I arrived at the northern edge of town. Exhausted, I weakly trudged up to the top of the sand dune and peered down. To my amazement, a hundred-and-fifty-foot-wide purple-colored road ran from inside the edge of town across the desert to the mountains. I walked toward it for a closer examination. The purple was dried blood from the Vietcong casualties that our air strikes had inflicted. From a distance I heard the deep boom from the jet jockey's bombs exploding on Vietcong targets near the mountains.

Later intelligence reports stated that our battle had inflicted at least 4,500 Vietcong casualties, including the Women's Action Company, which had led the September attack on our compound. The enemy regiment no longer existed. Over five hundred Vietnamese townspeople had been kidnapped to help the Vietcong carry off their dead and wounded. It was usual Vietcong practice of not leaving behind any of their casualties so as to mislead their enemy about the manpower losses. The noisy movement and agitated yelling were probably from the kidnapped Vietnamese, as Riley had thought. The South Vietnamese company had suffered only twelve minor casualties and no one was killed in action. We had saved Phan Ri Cua from enemy occupation and devastation.

Five days later, I walked along Highway 1, where I discovered several crudely printed leaflets stuck on buildings and on two roadblocks that had appeared overnight. On these leaflets appeared a recent picture of me for which I had unknowingly posed. The leaflet was a "wanted dead or alive poster" that offered $20,000 reward. Apparently the Vietcong had figured out that Captain William Haneke had controlled the air strikes. I was now a marked man living on borrowed time.

CHAPTER 2
Training of an Officer

My military life began at birth on April 27, 1942, at Scott Air Force Base, Belleville, Illinois, where my father, General William C. Haneke, was stationed along with my mother, Marion Guernsey Haneke. I was the middle child between two sisters, Carolyn and Margaret. My family left Scott Air Force Base while I was an infant. My father attended army finance school at Duke University, which secured him a U.S. Army finance job that carried him to all parts of the United States.

When the World War II armistice was signed in 1945, my father was transferred to Tokyo as a Far East Air Force Command finance officer. There he consulted with General Douglas MacArthur and his staff on strengthening the Japanese currency and rebuilding their economy. The move to Japan exposed me to a different culture and language. I spoke and understood the Japanese language quickly, which frightened my mother. She was afraid that my Japanese was better than my English and forbade me to speak it when my family returned to the United States in 1947. My father attended Harvard Business School, where he earned his master's degree in business administration. This launched a series of moves and promotions throughout my youth. Sometimes my family was apart while my father served his country.

2nd Lt. Margaret (sister), Major General William C. Haneke (father), Marion (mother), 2nd Lt. William G. Haneke

From 1952-54, my mother, sisters, and I lived in Carlisle, Pennsylvania, while my father served in Tageu, Korea, as comptroller for the Korean Communications Zone during the Korean War. He played a major role in stabilizing and improving the Korean currency and economy. Major General Haneke's successful military career resulted in his appointment as the U.S. Army chief of the Finance Corps, a position he held from 1963 until his retirement on December 1, 1967.

In 1960, after graduating from Hampton High School in Hampton, Virginia, I attended Sullivan's Preparatory School in Washington, DC, to provide me with intensive tutoring in mathematics. It also gave me the opportunity to walk the halls of Congress to find and qualify for an appointment to the United States Military Academy in West Point, New York, from which my father had graduated in 1936. Hard work helped me to pass the academy's vigorous entrance exam in 1961, and the Honorable Jackson Betts from the Ohio Eighth District in the U.S. House of Representatives appointed me to West Point, as the U.S. Military

Training of an Officer

Academy is commonly called. That same year my father was promoted to brigadier general, and he was assigned as commander of the finance center and post at Fort Benjamin Harrison in Indianapolis, Indiana.

Being raised around the military had instilled patriotism in me. However, my first exposure to West Point injected a deeper pride, knowing that the academy and the leaders it produced influenced United States history. Near the end of my freshman, or plebe, year in 1962, I had the honor of attending the Thayer Award Ceremony where General Douglas MacArthur received the award and gave what turned out to be a landmark speech that is often quoted.

"Duty, honor, country" is West Point's motto, and his speech used this as the foundation of his remarks. MacArthur stated that, "Duty, honor, country are the three hallowed words reverently dictate what you ought to be, what you can be, and what you will be. They are the rallying points to build courage when courage seems to fail, to regain faith when there seems to be little cause for faith, to create hope when hope becomes forlorn." He spoke without notes, yet wove a vivid picture through his eloquence. The assembled masses of army generals, officers, enlisted men, and West Point's corps of cadets left teary-eyed. Two years later, General MacArthur passed away. My cadet battalion had the honor of escorting this "old soldier" to New York City's Grand Central Terminal for a journey to MacArthur's final resting place in Norfolk, Virginia.

My first year at West Point, I received new cadet basic training, or "Beast Barracks," which referred to the harsh treatment the upperclassmen inflicted on plebes to prepare the cadets for the harsh realities of military life and war. There was little talk of Vietnam or Southeast Asia. Our main concern was the Cold War. When the Soviet Union was caught sending large missiles to Cuba, President John

West Point cadet William G. Haneke

15

F. Kennedy and Secretary of Defense Robert McNamara ordered all U.S. military forces on alert, including West Point cadets. All cadets were given yellow fever, cholera, and other inoculations. We were made aware that this incident could turn into World War III, between the United States and the Soviet Union. Then, on November 22, 1963, President Kennedy was assassinated, putting the U.S. military on highest alert again. There were strong suspicions that the Soviets were behind the assassination.

By early 1964, the United States shifted their military interest from the Cold War to the wars being fought in Vietnam and Southeast Asia. West Point saw an increased number of highly combat-decorated officers reporting to the Tactical Department. These men had recently served as advisors or unit commanders in Vietnam, Cambodia, and Laos. Some wore their designated headgear, the Green Beret, which was reserved for U.S. Army Special Forces. These advisors taught the cadets concepts of insurgencies, ambushes, infiltrations, guerilla warfare, and civil advisory efforts. West Point's thinking and training emphasis had changed from memorizing and following leadership/tactical principles to humanistic principles. These principles served as situational guidelines to shaping, analyzing, and selecting the appropriate course of action. We cadets respected the advisors' teaching and advice, since they had served and survived tough combat assignments.

West Point was not the only thing changing—civilians were too. The attitude of civilians toward the military and cadets from 1961 through 1964 was one of acceptance and support. It was not unusual to be in New York City in cadet uniform and have strangers buy us a drink or pay for our meal. By 1965, hippies and war protestors yelled and hurled rotten fruit, eggs, and vegetables at us. The West Point staff advised cadets to wear civilian clothes when traveling outside of West Point. Unfortunately, the clothes were not enough to blend in, considering our haircuts. Thus we were eventually given permission to buy and wear custom-made long wigs to disguise ourselves from further harassment, if we so chose. I never did.

Spring of 1965 also brought West Point graduate casualties returning from Southeast Asia, primarily Vietnam. We averaged several burials per month at West Point Cemetery. Cadets from their former companies were asked to serve as pallbearers or honor guard. These deaths instilled in us an understanding of the high cost of war. Despite these negatives—civilian resistance and casualties—I was proud to be serving in the U.S. Army.

Academics at West Point were a challenge, given its engineering-based curriculum. One professor, who the cadets not so affectionately called "Baron Von Schilling," failed 48 of the 579 seniors, which required us to spend "June Week" studying for a re-exam. My father had had enough of this nonsense and went to see the dean of the academic department, General Jannarone, who happened to have been a plebe in my father's West Point company. He reminded General Jannarone that the class of 1966 had all successfully completed their military and academic training. These men were fully qualified to be commissioned and serve as U.S. Army officers. My father reminded the dean that our military was fully involved in both a war in Southeast Asia and the Cold War, and they badly needed well-trained officers to command our operational forces.

The test was modified. On June 8, 1966, I graduated from the United States Military Academy and was commissioned a second lieutenant in the U.S. Army Infantry branch, my father, Major General Haneke, who was then chief of Finance and Accounting of the U.S. Army, having given me the oath.

My first military assignment began as a platoon leader with the Ninth Infantry Division at Fort Riley, Kansas. There I trained soldiers to go to the delta area of South Vietnam. I was soon transferred to attend Army Ranger School at Fort Benning, Georgia, for an intense nine-week training program on small unit organization, planning, tactics, land navigation, reconnaissance, patrolling, resupply, casualty evacuation, and survival.

Several weeks into Army Ranger training, I was on night patrol and slid down a steep embankment into a ravine. I sustained torn ligaments and cartilage to my right knee, which required surgery and a cast. Twelve hours after surgery, I experienced numbness, swelling, and black discoloration, which I attributed to the cast. The resident surgical doctors appeared unconcerned, but one night nurse recognized the urgency of the situation. I conned the nervous nurse into cutting off my cast. I assured her that I would tell the doctors that I had acted on my own. She agreed. The next morning the surprised and angered doctors reluctantly admitted that the cast had needed to be removed.

Despite an injured knee, my marriage to Mary Dolores Keegan was held in Scarsdale, New York, on December 3, 1966. The doctors would not allow me to deploy to Vietnam, so instead I was assigned to the Cold War. In late February 1967, I reported into the 1st Battalion, 54th Infantry Regiment for a tour with the 4th Armored Division in Bamberg, Germany.

The Cold War was an active one. Germany was the first place I was ever shot at by what I believe was a Russian sniper. During this year-long tour, I served in several positions with two infantry companies, a cavalry troop, and finally as a member of the Third Brigade staff. This firsthand experience taught me the differences and responsibilities between the activities of a unit with an operational mission as compared to one with a training mission.

Bamberg was only twenty kilometers from the East German border, where the Communist Soviet Union was reported to have seventy army divisions. Our unit's state of readiness was always on high alert. These alerts required us to set up defensive perimeters outside our armored personnel carriers and periodically pull guard duty on the very sensitive local special weapons ammunition dump, which probably held nuclear warheads. My company received a superior rating on our readiness and reaction during this assignment.

Several months later our new commander, who had a reputation for disliking West Pointers, put me on "special assignment" to a cavalry troop at Camp Gates. I found the troops at Camp Gates to be poorly organized and poorly supervised. I called everyone together and explained the importance of our operational mission, defining how I expected their duties to be carried out. Any infractions would be met with punishment under the Articles of UCMJ (Uniform Code of Military Justice—the "Bible" of military law). The first couple days passed with everyone working well to perform their assigned duties and no incidents or conduct problems were noted.

When Saturday night arrived, however, several non-commissioned officers and a master sergeant could not be found in the camp. One soldier confessed that they had climbed over the south camp wall and gone to Nuremberg to have some fun. I assigned two men to accompany me to keep watch on the wall until the AWOL soldiers returned. About 4:30 A.M. on Sunday, the drunken and disorderly AWOLs climbed back into camp. A general court martial was held Monday morning, and all six were found guilty of multiples charges, causing them to lose pay and spend time in U.S. Disciplinary Barracks (prison). This information was officially announced to all of the men in the cavalry squadron. I had no other personnel problems the rest of my time as commander. Under my supervision and major reorganization, Camp Gates progressed from being the most poorly rated unit and camp to the best along the entire West German border system.

My final assignment brought me back to Bamberg to serve as the brigade assistant S-3 for plans and operations. There my team and I updated and upgraded the emergency defense plan for the German state of Bavaria, a 1015-page document. I also was a member of the nuclear release alert system. Fortunately we were never ordered to fire any nuclear weapons.

On December 26, 1967, my superior evaluation netted me a belated Christmas gift—orders to deploy to South Vietnam. Before deployment I would attend specific training at the U.S. Army Special Warfare School, Military Advisors Training Course and Defense Language Institute at Fort Bragg, North Carolina, where we would practice field training, navigation without maps, and Southeast Asia survival techniques. Other courses would consist of Vietnamese history, society, culture, religion, customs, and languages, as well as first aid, demolition, construction techniques, and servicing weapons in the dark.

We celebrated New Year's Eve 1968 with a group of officers and their wives with whom Mary and I had grown very close in Germany. Now she would need to return to her family in the States. We reflected on some enjoyable times and tried not to think or talk about the coming deployment to Vietnam. At midnight we rushed to our apartment balcony and watched the elaborate fireworks display that came from all around Bamberg. We held each other tightly as we silently wondered about our fate.

CHAPTER 3
Vietnam 1968

In June 1968, a charter Continental Airways Boeing 707 took the Vietnam-bound troops due west into the setting sun. It was amazing to see the sun stay above the horizon for the next two and a half hours. The beauty ended when the stewardess told us to buckle up well because we would be making a non-routine landing at Honolulu International Airport. The pilot mentioned that the plane had lost all of its hydraulic fluid over the Pacific Ocean, so there would be no brakes to slow us down upon landing. He instructed us on the necessary precautions as he slowed the engines and coasted to a stop. The mechanics discovered a crack in the hydraulic fluid pan, which forced the airline to either find another aircraft or fix the problem. Thanks to Continental, the troops received a pass to go into Honolulu, the airline picking up the tab for lodging, food, beverages, and civilian "Aloha" clothes for the beach.

The Hawaiian vacation was short-lived before the troops were once again bound for Vietnam. The jumbo jet followed the coast of South Vietnam well out in the South China Sea for some distance before turning and heading straight to the base at Bien Hoa. The pilot wanted to avoid being hit by North Vietnamese ground fire.

All of Vietnam was a combat zone in 1968. A plane could be shot, no matter where it flew within the country. We approached the runway from the south, where I saw several large plumes of smoke rising from the jungle. The pilot informed us that the smoke was from a B-52 bombing raid that had just occurred. As we prepared to land, I saw four F-100 Super Saber jets loaded with bombs take off, while fifty helicopters and a number of U.S. Air Force C-130s, C-123s, AC-47s, B-50 Canberras, U.S. Army Caribou, Mohawk, and L-19 aircraft were parked along the runway. It was evident that this air base played a leading role in combat and supply operations in Vietnam.

The plane finally rolled to a stop near the small terminal building, which had two large field tents set up next to it. In each, rows of wooden benches were lined with sweat-drenched, khaki- or jungle fatigue-uniformed soldiers, who sat restlessly with their duffle bags at their feet. These soldiers had completed their tours in the Vietnam War and were waiting to fly back home to the United States on our plane. After a few minutes, the plane's door was opened and the ramp locked in place to allow us to deplane. We travel-weary soldiers slowly descended the plane's ramp. A wave of extreme heat and humidity hit me hard. I struggled to catch my breath and wondered how I would survive, much less operate, in these extreme conditions.

We were herded into the tent on the left end of the terminal building to await the arrival of buses that transported us to the Ninetieth Replacement Company in Long Binh for our in-processing to Vietnam. We sat down and the leaving troops greeted us. They shouted numerous catcalls: "Cherry," "You'll be sorry," and "I hope you made funeral arrangements before coming over here." Through the mass of troops I saw a West Point classmate, Captain John H. Eckert. He walked my way and welcomed me to Vietnam. Captain Eckert said that he had been waiting for two days for this "Freedom Bird" to take him home. I explained the plane's maintenance difficulties encountered in Hawaii. He joked that he would rather be delayed in Hawaii than in this godforsaken war zone.

Captain Eckert wore a Silver Star medal for exceptional valor in enemy combat. I questioned how he had earned the honor since he had been assigned to a "Rear Echelon Artillery Unit," where there was to be no direct contact with the enemy. Captain Eckert sighed and replied that he had thought the same until the Vietcong had overrun his unit several times during the Tet Offensive. *Tet* is the Vietnamese word for New Year. The North Vietnamese Communist forces attacked South Vietnam cities and communities in January 1968 and continued for several months in some areas.

Captain Eckert said that during these attacks, his unit had been surrounded on all sides. They had no choice but to lower the barrels of their cannons to fire anti-personnel rounds of the steel pellet canisters and nail-like projectiles, called flachette shells, into enemy attackers. This tactic was extremely effective and eventually caused the North Vietnamese troops and Vietcong units to turn back after exacting a heavy casualty toll. His unit had experienced some casualties, with a few men killed in action and a number of others wounded.

Captain Eckert looked very tired and relieved to be ending his tour in Vietnam. We talked a bit more before the transportation officer called the departing soldiers to pick up their baggage and board the plane to return to what the American troops referred to as "The World." He wished me good luck.

Five buses had lumbered up to the tent where we were sitting. I grabbed my gear and boarded. Our bus driver was Vietnamese, in accordance with the Status of Forces Agreement between South Vietnam and the United States. This agreement essentially governed the United States' activities while serving in South Vietnam. A military policeman, armed with an M-16 rifle for security, accompanied each bus. The windows were opened for ventilation but covered with a heavy mesh wire screen to prevent Vietcong terrorists from throwing a grenade into the vehicle. I was assigned to be an American advisor so I needed to endure the thirty-mile trip to Saigon to begin my military advisory training.

The buses passed complex rows of Quonset huts that housed the 24th Evacuation Hospital, the main surgical medical center for life-threatening casualties, where the injured were first treated before being medically evacuated. It was somewhat reassuring to know that such a facility did exist in case we were wounded or injured.

Outside the main gate we traveled the two-lane road to Saigon. Lush, thick tropical trees, bushes, and vines lined these roads. Vietnamese villages often featured a small marketplace surrounded by thatch huts or homes hammered out of Coca-Cola and beer cans. Farther inland a series of small canals ran off of the rivers. These sophisticated canals of gates and paddle wheels controlled the water source for the rice paddies. A putrid odor, consisting of a mixture of vehicle exhaust fumes, damp mold, rotting plants and flesh, and punctuated with animal/human feces, accompanied the tropical countryside. Vietnamese farmers generally fertilized their fields with human manure. While we covered our noses, the odor apparently did not seem to bother the Vietnamese women and children we passed.

Nearing Saigon, the buildings changed to mud/tile, cement blocks, and wooden planks. The homes of wealthier folks had a closed front gate surrounded by a walled compound. Many of these walls had sharp pointed objects, such as metal spikes, broken glass, and razor blades, imbedded in the cement on top of the wall as a deterrent to any would-be trespassers. Larger towns had a schoolhouse and a few businesses, which generally included a small restaurant, store, and barbershop for those needing minor medical assistance.

Traffic, too, changed. There was an increase of civilian vehicles as well as American, Korean, and Vietnamese military trucks, jeeps, and buses carrying troops and supplies. Civilian transportation consisted of European trucks, French Citroen cars, and three-wheeled Lambrettas. The Lambrettas fascinated me. This motorized tricycle had a small truck bed on the back and a two-cycle motorcycle engine. The driver sat in a single seat compartment in the front while the passengers sat on benches or on the floor in the back. They carried cargo on their laps, hung it on the sides, or piled it on the top. Cargo might include pigs, chickens, fish, vegetables, lumber, or other items heading to or from market. This unusual vehicle provided cheap and durable transportation to the natives.

I thought there was no limit to the number of people or amount of cargo until I encountered a Lambretta tilted back with the front up in the air. When this overflow happened, the Vietnamese just loaded up their livestock and other cargo onto the civilian buses to reach their destination.

The two-lane roads turned to four-lane highways with floral median strips and occasional palm trees. Homes, hotels, office buildings, and small factories lined both sides of the highway. Our bus turned down a side street that led to the main gate of the Keppler Compound, a hotel-looking building surrounded by a containing wall. Here we were to be housed for several days as we underwent our training.

It was late afternoon when we arrived, so we were sent to the mess hall to eat our first meal in Vietnam. All of the cooks and workers were Vietnamese, which I assumed was another requirement of the Status of Forces Agreement. We ate our tasty American-style food before we retired for the evening. I was assigned to room with Captain Mike Fellenz, another West Point classmate. We made up our beds and passed out from exhaustion.

At 6:00 A.M., a bugle call of reveille sounded over the PA system throughout the compound. Mike and I quickly showered, shaved, and put on a new set of the jungle fatigues and boots, designed for tropical climate that we had been issued just prior to shipping out. They would dry quickly after fording rivers or getting caught in Vietnam's frequent rainstorms. The uniform material was lighter than the traditional fatigues and we were not allowed to starch it, so that air would circulate more easily. It was worn with sleeves rolled up above the elbows. The shirt was not tucked in for added ventilation. The trousers had a series of pockets in the back, in the front, and deeper ones going down the sides of each leg. These were great assets in the field, since they permitted the troops to carry a greater number of essential items such as maps, extra ammunition, rations, and medical supplies. The jungle boots had green canvas sides that ran up to mid-calf on the leg. They also had a treaded sole made of synthetic corfram and thick rubber, which allowed better traction in slippery terrain. Placed between the treaded sole and the inner pad of the boot was a thin metal plate, which better protected the foot from the hazard of metal spikes or "panji sticks": sharpened bamboo stakes dipped in human feces. Mike and I admired our new wear like it was our outfit for the first day of grade school.

The new arrivals were assembled in an auditorium to begin the in-processing procedures to South Vietnam and assignment to Military Assistance Command Advisory (MACV) teams. This procedure included reviewing our orders, checking our immunization records, and exchanging all of our American "greenbacks" for either U.S. military pay certificates, referred to as "script," or South Vietnamese currency called *piasters* or *dong*. We then headed toward the supply area for the issuance of our weapons and equipment.

The major who had reviewed my orders stated that I would be assigned to an advisory team in the very mountainous Central Highlands. Out of my pocket I pulled my permanent Profile 3, which I was given for my severe knee injury during ranger training. Profile 3 meant that I was allowed to remain in the military with a few restrictions in the infantry branch.

Showing the major my profile, I requested a less mountainous terrain that required less physical strain on my knee. His first response was a scoff and a "no way in hell" look. Then one of his non-commissioned officers leaned over and whispered something to him. The major looked at me. He mentioned that a new advisory team was being formed in the coastal lowland region near the South China Sea and asked if I would be interested. I responded in the affirmative. My assignment was then firmed up to serve as deputy district advisor for the Hoa Da District, MACV 37, Binh Thuan Province, II Corps, South Vietnam.

At the supply area, the supply officer tried issuing me a .45-caliber pistol, which I turned down. I told him that I could throw a pistol more accurately than I could shoot it. He next handed me an M-1 carbine. Again I turned it down because it had too little firepower and it was difficult to acquire ammunition. After some further discussion, I was issued an M-16 rifle with its basic load of 120 rounds of ammunition. This was accompanied with metal magazines, a pack harness, a Special Forces rucksack, one- and two-quart canteens, four ammunition pouches, an entrenching tool (a small fold-up shovel), two pouches for medical supplies, a steel pot camouflage combat helmet, round-soft bush hat, waterproof map case, two rolls of extra-strength duct tape, two small bottles of insect repellant, and a bottle of anti-malaria tablets.

While I was hanging out in the supply area, I met another West Point classmate, Captain John E. Burger. He was turning in his equipment at the end of his year-long tour as an advisor in South Vietnam. We talked a little about his experiences, and he cautioned me to trust not a soul. I listened intently as Burger related his experiences. He had seen many of the South Vietnamese soldiers, local militia, civilians, and local police work by day for the South Vietnamese and/or U.S. forces and then for the Vietcong at night. He shared his frustrations, advising me about the South Vietnamese military units as well as methods he found successful in getting them to perform better. I thanked him.

That night some thunderous explosions and concussions awoke Mike and me, almost knocking us out of our bunks. We ran to the door and saw a series of very bright explosions near the edge of Saigon. The concussions from these explosions finally reached us nearly forty-five seconds later. Somebody hollered that this was a U.S. Air Force B-52 bombing raid on Vietcong targets outside of the city and not to be alarmed. The firepower from this concentrated bombing impressed me, and I realized I was witnessing my first military encounter.

The following two days were less dramatic, featuring general orientation from various personnel of MACV, CIA, Agency for International Development (AID), and Special Operations Command for the army, air force, and navy. The third night, a group of us went to the five-star Rex Hotel in Saigon for a nice French dinner at their rooftop restaurant. There was a floor show in which a number of young, attractive Vietnamese women and men performed a series of songs and dances that were currently popular in the United States. It seemed a little strange to witness these very Asian-looking people performing hits from our country.

After the show, we took a Vietnamese taxi back to Keppler Compound. I became aware that the taxi driver was taking us in the wrong direction. In Vietnamese, English, and French I ordered him to turn around. He did not reply nor did he turn the taxi around. Under the assumption that the streets of Saigon were generally safe for U.S. soldiers, we were required to keep weapons locked in the arms room at Keppler Compound while visiting the city. Fortunately I had had the good sense to strap my KA-BAR knife with its eight-inch blade on my leg under my fatigue uniform. Sitting behind the driver, I drew the knife out of its scabbard and put it up to his neck. In French, I told him again to turn the cab around and take us to Keppler Compound or I would slit his throat. He immediately turned the taxi around in the middle of the broad avenue and drove us quickly to Keppler Compound.

At the main gate, we piled out of the taxi. One of the men tried to get the Vietnamese security guards to arrest the cab driver, who quickly sped off. We reported the incident to the U.S. Military Police. They informed us that over a period of several months, a number of American soldiers in Saigon had taken taxis and were later found dead on the outskirts of town—all having been badly tortured. We were very lucky.

On the morning of the fourth day, we went to Than Son Nhut Air Base in Saigon to begin our respective trips on the "MACV merry-go-round." The tour showed the various MACV headquarters in the corps area to which we were assigned. Most of the men were assigned to either the III or IV Corps areas, while I headed for II Corps, an area north of Saigon. I tried to manage all of my baggage, which consisted of a footlocker containing required army manuals and equipment, a B-4 bag for clothing, a duffel bag filled with combat gear, and my M-16 slung across my back. As I laboriously dragged this baggage across the terminal building, I sensed the derogatory looks and comments from the combat-hardened troops I passed. This overload of equipment had marked me as a novice to Vietnam and untested in combat. None of the soldiers volunteered to help me with this load nor were there any skycaps. I was clearly on my own.

When the Air Force C-130 Hercules was ready to board, a mixture of passengers lined up. American and Vietnamese military had written orders that served as priority reservations for a seat or a space on the plane. Vietnamese civilians were boarded last, as room permitted. The Vietnamese carried all their worldly possessions with the exception of livestock, which were not allowed aboard, no matter how they were crated. Several of the plane's crewmen helped me onto the plane with my load, I'm sure just to hurry the boarding process.

The plane had only a row of canvas-webbed seats, facing inward, running down each side of the plane. Those passengers without seats had to find an unoccupied space on the floor and gather their gear close to them, allowing space for others. I was pleased to receive a space midway on the left side so as to store my footlocker and other baggage under my legs. Civilian travelers, consisting of grandparents down to children, sat among the military wherever they found unoccupied space. The air crew had to judge when the plane was completely filled within safety limits and then send the remaining passengers back to the terminal to await the next flight to Nha Trang. There were no seatbelts on the flight, so every passenger had to hold on to whatever was available for take-off and landing.

During take-off, everyone on the floor slid en masse toward the rear of the aircraft. Passengers were packed in so tight that nobody slid very far or got injured. The temperature was well over a hundred degrees, and we were ecstatic when we reached our assigned altitude of five thousand feet where the air became refreshingly cooler. The flight took about an hour, and upon landing, the reverse slide en masse toward the front of the plane occurred.

Nha Trang was a military hub in Southeast Asia for American, Australian, South Vietnamese, and Korean military forces. MACV Headquarters was located across the street from Nha Trang's beautiful beach, a former French tropical paradise getaway on the South China Sea. Behind the base was a small single-story hotel engulfed by a thick grove of palm trees that housed our accommodations.

I had reported to the headquarters only to discover that it was co-located with the First Field Force Command-Vietnam (IFFV) and the Civil Operations and Revolutionary Development Support (CORDS). The IFFV combined Vietnam's military divisions of Corps I and Corps II into a single organization under the command of Lieutenant General William Peers. The CORDS operation was founded in late 1967 as a joint operation of the U.S. Military, the CIA, the State Department, and other agencies involved in the routing out of the Vietcong infrastructure and pacifying the Vietnamese people. This operation was designed to gain control over people and territory while finding a more permanent solution to the conflict between North and South Vietnam. It was hoped that this approach would quickly "win the hearts and minds" of the undecided Vietnamese people over to the South Vietnamese government side. A large component of this involved civic action programs, which advisory teams would initiate and operate in an assigned territory.

Upon reporting, we were led into a large conference room where an army major welcomed us and collected a copy of our orders. From there a medic told us to drop our trousers so he could give us an injection of gamma globulin to help prevent hepatitis. We all protested, saying that we had been given several doses in the States and then again at Keppler Compound two days before. The medic snarled back that he had been ordered to give "every swinging Richard" that passed through this headquarters a dose of "Double G." Reluctantly we all submitted our already sore buttocks.

The medic seemed to take sadistic pleasure as he slowly massaged the thick, gelatinous vaccine into our muscle tissue, while commenting on the big bulge it made under the skin. Gingerly, we all hobbled back into the conference room where we underwent a series of briefings about the MACV/CORDS organization.

When the afternoon session ended, several of us walked across the street to admire the sun setting over the beach before we headed to a small French restaurant. Since South Vietnam had a thriving lobster industry off its coast, I decided to dine on lobster over a bed of rice accompanied by locally grown salad greens, with lemon custard for dessert. I was staring at the dark-green tea grounds decorating the bottom of my cup when a Korean contractor, speaking perfect English, struck up a conversation. I introduced myself, and when he heard my name his face lit up.

He asked, "Are you related to Colonel William Charles Haneke, who served in Tageu, Korea, during the early 1950s?"

Proudly I told him that was my father. The gentleman nodded and complimented my father. He told me how my father had worked with several local companies to help South Koreans get construction projects implemented in a very poor economy, and that many local people in Tageu still appreciated my father's support and integrity for helping them get jobs. The Korean gentleman worked for Pacific Architects and Engineers, an engineering firm that supervised the large majority of building projects for the American bases in Southeast Asia. Lady Bird Johnson purportedly owned a large share of this business, which I thought was quite unusual, but lucrative, for a First Lady. We talked a bit longer, and I enjoyed the insights into what my father had accomplished during the Korean War.

The next morning we were introduced to a representative from CORDS, Lieutenant Colonel Ferdinand C. Bidgood, and several assistants. They oriented us on the Pacification Program, the major emphasis of our advisory teams, and the newly initiated Phoenix Program. The Pacification Program was aimed at pacifying and "winning the hearts and minds" of the South Vietnamese locals by providing humanitarian aid and security.

The Phoenix Program was planned to defeat the Vietcong by combining military, paramilitary, special operations, and civic action elements. Colonel Bidgood warned us that one of their action teams, the Provincial Reconnaissance Units (PRUs), might come to operate in our area from time to time if the need arose. It was an extreme way of dealing with the Vietcong. Vietcong defectors, murderers, rapists, drug dealers, and other criminals composed the PRUs. The CIA led them to ferret out the hardcore Vietcong political cadre members. PRU units showed up in an area with a hit list of confirmed communist suspects and orders to "exterminate with extreme prejudice." This meant that the PRUs needed to round up and interrogate the Vietcong suspects and finally kill them to ensure no future problems. It sounded to me as if the presence of PRUs would be a contradiction and a detriment to making progress with the Pacification Program.

Another program was the Kit Carson Scouts. This program granted amnesty to Vietcong soldiers after they screamed "*Chieu Hoi!*" (open arms), threw down their weapons, and surrendered to the South Vietnamese. These soldiers were then put into a re-education course and trained to work with the South Vietnamese as elite scouts. The Kit Carson Scouts joined patrols and were in charge of identifying and reading Vietcong signs. This program was not always successful, as some Vietcong would become double agents.

After all of these orientations, it was apparent that the overall plan was to phase out the Special Forces from the advisory programs. We advisors were to train the South Vietnamese to operate on their own so we could send all our forces back to the United States.

Early the next morning, I boarded a C-130 aircraft and flew to the city of Pleiku in the mountains of the Central Highlands. This city was in the midst of its three-month monsoon season with temperatures in the mid-sixties, causing many of us to put on our field jackets in order to stop shivering. We were directed to a one-story building that housed the bachelor officer quarters. The building was surrounded up to the roof-line with sandbags three layers deep. These sandbags were to protect us from the frequent Vietcong mortar and rocket attacks.

A short distance in front of the building stretched a line of trenches and bunkers. Should an attack occur in Pleiku, we were instructed to assemble and head toward the trenches with our rifles and steel pots, or helmets. Over the previous three years, this area had been heavily contested and had experienced intense Vietcong fighting. The North Vietnamese Army had reinforced the Vietcong during the recent Tet Offensive. They had overrun a large part of the military base and airfield before American units pushed back and defeated them.

That evening, several of us were sitting in our barracks when we heard a series of explosions close to our building. Our adrenalin flowed and our hearts raced as we instinctively ran to our respective rooms, grabbed our rifles and steel pots, and assembled in the muddy trench in front of the building. A second lieutenant responsible for the trench asked for a show of hands of all who needed ammunition for their weapons. About fifteen of us raised our hands and were each issued 120 rounds of ammunition.

Distant explosions echoed on the other side of this compound—and then silence. Something burning flickered in that area and was soon extinguished. Light rain had soaked us by the time the all clear was announced. Word filtered through the trenches that small Vietcong rockets had caused no injuries, but some limited damage to one building. *If these were small rockets, I sure do not want to face the big ones,* I thought. That night I slept fitfully with anxiety-fueled dreams of an enemy attack coming right though our building and men shot in their bunks. I didn't want to end up that way.

The next morning I was thankful to be alive to continue my MACV merry-go-round tour to Ban Me Thout in Darlac Province. The fifteen-mile drive to the MACV Headquarters was on unpaved road made up of red clay that had turned muddy from the steady rain. Once again we were trapped in the heat and humidity that the double and triple canopies of the rainforest caused. Little air circulated through these canopies, causing it to feel like a sauna. Passing out was common among Americans. It was necessary to carry and use an abundance of water and salt tablets when operating under these conditions.

The road wound through small villages with long, stilted houses, which identified them as belonging to a local Montagnard tribe. The Montagnard people resembled the Polynesians in Hawaii with their dark brown skin, round eyes, medium stature, and strong legs. Most of the men wore shorts or loin cloths, no shoes, and a shirt. Some carried rifles and others toted a primitive crossbow and crude wooden quiver of wooden darts. The women dressed in dark wraparound skirts and were generally topless. Children under two years of age just wore a crude shirt and nothing on their bottoms, making it easy to relieve themselves. These youngsters were generally carried on an older sister or brother's hip.

As we slowly rounded a sharp bend in the road, the traffic forced us to slow to a stop. The side of the road was full of thick vegetation and looked to me like a perfect place for an ambush. After a few minutes I heard two shots zip past my left ear. I swung my rifle around, took off the safety, and pointed it in the general direction of the jungle. By then the jeep was moving again. At first I questioned whether I had actually heard the shots until I looked at the windshield and saw two new bullet holes.

The jeep pulled up to the gate of MACV Headquarters, which turned out to be the hunting lodge of the former emperor of Vietnam. It was a spectacular set of buildings constructed out of solid red mahogany. The entrance was raised off the ground to prevent unwelcomed animals, snakes, and crawling insects that might venture in from the rainforest. A series of manicured trees, flowering bushes, and decorative plants that opened into a formal garden surrounded the building. The front yard of the main buildings sloped into a terraced embankment that dropped into the rainforest. I wasn't sure how the American military had ended up occupying this magnificent place, but I felt privileged to partake in the beauty.

I asked one of the officers what kinds of animals were in the area that could be hunted. He sighed and said that this region of Vietnam had more types and greater abundance of animals and large birds than any other place in the world. These included elephants, tigers, several types of apes and monkeys, gibbons, deer, wild boar, Cape buffalo, and peacocks. The officer also cautioned that the jungle housed pythons, cobras, bamboo vipers, and other poisonous reptiles. He scared the living hell out of us.

The senior advisor met us and conducted the orientation concerning advisory procedures in dealing with Montagnard and Khmer tribesmen and/or mercenary military units. He explained that one of the largest crops many of the Montagnard tribes raised was poppy, which only grew in the Central Highlands. The poppy sap was processed into high-quality raw opium. The CIA allowed this process because they bought the opium and then resold it to area Vietnamese or Chinese drug czars to pay for intelligence and military service of the Montagnards. The orientation was very instructive and helpful.

Afterward, I met up with a West Point classmate, Captain James A. Whicher, who was now the commander of the local military intelligence detachment. Whicher shared information about the setting up of an effective intelligence network and the inner workings of the intelligence operations in Vietnam. He stated that the various intelligence operations shared very little information with the advisors, who needed it the most. While we ate dinner, I recounted my story about being shot at. He confirmed that snipers were working that stretch of road, averaging three deaths a week in spite of local forces efforts to catch them. Again I was lucky.

The next morning we continued our training tour, making flight stops in Tuy Hoa, Hau Bon, Qui Nhon, Kontum, Dalat, and Phan Rang. My final destination was Phan Thiet, the capital of Binh Thuan Province located northeast of Saigon along the Ca Ty River and South China Sea. Phan Thiet was a moderate-sized city of about one hundred thousand people. It was famous for its production of *nuoc mam*.

Nuoc mam is produced from an anchovy-like fish that is placed in large clay urns. These urns are filled using alternating layers of palm fronds, then a layer of fish seasoned with a coating of salt and herbs until the urn is completely filled. At this point, the urn is sealed and left in one place throughout the curing period. The fish by-product is then strained off and the remaining liquid diluted into a less-concentrated solution that is then bottled and sold. Phan Thiet annually produced between sixteen and seventeen million liters of *nuoc mam*. This business required the whole family's involvement, so while the men were at sea fishing, the women and children remained at home repairing damaged fishing equipment and mending nets.

The headquarters for MACV 37 was located in the capital city, Phan Thiet. I spent two days in Phan Thiet receiving the basic training in-processing and orientation. At night, off-duty soldiers assembled on the roof of the headquarters building and watched an episode of the television program *Star Trek*. While watching, we saw two flashes of light followed by a muffled boom. This went on for fifteen minutes, and then silence. A number of relaxed enlisted men told me not to be concerned: a couple of Vietcong guerrillas were living in a cave by a Vietnamese graveyard next to the airstrip. After dark, they would lob a couple of mortar rounds harmlessly into the open airfield, resulting in no damage. They'd call it a night and return to the comfort of their cave. These harmless Vietcong were referred to as the "Phantom Regiments of Phan Thiet."

The next morning Province Senior Advisor Lieutenant Colonel Thompson welcomed me and told me that I was being assigned as the acting senior district advisor for the Hoa Da District in the northern part of Binh Thuan Province. My mission was to establish and operate a new site for a district advisory team. I would be starting from scratch at this location. This team would require personnel, equipment, housing, supplies, weapons, defensive perimeter, and medical support services. I was shocked. No one had informed me that I would be expected to start a new compound and advisory effort!

Thompson concluded that he was going to send me to the Tuy Phong Compound, north of the Hoa Da District, where I would spend three to four days training with Senior Advisor Major John C. Bennett, who would explain the setting up and running of an advisory effort in this region. My stomach churned. What did the army really want from me? I feared that my military mission would be like no other.

CHAPTER 4

Major Bennett

My MACV merry-go-round continued the next morning for the next phase of my training. I rode a Huey helicopter, where I had a bird's-eye view of the different types of terrain that made up Binh Thuan Province. My eyes focused down on some arable soil inland, where I saw peasant farmers in their characteristic black pajama outfits and cone-shaped straw hats wading through rice paddies and hoeing their vegetables. Small rivers and streams running from the base of the rugged, jungle-covered mountains irrigated their crops. A heavy bank of clouds passed over the arid coastal lowland area and then, upon reaching the mountains, dumped its rain. No wonder the mountains were lush with vegetation.

Northwest of Phan Thiet was a lone mountain shaped like a woman's breast, rising above the flat lowlands. This was what the American men referred to as "Titty Mountain." Below it were a number of widely scattered villages and three larger towns: Hai Ninh, Song Mao, and Phan Ri Cua. Along the coast of the South China Sea was a wide strip of sand dunes, an occasional small grove of palm trees, and an extensive network of small fishing boats. The light-colored areas around Phan Ri Cua and Tuy Phong turned out to be drying fields for the briny solution that became salt used to produce *nuoc mam*. I was amazed that one province could be so diverse geographically.

I arrived at Tuy Phong Compound. Major Bennett had been assigned an eight-man advisory team due to Tuy Phong District's low population along the coastal lowland desert. During his tour, Bennett had developed an excellent rapport with Tuy Phong's district chief, which helped present the ideal working circumstances for an advisory team. Together they extended an intelligence network of reliable agents while organizing a dependable military and paramilitary organization of regional and popular force units that were dispersed throughout the entire district. Tuy Phong District had had trouble with widespread Vietcong presence. Through Bennett's advisory team and South Vietnamese efforts, the area north of their compound had been completely pacified and the villagers were friendly with the Americans and the South Vietnamese forces.

Bennett had no idea that I was coming. He commented that this was not unusual; the military personnel in the southern half of Binh Thuan Province rarely communicated with the district compounds in the northern half. Bennett shrugged it off and walked me through his compound to explain the layout. He had set up his compound in the shape of a giant triangle, with an extensive reinforced bunker system at each of the three points. Each of these was supported by a system of covered tunnels running from the center of the compound. This allowed a safer way to resupply and reinforce the critical points under enemy attack without unduly exposing the men.

In the center of Tuy Phong Compound was a large masonry tower standing about three stories high. It had a fortified observation deck that overlooked the rolling countryside and was the main source of observation, command, and resource control. Bennett stated that during an attack, the tower was the first thing the Vietcong would try to knock out. I asked if the tower had experienced any direct hits from mortar shells. Bennett shook his head and noted that the odds of a direct hit on such a high and narrow tower was low. The usual Vietcong tactic was to shoot at the open observation deck and fire port holes at the top of the tower in hopes of killing or disabling the soldiers.

Major Bennett

The firing point was armed with two .50-caliber machine guns, two M-79 (40mm) grenade launchers, an M-60 (7.62mm) machine gun, and a two-way radio capable of talking within the compound to coordinate air strikes or artillery fire. It had the means of setting off the network of claymore mines that were situated as a part of the defensive perimeter in layers around the entire compound. The tower was well reinforced with layers of sandbags, which Bennett guaranteed would withstand direct hits by mortars, rocket-propelled grenades, and recoilless rifle hits. Out of curiosity I asked how they got the layers of sandbags on top of the observation tower. Bennett smiled and said that there was a swinging trap door to the top with sandbags affixed to it so that when it was swung shut, the sandbags over it would automatically be in place. *Clever,* I thought.

Bennett told me that MACV 37 had his permission to place communication men on Titty Mountain's communication relay station. This station was a well-defended network that was part of the Military Intelligence and Army Security Agency. He explained that Binh Thuan Province was so large that radio communication from the southern regions to the northern half was impossible without the aid of this station. Radio communication depended on a direct line-of-sight from radio antenna to radio antenna. The mountains in the western parts of Binh Thuan Province interfered with this. Communication with MACV Headquarters in Phan Thiet was essential for advisory compounds, especially when under attack. Sometimes a compound needed to request direct air support or medical evacuation.

I asked Bennett if Titty Mountain's communication relay station was ever shot upon. He admitted that periodically the station had been the object of Vietcong attacks. Up to this point, the Vietcong had not been successful in knocking it out. He added that for the last six months the largest enemy contact in Binh Thuan Province had occurred in the four northern districts. It appeared that the Hoa Da District, where my compound would be stationed, was the exception. There had been little or no effort against the Vietcong there since the French left in 1954.

Hoa Da District had the reputation as being the local Vietcong R & R spot. The Vietcong felt safe and unmonitored there.

Bennett's Vietnamese counterpart, the district chief of Tuy Phong, met us. The seasoned major had fought with the Vietminh against the Japanese, then the French, and had trained with the American Special Forces. He had served primarily in the I Corps Tactical Zone in operations against the Vietcong and was accustomed to working with troops and people from a variety of different racial, religious, and ethnic backgrounds.

The troops at Tuy Phong Compound were mainly Vietnamese and were almost all Buddhists or Cao Dai (*cow-die*). Regional and popular forces units composed most of these, with the assigned tasks of defending his compound, several key bridges, and important points along Highway 1, the main north-south route along the coast. Bennett complimented his counterpart, stating that he did an excellent job of weeding out the Vietcong and other problems within the South Vietnamese units.

The next day Bennett drove me north along Highway 1 to Phan Rang, where we met for several hours with the American military advisors at their compound. These Vietnamese units were a mixture of Vietnamese and Chams. They were a well-trained military force that had been instrumental in effectively pacifying this region of Ninh Thuan Province.

Their district chief hosted a very nice luncheon for us. We were seated around a large table; he served the feast family-style. In the center of the table were platters of chicken, several types of seafood, boiled oriental vegetables, slices of bananas, and their local sour watermelons. Each person was provided an individual bowl of rice. It was assumed that everyone brought his own chopsticks. For those of us without a set, "loaners" were provided. These chopsticks were ceremoniously rinsed with boiling water. Even so, I was very nervous about the many types of exotic and toxic bacteria that I was being exposed to by using these "loaner sticks."

During the course of the meal, everyone used their chopsticks to serve themselves from the common platters in the center of the table. They used these same chopsticks with which to eat. I was glad that I had mastered the art of eating with chopsticks as a toddler when my family lived in Japan. The meal was topped off with cups of Vietnamese coffee, which contained two inches of sludge from the grounds, and bottles of Ba Moui Ba, Number 33 beer, a typical Vietnamese beverage containing a large amount of formaldehyde as a preservative. After this leisurely meal, Major Bennett and I expressed our thanks to the Phan Rang district chief and the district senior advisor. We then drove off in the jeep for our return trip to Tuy Phong Compound.

On the outskirts of Phan Rang, Bennett stopped at a small shop. He went inside and returned with a set of ivory chopsticks for me as my "welcome to Vietnam" present. He showed me a place in the right top pocket of my fatigue shirt where these sticks would fit. It was the perfect storage place. These sticks were to serve me well through all the Vietnamese meals I would experience during my tour. This was a part of the advisor's lore that had not been taught prior to arriving in-country.

We took a leisurely drive back. Bennett wanted me to become familiar with some of the landmarks and symbols of the culture and society in this region. On top of the two tallest hilltops were a set of pyramid-shaped pagodas from the Cao Dai religion. We continued our journey through several small hamlets and freshly planted and well-irrigated rice paddies. A boy of about seven years of age was herding six water buffalos with a long switch. Bennett pulled the jeep over to the side of the road to let them pass. He then tried to restart the engine, which coughed and sputtered and would not turn over.

Something suddenly told me to turn around: a water buffalo was charging. I yelled a warning to Bennett, who was still trying to start the flooded engine. Immediately the water buffalo butted the spare tire mounted on the back of the jeep, jolting the jeep and its occupants. Mr. Water Buffalo backed off a short distance and took another stab at the spare tire, which exploded with a loud bang. This caused the angry beast to back off again, but this time he took aim at me.

Bennett hollered, "Kill it!" I immediately complied and fired one shot into its neck and three shots into its chest. The determined buffalo kept charging, but then suddenly fell to the ground a foot away from me. He let out a final breath as his eyes rolled upward. Blood gushed.

Scared to death, we gazed at the now lifeless beast and shook.

Bennett regained his composure and tried once again to restart the engine. It worked. He turned around and drove back into the hamlet where a small crowd of agitated people had gathered. From their apparent level of anger and their increasingly aggressive behavior, I feared that they would do us bodily harm. For that reason, I kept my rifle in position.

Bennett put his hand on my rifle and had me lower it, in a symbolic gesture of approaching peace. He explained to the irate group, in Vietnamese, what had happened. The farmer who owned these water buffalo confronted Bennett. After several minutes of strong conversation, Bennett handed the farmer a wad of Vietnamese piasters. The satisfied farmer parted, and we resumed our trip.

Bennett explained that the farmer had gained big time from this incident. First of all, he had gained face in his village through his hard and aggressive negotiations with "the foreigners." Secondly, he acquired more than enough money to purchase a replacement water buffalo; finally, the farmer and his family now had plenty of fresh buffalo meat to eat and share with their fellow villagers. As for Bennett, he would receive reimbursement from the advisory team since it helped to offset what could have been a negative incident. In short, it turned out to be a win-win situation.

We drove along the coast. The untouched natural beauty amazed me: deserted beaches and the clear blue ocean were punctuated with isolated palm tree groves filled with ripening coconuts free for the taking. I couldn't help but contrast the Unites States and Vietnamese beaches. We used our beaches for leisure activities, versus the Vietnamese, who have little or no leisure time. They worked just to survive.

The hamlets grew farther apart and the presence of people along the highway dropped off dramatically as we continued our journey. Salt flats laid out in symmetrical patterns indicated that we were at the edge of Tuy Phong District with its small villages. Several times, Bennett stopped to talk to the villagers in Vietnamese about some local matters. The major explained that creating a good rapport with the villagers was important to prevent future difficulties. When he began his tour, there was initial distrust toward Americans. Gradually, normal conversations between the villagers and him evolved, making life easier for everyone.

Back at Tuy Phong Compound, Bennett took time to explain the differences in the racial, ethnic, and cultural backgrounds in Tuy Phong and the surrounding districts. These differences impacted the way the people interacted or refused to interact with one another. The Hoa Da and Tuy Phong districts were composed of Vietnamese people whose religion was Buddhism, Cao Dai, or Roman Catholicism. A neighboring district, Phan Ly Cham, was a combination of Cham and Montagnard, who believed in ancestor and spirit worship or Hinduism, while the Hai Ninh District was Chinese, believing in Confucianism or ancestor worship. Bennett expressed that it was a challenge to get mutual cooperation in civic action programs as well as joint military operations with these multicultural differences.

That night after I fell asleep, there were several short bursts of gunfire, the characteristic sound of a Vietcong AK-47 automatic rifle. Single shots from several rifles of Regional Forces guards within the compound perimeter followed. Bennett and I quickly grabbed our rifles, web gear, and spare ammunition and ran to the tower command post to access the developing situation.

An American sergeant and a South Vietnamese first lieutenant on duty informed us that it was a limited probing attack by the Vietcong to check the alert status of Tuy Phong Compound. The attack appeared to be directed from the northwest and seemed to involve random rifle fire from only a few Vietcong, who were easily driven off. Just then, several more bursts of rifle fire came from the southwest, two of which had a stream of green tracer rounds. They arched high and harmlessly over the compound.

Bennett pointed to the tracers and told me that the Vietcong and North Vietnamese Army routinely used green or purple tracers that the Russians, Czechs, or Chinese communists furnished. Our side used red or orange tracers, so it was very easy to differentiate which side was firing. He had no more than finished his sentence when three flashes of light swarmed from the southwest followed by the whump-whump-whump of mortar and additional rifle bursts.

Bennett yelled to take cover. He quickly picked up a field phone and turned the handle a couple of times, which sounded the ringer in the compound mortar pit's phone. He rattled off a compass azimuth reading and a range from the compound to the attacking mortar's location. Suddenly three mortar shells impacted the mess hall, resulting in little damage but no casualties. Almost immediately there was the sound of three outgoing 4.2-inch mortar shells being launched from the compound. The shells impacted the exact area where we had seen the flashes from the Vietcong mortars.

Silence fell and a half hour of firing ended. Bennett suggested we get some sleep, because the next morning we were going to patrol the area from which the attack was launched, as well as an area of increased Vietcong activity as reported by intelligence.

The following morning we formed up for the patrol with our rifles, ammunition, hand grenades, web gear, radios, canteens, rations, and other special equipment. Bennett asked me to follow him around as he inspected the men who would be accompanying us on this overnight patrol. I noted that he inspected each person's equipment to ensure that all was clean, serviceable, and properly secured to make as little noise as possible. He made sure each man had the necessary amount of food, water, and ammunition. Finally, he had the men take a break in place. Bennett briefed us on the objectives, responsibilities, and routes for the operation. One squad served as the point and flank security for the first night objective. Another squad was responsible on the return trip. He then checked to make sure that those who needed maps and compasses had the proper items. We reassembled and began our march out the gate.

Early in the patrol the leaders insisted on noise discipline, so there wasn't loud talking or laughter to alert local civilians to our presence or route. The men were allowed to smoke on the march, but soon that was reduced to smoking in specified break areas. Our first objective was to search the areas near the perimeter of the compound to get an idea of the possible number of our night visitors. The area to the northwest had revealed only a few empty AK-47 cartridges, which proved that there had only been about three Vietcong at the initial point of fire. This area had provided very poor access to the compound, since an enemy force would have to get through a defensive perimeter of barbed wire, tangle-foot wire, land mines, and claymore mines. We concluded that this was a diversionary force; the main focus of the attack was from the southwest.

Upon reaching the southwest area, we discovered positions from where at least a dozen Vietcong had fired their rifles. Nearby was the place where a 60mm mortar had been fired. There was a distinctive impression from the Vietcong mortar, evidence of the three 4.2-inch mortar explosions, and at least four blood trails, indicating that our counter-fire had had desired results in breaking up the Vietcong attack. Bennett pointed out that there was enough abdomen flesh on the ground to verify that we had killed at least one of the attackers, as well as a man's black shirt.

Bennett said, "Nobody can lose that much of his gut area and still keep on living."

A Vietnamese trooper pointed to a heavily soaked, bloodstained Vietcong "bush hat." This soldier had either died or would not be fighting us anytime soon. One of the American team sergeants showed us three crude black rubber "Ho Chi Minh sandals." The sandal consisted of a strip of tire tread to fit an individual foot; this was affixed with two strips of a tire inner tube and fashioned into an Asian-style sandal. Bennett explained that this was typical footwear of the Vietcong. He was amazed to hear about how far the Vietcong could walk using this primitive footwear.

After searching the area for about half an hour, we found nothing else. Bennett directed us to follow the blood trails that led toward the northwest mountains. Initially the terrain was mainly sandy and desert-like, but an hour into our patrol this turned into lowlands between two rivers and a series of streams. The ground went from firm to marshy and back again. My strength was sapped between the difficult terrain, heat, and humidity. From the profuse amount of sweat that I was emitting, I was convinced that the water was running out of me faster than I was putting it in.

Thankfully, Bennett gave us a water break. He looked at my drenched clothing and told me to cheer up—the weather could be much worse. It was only about 110 degrees; there were many days when it got over 120. Bennett pointed to his canteen and reminded us that water was the most valuable commodity to any soldier and was not to be wasted. I understood, and from that point on I kept reminding myself that I had worked hard to become acclimatized to this godforsaken country to participate in these patrol operations, so keep moving.

About late afternoon, we approached a main river that flowed down from the mountains and jungles, branching out into three smaller rivers and several streams that flowed toward the South China Sea. There were several blown-up bridges and an old set of railroad tracks near a town called Tuy Tinh Viet. Bennett informed me that the French and Vietnamese had used this rail line to travel and haul cargo from Saigon to Hue. During the Indochina War, it had been a frequent target of Vietminh *sappers*, those who handled explosives. Sappers blew up sections of tracks and bridges, eventually rendering the line unusable. The handiwork of the sappers was readily apparent on two of the four bridges crossing a stream. They had been blown up; sections of track and wooden crossties were missing. It was here that Bennett had the patrol stop to prepare our dinner of dried fish, rice, and vegetables. Our two-hour break revived us after a long, arduous march.

We reassembled and moved out quietly across the rail line to a point at the base of a nearby mountain where three well-worn trails converged out of the thick jungle. Major Bennett smiled and commented that this was a perfect position for an ambush. Our chosen site had a steep hill in front of us, making it difficult for an attacking force to scale. It also provided surveillance of the three trails turning into a single long trail leading out of the mountain, while the swift-moving river on the other side blocked any escape on the trail.

Bennett and his team sergeant deployed an observation post at the far right end of our group. The post was instructed to click the radio handset twice when any enemy force was spotted on the trail coming out of the jungle. Three clicks indicated that the enemy troops were centered in the designated "kill zone." Bennett would then initiate the ambush by firing his Swedish K automatic sub-machine gun, which had a distinctive sound all of the troops in our patrol could easily recognize. Upon hearing the Swedish K, we would all commence firing in the kill zone.

Two M-60s were placed in a position near the opposite ends of the patrol positions to ensure maximum coverage over the entire area. The American demolition sergeant and two Vietnamese assistants set up and camouflaged several claymore mines along the kill zone. They ran the wires from the mines up the hill to the detonating handles that key members of the patrol held. We all were assigned a position, a lane of fire, and instructed to maintain strict noise control. We were cautioned not to use any tracer ammunition in our weapons, as that might alert the enemy to our location.

Settling into my assigned position near Bennett, I applied a fairly thick coat of insect repellant on all of the exposed patches of skin and hoped that the increasingly thick cloud of hungry mosquitoes would leave me alone. There were three types of mosquitoes that we needed to endure: dawn to noon had the medium-sized biting ones; mid-afternoon to ten in the evening had the small non-biting; and nighttime to dawn were the huge anopheleses. The anopheles resisted repellant and could be heard and felt when they landed on your skin. This mosquito carried two kinds of malaria; we took anti-malaria pills daily for one and weekly for the other strain of malaria.

The temperature had dropped to a balmy one hundred degrees with no breeze at all. It felt like a steam bath. I struggled to breathe. My perspiration increased, and I had doubts about the repellant staying on my skin long enough to discourage the myriad of mosquitoes looking for their next feast. The average time for insect repellant to stay on your sweaty body was ten to fifteen minutes; I was past the time limit. While I silently complained about the climate, Bennett nudged me and whispered that the radio had just clicked twice. We each quietly alerted the man next to us. They, in turn, passed on the warning of approaching enemy force.

I gently took the safety off my rifle and felt for the extra magazines of ammunition. Although there was no moonlight, our eyes had adjusted to the dark. The river behind the trail silhouetted men carrying weapons and equipment. A few were wheeling bicycles loaded with supplies, while others had large frames or packs with supplies on their backs. Several were whispering to one another as they walked.

After another minute, the radio clicked three times and Bennett whispered, "It's time." He started firing his Swedish K weapon into the center of the enemy column, which the loud noise of fire from the patrol members' rifles immediately joined, the rapid machine guns and the blasts of five claymore mines along the trail punctuating it. I aimed my rifle into the kill zone and remembered the instructions in my training for night combat: aim low, since there was a natural tendency to shoot high after dark. A couple of Vietcong AK-47s fired back, but that quickly ended as our machine guns raked the entire line of enemy troops.

Bennett hollered, "Cease fire." The Vietnamese troopers followed orders, which was a great testimony to the effectiveness of Bennett's advisory training efforts. What had seemed like an hour was actually three minutes of intense firepower, but now there was eerie silence. We listened intently to detect the sound of men moving away from the ambush or maneuvering behind us. With the exception of two noticeable groans from the front trail, all was quiet. My hands trembled. I wiped the sweat off my brow with my sleeve. This was my initiation; my official welcome to actual combat operations. I had fired my weapon with the intent of killing another human being, which unnerved me to no end.

We waited a half hour, and when no additional movement was detected, ventured carefully onto the trail along the ambush site with our weapons ready to fire. Twenty-one Vietcong had been killed in action. They were all dressed in the typical black pajama outfits. From the cargo, we determined that this was a small supply patrol with the mission of providing food and ammunition to the local Vietcong force. The American team sergeant and a small team of Vietnamese troopers went from body to body, checking their pockets and packs for any papers, orders, or pertinent items that would provide insight into the destination of their cargo or any other useful intelligence.

Bennett assigned five of our troopers to wheel the bicycles loaded with bags of rice back to Tuy Phong Compound. The weapons and other supplies were divided among us. The few items that were of no use were thrown into the river, where the strong current carried them away. We left the stripped Vietcong casualties where they lay. It was hoped that they would serve as a warning to the other Vietcong. Before we parted the scene, Bennett took an ace of spades playing card from his pocket and placed it in the hand of the Vietcong leader. He explained that the ace of spades was a bad luck omen to the Vietnamese. The card would play with the psyches of those who might find these bodies. He said, "This one load of food and supplies won't reach the Vietcong, but instead will help the friendly troops."

Our patrol went back to the ambush site to gather our belongings and ammunition. One trooper noticed fresh tiger paw prints directly behind our standing position. We had never heard or detected its presence. The fact that this feline carnivore had been behind us was eerie. I searched my surroundings carefully, grabbed my gear, and scrambled.

We headed due east instead of retracing the route we had taken to the ambush site, to prevent walking into a possible enemy ambush set up for our return trip. The trip back was a strain on the troopers who wheeled the heavily loaded bicycles through mud, sand, and other adverse terrain. Our Vietnamese troops were aware that the rice would add to the food supply for themselves and their families. This motivated them to continue forward. The cumbersome journey gave me a new appreciation of the intense effort on the part of the Vietcong to transport their supplies to local forces.

Back at the Tuy Phong Compound, Bennett asked me if I had been able to detect the enemy before we saw them pass in front of us. I responded that they had made very little noise, but I had smelled a sickeningly sweet odor just before they came into view. He said that this smell was a typical Vietnamese characteristic due to their diet. The average American or Westerner emits a sharper and more acrid odor from consuming beef and sweets. Bennett looked me in the eye and went on to say that when a force is going out into enemy territory, it is important to avoid detection, which includes noise as well as smell.

The Vietcong were aware of the Americans' body odor. He advised me to overcome the differences in smell by having my advisory team eat the same foods as the Vietnamese at least five to seven days before going into enemy territory. They must also refrain from bathing with scented soap and wearing deodorant and aftershave lotions, which are distinctly Western behaviors. When following these guidelines, the Americans have the advantage over the Vietcong because we smell like them yet we can easily detect their sickeningly sweet smell.

My tour on the MACV merry-go-round had ended. The time spent with Bennett and the Tuy Phong advisory team was extremely helpful. It was an example of an American advisory team program that was going well. Major Bennett had had a positive impact on the local Vietnamese soldiers, police, and villagers. In short, he and his advisory team had won the battle of winning the hearts and minds of the local people to support both the South Vietnamese and American efforts. It was now my turn.

CHAPTER 5
MAT Team

The next morning, I loaded my gear into the back of Major Bennett's jeep. I thanked the Tuy Phong advisory team and their South Vietnamese counterparts for their help. Following Bennett's advice, I made a special point of going to see the Tuy Phong district chief last, and presented him a small gift as a token of my appreciation for the time spent in his district. This was well received and he offered to help me when I assumed my duties as district senior advisor of the Hoa Da District. Finally, he warned me to be careful in my dealings with *Dai Uy* (Captain) Manh, the district chief of the Hoa Da District. When I asked him why, he said that in time I would learn Manh's true nature. I thanked him again and hopped into the jeep with Bennett.

We headed south along Highway 1, which paralleled the coast of the South China Sea and wound its way through the barren, white-colored sand dunes. Bennett explained that we would first visit the Hoa Da District Compound to meet District Chief Manh and then continue to the Song Mao Compound in the Hai Ninh District. I would stay at Song Mao Compound until the Hoa Da District Compound had created space for our advisory team. I was very excited about establishing the advisory team at Hoa Da District, yet I was also fearful of what difficulties I would be facing in a rumored Vietcong stronghold.

We passed a series of football field-sized basins used to gather raw salt deposits through the evaporation of local water sources. This large production of salt was used for a variety of purposes including the production of *nuoc mam*. I commented on a large number of sand-colored, igloo-shaped, mud-covered domes scattered across the extensive dunes. Bennett said that these were kilns the local industry used for producing charcoal sold throughout South Vietnam. I asked where the source of wood was located since there were no trees growing locally.

His response was that the Montagnard tribes, particularly the Chams, served as wood cutters in the jungles of the Central Highlands. These tribes transported their harvested wood via oxen or water buffalo-drawn carts to the kilns. The cut wood was then smoked to seal the outside layer of wood. After that, it was placed in layers in an igloo kiln and allowed to stay there for a number of weeks as the daytime temperatures inside ranged from around 150 to over 200 degrees. This allowed the wood to slowly dry out. These eco-friendly processes allowed the sun and the desert sand to heat and dry the wood, while the rainforests provided a limitless source of wood. It ultimately resulted in the world's best charcoal, which burned hotter and longer than any other.

The drive continued through several small hamlets where the people appeared to be incredibly poor. Those standing or squatting in front of their thatched huts glared with obvious hatred. Bennett commented that these were either Vietcong or Vietcong sympathizers and were certainly no friends of either the South Vietnamese or the Americans. He nudged me and reminded me that my advisory mission would be to rout out the Vietcong and win the hearts and minds of the South Vietnamese in order to pacify this region. "As you can see, you and your team have your work cut out for you," he said.

Our journey led us through Phan Ri Cua, which had a population of over thirty-five thousand. The city is located on the South China Sea and the mouth of the Song Luy River. It served as a large fishing center and stopping place for junks ferrying cargo and charcoal. The U.S. Navy maintained a presence along this stretch of coast with the mission of checking the Vietnamese boats for Vietcong and/or illegal cargo. They also had the duty of providing on-call artillery support for the advisory teams. Their available ships alternated between swift boats armed with a gyroscopically-controlled 81mm mortar and quad .50-caliber machine guns, and a destroyer armed with five-inch guns and .50 caliber machine guns.

Heading south from Phan Ri Cua on Highway 1, we crossed rivers and streams over several makeshift bridges called Bailey bridges. These bridges were prefabricated and designed to replace a bridge that had been destroyed. The approach and exit from a Bailey bridge was very rough, and it required vehicles to drive slowly. A local Vietnamese Popular Forces platoon was assigned to guard each bridge twenty four hours a day. Arriving at the first Bailey bridge, we saw a small river surrounded by sand-bagged defenses on the roadsides and manned by heavily armed men. There was a large bunker at both ends, each equipped with a World War II vintage U.S. .30-caliber machine gun.

A line of vehicles made up of trucks, buses, three-wheeled Lambrettas, two very old civilian cars, two military jeeps, and several bicycles was in front of us waiting their turn to cross the bridge. The guard leaning against the sandbags was paying little attention to those vehicles or people crossing the bridge. I suspected that the guards provided little or no deterrent to an enemy trying to kill them or blow up the bridge. I made a mental note that improving their state of alertness and security would be a high priority for our new advisory team.

Shortly thereafter, we reached the village of Phan Ri Tanh; the Hoa Da District Compound was located here in an old French hospital complex. We stopped at the headquarter building and learned that District Chief Manh was unavailable. It was rumored that he was still asleep after a long night of heavy drinking and that he rarely got up before noon anyway. Bennett shrugged his shoulders and motioned me to the jeep. We resumed our trip.

Before entering the town of Phan Ly Cham, a strong smell of burning charcoal, cooking food, animal manure, poultry, and fish, all mixed with other unidentifiable aromas, assaulted our noses upon entering the marketplace. I noticed a difference in the people walking along the road. They were darker-skinned and looked more like Polynesians with their round eyes than did the almond-eyed Vietnamese. Their stature was noticeably taller and the women and girls were dressed in brightly colored sarong-like outfits that covered them from their necks down to their ankles. Many also wore scarves on their heads, covering their hair. The men dressed in a similar fashion. These were the Chams.

Cham pedestrians crowded the streets to go to market, which was a semi-weekly routine since they had no refrigeration. Many carried two fully loaded baskets, each on the end of a strong pole for easier carrying. Their cargo included rice; beans; varying types of vegetables and fresh fruits; live poultry such as chickens, ducks, geese, and guinea hens; a variety of fish; types of lizard-like reptiles; several kinds of monkeys; a small furry animal that looked like a cross between a raccoon and an opossum; eggs; salt; charcoal; flower; raw herbs; and a variety of other necessary household items. Our jeep crept slowly through this mass of people until we passed the marketplace and headed out of town.

A sea of light green geometric patterns stretched out on either side of the roadway. These were rice paddies and irrigational canals or ditches. It was a marked and pleasant contrast to the never-ending sand dunes through which we had been driving all morning. As we rounded a slight bend in the road, a small, light-green ribbon slithered in front of our jeep. Bennett came to a stop and stated that this was a rice snake, sometimes called a bamboo viper or a "two-step snake." He pointed out that about a quarter of this two-foot-long snake's body was its head. The venom was an incredibly potent neurotoxin. The venom from this snake's bite allows the victim to take two steps before completely disabling the muscles and lungs. The result was always fatal. There was no antivenom for this poisonous reptile.

Due to its frequent presence in rice paddies and its protective camouflage color matching the rice stalks, its most frequent victims were those barefooted villagers tending their rice fields. Fortunately, the snake had no fangs, but instead a row of teeth, only the back teeth capable of injecting venom. Consequently the rice snake must open its mouth extra wide to get a firm grip on its prey.

Bennett warned me that rice snakes liked to crawl into unoccupied boots, as did scorpions, roaches, and tarantulas during the night. He recommended a morning ritual of knocking the boots over with a rifle butt and then hitting each boot a few times. "Allow about a five-minute crawl or slither time," he said, "then turn the boot upside down and whack the sole and heel. When satisfied that all interlopers have left, put boots on feet."

How nice, I thought, *another fact deleted from our military training.*

After my nature lesson, we arrived at the city of Song Mao, a population of over fifty thousand people. The houses and buildings were constructed of solid-colored masonry of white or light shades of green, yellow, gray, pink, orange, or cream. The areas around the buildings appeared to be kept fairly tidy and clean, which reflected community pride. Farther into town the buildings became two-story structures and the streets teemed with activity and heavy traffic. There were many old cars, trucks, Lambrettas, motorcycles, bicycles, along with a lot of Vietnamese military vehicles.

Bennett said this was local traffic since Highway 404 ended on the far side of Song Mao. After the highway ended there was a series of marshes, sand dunes, areas with scattered scrub-growth of low trees, scraggly bushes, and clumps of grass or weeds. Civilization ended at the far end of Song Mao.

Before the highway ended, we came to an intersection that had a large wooden sign with the MACV crest painted on it. An arrow pointed to the left, indicating the direction to the Song Mao Compound. We turned in that direction and traveled several blocks. About a block from the compound, I noticed a low, one-story, dark-colored structure. In front was parked an unsupervised American military jeep containing four M-16s and accompanying packs, hand grenades, web gear, and a military PRC-25 two-way radio with its carrier strap hooked over the driver-side outside rearview mirror. Bennett voiced that this equipment should never be left unattended; there were too many Vietcong and black marketers around looking for the opportunity to grab some American military equipment. He slowed down for a closer look. The soldiers whose gear was in the jeep were nowhere in sight. The rear bumper markings on the jeep read "American 173rd Airborne Brigade," which indicated that the jeep was not associated with any advisory programs.

We continued our drive until we approached a long, one-story building with a sign that said "Song Mao Advisory Team Headquarters." Bennett parked the jeep, and we entered the main door. An orderly was seated near the entrance. Bennett made the introduction and informed the orderly that we were here to see Major Harlan Elliott, the Song Mao District senior advisor. The orderly walked down the hall to an office, and Elliott immediately came out and greeted us both as if we were long-expected and welcomed guests. He told Bennett that it was great to see him again. Then, turning to me, he expressed that he had been anxiously expecting my promised arrival for over a month and that my being here was a tremendous relief; the Hoa Da District badly needed the active presence of an organized American advisory team. He further indicated that at present the Hoa Da District was a Vietcong sanctuary that was causing numerous problems for the adjoining districts.

Elliott welcomed me to stay at the Song Mao Advisory Compound until the members of my team arrived and we had established a place in the Hoa Da District Compound. He directed his orderly to carry my gear from the jeep to the room next to his. This was great news, since I was very tired of single-handedly lugging all of the equipment and supplies. I asked Elliott if any of the men assigned to the Hoa Da District had arrived. He replied that four MAT team members with orders for Hoa Da District had arrived almost one month before and were currently living and operating out of Song Mao. I asked if they were working on any projects, since I saw no signs of their presence or activities when we stopped at the Hoa Da District Compound earlier this morning. Elliott said that they had gone to Hoa Da District Compound a couple of days after their arrival, but had experienced a very severe run-in with District Chief Manh. As a result, these men had decided not to return until the rest of the team arrived.

I asked if they were around the Song Mao Compound now. He replied that he had not seen the men in about three days. I then asked if they were here on temporary duty or were permanently assigned to the Hoa Da District advisory team. Elliott smiled and said that their orders indicated that they were permanently "mine." I stated that these soldiers were reassigned to this duty from the 173rd Airborne Brigade. The accuracy of my information amazed him.

Bennett interjected and said that we had noticed an American Army jeep with 173rd Airborne Brigade bumper markings parked unattended with weapons, web gear, and a PRC-25 radio. Elliott was sure it belonged to them. He suspected they were probably frequenting the Ba Phong (*bah foong*) house, a local "joy house," or whorehouse, that the local Vietnamese and American troops often visited.

Elliott changed the subject and invited us to join him for lunch. Bennett politely declined, saying that he needed to drive back to Tuy Phong while it was still daylight as there was less chance of a Vietcong ambush. I told Elliott that I would be happy to join him after I had completed a necessary errand that would take about fifteen minutes. I thanked Bennett for all of his guidance and asked him if he would drop me off at the Ba Phong house to retrieve the jeep and its contents and await the return of the wayward team. Like Camp Gates in Germany, I wanted to introduce myself and begin my relationship with my team with an understanding of what their duties and conduct would entail as a part of the Hoa Da District advisory team. Bennett gave me a thumbs-up.

Bennett dropped me off in front of the joy house. I jumped into the jeep, took the radio harness off of the rearview mirror, and started the jeep with the key that had been left in the ignition. I beeped the horn twice and looked around for a couple minutes. Seeing no response, I drove the jeep with all of its equipment back to Song Mao Compound, being careful to park it behind the headquarters building where it could not be seen. I then carried the four rifles, web gear, grenades, and PRC-25 radio into Elliott's office and joined him for lunch.

The Song Mao mess hall seated a hundred men. I suspected that this large hall was a carryover from the compound's previous mission as a combination U.S. Army Special Forces team and CIA operations base. An all-Vietnamese staff manned the kitchen and mess hall as a part of the Status of Forces Agreement. Elliott said that the staff was well versed in the preparation of American-style meals. That meant the cooks had been there working with Americans for quite a while. This luncheon consisted of corned beef hash, mashed potatoes, gravy, peas, corn, and applesauce. All of these American selections had come from cans, as was common in Vietnam. Song Mao, being a more established compound, had constant electrical service, refrigeration, more food options, and some freezer space to produce a supply of sanitary ice for iced tea. I figured that I better enjoy these comforts now, as I sensed an impending state of hardship at Hoa Da District Compound.

After we finished our lunch, we walked back to his office. He pointed out the various parts of the Song Mao Compound on the way, confirming my suspicions that this compound formally housed both the Hai Ninh and the Phan Ly Cham advisory teams, two companies of Vietnamese Regional Force soldiers, a CIA field team, AID representatives, the advisory team for the 44th Army Republic of Vietnam regiment, and two Mobile Advisory Team (MAT) teams.

MAT teams were a precaution added after the Tet Offensive. They were assigned to perform specific military training tasks with the Vietnamese regular and popular force units or neighborhood defense groups. Although not technically a part of MACV advisory teams, they lived in nearby advisory team compounds when possible for greater security and support. MAT teams consisted of five members: a team leader, assistant team leader, operations sergeant, communication sergeant, and weapons sergeant.

Song Mao Compound's buildings were not air-conditioned. Each building had one or several large exhaust fans in their ceilings to aid air movement. Finally, a number of large trees were placed strategically near buildings to offer welcome shade and coolness. The compound did have some amenities: running water from its water tower in the compound's center, showers with hot water, sinks in the barracks, and sit-down "burn-out style" latrines. This type of latrine, located in enclosures behind the barracks, featured a row of wooden seats with holes. A half of a fifty-five-gallon drum was placed underneath each hole. At least once each day, a crew of hired Vietnamese laborers removed these waste-containing drums. They would drag the drums some distance away, douse the contents with diesel fuel, and set them on fire. Everyone in the compound was very careful not to be downwind of the putrid odor while the burning process was under way. When that process was complete, the laborers would return the empty drums to their appointed places under the latrines once again.

Near each latrine was the urination station or "peeing place." Several large, empty, tubular, artillery shell containers were inserted into the ground to a depth of about two feet and canted at an angle to allow men to easily stand and urinate into them. Gravel that was about a foot and a half deep surrounded these tubes. The same crew of laborers would spread lime on the entire area at least once each week so it did not smell and was not an attraction for bugs or critters. I hoped my future compound would be as fortunate to have some rustic comforts of home.

We had just returned to Elliott's office when we heard a loud ruckus of cursing outside the headquarters building. An anxious orderly came in and informed us that the four men from the

Hoa Da District MAT team had just returned to the compound and were very upset that someone had stolen their jeep and equipment. This was what I had been waiting for. I asked Elliott if I could borrow a nearby office to have a heart-to-heart discussion with these men. He grinned and suggested gladly that we use the conference room.

I went in to the conference room and asked the orderly to invite my team members to join me. The MAT team, all of whom looked very irritated by this unexpected chain of events, reluctantly came in. The dirty, ruffled, uniformed men were two first lieutenants, Blevins and Hale; a staff sergeant (E-6), Whitehead; and a "buck-sergeant" (E-5), Amos. I told them all to take a seat at the table. I then reached down at my feet and picked up each of the packs, attached web gear, and M-16s and abruptly deposited one in front of each of these men whose uniform nametag matched the name on the packs. I placed the PRC-25 radio in the center of the table.

I waited a few seconds for this to sink in and then introduced myself as the new senior advisor for Hoa Da District Compound, their new commanding officer. Coolly, I informed them that I had seen their military orders permanently assigning them to the Hoa Da District advisory team. Effective immediately, they would report to me daily at 0600 hours to get their assignments for that day and evening. They were confined to the Song Mao Compound until they received a direct order from me to the contrary.

I told them that upon arriving in Song Mao, I had observed a jeep, rifles, and gear sitting unsupervised outside of the Ba Phong whorehouse and learned that it all belonged to them. The unattended jeep and equipment were in jeopardy of the Vietcong or some black marketer stealing them. For that reason, I went back to the whorehouse. I also discovered the key had been left in the ignition, and when no one responded to my beeping of the jeep's horn, I drove it with the rifles and equipment back to Song Mao Compound. "The jeep," I added, "is parked behind the headquarters building."

I looked at their hands and pointed out that three of the four were wearing wedding rings. If they were consorting with prostitutes, they were violating military law under the Uniform Code of Military Justice and could well be prosecuted for this offense. I reminded the motley crew that being off base without permission could also be interpreted as being AWOL. This was another prosecutable offense and could end the career aspirations of either of the two officers.

At this point, Blevins stood up and started to lodge a protest. I quickly cut him off and advised him that "when you find yourself up to your asshole in blame, it's best to keep your mouth shut and see where the situation is going." He sat down. I had enough on each of them to bring disciplinary action should I choose, and they were beginning to comprehend this fact.

Glaring at the MAT team, I outlined the standards of conduct and performance that I would expect from my advisors. Under no circumstances would they be allowed alcoholic beverages, use the readily available illegal drugs like marijuana, opium, heroin, hashish, or the services of a prostitute in this area. We would not present the Vietcong any situation or instance of misconduct to give them any leverage.

I paused for a minute to let that sink in and then reminded them that we were here to establish a new advisory team in Hoa Da District. If they performed their assigned duties well and their conduct was good, I would try to give them a chance to go to Nha Trang, Cam Ranh Bay, or Saigon at least once each quarter to relax and let off some steam. I asked if we all fully understood one another. They each replied, "Yes, sir." I said that at this time I would be happy to answer any questions. There were none. Moving on, I explained the next day would be spent with Elliott and his team. They would provide us with a general orientation about issues facing this region. I asked again if they had any questions and they all answered in unison with a snappy, "No, sir!"

To lighten up the situation, I asked how long each had been in Vietnam and where they had served prior to being assigned to this advisory team. Blevins responded that he and Hale had each been in-country for six months, while Whitehead had been there for seven months and Amos four months. He said that they had all been with the 173rd Airborne Brigade before they were reassigned to form this new MAT team. I asked if each of them had served in an infantry assignment in the 173rd and whether any of them had seen any combat. The response from all was a loud "Yes, sir!" I told them to go get cleaned up and to meet me in the mess hall to eat dinner at 1800 sharp.

After the MAT team left the building, I went and thanked Elliott for his kind indulgences in letting me meet with these men to get their attention and to get the Hoa Da District advisory effort off on better footing. Elliott patted me on the back and said that he was glad to assist. He felt that I had taken charge of a group of men that probably were not too happy about being reassigned from their elite airborne unit to an unproven advisory effort. He also guessed that several or all of these men did not have a sterling performance with the 173rd, which is why they were "volunteered" to join the new advisory team. From his brief contact, Elliott figured they had little or no idea about an advisory team's mission. I sarcastically responded that I knew where to start this advisory effort. Elliott laughed and wished me luck.

Back in my room, I began to organize my gear and hang up my uniforms that had been folded in the B-4 bag since my odyssey through the MACV merry-go-round began. Everything smelled musty, and I was glad to have the chance to air it all out. It was also great to have a desk and comfortable chair at which I could spread out the maps and materials. I took a moment to sit and was suddenly overcome with the enormity of the responsibilities and tasks ahead. I was assigned to establish a new advisory team in a region where the people were openly hostile to the South Vietnamese government and the Americans. The prospects scared the living daylights out of me.

At 1800 sharp, my four MAT team members were waiting at my door. All had showered, shaved, and were dressed in clean, pressed uniforms and proper hats. What a transformation from the ragtag bunch that I had encountered earlier in the afternoon. They all saluted as I exited the room. I commented on the appropriateness of their appearances, which was how I expected them to look from now on unless they were out on a patrol or field operation. Each acknowledged that they had heard and understood my comments. We walked the short distance to the mess hall and found Elliott, along with a couple of his officers and non-commissioned officers, sitting at a table. He invited us to join them.

The meal consisted of a choice of corned beef hash or dehydrated beef patties, canned peas or carrots, instant mashed potatoes and gravy, canned pound cake with applesauce, and either hot coffee or tea. It all smelled very good and reminded me how hungry I really was after a long, stressful day. Elliott welcomed us and introduced us to his team. The conversation began with getting to know one another, which then wove into seeking advice and support from this veteran advisory team. All had arrived at Song Mao Compound about the same time and had been there for slightly over seven months. Major Elliott pointed out one big difference that existed between the two districts: the Hoa Da District advisory team would be establishing and building a new team from scratch, while the Song Mao advisory team had inherited a well-established advisory effort and compound from their U.S. Army Special Forces predecessors. Elliott finished his coffee and suggested we meet with him tomorrow to discuss further information and concerns.

The following morning my team and I gathered in the conference room next to Major Elliott's office. Elliott and his deputy senior advisor soon entered and wished us a good morning. Then Elliot's face turned serious. He began the orientation by stating that the alleged information about the Hoa Da District was neither entirely complete nor verifiable. MACV was attempting to reorganize its advisory team concept from one that contained only military members to one that alternated civilian and military in its organization. Elliott explained that this was some "Whiz Kid's" idea of the approved means of putting a greater emphasis on civic action programs as a basic part of the advisory operations.

I responded that this smacked heavily of a State Department spin on the advisory program in Vietnam. He acknowledged that this was very perceptive. The last three months the "powers that are" had assigned a representative from the AID to be senior advisor of the new Hoa Da District advisory team. This representative had absolutely no training or experience working with a military team. In fact, he was a professionally trained career service member of the U.S. Diplomatic Corps; he was well paid and held the military and their programs in great disdain and had stated several times that he did not approve of nor would he permit "his" advisory team to conduct or take part in combat operations in the Hoa Da District. This guy had only been in Hoa Da District a few days and had hit it off very well with District Chief Manh.

Elliott let this information sink in a bit and then hit us with the blockbuster. According to numerous sources, Captain Manh came from a very influential Vietnamese political family, had bribed his way into his job, and was a major crook—even by Vietnamese standards. It was believed that Manh was at the center of an opium and hashish drug exporting business, as well as a murder-for-hire, illegal financial shakedown ring and a smuggling operation in the region. My response was that I previously had heard none of this, and I suddenly felt like a sacrificial lamb being led to the slaughter. Elliott nodded and continued that it was unknown what the AID advisor's relationship was with Manh. There was a suspicion that he may be involved in the smuggling, sale, and export of illegal drugs, since he spent very little time in Hoa Da District and traveled frequently to places like Bangkok, Hong Kong, Taipei, and Vung Tau.

Turning to me, Elliott informed me that my immediate task would be to formally document enough on Manh to give the higher-ups sufficient justification to remove him as district chief. I questioned if this matter could be referred to the CIA. Elliott acknowledged that the CIA was aware of the situation, but they wanted to keep a low profile and let an independent source (i.e., me) do the investigation and reporting.

I suggested that either the State Department and/or the CIA should eliminate Manh, his henchmen, and the AID senior advisor from the Hoa Da District so that our advisory team would not be plagued with their negative influence. Elliott assured me that they would be dealt with very quickly and permanently. I asked why these people had not been dealt with sooner if the American and South Vietnamese officials had all these suspicions and proof readily available. He responded that the timing had not been right until now. The other American advisors and he were in no position to act on these matters because their actions may jeopardize their district advisory efforts. I told him that in spite of all this, I still felt I was being set up.

Internally I was fuming. I was more than a sacrificial lamb. I had been used and set up to do the dirty work and to potentially take the fall in case everything blew up in our faces. This, in turn, would allow the more senior advisors in the region to sidestep the issues, the blame, and the career hazards. They probably would just chalk me up as another casualty of a sticky wartime circumstance and allow everyone to think that things went badly because of my inexperience and mishandling of the situation. I felt backed into a terrible corner with no options available. My mind raced as I wondered how many people knew about the Hoa Da District's sketchy problems and how high up the chain of command it went. At this point, I decided to keep a personal journal to record all pertinent details in case something happened to me during my tour in the district.

Elliott was not finished with his bombshells. He told us that the Vietnamese senator from the Hoa Da District in the South Vietnamese National Congress was acknowledged to be the biggest supporter of communist interests and operations in South Vietnam. It had even been rumored that this senator could well be the top Vietcong commander in the region and was the one who gave the final command to kick off an attack. Every time the senator flew a South Vietnamese Army helicopter to carefully inspect area defenses, road and bridge improvements, and/or trained Vietnamese military units, "coincidently" a Vietcong attack would occur within a twenty-four to forty-eight-hour period. These attackers all appeared to be well versed on the latest defenses, thus allowing them to score victories by destroying key places and eliminating or seriously weakening the South Vietnamese.

I realized that our advisors would be facing the Vietcong, corrupt South Vietnamese officials, smugglers, illegal drug producers and transporters, warlords and their military forces, and a number of plain old bad-assed bandits and pirates. I looked at the now very worried expressions on my MAT team's faces. I told Major Elliot that if he was trying to make us more nervous or just out-right scared shitless, he had definitely succeeded.

Elliott said that this was not his intent. He wanted to heighten our awareness of unfriendly elements so we would be better forewarned and prepared. He noted one major benefit to this situation: none of these bad guys ever worked together on anything. He suggested that if I were to work things carefully and negotiate supportive relationships, I might even be successful in forming an alliance with the warlords, drug producers, and smugglers to deny further support to the Vietcong, who none of them liked. Besides, the troops for each of these criminals were more numerous, better armed, and better trained than any of the Vietcong units operating in the Hoa Da District. He cautioned me that coming to terms with the drug producers and smugglers would mean that we would have to allow them to continue to ply their trade in exchange for their reporting on and/or interdicting the Vietcong and their activities.

I commented that all this made it sound as if I were working in a different country than South Vietnam. He responded that I was correct. The South Vietnamese government had very little influence or impact here. From his description of the situation, it sounded to me that the most effective approach would be to bomb them all and let God sort out the innocent. I kept my thoughts silent.

After the bombshell, Elliot shifted the meeting to the Song Mao Compound. He stated that the Song Mao advisory team served as advisors for the Hai Ninh District with its headquarters in the city of Song Mao along with the 44th regiment, Army of the Republic of Vietnam (ARVN). Their senior advisor was Captain Tim Simmons, a West Point graduate, Class of 1965. I knew Simmons very well and mentioned the fact. We had been in the same company at West Point for two years and had run on the intramural track team together. Elliott suggested that maybe I could possibly use that friendship to get some needed military equipment and support.

Besides the advisors, Song Mao Compound housed the CIA field team, the PRUs, and the AID teams for the northern region of Binh Thuan Province. Elliott felt that these AID teams were involved in more than they acknowledged. In his opinion, some of them were involved in an intelligence gathering and security operation that was different from that of the CIA. Any information was sent through State Department channels and was not shared with either the CIA or Department of Defense. I was beginning to get the big picture: the United States government had a variety of operations in Vietnam gathering intelligence and few, if any, were sharing what they knew with one another. This did not bode well for an advisory team trying to establish itself.

I spent the remainder of the day meeting with the district chiefs and their staff from the Hai Ninh and Phan Ly Cham districts. They all seemed genuinely glad to see that I had finally arrived. The two district chiefs assured me that I would have their full support regarding changes in the Hoa Da District, such as the removal and replacement of Manh. The meeting went very well and ended positively, which led me to believe that I would have strong support from my district chiefs.

Late that afternoon, Elliott informed me that a meeting had been scheduled for my advisory team with District Chief Manh the next day at the Hoa Da District Compound. He said that the purpose was to introduce me to Manh as the new deputy district senior advisor for the Hoa Da District, since the American AID representative was to be considered the district senior advisor. I mildly protested, stating that my orders clearly specified that I was assigned as the district senior advisor for Hoa Da District, not the deputy senior advisor. Elliott cautioned me to play the game for the time being and accept this lesser role until the situation in Hoa Da District could be better defined. I reluctantly agreed.

I met privately with my advisory team to alert them of the meeting and the situation with the AID senior advisor and Manh. Blevins asked if this senior advisor would be attending the meeting. I confessed that I had no idea, but at this point anything was possible. I asked if either he or any of the other team members had met the AID senior advisor. All shook their heads. They had only heard a few indirect rumors of his existence and assigned role in the Hoa Da District. I told them that we would all meet the following morning in Elliott's conference room to plan our roles at the Hoa Da District Compound. I had become very uneasy with the turn of events and with the uncertain prospects of the following day.

The next morning I met with Elliott and my MAT team. We agreed that we would all partake in the initial introductions between District Chief Manh, his staff members, and our team at Hoa Da District Compound. Elliott and I would then remain with Manh and discuss the plans for establishing the district's new advisory team. At the same time, Lieutenants Blevins and Hale would spend time with the other officers from Manh's staff. My two sergeants would casually walk around the Hoa Da District Compound making mental notes on the presence and type of existing defensive positions, weapons, bunkers, machine guns, mortars, barbed-wire barriers, minefields, and any other interdefensive measures that might be in place.

I asked Elliott if he had two or three reliable interpreters that he could provide to help us during our visit. He indicated that he could make two available, and he recommended that we use one in our meeting with Manh while the other would go with Blevins as they discussed things with the other Vietnamese officers. I wondered aloud if they were good interpreters, or what I called "pseudo-interpreters," meaning did they give an accurate interpretation or what they thought you wanted to hear.

Elliott assured us that they would give a good interpretation no matter how rude or contentious the conversation may become. This was exactly what we needed considering Manh's negative reputation. Elliott cautioned us that there was a strong possibility that Captain Manh and one or more of his staff officers understood and spoke some English. We should not openly comment about our thoughts and feelings about Manh, his staff, or the Hoa Da District. This would help us from falling into Manh's potential trap. The MAT team and I were facing unfriendly territory.

CHAPTER 6
Hoa Da District Compound

The following day our mini-convoy of two jeeps drove through the main gate of the Hoa Da District Compound. We stopped to the right of the flagpole in the center of the courtyard. The compound was built in a U-shape, with the Hoa Da District government offices housed in the one-story building to the right of the courtyard, the district chief's quarters and conference room in the building at the bottom of the U, and the police office and jail in the building to the left of the courtyard.

Major Elliott pointed to a fenced-in lot behind the jail, which served as an exercise and outdoor cooking area for the POWs and their families. He explained that it was Vietnamese custom for family members to be lodged at POW compounds when a loved one was jailed. The family was responsible for doing the inmate's laundry, shopping, and preparing all of his meals. I asked if any of these inmates were dangerous. He shook his head. Those inmates held in the jail were there for only petty crimes such as failure to pay taxes, debts, petty theft, or because they had displeased Manh or his police chief in some manner.

I expressed that Manh had set himself up as tax collector, judge, jury, and executioner, which was his right to do in this local system of government. Elliott agreed. Unfortunately, he added, in this local system there was no way to actually monitor the law or audit his tax collection efforts to determine what percentage went to the Hoa Da District, to Saigon, or how much ended up in Manh's own pocket. This form of corruption was common practice, along with buying one's position. Elliott reminded me that Manh came from an old aristocratic Vietnamese family with little military experience. He had bought his way into this district chief position.

"Terrific," I said.

The deputy district chief, First Lieutenant Con, along with two other Vietnamese officers on the staff greeted Elliott and me cordially. One of our interpreters translated our exchange of greetings. Then we were led into the Hoa Da District government office. We had arrived a couple minutes early, trying to make a good impression for our advisory effort. After about twenty minutes of polite exchanges through our interpreters, the atmosphere was beginning to get tense due to the noticeable absence of Manh. Con politely excused himself and went through a door in the back of the office. After about ten minutes he returned looking very flushed and nervous. He invited us to follow him to the district chief's conference room where the meeting would be held shortly.

The large conference room housed a number of comfortable easy chairs, several side tables, and a large central table. A South Vietnamese flag hung on the wall behind the table. On the center of the table was a large bowl filled with an arrangement of local flowers I had never seen before. Beside the flag hung a large map covered with a sheet that had a Vietnamese word *mat,* meaning "secret." Pictures depicting scenery in Vietnam adorned other walls. There were also several ashtrays made of Vietnamese china placed on the main table along with several unopened packs of Vietnamese cigarettes, a polite custom in Vietnamese society. At the head of the table rested a nicer chair and a stack of official-looking papers, which denoted the place reserved for District Chief Manh.

We were invited to sit down and told that Manh would join us momentarily. After an additional period of waiting, I glanced at my trusty Timex and noted that we had been there for almost an hour. As we continued our wait, we asked Con about the buildings in this compound. He told us that this had been a French hospital built sometime before World War II and then reoccupied after the French returned following the ousting of the Japanese in late 1945. The French had used it until they were forced to abandon it following the signing of the armistice ending the Indochina War in 1954, marking the independence of Vietnam and its division into North Vietnam and South Vietnam. The majority of the compound buildings were well constructed with walls of solid masonry that were at least two feet thick. This feature offered good protection from man, animals, reptiles, insects, and the environment. The roofs were made of red clay tiles, which also served as fairly good insulation, while the windows were either open or covered with heavy wooden shutters.

The larger building where we were seated had served as the main hospital building and was shaped like a large rectangle with a small, open, central courtyard. The front part of that building now served as the district chief's living quarters and conference room. The side section and half of the back section housed the other Vietnamese officers and senior non-commissioned officers serving at this compound. The remaining part of the back section contained several varieties of pigs, goats, chickens, ducks, and guinea hens. Behind the hospital was the district chief's small private shower/washing building.

To the left of the former hospital building was a newer large building of white-washed masonry with a galvanized steel roof that AID had constructed. This building was used for the storage of agricultural materials, tools, seeds, fertilizer, and a few crude wooden plows. All were intended to be used to help the local peasant farmers farm their land. At some point, the State Department, through AID, would permanently assign an agricultural advisor to the Hoa Da District to help the local farmers improve their crop yield per acre. This was a part of the loosely fabricated American plan to "win the hearts and minds" of the South Vietnamese.

Unfortunately, the local people did not know how to perform this mission. The assigned American representative for AID had failed to communicate or institute the agricultural techniques and supplies. After seeing the arid nature of this region, I was beginning to suspect that this project was a bit of a boondoggle with the district chief actually using the warehouse for another purpose. I made a note to look into this matter in more detail later.

To the right of the agricultural building was a long, one-story brick building shaped like a giant "L" that housed all of the enlisted troops serving at the compound. These troops were a combination of South Vietnamese Regional Forces recruited from the Binh Thuan Province and Popular Forces from within the Hoa Da District. They were better trained and equipped soldiers, looking professional in their complete South Vietnamese Army uniform. They were comparable to the American reserve forces and armed with an assortment of U.S. M-1 Garand rifles, U.S. M-1 and M-2 carbines, U.S. .45-caliber pistols, U.S. 40mm grenade launchers, .30-caliber Browning automatic rifles (BARs), four U.S. .30-caliber machine guns, a U.S. 4.2-inch mortar, and three U.S. 60mm mortars.

The popular forces resembled a local recruited militia, minimally trained, wearing either no uniform or only parts of a uniform and no shoes or Ho Chi Minh sandals. They were armed with a varied assortment of American, French, British, Japanese, German, Italian, Chinese, Czech, Russian, and unknown nationality weapons that included a variety of rifles and pistols on which they had managed to get their hands.

Popular Forces Units were assigned to defend specific areas such as bridges, critical road junctions, villages, or the district headquarters. Their military work was on assigned shifts during the night. The Popular Forces were considered local militia, which meant no housing when they were off duty. After their shift, they returned to their homes where they worked by day at their normal jobs such as farmers, shopkeepers, brick makers, builders, tailors, bakers, fishermen, and woodcutters.

After almost two hours of tense waiting, Manh made his dramatic entrance into the conference room. As if he were royalty, his staff snapped to rigid attention and saluted. Elliott, my MAT team members, our interpreters, and I got to our feet. We greeted the district chief, introduced ourselves, and thanked him for agreeing to meet with us. Elliott and I offered our hands, but Manh failed to either shake our hands or acknowledge that we had even done so. He was dressed in a crisply starched and tightly tailored South Vietnamese Army uniform adorned with many ribbons and badges. I did not see the Vietnamese Airborne Wings, the Vietnamese Ranger Badge, or the Vietnamese Special Forces Badge anywhere on his uniform so I concluded that he had received no special military training through either the Vietnamese or American military.

Elliott began by introducing me as the new Hoa Da District deputy senior advisor who had been assigned to help organize, equip, supply, and train Hoa Da District's military and police forces, as well as provide resources of food, construction materials, shelter, and medical care for the Hoa Da District people.

Manh responded coldly and reminded us that the AID district senior advisor representative had already been assigned to Hoa Da District. He would be returning the following week. Elliott replied that although the U.S. State Department had assigned this individual to work on civic action programs in the Hoa Da District, he was not an advisor for the MACV. This was to be Captain Haneke's role.

Manh appeared to mull over this information along with the fact that we were here to stay. He glared and studied us. Suddenly he displayed a change in attitude. A wide smile beamed as he cheerfully launched into a much more cordial welcome to "his district" and greeted each of us by name. He then expressed his difficult task of dealing with the Vietnamese government, Vietcong, warlords, bandits and pirates with a small police force and an ineffectual volunteer military force. He complained about being responsible for raising money locally to pay his Regional and Popular forces. Collecting taxes in this poor rural region was nearly impossible. To make matters worse he had to scrounge to get most of the necessary weapons, ammunition, uniforms, military equipment, medical supplies, and food for his troops. Overall, Manh painted a very grim picture of the situation in the Hoa Da District.

Elliott's interpreter, who seemed to be taking great care to guarantee an accurate interpretation, repeated Manh's statements. As the meeting unfolded, I had the distinct impression from Manh's crafty look that he probably spoke very good English and was playing charades. He proudly mentioned that his family had come from the ancient city of Hue, the old emperor's capital of Vietnam. He had gone to Paris and London to receive his formal and military education and training. I asked him in French if he had enjoyed his association with the people at Saint Cyr, the French Military Academy. He automatically responded in French that this had been an exceptionally good experience for him, and he particularly liked the French food.

In turn, I asked in English if he had enjoyed a similar experience with Sandhurst, the English Military Academy in England. Manh started to reply in English and, upon realizing his mistake, lapsed back into Vietnamese. He knew that his ruse would no longer hold up. I followed up by asking if we could conduct the rest of our meeting in English for greater ease of understanding. He smiled somewhat sheepishly and replied in good English that this was a satisfactory approach, since he and his whole staff were fluent in English, French, and Vietnamese. Through this verbal maneuvering, he was beginning to realize that we Americans were not fools.

Elliott explained to Manh that I was assigned in the Hoa Da District to lead an advisory team of thirteen American army officers and enlisted men. Although this statement appeared to encourage a couple of his staff officers, Manh did not react favorably. He probably realized that he would soon be under more direct scrutiny, which would curtail some of his illegal activities. I asked Manh if he could designate a space in this compound to house our advisory team. He replied that he would have to discuss this with his staff and get back to us within the next two days. The meeting lasted a little while longer before Manh told his deputy to give us a tour of the compound. He made his excuses and left the room.

Con instructed us to follow him for a tour. Our group was divided for the tour. Con led Elliott and me, while the remainder of the group followed another Vietnamese lieutenant, who we thought might be an intelligence officer. Con led us down the dirt road that went around the left interior side of the compound. He pointed out the surrounding buildings and offices that he had described for us earlier. We followed the small road that a masonry wall bordered. The five-foot-high wall was composed of rocks, cement blocks, iron stakes, and other reinforcing materials. It was erected along the entire left side of the compound as a barrier to enemy forces. Along the wall were a number of regularly spaced firing points that housed sentries. Embedded along the top was an array of spikes and broken glass to keep people from climbing over. Midway along this wall on the inside of the compound was one lone, large tree.

I observed that three mortar pits were crudely constructed and located together between the district chief's latrine and the end of the security building and jail. These pits contained a 4.2-inch mortar, an 81mm mortar, and a 60mm mortar that a barrier of empty wooden ammo boxes filled with dirt and stacked about four feet high encircled. At the end of the pits farthest from the jail was a partially buried steel connex container with a ramped entrance that served as the ammunition storage facility for the compound. A barrier of the same kind of stuffed wooden ammo boxes, stacked to about a foot from the top of the container, surrounded the container. There was no protective covering on the top of the connex container, and it was sitting in direct sun. The containers were not labeled with the types of ammunition and explosives, which also concerned me. I certainly didn't want this to become a large bomb that would explode, either from the heat or enemy contact. I made another mental note to correct this deficiency.

During this inspection, I was impressed that the mortars appeared to be well maintained; each had a canvas cover over the end of the muzzle to keep the continually blowing sand out when the weapons were not in use. I commented on the good condition of the mortars to Con. His chest puffed over this compliment and he barked an order to one of his assistants, who immediately ran off and quickly returned with a nervous-looking Vietnamese soldier. He was the sergeant in charge of the mortars and their crews. I introduced myself and repeated my compliments about these mortars, which relaxed him. Bowing his head, he thanked me and proudly stated that his mortars and crews were "number one," which meant that they were in good condition and well trained. I told him that I was looking forward to working with them. His wide smile expressed his satisfaction.

Con next showed us a prepared bunker along the middle point of the wall that housed a WWII vintage U.S. Browning .30-caliber machine gun and firing ports for several supporting riflemen. This bunker had been constructed from empty mortar ammo boxes filled with sand and stacked so that they completely covered the sides and top of the emplacement. Con said that this was a typical bunker for this compound. Elliott whispered that it was sized for the shorter and smaller Vietnamese.

Noting the lack of sandbags, I asked Con if some sandbags were available to reinforce the bunkers and gun emplacements. Any hits on these wooden boxes could potentially produce wooden splinters, which were as dangerous as metal shrapnel. He acknowledged that fact, but said that after numerous attempts through normal supply channels, they were unable to acquire sandbags. They had no other choice but to use the wooden boxes. I agreed that this was probably true, but we still needed to find a way to upgrade these defenses. This would be an immediate priority on my part.

He pointed to bunkers on each of the four corners of the wall, another at the midpoint of the two sides and rear wall, and one to the right side of the main gate. The bunkers on the four corners each had a .50- and .30-caliber machine gun. The main gate bunker was equipped with two .30-caliber BARs. He indicated that a minefield surrounded the entire compound, with the exception of the main road and a cleared path to the helicopter landing pad. I asked him how long these mines had been in place. Con responded proudly that they had been there since the French left in 1954, while others were from the Japanese occupation during WWII. He quickly added that the Vietcong and the bandits were too scared of these mines to attack the compound. I looked out at the minefields. Many mines were partially uncovered by fifteen years of weathering. Another mental note: dismantle the mines and update the outer wall defense.

Beyond the mines a series of low, rolling sand hills dotted with occasional scrub grass, low bushes, and prickly pear cactus graced the terrain. Some stands of this cactus were about twenty feet tall with broad, thick, fleshy, leaf-like projections covered with an abundance of long, sharp needles. They looked quite menacing, a deterrent to anyone trying to get close to the compound on at least two sides. Several rows of barbed wire surrounding the compound were notably old, rusty, and falling down in several places. I asked how long the barbed wire had been in place. Con told me that it was put up just after the mines. This meant prior to 1954. Another mental note: barbed wire must be replaced.

The back of the compound faced an expanse of white sand. A greater distance away stood the mountains where the jungles began. I asked how far the mountains were from this compound and was told over twenty-eight kilometers. The mostly collapsed wall along the rear of the compound left a wide open section. The only form of protection depended on rusty barbed-wire fencing, a questionable minefield, and occasional stands of cacti. We walked farther and a foul smell and a concentration of flies hit us. I assumed, correctly, that this wide, dugout depression served as the compound's latrine. The pit also served as the compound's garbage disposal—an all-in-one waste station. Swatting away the flies, Elliott suggested that South Vietnam designate the fly as the national bird.

Both groups returned to the main courtyard. We thanked Con and the other Vietnamese lieutenant for their informative tour. Con politely acknowledged our thanks. He and the other Vietnamese officers saluted sharply as we drove out of the compound on our return trip to Song Mao Compound. None of us talked much as we each processed what we had seen. Elliott interrupted the silence and told us to meet in his conference room after dinner. There we could compare our observations and impressions so that we could better plan the basis for our future approaches with District Chief Manh and the Hoa Da District Compound.

When we assembled in the conference room, I began with some of my observations, which centered on the perceived weaknesses in the compound's defenses: inadequate barriers, bunkers, manpower, and weapons at the main entrance. Secure defenses would be necessary to block and repel any enemy attempt to gain access to the compound from all sides. Next I stated that it was vitally important to remove the old mines, which were of questionable effectiveness, and replace them with a combination of modern, in-ground, anti-personnel mines and above-ground claymore mines. The rusty old barbed-wire fences should be removed and rewired with a new series of barriers both outside and at strategic places within the compound. These barriers would include rolls of concertina barbed wire in between strands of barbed wire at several heights on six-foot-high stakes firmly mounted in the ground. An extensive network of tanglefoot barbed wire needed to be installed along the outside of the barriers closest to the approaches.

Critically important was a sufficient supply of sandbags to replace the potentially hazardous sand-filled wooden ammunition boxes. We also needed to reinforce bunkers and construct a command bunker and an underground medical aid station. These were currently nonexistent. I suggested a security barrier around and on top of the connex container that was being used as the ammunition supply site.

Whitehead interjected and questioned the defensive wall network around most of the compound. It required repairs or replacement, as well as the construction of a wall across the entire back section of the compound. The latrine situation needed revamping, preferably of the burn-out type. This would help isolate and sanitize the area for the soldiers and civilians. Of course this would also necessitate an extensive effort to try to teach the local people about the need and benefits of following proper sanitation practices as a guard against insects, rodents, and disease. They apparently had no knowledge or understanding of any toiletry hygiene.

I identified the importance of having several military radios in the compound to allow communications with Binh Thuan Province Headquarters; Popular Forces Units platoons manning local bridges and highways; patrols or groups on operations; and American military forces to provide artillery support and air strikes, resupplies, and medical evacuation. I suggested a telephone-line system be set up between the bunkers, the mortar pits, the command bunker, and the medical aid station. This web of lines would allow necessary communications when the compound was on alert or under attack. As for compound defense weapons, I suggested additional and newer machine guns, a replacement 81mm mortar, several BARs, several 40mm grenade launchers, ample supply of appropriate ammunition and grenades, and three 90mm recoilless rifles. Elliott complimented me on the assessment given the brief tour and time that we had spent at the Hoa Da District Compound.

The other team stated that their tour allowed them to briefly see the inside of the Vietnamese soldiers' barracks. The Vietnamese proudly pointed to the one open entrance available to them. All the other openings had been totally blocked and barricaded so that the Vietcong could not sneak in during the middle of the night. Our team, however, felt that this presented a potential hazard to these troops when under attack. There was no sandbag protective barrier around or on top of this building, which added to its vulnerability. Another shocking observation was the lack of a kitchen and mess facility to store or provide food for the troops, which caused them to go to market daily.

The troops used four sites to make their fires, cook their own meals, and sit and eat wherever they could find room on the ground. This lack of saved rations meant that there were no provisions for the compound if they were under attack for an extended period of time. We surmised that they used their pay from Manh for food purposes. This made it all the more critical that Manh pay them all in a timely manner so they could each afford their food.

Another concern was the fact that there were no wells in the compound. Each soldier obtained water by crossing Highway 1 and walking the block to the river to fill his canteen, jug, or pot. The water was then consumed without being purified. This practice was unsafe, considering that the towns and villages upriver used the river to wash and to dump garbage, animal and human sewage, farming insecticides, and oil from vehicles. These substances turned the river into a toxic cesspool from which our troops and the local people were regularly drinking. It was no wonder that everyone we saw had runny noses and a case of diarrhea. A better source of suitable drinking water and sewage disposal would be high on the priority list for our new advisory team.

Amos mentioned that he had taken a few minutes to look at the small POW compound, jail, and its enclosure. There appeared to be few restrictions placed on either the prisoners or their family members. Family members moved in to the small site and roamed without any restrictions. They ambled to the village marketplace daily to shop for food or waded in the river to bathe, wash clothes, or retrieve water for the incarcerated family member. Entirely too much freedom was allowed with this prison operation—another matter that needed to be redefined and controlled.

The MAT team leader, Blevins, had looked around the large white AID warehouse and commented that it was unusually secured for a building that was supposed to be storing only agricultural supplies and equipment. He asked several of the Vietnamese officers and non-commissioned officers questions about the warehouse and its contents, but they appeared reluctant and almost scared to say anything. Their reactions to these questions spoke volumes about the real utilization of this building. The warehouse probably had little or nothing to do with agriculture. I stated that the warehouse and its actual usage was a matter I would have to pursue with Manh himself. I theorized that he would stall under the guise of waiting until the American AID senior advisor representative returned to the Hoa Da District.

Whitehead said the Hoa Da District troops had poor training. The majority seemed to be fairly disorganized, disorderly, and undisciplined. He felt that an aggressive plan of orientation and training would have to be developed and carried out if we were to have a reliable and effective military force. Everyone agreed. Elliott spoke up. He assured my team that he was here to help. There being no other issues to hash over, we all went to our respective rooms for the night.

I wrote a letter home to my wife expressing my grave reservations over the negative factors stacking up with this new advisory effort for the Hoa Da District Compound. At least I had Elliott's backing and support, which helped me to feel somewhat better. It was comforting to know that I was not facing this situation all by myself. When I finally put my pen down, I sank into my bunk and fell into a deep sleep in spite of the temperature still being over a hundred degrees.

CHAPTER 7
Cleaning House

The next morning I got up early, shaved, showered, and dressed in a clean set of fatigues. I paused briefly to enjoy the sweet flower fragrances accompanying the early hour. While I sipped a cup of coffee at the mess hall, Blevins, Hale, Whitehead, and Amos approached me. They said that our visit to the Hoa Da District Compound had raised more questions than answers. It had shown them the enormity of getting the Regional and Popular Forces Units fully trained, equipped, and operational to American military standards. What seemed to worry the MAT team most were the uncertainties that the seemingly hidden agenda of District Chief Manh caused us to face. The district chief's operation did not appear to be in line with American advisory efforts. My team's comments and concerns further mirrored my thoughts.

They asked if I had heard anything about the status of the incoming advisory team members. I revealed that the remaining members had been selected and were expected to begin arriving within the next couple days. They had been chosen from military units in the United States with a few scarce specialties being found around Vietnam. I wasn't sure what that all meant, but we would find out when they all showed up. After the recent Tet Offensive, available military personnel were being assigned to replace the casualties suffered in the regular American military units. Unfortunately, the military advisory program was low on the military totem pole so it received the personnel "leftovers." This piecemeal manner in which the MACA was currently running followed the adage that if an available soldier had a pulse and was conscious, he qualified to serve on one of these advisory teams. I was destined to make use of our assigned team members and train them to be advisors on site. I sure hoped and prayed that we would not encounter enemy activity too early in our tour.

The only team slot unable to be filled was the head medic position. Blevins and Whitehead shouted the name "Billy J. Bolling" in unison. Both had worked with Master Sergeant Billy Joe Bolling and complimented him as a very experienced medic in the 173rd Airborne Brigade. He had been sent back to Nha Trang to await further assignment when they were reassigned to the Hoa Da District advisory team. Bolling had received his training as a medic with the U.S. Army Special Forces and had already served three tours as a member of a Special Forces "A" Team somewhere in South Vietnam and Laos. Whitehead said that Bolling had spent over five consecutive years in Southeast Asia already and wasn't agreeing to go back to the States any time soon if he could avoid such a transfer. Blevins added that he spoke Vietnamese and several Montagnard dialects fluently. They all agreed that he was a very good combat medic.

It sounded to me as if he had either "gone native" or become a "homesteader" in Southeast Asia. Either way, he sounded well experienced in dealing with the Vietnamese people. I asked Lieutenant Blevins if he could track him down by radio in Nha Trang and ask him to join our team. If he was agreeable, I could get his military orders cut immediately, and we could arrange for him to come to Song Mao Compound the next day. Blevins seemed very excited by this prospect and left running to use the Song Mao team radio.

Elliott entered the mess hall and sat with us. The head cook placed a made-to-order breakfast in front of the major, a perk for the commander. Elliott leaned over to me and whispered that he had some new information about Manh to share with me later.

I took the hint and changed the subject to discuss a potential medic for the Hoa Da District advisory team. I mentioned that Blevins had gone to the radio to try to track Bolling down in Nha Trang. He agreed that this sounded very promising, since a good medic was one of the most important members of an advisory team. A medic provided health care services for the team members and conducted the MEDCAP programs throughout the district villages. This was a major tactic in "winning the hearts and minds" of the local people. Major Elliot mentioned he was meeting with the two district chiefs from the Hai Ninh and Phan Ly Cham districts. He suggested that I accompany him to the meeting to develop an understanding of regional matters and get better acquainted with the two district chiefs and staff members.

After breakfast, Elliott and I got into his jeep along with his deputy senior advisor and interpreter and drove the short distance to the Hai Ninh District Compound. The district chief greeted us warmly and invited us into a conference room. Hai Ninh's district chief began the meeting by formally introducing me to everyone present. I noted that I was the only representative from the Hoa Da District present. I immediately suspected that this was indicative of the problematic situation in Hoa Da District. During the course of the meeting, the issues of concern were identified and carefully discussed, including their impact on each of the surrounding districts in the region, as follows:

    1. The Vietcong are now operating freely within the Hoa Da District and setting up camps to use as their base of operations in the northern Binh Thuan Province region. There are strong indications that weapons, ammunition, and food are being procured and distributed through Hoa Da's district chief to these Vietcong units. There are suspicions that the details for these activities are being coordinated through the South Vietnamese senator who represents the Hoa Da District in the National Legislature. It is firmly suspected that the Vietcong base camp in the mountainous region of Hoa Da District is the central point from which the Vietcong Political Action Cadre is being

coordinated in the northern region of Binh Thuan Province and possibly the southern part of neighboring Ninh Thuan Province.

2. The Vietcong cadre forces, accompanied by Vietcong military detachments, go from hamlet to hamlet, mostly at night, and force the villagers to undergo indoctrination of the basic Vietcong doctrine and principles. The Vietcong selectively identify villagers who they accuse of working with the South Vietnamese and/or the Americans. They torture and execute them in front of the rest of the villagers as an example. By establishing and maintaining a level of fear over the villagers, the Vietcong hope to control the loyalty of the people.

3. Bandits and pirates are known to be actively using Hoa Da District ports as routes for their smuggling operations. It is strongly suspected that these forces are acquiring weapons, ammunition, and supplies through the Hoa Da district chief.

4. Several drug lords are routinely using routes through Hoa Da District to send their products, mainly raw opium from poppies raised by Montagnards in the Central Highlands, to ports for export to their external markets. This practice is being allowed to go on unimpeded by Captain Manh.

It was further believed that Manh was personally making an obscene profit for allowing and aiding all of these activities. Everyone was in agreement that Manh was very corrupt and must be replaced immediately. The role the American AID senior advisor played was not known. They suspected that he was assisting with both the smuggling and drug operations for personal gain. At any rate, he was accomplishing little or nothing in his assigned duties to improve the various aspects of civil affairs in the Hoa Da District. Furthermore, he had rarely been present in the area since his assignment began.

It was decided that the district chiefs for Hai Ninh, Phan Ly Cham, and Tuy Phong would go to Phan Thiet tomorrow to meet with the Binh Thuan province chief to list these problems and ask that District Chief Manh be replaced immediately with somebody having extensive military and civil governing experience. These district chiefs asked Major Elliott, Captain Simmons and me if we could transfer the American AID senior advisor representative, since his presence and actions appeared to be disruptive. We all agreed to accomplish this request. The district chiefs offered me their support and stated that my team's success in Hoa Da District would make all of their lives and operations much easier.

As we drove back to the Song Mao Compound, Elliott stated that Manh would be removed very soon. When a unified group of district chiefs made such an appeal, the province chief usually took their comments very seriously and took quick action to correct the problems.

He commented on another issue: the three district chiefs and the province chief were originally from Binh Thuan Province, while Manh had come from the city of Hue far to the north. I was beginning to discover just how regional loyalties worked in Vietnam. Elliott said that I should keep my meeting with Manh the next day as scheduled and say nothing about this meeting. I agreed with this secrecy and said that my main reason for meeting with Manh was to procure a space for my team of advisors. Elliott cautioned me not to be optimistic since he fully expected Manh to assign us one of the least desirable spaces in the Hoa Da District Compound.

Back at Song Mao Compound, I met with the MAT team and informed them about the meeting. I stressed that this information was highly classified and not to be discussed among themselves or shared with anyone else, period. They acknowledged that they fully understood and would comply with my orders. With that information behind us, we prepared for bed.

A mosquito net hung over the frame mounted on each of the bunks. Although Song Mao Compound was sprayed frequently for mosquitoes and a few other highly undesirable insects, there was still the hazard of a number of these pests biting one throughout the night. We had all been shown a recommended process of ensuring that our bunks and mosquito netting were almost guaranteed to be mosquito-free when we went to bed at night. This process required that we take a spray can of DDT and thoroughly spray the interior of our mosquito netting about fifteen minutes before bed then tuck the sides of the netting under the mattress to ensure that no other insects could enter that area. During this time period, any mosquitoes inside the netting were sure to die from the insecticide. After that time, we could safely enter the netting to sleep with our shirts off for greater comfort from the intense heat. That night we went to sleep feeling better organized and hopefully prepared for whatever we were to encounter in Hoa Da District Compound the next day.

The following morning, a jeep entered the main gate with an American second lieutenant driving, a sergeant first class wearing the Green Beret of the U.S. Army Special Forces and an uncharacteristically tall Vietnamese wearing the tiger-striped uniform of the Vietnamese Special Forces accompanying him. They parked in front of the headquarters building. Blevins and Whitehead ran over and warmly greeted the sergeant, who turned out to be Billy Joe Bolling, our new medic.

The second lieutenant was introduced to us as Second Lieutenant Carl Zender, the team intelligence officer, who was wearing infantry branch insignia on his uniform. I asked if he was in the infantry and he answered, "Absolutely not! I'm in the Army Intelligence Branch. I'm wearing the infantry brass so none of the local people will detect my true mission." He had just completed the Intelligence Branch Officer Basic Course at Fort Holabird, Maryland, prior to arriving in Vietnam. Zender said that he flew to Nha Trang where he met with several MACV intelligence officers who briefed him for several days on the area, the people, and the nature of his duties with an advisory team. What bad luck! My intelligence officer was a newly assigned, newly commissioned officer who had received less than a full week of military advisory training. At least he had been issued a brand-new American jeep that we could use.

The tall Vietnamese man turned out to be an interpreter named Tony Nha, who had formerly served with a U.S. Army Special Forces "A" Team and had been sent to join our team along with Sergeant Bolling. They had taken advantage of

Zender's jeep to transport them to Song Mao Compound. After we introduced them to Elliott, Whitehead took them over to our team's temporary quarters and showed them their assigned bunks.

Later I walked back to our quarters and again welcomed Sergeant Bolling to our advisory team. Bolling told me he was originally from Tennessee and had been serving in several assignments in Southeast Asia for about five years without rotating back to the United States. I asked if that was legitimate since the normal job assignment in Vietnam was typically eighteen months at the most. He stated that this normally was true, but the Special Forces needed qualified medics so badly that they allowed volunteering personnel to extend again and again to help fill these extreme needs. Bolling said that he had no commitments back in the States and liked living among the Vietnamese people, so he kept on extending his deployment. He said that his first tour in South Vietnam was with a Special Forces "A" Team in I Corps, where he experienced a fair amount of combat operations. The extensive training as a Special Forces medic qualified him to perform a wide range of medical services, including minor surgical procedures to save someone's life.

When that tour had ended, he volunteered to transfer to an "A" Team serving with the Hmong Tribe in the mountains in Laos near the Plain of Jars, followed by an assignment with another "A" Team in the IV Corps area near the Cambodian border. These tours gave him a lot of experience in dealing with and treating a wide variety of tropical conditions and diseases, as well as handling the superstitions and customs found in native cultures in several regions. He said that most recently he had served a tour with the 173rd Airborne Brigade. He spoke French, a dialect of Vietnamese, and a couple of Montagnard dialects. I felt fortunate to have been assigned a combat-seasoned and well-trained medic to handle our medical needs and services.

Bolling mentioned that he had recruited Tony from the Vietnamese Special Forces to serve as our interpreter. He and Tony had served together in both I and IV Corps. Tony was a very reliable interpreter who would tell you exactly what was being said and not just what the Vietnamese wanted the Americans to hear. He originally came from Saigon and learned to speak English while attending courses there. His English was unusually good but liberally peppered with a variety of profanity and obscenities he had picked up during his associations with the U.S. Army Special Forces. Bolling mentioned that Tony's true loyalties lay mainly with the Americans, as he didn't really trust the Vietnamese because too many of them were working both sides and it was difficult to tell where their loyalties really were. It was refreshing to know that Tony's loyalty to the Americans would not be in doubt.

I noticed that Zender was missing and questioned his whereabouts. Bolling said that Elliott had asked him to spend some orientation time with the Song Mao advisory team intelligence sergeant and the local CIA area specialist. This sounded like an excellent way to get him quickly accustomed to working in this region.

A while later, I talked to Zender and found out that he came from Hartford, Connecticut, and had received his college degree from the University of Connecticut, as well as his army commission in the Intelligence Corps through their ROTC program. I told him that we were glad to have him as a Hoa Da District team member and that I wanted to support his efforts in establishing an intelligence network. As a member of this team he would be expected to help with the establishment of the new compound as well as the organization of plans and operations. This also meant that he was expected to serve his fair share of nightly shifts on operational and radio watch.

Zender scoffed at helping with these activities. It was his understanding that he would only be responsible for intelligence gathering and interpretation activities for the advisory team. I responded that my understanding of his job description was that it also included the term "all other duties as assigned by the commanding officer." As his commanding officer, I was herewith assigning him the additional duty of helping with all necessary activities in getting this advisory team established, organized, and fully operational. We only had a team of thirteen Americans. It was important that we functioned together for our mutual survival.

I offered him a copy of his assigned duties in his Army 201 personnel file to clarify this matter. Zender said that this was not necessary. I asked if we now fully understood each other and he replied, "Yes, sir." This need to get all of the new team members' attention to orient their priorities and actions was really beginning to wear on my patience.

The MAT team and I got into our jeep and drove to Hoa Da District Compound for our meeting with District Chief Manh. Along the way, I again reminded them to say nothing about the results of yesterday's meeting with the area district chiefs. "If any questions should arise involving our presence or planned involvement with the Hoa Da District, please don't try to answer. Defer the question to me," I said. They all agreed to this course of action as we drove through the main gate of the compound.

We entered the headquarters, and I told Manh's administrative assistant that we were here for our scheduled meeting at noon. We assumed we would be invited to lunch given the hour of the meeting. This proved to be wrong. Instead, we were shown to his conference room. After about a half-hour wait, he entered. In his haughty manner, he invited us to sit down. I introduced each of us and told him that we had scheduled this meeting to secure an area within the Hoa Da District Compound for the new advisory team.

Manh paused a moment before making his reply. If it were his decision alone, we would not be allowed to use any space in his district, because our services were not needed or welcomed. There was no doubt about exactly where we stood with him. He went on to say that since the South Vietnamese military and MACV had decided to start up a new advisory team here, he had no other choice but to comply with their orders. He would show the assigned place to us now.

Captain Manh stood and led us through a small inner courtyard behind his conference room and into another complex. He eagerly opened the large wooden double doors to our assigned place. An overpowering smell of excrement made us nauseous. This area had been used to house chickens, guinea hens, ducks, pigs, and some other unidentifiable small animals since the French left in 1954. These animals, fowl, and their products were a source of food for the district chief, his staff, and selected members of the Regional Forces company assigned to the Hoa Da District Compound.

Looking at the accumulated manure on the floor, walls, and doors, I immediately protested that this space in its current condition would be totally unsuitable. With an evil smile, Manh responded that this was the only available area, and we could either take it or do without any space in the compound. I realized that we had no other choice. Manh was determined to play his game of making our advisory efforts difficult and unpleasant in the hopes of dissuading us from the Hoa Da District.

Thanking him with a plastered-on grin, I told the district chief we were very happy to be assigned this space and asked when the animals would be removed. His sadistic smile immediately turned into a deep frown as he realized that we had trumped his last attempt to discourage us from coming to his district. He reluctantly replied that they would be removed by early the next morning. We each thanked him for his cooperation. I told him that my team would be here the next day to begin cleaning up the area.

As it turned out, my visit to the Hoa Da District Compound that day and the commotion it created effectively diverted Manh and his staff's attention away from the activities happening in Phan Thiet, where the district chiefs were meeting with the province chief. He had no clue that a meeting was taking place and the main topic was him.

While we were driving back to Song Mao Compound, Blevins was very aggravated with Manh's antics, stating that he just wanted to punch him one time in his "cocky, smirky, smart-assed mouth." I told him to be patient and remember that Manh

Cleaning House

would soon be history if all went well during the district chiefs' meeting in Phan Thiet.

Turning to Whitehead, I instructed him to visit the supply sergeant and requisition as much Phisohex cleanser as he could get, along with several shovels, buckets, sturdy brooms, mops, bleach, and rags. We were cleaning house in our assigned space at Hoa Da District Compound.

At Song Mao Compound, I caught up with Elliott and told him what had happened during our meeting. He did not seem surprised about Manh's discouraging attempt and stated that my reaction in accepting the designated space was about the only acceptable option. I was planning to take the MAT team with me tomorrow to begin the process of getting the space cleaned and ready for our occupancy. Elliott agreed that I had made the right decision to begin immediately clearing and cleaning our assigned space. This would give us legitimate claim to the Hoa Da District Compound and a sign that our advisory team had officially arrived and started to operate in the district.

I asked Elliot if we could borrow thirteen bunks, mattresses, pillows, and mosquito netting necessary until we received issuance of equipment, as we hoped to move in within the next week. He said that he would be happy to help us out. We could take the bunks we were now using to the compound. Elliott did have some good news to report: an external contractor would construct our new advisory team quarters late this summer or early in the fall. This meant that our original living arrangements at Hoa Da District Compound would only be temporary, allowing us time to get our full team on board and get organized.

The next morning the MAT team and I prepared to begin the clearing and cleaning task. While we were cleaning house, I assigned Bolling and our new interpreter, Tony, to spend time with the medics of the Song Mao advisory team to familiarize themselves with the varied ethnic groups, typical medical conditions, and medical problems unique to the area. They were also ordered to make local village rounds with Song Mao's MEDCAP. Lieutenant Zender would continue to work with the area CIA representative and the intelligence representatives for both the Song Mao advisory team and the 44th ARVN. I wanted our team to become completely oriented to the regional situation and attain direction on setting up an effective intelligence network. Zender seemed relieved that I did not ask him to help clean out the dung-filled rooms.

Whitehead had packed the necessary tools and materials in the trailer, which he hooked up to the back of the jeep while Amos revved up the engine. We exited the main gate and drove to the Hoa Da District Compound. When we checked in, Manh's administrative assistant informed us that there were several men presently taking the last group of chickens and animals out of the assigned area. We told her we were here to begin the process of cleaning that space so that it would be suitable for our occupancy. She smiled, bowed, and said something that we didn't understand, but from the giggling of two of her coworkers, I took it to mean something sarcastic like "good luck!"

We drove around behind the big hospital building and parked by the back door of our assigned two-room complex. Loud, frenzied clucking noises greeted us. Two Vietnamese men slowly emerged dripping sweat and covered with spattered fowl droppings. Each held two chickens upside down by their feet. They announced that these were the last of the animals, and we were now free to move into the space. In French, I thanked them for their help in accomplishing this difficult job. The men bowed and told us we were welcome. Quickly they scurried off with the hens to the back part of the compound where they deposited them in a small shed with the other animals and fowl.

The temperature that day was over a hundred degrees and the smell of animal manure was incredibly strong and nauseating even from the outside of the building. I took a deep breath then led our group through the door to determine how and where to begin. The large room in the back appeared to be the worst, with the manure a little over six inches deep. The front room contained only about three inches of accumulated deposits. I suggested we start in the back room and work our way through the front room to the main door. With no other opinions stated, the plan was accepted.

To tackle this vile task, we decided to roll our shirtsleeves down to protect our arms, button our collar buttons, turn our collars up, and wear cotton work gloves for protection. We soon realized we needed a barrier from the intense smells. Whitehead suggested we rig some of the clean rags as bandannas to cover our noses and mouths. We all nodded in agreement, but after the first hour we had to sprinkle some aftershave lotion on them to further block the strong odors. We had only been issued three shovels and four buckets, so we initially began our project with three of us shoveling the shit into the buckets while the fourth person dumped the filled buckets, two at a time, in a pile in the far rear section of the compound.

The manure in the back room, which pigs and other four-legged animals had mainly occupied, was quite damp and firmly packed. It was easier to shovel and chop it into solid sections to be lifted outside, which left only a little amount of manure remaining stuck on the concrete floor. Significant patches of manure also remained on several walls beneath where some fowl had repeatedly perched. The shovels were very helpful in removing most of this accumulation. We started slowly, each trying to think up easier and quicker approaches to accomplish this onerous task. It was decided after the first two hours of work that, on a rotating basis, two people would shovel, one would carry and dump the filled buckets, and one would take a much needed break to partially recover from the smell, heat, and intense work. We also came to the conclusion that a greater supply of drinking water and salt tablets were needed to take during our breaks. The intense heat and humidity, along with the noxious odor, left us light-headed, nauseous, and at times faint. We decided to bring along a spare outfit for each of us to put on after we finished working for the following days.

Back at Song Mao Compound we each took a long, cleansing shower finished off with a scrubbing of Phisohex, which helped decrease the strong shit smell. We then gave our soiled laundry to the Song Mao laundry ladies. They took one whiff of our uniforms and refused to wash our "stinky" uniforms. So we brought them over to the Hoa Da District Compound and got a lady and her daughter who lived near the front compound entrance to agree to wash and press our uniforms. We assured them that if they did this right, all of the advisors on our new team would be using their services. The mother seemed very happy to get this new line of business and not at all offended when we provided her with soap to wash our clothing. This measure of providing soap was important, as we had discovered that very few people in the Hoa Da District had access to any laundry products. Fortunately, these women knew what the products were and how to properly use them. They simply couldn't get access to and/or afford the soap.

While the manure management project was in progress, the laundry lady met us by the front gate each afternoon. She smiled and bowed while taking our very dirty clothing from us and giving us our freshly washed and pressed uniforms and underwear. Each outfit cost only the Vietnamese equivalent of twenty-five cents to be cleaned.

Word spread quickly throughout the Hoa Da District Compound regarding our housecleaning efforts. Vietnamese troops came by the building to see the strange Americans tackle this crappy work. I got the impression that Manh had given them all strict orders not to provide us with any assistance or encouragement. Occasionally we would catch a glimpse of either Manh or one of his staff members quietly observing and hoping not to be noticed. It was obvious that our presence was not wanted, welcomed, or encouraged. At least we could take comfort in the fact that the Vietnamese and Manh were not trying to block or openly harass us as we tackled this disgusting project. I believe that they were genuinely surprised at the intensity, organization, speed, and thoroughness that we displayed as we tackled the mess.

The audience of changing Vietnamese faces increased. There was a constant murmur among the Vietnamese as they discussed us, our work, and God knows what else. We occasionally had to ask them to move out of our way. After a while, this was no longer a problem. They backed off quickly, covering their noses and making some rude comments in Vietnamese about the strong, unpleasant smell. Every so often one of the Vietnamese sergeants would come by and yell at the troops, causing them to scatter temporarily. Soon, however, these soldiers filtered back to resume their watch. It appeared that we were the featured performance for the compound that week.

When we had shoveled out as much as we could from the back room, we moved to the outer room, which had a different type of excrement pile. This manure was dryer, less compact, stuck to the floor, and much harder to break up and shovel out. It required greater effort with lesser results. As the pile of manure grew rapidly at the back of the compound, I suggested to one of the Vietnamese staff officers to ask the local farmers if they wanted the manure as fertilizer for their crops. At first he was puzzled and thought I really was nuts. Then he showed a glint of understanding of the true meaning of my words. He wandered off and about an hour later returned with a big smile and reported that a suitable farmer had been located. The farmer would come to the compound and haul away the manure to use in his fields. He let it slip that an appropriate fee for this fertilizer would be paid to Manh. This helped confirm my suspicions that Manh made use of every opportunity possible to pad his pockets.

After we had shoveled the bulk of the solid manure out of the two rooms, the next phase required a mixed solution of Phisohex and water to wash down the floors, walls, ceilings, windows, doors, and doorways. This presented a challenge since there was no source of water in the entire compound. In recognition of this deficiency, we arranged to bring an empty fifty-five-gallon barrel from the Song Mao Compound. The nearest source of water was from the river that ran on the other side of Highway 1 at a distance of about a thousand feet from the compound. Our hard-working team initially drove the barrel to the river and used the buckets to fill it up with water. We soon found that this required a lot of time and effort that took us away from our primary job of working on the two rooms. In a very short time, we were able to negotiate a deal with several of the Vietnamese soldiers to fill the barrel with water. We paid for this service with packs of American cigarettes, which were much prized.

When some of the more reluctant soldiers saw what was happening and how well we were paying our work party with American cigarettes, we had no end of volunteers. This necessitated the appointment of a Vietnamese sergeant to coordinate the volunteer party, which netted him a couple packs of Marlboro cigarettes, much to his delight. For an extra pack of cigarettes, he also volunteered to watch our water barrel while we were gone to make sure it didn't disappear. It seemed that Vietnamese free enterprise was alive and well in Hoa Da District.

We hoped that our supply of cigarettes would not run out before the project was over; we would be hard pressed to find another type of payment that would be as universally acceptable, although we had heard that bars of soap were another popular commodity.

Thoroughly scrubbing the rooms required a six-step process. Step One: apply a concentrated solution of Phisohex and water thickly and leave for about a half hour to interact with and soften any deposited materials still sticking to the surface. Step Two: use the strong brooms dipped in water to thoroughly scrub the area to loosen the remainder of the stuck material. Step Three: douse the scrubbed area with buckets of water and use the strong brooms again to move all of the loosened material out of the door into the backyard. Step Four: wipe down the cleaned area with rags dipped in pure, undiluted bleach to kill the germs. As an additional precaution, Step Five: use rags to scrub down the same area with a dilute solution of Phisohex and water, which helped kill most of the remaining germs. Step Six: let the area dry out completely for about twenty-four hours to discourage the growth of any mold or mildew, as well as to let any remaining dust settle.

By step six, the prevailing smell of manure had vanished and the more medicinal smell of Phisohex and bleach replaced it. All of the many varieties of insects and rodents that had been present in these animal coops when we began had also been driven out during the cleaning process. After that, it would be all right to move our bunks, bedding, furniture, and personal possessions into these rooms.

We amazed Manh, his staff, and the Vietnamese troops. By way of this project, we earned the respect of many of the troops and the Hoa Da District staff. Manh scowled at the prospect of his new and constant American neighbors.

Our intense activities during this cleaning project had provided the necessary diversion to keep Manh's attention focused locally. He didn't get a hint of what was taking place between the other three district chiefs and the province chief. On the fourth day of our labors, Elliott pulled me aside and mentioned that the province chief had decided to relieve Manh within the next week. Manh and several of his staff members would be sent to a remote district in the far northern part of I Corps, not far from the Demilitarized Zone (DMZ) between North and South Vietnam. Manh's family had too much political power to allow full, proper disciplinary measures to be taken against him.

I was glad that I never had to spy on Manh. The issue was resolved before the task started. Soon Manh would no longer be a problem for the Hoa Da District and the neighboring districts. The fear that the replacement district chief would be another "political hot potato" registered in my mind, and I expressed my concern to Elliott. He assured me that this was not the case. The new district chief was named Major Xuan (*Swan*), a senior Vietnamese military officer who fought against the Japanese during World War II, then against the French with the Vietminh during the Indochina War, and now with the South Vietnamese Army.

Elliott was quick to add that Major Xuan was not a Communist but a Vietnamese Nationalist. I speculated that Xuan would not be pleased to work with a foreign advisory team when he realized that he had more combat experience in his little finger than anyone on our team. Elliott replied that only time would tell. He added that the State Department was having trouble tracking down the American AID senior advisor, but he assured me that when they did, he would no longer be assigned to the Hoa Da District. That was great news, too.

Conditions were rapidly lining up for the Hoa Da advisory team. We had "cleaned house" literally and figuratively with the transfer of Captain Manh and the American AID senior advisor. Our assigned space was ready, and a combat experienced military leader would be the new district chief. I welcomed these sudden turns of events and anxiously awaited my responsibility as senior advisor to the Hoa Da District Compound.

CHAPTER 8
Major Xuan

The province chief summoned Manh to Phan Thiet on Saturday, who told Captain Manh of his transfer to the northernmost district in I Corps, where he would serve as district chief. Three of Manh's staff officers would accompany him to his new assignment. He was ordered to be packed up and ready to catch his flight from Song Mao on Tuesday morning. We heard that Manh launched into a very loud protest. His tirade was halted when the province chief stated that this action served as a lateral transfer with no loss of position or prestige. If he chose to question or fight it, the other district chiefs would turn this lateral transfer into a disciplinary action that would lead to a court-martial and prison time in light of all of the evidence stacked against him. Manh was said to have fallen silent and then agreed to gratefully accept this lateral transfer. His game in the Hoa Da District was over.

It was a great joy and relief for all of us to hear that several of the "Hoa Da problem children" were being exiled together to a far, faraway place. I had hoped that the Hoa Da District police chief would be one of the designated people to follow Manh, but that was not the case. The few times I had met with the police chief, his vitriolic statements aimed at Americans sounded like they came straight out of the Karl Marx primer for good little Communist comrades. I told my team not to turn their backs on the police chief or any of his men since they were strongly suspected of working for the Vietcong. A lot of organizing and evaluating had to be accomplished before our advisory efforts were fully started, and determining the true loyalty of each of the Vietnamese was essential for our survival.

At breakfast, Elliott told me that Major Xuan would be arriving in Hoa Da District by helicopter Tuesday afternoon. All members of the advisory team were expected to be on site at the Hoa Da District Compound at that time. I was keeping my fingers crossed that Xuan and I would establish a strong working rapport. I also hoped that he would recruit and organize a good staff that would be cooperative with the American advisors. This would not come easy after Captain Manh. He had been verbally and physically abusive to the Vietnamese soldiers as well as the local civilians. New beginnings included new challenges for winning the hearts and minds of the Vietnamese.

Shortly after lunch a South Vietnamese Army three-quarter-ton truck drove into the Song Mao Compound and unloaded two U.S. Army sergeants and their gear. They turned out to be Master Sergeant Wilson, who was to serve as our head noncommissioned officer (NCO) sergeant, and Sergeant First Class Cuthbert, who was to serve as the infantry small unit NCO advisor. After introducing myself and welcoming them both to Song Mao, I asked Wilson where he had served before coming to Vietnam. He replied that he had been stationed in Augsburg, Germany, with the 24th Division where he had served over five years, first as the top NCO for an infantry battalion and then as the top NCO in a Brigade G-3 section. Sergeant Wilson had arrived in Vietnam with no real training as an advisor, but admitted that he was very good at getting a unit organized and keeping it supplied and fully operational. Wilson had never served in combat, which might have proven to be a large shortcoming for the top NCO. He did have twenty-six years in the army, which would be of great assistance to us.

The tall African American, Cuthbert, looked very familiar. From the Airborne wings and ranger tab worn on his uniform

I could tell that he had gone through rigorous army training. I asked Cuthbert if I knew him. He smiled broadly at me and said that he remembered me when I was a West Point cadet. I suddenly remembered that he had served as an NCO in the department of military tactics and had worked with a number of my classmates and me. We worked on classroom-based tactical exercises, patrols, and recon during the infantry phase and recon training course. I encountered him again when we were receiving our training in military instruction on how to plan, organize, and carry out all aspects of a military unit. Cuthbert admitted that he had served in that capacity at West Point for the past seven years, but the downside was that he had no actual combat experience or advisory training despite a number of insurgency and counterinsurgency training exercises with both cadet and army infantry units. I told him that it was great to be working with him again. He smiled in agreement.

That evening I brought the team up-to-date on the situation involving District Chief Manh's sudden departure the following morning as well as the arrival of Major Xuan and his welcoming formation at the Hoa Da District Compound in the afternoon. The members of the MAT team were all extremely glad to hear of his departure and summed up their feelings of him by stating, "What an asshole!"

Early the next morning the CIA case officer for the northern Binh Thuan Province region visited Elliott, the Song Mao intelligence officer, Zender, and me. Two dead bodies had been discovered on the edge of the village of Hoi Tam, not far from the Hoa Da District Compound. The CIA case officer suggested we join him to save time with the explanation process. Elliott arranged to have, as added precautions, an extra jeep with four men armed with three automatic rifles, a 40mm grenade launcher, and a number of special grenades and ammunitions designed to handle a variety of combat situations. The rest of us each carried eight grenades, an M-16 with two bandoleers, and 120 rounds of ammunition loaded into magazines of twenty rounds for quick loading. We each wore our flak jacket. Our steel pot helmets covered with a camouflage cloth cover protected our heads. The CIA case officer carried a Thompson sub-machine gun and several grenades with him.

The drive down the road was slower than normal due to an unusually large number of people, cargo, and animals headed for the local marketplaces. Even when we cleared the throngs of people, we were forced to drive slowly to avoid the myriad of large potholes that pockmarked most of the local roads. Severe weather, traffic, and a lack of maintenance, punctuated by occasional landmines and booby traps being detonated at roadblock sites, which were often erected by the local Vietcong guerillas under cover of night, caused these.

Our three-vehicle convoy drove into Hoi Tam. On the far side of the village, two civilian vehicles, which turned out to be driven by three other CIA agents, stopped us. The CIA agents assured us that proper security was set up and led us on foot behind the line of houses where a crop of peanuts was being grown. To the side of a low berm lay the two bodies that appeared to be dressed in the tattered uniforms of U.S. Army officers. The lead CIA case officer said that the Vietcong had tortured these officers to death by and left them there overnight. From the dog tags and nametags on their uniforms, they could confirm that these were a pair of U.S. Army military advisors who had disappeared about a week ago in Lam Dong Province. One of the officers was a major and the other a captain. The stench of death was overpowering and nauseating, causing several of us to take handkerchiefs and cover our noses to keep from vomiting. The exposed flesh was covered with masses of swarming flies and several types of small beetles. We quickly learned firsthand that in the heat of the tropics, dead flesh starts decaying very rapidly.

The CIA agents brushed away the insects and showed us in great detail how these officers had been tortured and murdered. I noted that both of these men had died with a look of extreme pain permanently etched into their faces. One agent pointed out that their backs showed that they had been severely whipped with some kind of belt or rope that had a metal attachment on the end. Another agent showed us at least twenty places on their legs, arms, and torsos where patches of skin had been stripped off by a knife or some other sharp device. Some of the bones in each of their hands and forearms had been systematically broken. It also appeared that they had been struck in their faces and heads with a rifle butt, which had caused severe bruising along with several broken bones, gouged eyes, and a number of missing teeth. Finally, and most disgusting and unnerving of all, the CIA case officer showed us that they had each been castrated and their testicles had been shoved down their throats. He added that they had probably not died from the severe pain, but had instead choked to death during this process.

By this time we were all in shock and several in our group turned aside and vomited. What a horrendous display of barbarism and extreme cruelty. The CIA case officer apologized for putting us through this process, but stated that we needed to know the enemy and their capabilities. He added that the Vietcong's basic beliefs and values were different than ours and they should be regarded and treated as uncivilized barbarians. The only thing the Vietcong seemed to comprehend was that if they felt you could hurt them worse, then they might respect and treat you better. Because of this extreme brutality, the members of the Hoa Da District advisory team and I made a pact that we would never surrender or be taken alive if at all possible.

Earlier in the day, the CIA agents had questioned the villagers about what they had seen and heard during the night. The villagers, consisting of a few elderly, children, and young women (most of whom were pregnant), claimed that they saw and heard nothing. This seemed odd to the CIA agents, since a number of local dogs had been barking since their arrival. The CIA agent wondered where the village men were. The villagers responded that they were either off in the army or had been killed. When asked how long it had been since any younger men had been in the village, they said that it had been at least two years.

The CIA agents then asked themselves how all of these pregnancies were possible if no men had been around. Their conclusion was that this was obviously a Vietcong village and the men were off with the army; that is, the Communist Vietcong Army. They probably visited their homes under cover of darkness when they were in the area.

One CIA agent looked away and informed us that they would arrange for the bodies of these officers to be accounted for through the Army Graves and Registration Unit and finally shipped back to their families in the United States. The agents would work through their intelligence sources to try to pinpoint the exact Vietcong unit and people responsible for this despicable and barbaric crime. They assured us that when that happened, appropriate measures of "extermination with extreme prejudice" would be taken. We thanked the CIA agents for giving us this tragic but important lesson. With the stench of human death burned permanently into our noses and memories, we solemnly left with weapons ready and a higher awareness of our enemy and surroundings.

That afternoon our jeeps rolled through the main Hoa Da District Compound for the installation ceremony of Major Xuan as the Hoa Da District's new district chief. Thin ropes with a number of small South Vietnamese flags on each had been strung from the edge of the buildings surrounding the central courtyard to the flagpole in the center. These ropes were arranged in such a manner that they resembled the spokes of a giant wheel. The main flagpole had a large Vietnamese flag, with its yellow and red stripes, flying above the layer of thin ropes. The American flag was not displayed anywhere since the Status of Forces Agreement with the Vietnamese forbade American advisory teams from flying their country's flag in a Vietnamese compound. The entire compound appeared to have been greatly cleaned up and all of the driveway and surrounding dirt or sand had been carefully cleaned and raked.

The district chiefs from Phan Ly Cham, Hai Ninh, Tuy Phong, and their staff officers drove in to the courtyard. We all politely greeted one another. Two of the district chiefs stated that this was a long overdue occasion. They had heard that Xuan was regarded as a professional soldier who would absolutely not permit any type of illegal activities in his compound or military units. I thought that this would come as a major shock to everyone in Hoa Da District. Someone like that would be a refreshing and rare commodity in South Vietnam.

All of us were asked to stand to the left of the podium, which had been set up in front of the headquarters building. There several men, who appeared to be dressed in religious ceremonial robes, joined us. I recognized two of them to be Roman Catholic priests with their black robes and high, starched white collars. Three others with shaved heads and bright yellow robes were Buddhist priests, and three more men with short hair and dark-colored robes I guessed might be Cao Dai priests. At the last minute, the local Hoa Da District police chief hurried in and stood next to me with a real scowl on his face. He made no secret of the fact that he did not like Americans.

The soldiers serving on the honor guard were all dressed in tailored, starched Vietnamese fatigue uniforms with bright yellow Vietnamese ceremonial neck scarves. Their black boots were freshly polished and they wore military helmet-liners that were painted white for this occasion. Each carried a carbine rifle for the ceremony. Con commanded the honor guard to fall to attention and then to the position of parade rest.

Major Bennett leaned over to Major Elliott and me and whispered that these yahoo troops were on their best behavior trying to make a great first impression on their new boss. We laughed and I added that in time Major Xuan would discover what a bunch of disorganized troops they really were.

Just after 1400 hours, two Huey helicopters flew in to at the landing pad just outside the right-side fence of the compound. The honor guard and visitors were all called to attention and a record of Vietnamese marches began playing over the compound's PA system as the Vietnamese province chief, Major Xuan, a couple of Vietnamese province staff officers, Province Senior Advisor Lieutenant Colonel Thompson, and three of his staff officers dismounted from their respective helicopters. The honored men walked through the compound fence opening, filed into the courtyard, and took their assigned places to begin the ceremony.

The Vietnamese marches continued to play on for a few more minutes until a red-faced Con scurried out of formation into the doorway of the headquarters building and barked some orders at someone inside who immediately grabbed the arm of the record player and dragged it off the record with a loud scratching sound. Con then hurried back to his place in formation, red-faced, head bowed, and with eyes looking at the ground. The Vietnamese province chief took his place at the podium and launched into his welcoming oration to Major Xuan as the new Hoa Da district chief.

The speech, in Vietnamese, droned on for the better part of an hour. The high heat and humidity slowly began to take their toll among the troops in the honor guard. Since they were positioned directly across from the visitors, we had a good view of them. When the speech began, they all stood at rigid attention and looked very sharp. After about twenty minutes some began to look frazzled and to wobble a bit as their legs got weaker and shakier. My guess was that they had never been instructed not to lock their knees, which in time could cut off the circulation to the lower half of the body and cause them to pass out. The soldiers, wanting to look sharp and give the best impression to the new district chief, tried to hold that rigid pose as long as possible.

After thirty minutes, their wobbling became much more noticeable, until several passed out and fell where they stood. When this happened, nobody made a move to come to their aide, nor did the Vietnamese province chief seem to take note of it or make any attempt to hurry or shorten his presentation. After spending a few minutes on the ground, they each came to and regained their standing position in ranks appearing to be rather unsteady for a few minutes more.

One of the soldiers in the back row threw up a little when he came to again, while the other fallen soldiers stood up but were too weak and wobbly to lock their knees as they had before. This

Major Xuan

worked in their favor: none of them passed out a second time during the ceremony.

The Vietnamese province chief's message emphasized honorable changes that would be occurring in the Hoa Da District through the direction of Xuan. This seemed to please the other district chiefs, their staff members, and the religious leaders, while the Hoa Da District police chief appeared very annoyed. His negative reaction convinced me he was working for the Vietcong. Eyeing the police chief, I wondered what his connection was, if any, to the deaths of the two American advisors that we had found earlier in the day. I needed to determine for which enemy group or groups he was actually working and take appropriate action at that time. It appeared that my advisory work would involve a fair amount of detective work to accurately assess the situation.

The Vietnamese province chief finally reached the end of his address and called Major Xuan up to officially welcome him asced the new district chief. Xuan was wearing a well-tailored, starched fatigue uniform with Vietnamese and American parachute wings, as well as the Vietnamese Ranger Training patch, all of which indicated his extensive military training. On his head he wore the tan beret of a Vietnamese Ranger, an honor reserved for only an elite section of the Vietnamese military who had served in extended combat operations with that type of unit. A couple of deep-set scars were etched on one side of his face, which I guessed to be old shrapnel wounds. His skin looked like tanned leather from all of the sunlight he had been exposed to during his years in the military. Overall, he was the picture of military experience, discipline, and leadership, unlike the soft, deceptive, and totally corrupt Captain Manh.

Xuan thanked the Vietnamese province chief and told those assembled how glad he was to be at the Hoa Da District Compound. He was a man of few words and high expectations; he remarked upon the enormity of work required from all of us in order to straighten out the situation in the Hoa Da District. On behalf of the American advisors, Lieutenant Colonel

Thompson then offered a few words of welcome and support for Major Xuan. Thompson then presented him with a highly decorated swagger stick and a MACV 37 Advisory Team coffee mug with his name embossed on it as a symbol of American support. With that, the ceremony concluded. Xuan was introduced to the other Vietnamese district chiefs, the staff, local dignitaries, religious leaders, and American advisors. He spoke only in Vietnamese but politely greeted us. I was sure from his age and experience that he also could speak French and perhaps even understand some English.

The Vietnamese province chief returned to his helicopter, and I accompanied Thompson and his staff to their helicopter. Thompson briefly mentioned that a decision had been made at MACV Headquarters to have a more senior American military officer, Major George Dramis, was sent to the Hoa Da District to serve as district senior advisor. He was expected to arrive in mid-August, and with his arrival, I would serve as the deputy senior advisor. With that news, Thompson boarded his chopper and was soon in the air for the return trip to Phan Thiet.

This news came to me as a total shock. I suspected that this change-in-command might be due to the fact that a very senior Vietnamese major had just been appointed district chief and the Americans wanted to be equal, seniority wise. When I announced the change of command to the other advisors, Bennett shrugged it off and stated that this was a typical example of the lack of communication the American Binh Thuan Province senior advisor, Thompson, and his staff practiced.

Major Xuan spoke to us through an interpreter and informed everyone that he would be meeting with the other district chiefs for the next couple hours and would like to meet with the American advisors the next morning. In effect, the afternoon's meeting was to be an all-Vietnamese meeting excluding all American advisors. We, in turn, got back in our jeeps and drove to Song Mao Compound where we had planned to meet in Elliott's conference room to assess this developing situation and our future course of action as advisors in this region. Before leaving, I quickly looked into our assigned advisory team space and was pleased to see it still intact after our many hours of arduous cleaning. All appeared ready for our move to the compound.

Back in Song Mao Compound, Elliott called a meeting for Bennett; Simmons; Major René Dufort, the senior advisor for the former Special Forces camp at Luong Son; team sergeants for Tuy Phong, Hai Ninh, Phan Ly Cham, Hoa Da, Luong Son; the CIA regional representative; and me. Bennett expressed his grave concerns over the torture and deaths of the two American advisors. He said that this represented a new, more brazen approach on the part of the Vietcong operating in this area. Elliott cautioned Bennett not to jump to conclusions too fast, since there was yet no proof that the Vietcong had performed this barbaric deed. Several possible Vietnamese groups known to be operating in the northern Binh Thuan Province as well as the neighboring provinces could have carried it out.

The CIA representative interjected that while this might be true; this heinous act had all of the characteristics of a Vietcong cadre-directed action. The Vietnamese senator, who was suspected of being a Vietcong mole, may well have ordered it. Another possibility could be a parting statement from Manh or one of the regional drug lords, who were reported to be very unhappy with those two advisors for directly interfering with the processing and shipment of their drugs. The CIA representative felt very sure his sources would be able to pin down and identify both the group and individuals who had ordered and carried out the act. When that time came there would be abundant opportunities for appropriate retribution.

Dufort reported an increased level of Vietcong activity in the Luong Son District since the start of the Tet Offensive in late January. Of even greater concern was the better organized, equipped, and trained Vietcong units. He hoped this was not indicative of a larger offensive being prepared for this region. Bennett asked him to elaborate on the type of activities they were experiencing. Dufort replied that there were roadblocks, punctuated with land mines and booby traps, which the Local Force

Vietcong placed along the main roadways nightly. He explained that these roadblocks provided a distraction from the Main Force Vietcong who were visiting a couple of the hamlets each night to "recruit" (kidnap) available young men and train them to become Vietcong soldiers. Anyone who resisted was taken in front of the other villagers and shot on the spot, along with the rest of their immediate family members. The Vietcong then labeled them as sympathizers of the American puppet government who must be weeded out for the good of the community.

The Vietcong political cadre would spend a couple hours indoctrinating the villagers on communism and the consequences for supporting either the South Vietnamese or American forces. This was their way of spreading terror throughout the countryside in order to keep the local people from supporting the Vietcong's enemies. Dufort added that most of the young men had been taken from the Luong Son region, and the locals had recently been reluctant to cooperate with either the South Vietnamese or the American advisors.

Majors Bennett and Elliott stated that they had not seen any signs of this type of activity in their regions. They also admitted that their districts were far more pacified than the areas around the Loung Son and Hoa Da districts. After some further discussion about how the Vietcong activity level was intensifying in northern Binh Thuan Province, it was generally agreed that the presence of the new Hoa Da District advisory team would be a step forward in blocking aggressive Vietcong activities. It was agreed that I should set up in the Hoa Da District Compound immediately to establish our presence and begin the process of working to better organize, train, equip, and discipline the Vietnamese Regional and Popular Forces in the Hoa Da District.

Major Elliott informed me that our advisory equipment kit would be issued at the Army Logistics Center at Cam Ranh Bay. We were to be notified by the MACV II Corps Headquarters when this was fully prepared for our team. He handed me a lengthy list of items that made up the kit: medical equipment, beds, mattresses, chairs, tables, field desks, field safe, kitchen supplies, gas lanterns, flashlights, batteries, electrical generators, latrine set-up supply, three one-hundred-gallon rubberized water bladders for storing purified water, mosquito netting, and pest-control supplies. Compound defense weapons included .50- and .30-caliber machine guns, 40mm grenade launchers, BARs, a recoil-less rifle or two, claymore mines, ammunition for these weapons, two jeeps, and a three-quarter-ton truck. To help establish and maintain communications with Binh Thuan Province Headquarters and surrounding advisory teams, two VRC-47 radios, four PRC-25 radios, and two large radio antennas would also be sent.

I thanked Elliott. He acknowledged this and then strongly expressed the importance to train and supervise the Regional and Popular Forces. Elliott doubted that Manh had arranged for the Popular Forces platoons to receive much training, never mind supplying them with appropriate equipment or supplies. He theorized that Manh was involved in working with the Vietcong, drug smugglers, pirates, bandits, and other bad guys and thus would not have wanted the Popular Forces to be very effective.

The CIA representative agreed with Elliott, but he added the importance of developing, maintaining, and utilizing an extensive and effective intelligence network in the Hoa Da District, a resource that currently did not exist. He said that there were many people in the region who did not like either the Vietcong or the North Vietnamese. It was essential to find a number of these people and qualify them as reliable informants for the South Vietnamese and/or American advisors. We needed to train them on accurate observing and reporting. All informants were to be given a contact person and a time frame. They were rated on the quality and reliability of their reported information from R-1 to R-5, with R-5 being the most reliable. Their efforts needed to be quietly rewarded.

The CIA representative cautioned me that it would take time to accomplish this search and that we would undoubtedly encounter a number of people who were imposters. Their real loyalty was for the Vietcong in hopes of gaining information about us, our intelligence network, agents, and contact people. For these reasons, it was vitally important that we not reveal any network members other than their contact representative. If our informants were captured and interrogated, they would not be able to give the Vietcong any information that would further compromise other agents or our intelligence network. Other CIA agents on his team would be available to help us choose appropriate agents, evaluate their information, and devise an appropriate reward for their services. I found this to be somewhat reassuring.

The CIA representative concluded his comments by saying that it was essential for my team to set out immediately to establish an open and friendly presence in the local villages and throughout the Hoa Da District. We were to let the locals know our presence and willingness to help improve their security and social conditions. We should then be prepared for people to quietly approach us who would give us vital information or who wanted to serve as a part of our intelligence network. It was up to the advisory team to handle these people and their information appropriately.

I assured the group that I would begin the process of directing the movement of supplies and equipment to the Hoa Da District Compound the first thing in the morning. We planned to begin staying there as of the next night. I then coordinated the radio frequencies, call signs, and code words with the advisors from Song Mao, Tuy Phong, and Luong Son compounds and the 44th ARVN. Finally Elliott and I coordinated the use of appropriate vehicles and assigned drivers to transport our equipment. I thanked everybody for their advice, guidance, and support in the establishment of this new advisory team. They commented that the success of my team would ultimately help make things easier on all of the teams in northern Binh Thuan Province. I left Elliott's office and met with my team to brief them on the details of our move to the Hoa Da District Compound.

My alarm went off at 0500 hours the next morning. I realized this would be the last occasion to clean myself in a normal shower before becoming a "boonie rat." I met Major Elliott in the supply building just as two deuce-and-a-halves, a three-quarter-ton truck, and a Japanese-style jeep pulled up in front of the building along with my team. We loaded the vehicles. I thanked Major Elliott again. Patting me on the back, he mentioned that he would visit our compound in a few days to see how we were faring. He added that he had just received some information about Hoa Da District's new senior advisor, Major Dramis. He had graduated from Ohio State University and received an ROTC commission in army artillery; spent eighteen years in the army; had just completed a course at the Civil Affairs School at Fort Gordon, Georgia; had no combat experience and very little military experience in commanding troops. My heart sank. Dramis didn't sound like a very promising prospect for the senior advisor job, but I offered no comment in response. I would just have to make the best of this situation to get my job done properly. We exchanged salutes and I returned to my borrowed jeep.

We arrived at the Hoa Da District Compound, where First Lieutenant Con met us and led us around the back of the building to our assigned quarters. In his halting English, Con instructed us to unload. I asked him if we should first perform the courtesy of reporting to Major Xuan.

At first he appeared not to understand my question, but when Tony, our interpreter, prompted him in Vietnamese, he replied, "That will not be necessary. He already knows that you are here and told me to come and meet you." I hoped that this was not an indication of our future relationship and dealings with the new district chief. If we could not deal directly with the district chief, our efforts could fail, as subordinates were not permitted to make decisions.

When I entered our new area, I was very relieved to find that it was still clean and orderly. It was comforting to see that Xuan and his assistants were apparently not trying to work against us like his predecessor had. This encouraged me to think that in time we might be able to develop a decent working relationship with this new district chief and his staff. After all, he was an experienced military professional who would need all of our advice, support, and resources if he expected to be successful in this new assignment. I reasoned that he had not been successful and survived this long by being arrogant or stupid.

Late that morning, as we were unloading the last of the beds and mattresses from the trucks, Major Xuan suddenly appeared, and I called my team to attention. We all rendered him a hand salute, much to his pleasant surprise, which he returned with a slight smile on his face. He apparently respected the rendering of proper military courtesy. Through Tony, I told him that we were very happy to finally be in Hoa Da District Compound to begin working with him and his staff. We all saluted him again as he turned to leave.

Shortly after noon we completed the process of moving all of our furniture and equipment into our two assigned rooms. The two trucks then left to return to Song Mao Compound, leaving us with the MAT team jeep, Zender's assigned jeep, and the Japanese jeep on loan from Elliott. After taking a brief break to eat the sandwiches the Song Mao mess staff prepared us, we resumed the task of arranging the furniture and gear in a manner that would make the most efficient use of our limited space. This resulted in three sets of bunk beds with appropriate frames and mosquito netting being placed in the smaller room and designated for the team officers and the senior NCOs. Five sets of bunk beds along with their mosquito nets were also set up in the larger room for the enlisted men and interpreters. Our team space consisted of several work tables and chairs, individual footlockers for our clothing and personal effects, and hooks on the walls to hang each of our field packs and web gear.

In a recessed space off the large entrance foyer, we stored our cooking implements and food supplies. It was harder to find space for the small, upright field safe that we had been issued to safeguard any classified documents. Initially, we stacked boxes and items on the safe, but this was not secure. We then decided to clear everything off the safe and tape a thermite grenade to the top, using strong military duct tape. I gave all advisory team members the directive that if and when we evacuated under an enemy attack, the last man out was to pull the grenade pin.

Maintaining a good source and supply of potable water is important for any military unit. All previous attempts to drill wells in the Hoa Da District Compound netted only non-drinkable salt water. We had determined that the closest safe wells were in the town of Phan Ri Cua, which was ten kilometers away. This necessitated a negotiated agreement with the mayor. To obtain periodic access to two wells, we exchanged bars of soap, cartons of cigarettes, and piasters. Fortunately we were issued two one-hundred-gallon water storage bladders as a part of our equipment. Two fifty-five-gallon drums were intended for non-potable water taken from the nearby river. Non-potable water was mostly used for bathing or for other general purposes.

I sent three men and an interpreter across Highway 1 to the nearby river with one of our jeeps and an attached trailer containing the two fifty-five-gallon drums and two buckets with the assignment of filling up these drums and returning them to our quarters. One of the men had the mission of providing security for this work detail. Proper security was a standard part of every work detail and group sent out of the compound. This was an integral part of our security and survival in this hostile region.

Developing a proper latrine would be another undertaking. Xuan ordered a slit trench dug farther away from the buildings near the back of the compound. This was an obvious improvement over the practice of the previous administration, where everyone just went anywhere they felt like outside the building. Of course it would take time to develop and properly educate the local people on how to use the facility correctly. We soon discovered that there was a district-wide need to get the locals to develop and properly use local latrines.

We next identified a suitable area behind our quarters to cook. Since we had no grill, we used a field-expedient consisting of two metal mesh leg splints from our first aid kit that we set up across the top of two stacks of rocks. The Hoa Da District produced the finest charcoal in all of Vietnam, so we had an infinite supply of fresh fuel readily obtainable. We opened several cans of ready-to-eat foods and tried out our newly made grill. There was nothing like a full day of work to establish a good appetite.

While eating, we noticed that there was a small cyclo vehicle parked in such a way that a mounted movie projector faced the white side of the AID storage building. The American AID representatives normally used this vehicle to get to the villages and hamlets, where they would show informational movies on topics both the American and South Vietnamese forces deemed appropriate.

As the sun was beginning to go down, the area around the cyclo filled up fast with people from the local area and some that looked like they really didn't fit in with the rest of the locals. My advisory team applied a thick coating of mosquito repellant and joined the Vietnamese crowd gathering to watch the nightly movie. The generator of the cyclo was cranked up and the movie was started. It was entitled *Navaho Joe,* starring Burt Reynolds, and appeared to be quite popular with the locals, who couldn't understand a single word of English. Maybe the big attraction was the many scalps the very bloodthirsty Indians featured in this film took.

When the movie ended, I noted that there were several thousand locals who had entered the compound to watch the movie. This made me very nervous because there appeared to be no effective security on the front gate to screen who came and left, no matter what time of the day or night. I needed to speak to the new district chief about tightening the compound's security immediately.

We returned to our assigned space and used a Coleman lantern to finish setting up our personal spaces, getting undressed, and lining up our boots, rifles, and emergency web gear in places easy to locate in the dark in case we were suddenly attacked during the night. Finally we sprayed the inside of each of our mosquito nets with DDT. At this late hour, the female anopheles had arrived on-station for the night, and we certainly didn't want to be bitten and run the risk of catching malaria. Since I was the last one into the bunk, I had the additional chore of turning off the lantern. I volunteered to take the first radio watch for a two-hour period, after which I would pass it off to another team member, and so on.

    I stretched out on my bunk under the mosquito net with the radio next to me and reviewed the day's events in my mind. I doubted that much would happen our first night in the Hoa Da District Compound since we were not yet perceived as a threat to the Vietcong. We also were unable to communicate with any other Americans except those in Song Mao Compound due to the extreme limitations of our radio antenna. I had already assigned the task of raising a long-range antenna to our team radio operator and the communication sergeant the next day: they would lash it to the top of the only large tree in the center of the compound. That should help to increase our range of communications to the signal outpost on Titty Mountain, where our signal could be forwarded to the Province Advisory Team Headquarters in Phan Thiet. This would be our main means of establishing communication with important support elements such as the U.S. Air Force, Army Aviation Service, Navy, and medical evacuation. The harsh reality of establishing a new advisory team from scratch was really starting to set in big time. There were so many needs to be met. Most of my team was new to Vietnam and none had ever started a new compound. We were all going to have to learn by on-the-job training, but at least we could rely on Major Xuan.

CHAPTER 9
Survival of a New Advisor

The team member on radio watch enforced a wake-up time of 0600 hours. We poured the non-potable water that had been gathered from the river in the fifty-five-gallon drums into our steel pots. These helmets served as washbasins when we set them on top of an improvised washstand behind our building. The stand was constructed of several scraps of wood scrounged by Sergeants Whitehead and Amos. We hastily took turns washing, shaving, and brushing our teeth. During this personal clean-up process, we noticed a lot of interest from giggling young Vietnamese women who stopped and watched us. These women were the family members of prisoners.

Apparently we were of great interest to these women since we were the first round-eyed, non-Vietnamese men they had ever seen. We were all over six feet tall and most of us had blond hair and blue eyes, and we were young, attractive, and in very good physical condition. This increasing gallery of giggling Vietnamese women developed into a daily morning ritual. All of these women were aged dramatically from years of hard labor. None of them were very attractive and most lacked personal hygiene. You could smell them long before you could see them.

Most of them had smiles featuring teeth blackened by chewing betel nuts. Betel nuts were a type of berry plentiful throughout Vietnam. They were first dipped in powdered lime before being chewed. My guess is that the lime had a slight buffering effect on the tartness of the betel nuts. The constant practice of chewing them protected their teeth by layering a black coating on them and releasing a slight narcotic "high" alleviating any dental pain. The juice from the berry is red. When spit on the ground, it looks like blood. Many times we would follow "blood trails" to hunt down the wounded Vietcong. There were many false alarms when it was discovered that these "blood trails" were actually betel nut spit.

The Vietnamese women, who had no knowledge of or access to any dental care, toothbrushes, toothpaste, or dental floss, watched in amusement as we advisors brushed our teeth. This act of hygiene was foreign to them. They were amazed that a little bit of toothpaste filled our mouths with white foam that we eventually spat out. I stared at their blackened teeth and they stared at my foaming mouth. I chuckled to myself as they giggled aloud. Dental hygiene was just one example that presented an array of amusing and mostly confusing contrasts between different cultures and customs.

The women's interest initially amused the Vietnamese men, but then they became jealous of the attention we were receiving. Eventually it became a problem to both us and the Vietnamese men. We tried to convince the POW guards to keep their female prisoners moving along and not let them dally and watch us do the American hygiene routine. It occasionally worked.

After one of our morning hygiene rituals, the advisors and I met in the district chief's conference room. Xuan's main concern seemed to be the need for a new and more functional marketplace for the people of the village of Phan Ri Than, just outside of our compound. The Vietcong had blown up their old marketplace. The villagers had to walk several miles daily to and from Phan Ri Cua to get their necessary food, water, and supplies. This haul was especially hard on the elderly, infirm, and pregnant. Xuan stated that the Vietnamese could offer the land and manpower to build the market if the Americans would provide the cement for the foundation as well as the materials to build the support columns and the roof. He listed several villages that badly needed water towers for better drinking water. Once the projects were completed to his satisfaction, he would then take full credit for delivering these resources as promised to the people of the Hoa Da District, thereby raising his popularity with the locals. Xuan was an excellent politician as well as military leader. He was well versed at organizing and utilizing all assets available to him. The keen district chief was beginning his new relationship with our team by coercing us to accept his requests for helping the local people.

These projects required that our team react quickly. I turned to Lieutenant Blevins, who was temporarily assigned the responsibility of civil affairs for our team, and told him to look into these requests, determine their feasibility, develop construction plans, and hand me preliminary plans by the end of the first week. I had Tony translate to Major Xuan what I had ordered our lieutenant to do. Xuan was very pleased and asked me if we had any concerns or requests for the Hoa Da District Compound.

I paused a moment, then said that I had become very concerned about the current level of security and the relative freedom with which the local people entered and left the compound at all hours. Xuan said that he too was very concerned and would welcome any suggestions to improve the level of security. I suggested that an armed guard be assigned to the main gate twenty-four hours a day with specific instructions about whom should be allowed to enter and leave at various times. During the day there should be greater flexibility, since this was the Hoa Da District's headquarters. I recommended a double reinforced gate system, to be built immediately, that could be closed between sundown and sunup.

Out of my pants pocket, I pulled a crudely drawn sketch of the compound that I had prepared early that morning. Pointing at my plan, I showed Xuan where the bunkers should be placed: one on each side of the main gate, one at each of the four corners of the compound, and one at the midpoint along each of the long walls. I stated that the Americans would provide the appropriate armament to protect each of these bunkers. We would try to get new barbed wire to replace the disintegrating wire that had been in place since before the French left in 1954. Xuan thought about all of this for several minutes before approving the approach. He assigned two of his officers to work on the plan with us. I entrusted Blevins and two of our NCOs to help get this task started.

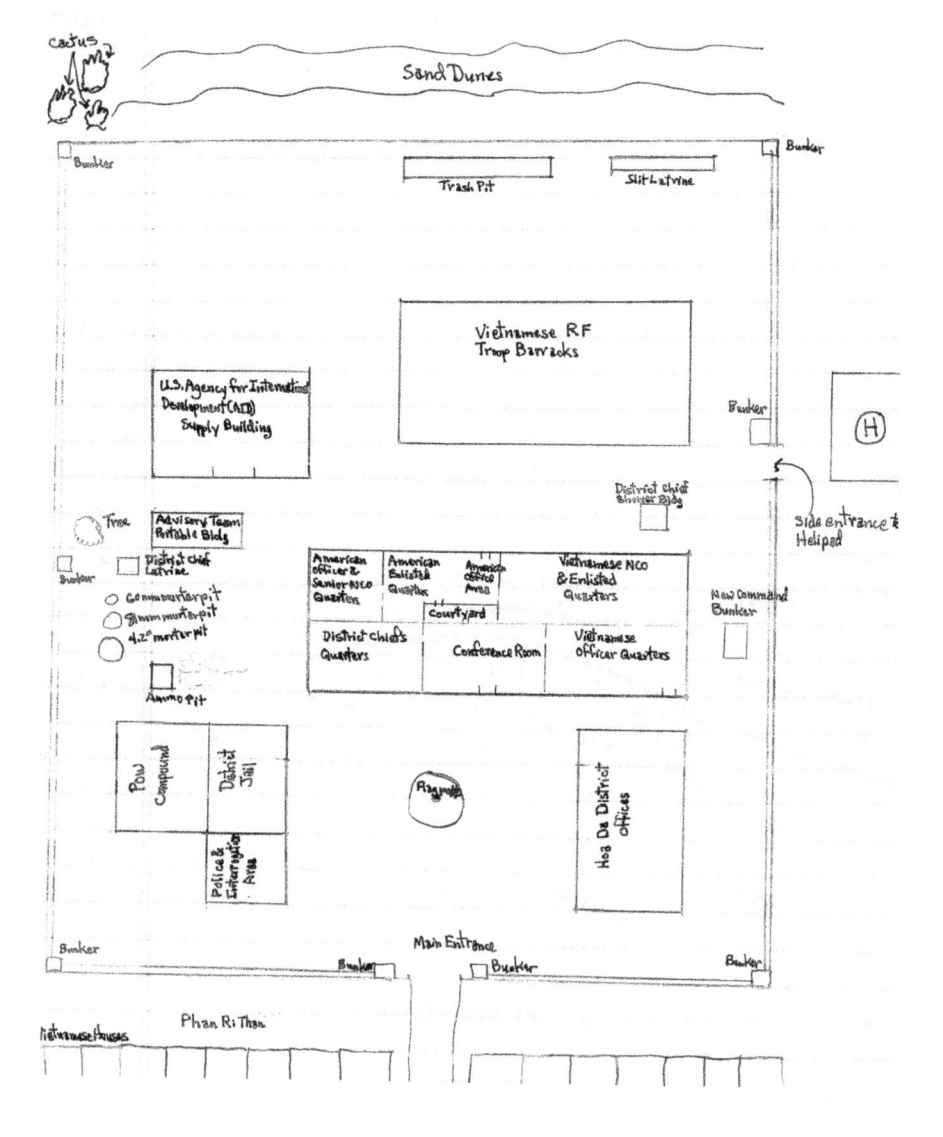

Survival of a New Advisor

The task force immediately started touring the compound in an effort to scrounge up the necessary materials to fashion the reinforced front gate. They rounded up a collection of metal poles, sheets of corrugated steel, metal bars, some rolls of non-rusty wire, and some other materials that would be very useful. They spent the rest of the afternoon laying out and constructing both layers of the double gate, to which they attached four sets of medium-sized metal wheels found with some other items in the AID warehouse. This design would make it easier to drag the gate in place each night and then retract it in the morning. A small, open-sided guardhouse was erected on the right side of the compound's entrance, and then two small two-man bunkers—one on each side of the main gate—were dug and emplaced complete with a .30-caliber machine gun in each.

Over the next two weeks, similar but larger bunkers were constructed at each of the four main corner points of the compound. Other bunkers were added to the midpoint of the two longest sides: the north and south walls. Each of these larger bunkers was designed to hold four men. Since we had no empty sandbags to use in reinforcing the sides and top of the bunkers, we reluctantly utilized the many empty wooden mortar ammunition boxes stacked high beside the warehouse. These we filled with sand, rocks, and dirt. They were stacked in staggered fashion to form the side and roof covering for the bunkers. A mixture of sand and dirt covered the outside around and atop each bunker, with the exception of space left for two firing ports in the front and a rear entrance. We were banking on the assumption that the outer covering of sand and dirt would better absorb the impact of any bullets or explosives, thus cushioning the wooden boxes. I still feared the boxes splintering under incoming fire, but as Con stated, without the availability of sandbags, we were left with no other choice. We couldn't wait any longer to upgrade the compound's security measures.

During our first week, Blevins, several of our senior NCOs, and I met a number of times with Xuan and several of his staff officers to develop a comprehensive defense barrier plan to be emplaced around the compound's perimeter. The plan incorporated three separate layers of barbed-wire fencing surrounding the entire compound. The outer barbed-wire fence line would be 150 yards from the compound and six feet tall. Outside of that would be a twenty-foot-wide band of tangle-foot barbed wire. Tangle-foot barbed wire is always securely anchored in the ground at a height of one to one and a half feet above the ground so as to trip and/or entangle anyone approaching. Ten feet inside of the first fence would be a second identical fence, with three stacked rolls of concertina razor wire between them.

The second layer of fencing would stand six feet tall and was about eighty yards outside the compound. This was constructed by double-line fencing similar to the first layer. Forty yards from the main wall of the compound would stand a six-foot-high barbed-wire fence. We all agreed to further enhance this array of fencing with a pattern of land mines, claymore mines, trip flares, and assorted booby traps. Claymore mines were a favorite, because the portable convex-shaped mines were quick to set up and deploy. They were used at base compounds and for pocket artillery in ambush attacks.

Someone suggested making noisemakers out of metal beverage cans containing small rocks, which could be suspended at various places along the barbed-wire fencing. The six-feet-high and three-feet-thick masonry walls around the compound were already well protected since they were embedded on top with broken glass and rusty metal spikes. This design would delay and injure anyone trying to climb over them.

After days of discussion, everyone was pleased with the exterior defensive plan, but one problem remained: the disposal of the old mines and booby traps that surrounded the compound. Exterior construction could not begin until the ground was clear of hazardous explosives.

We decided that when we picked up our military advisory team basic equipment kit, we would do our best to acquire an adequate amount of sandbags, barbed wire (both regular rolls

Survival of a New Advisor

of single-strand wire and bales of concertina wire), steel fencing stakes, anti-personnel land mines, claymore mines, trip flares, C-4 and TNT demolitions, blasting caps (both electric and percussion), detonation cord, compound defense weapons (i.e., .50- and .30-caliber machine guns, 90mm recoilless rifles, 81mm mortars, Browning automatic rifles, grenades-fragmentation, white phosphorus, thermite, smoke and teargas, a supply of ammunition for all weapons acquired, and anything else thought practical to utilize in our defenses.

The new security barrier on the main gate and the addition of a full-time armed guard proved successful. We began checking and limiting the people seeking entrance to the Hoa Da District Compound. The evening movie audience was reduced from a couple thousand to about four hundred people, all members of the Vietnamese Regional Force company, the assigned Popular Force platoons, and our advisory team. Gone were the faces of those who obviously didn't belong there.

Near the end of our first week, Major Elliott and his operations NCO visited us. They wanted to see how we were getting along. We went over our proposed compound security plan with them and Major Xuan. They agreed that it would be very good when implemented. Elliott took note of our progress in constructing our series of new bunkers and remarked that these looked good since we were hard-pressed to find any sandbags or barbed wire, both of which were in short supply throughout the region. As for the obsolete mines outside the compound walls, he agreed that their removal was top priority.

On our fifth night, we experienced our first enemy contact: a brief mortar shelling and a small, probing attack on the right rear side of the compound. It only lasted about fifteen minutes. It seemed that the Vietcong were testing us to see our new defenses and how we responded. The five mortar rounds landed harmlessly in the vicinity of our slit-trench latrine. The incoming rifle fire seemed to come from about five or six weapons and was very erratic, with the rounds going mostly up in the air.

Our Vietnamese troops managed to fire two 81mm mortar shells back in the attack's general direction. Our ready response that night may have been better than the Vietcong expected. We received more probing attacks on each of the next five nights. As Sergeant Wilson observed, it was as if the Vietcong were now trying to punish us for revoking their movie privileges.

Late one night I was serving my turn on radio watch when one of the guards from the front gate ran up and reported that a group of men were coming up to the gate area saying they were the survivors of a Vietcong ambush and asking to be let into our compound. I instructed Sergeant Amos to alert the rest of our team members, have them grab their weapons, and man their assigned posts for an emergency situation. I then followed the guard to the front gate near the outside of our secured gate.

I called out, first in Vietnamese and then in English, trying to determine the identity of the group. We had no personnel from our compound deployed outside that night, other than the Popular Force platoons that routinely secured several of the bridges over local streams. After a few minutes, an American voice answered me stating that this was a group of ARVN troops with American advisors who were traveling by truck convoy up Highway 1 from Phan Thiet to join the 44th ARVN in Song Mao. He said that the Vietcong had ambushed them about halfway between Luong Song and our compound. They had to walk and carry their wounded this far.

I asked how many men were with him and the number of casualties. The American replied that there were about thirty-five survivors, twenty dead, and ten severely wounded. I told him that it was extremely risky to keep our gate open for very long. I asked that he have the wounded gather in front of our gate so we could get them in first. He said that would be fine, but it would take a few minutes. I told him to call out when they were ready.

I squatted down so I could try to see the number of men gathering near our gate. I was very surprised to count about eighty-five, with the number still growing. I got up and grabbed Cuthbert and took him away from the gate area. I whispered

Survival of a New Advisor

to him to run and secure two machine guns, their crews, and adequate ammunition to sustain them through a long firefight. They were to be positioned where they could fire on the main gate and the approaches leading up to it. I would signal if it became necessary to open fire.

He immediately ran off to take care of this order. I ran to Major Xuan and, in French, informed him that I suspected a trick to get inside our compound defenses. He agreed, knowing that no convoys had been assigned to drive on this portion of Highway 1 in over a year. This was due to the fact that so many of the bridges had been bombed out and road sectors were impassible from bomb craters. His comments helped confirm my suspicions.

I again squatted down to better see what was happening outside the gate. This time I saw them in position and ready to enter our compound. A second American yelled that their wounded were really in bad shape and asked us to hurry and let them in. I said a short prayer about this being the right decision and then gave the command to open fire on all those gathered outside the gate. This consisted of concentrated fire from three .30-caliber machine guns, accompanied by rifle fire and grenades from about a hundred men.

At first there were a few answering bursts of AK-47 rifle fire with their characteristic Vietcong green tracers, and one rifle-propelled grenade flew high with a big whooshing sound and landed harmlessly near the dump. After that, there was no incoming fire of any kind. For a couple more minutes we continued firing, and then I called for everyone to cease fire. One of my team members brought up a large battery-powered spotlight to survey the area outside the gate. There were many bodies lying in random piles in front of the gate, and they all appeared to be dressed in Vietcong black pajama uniforms. There didn't appear to be any movement. We only heard one or two very slight moans coming from this mass.

After spending a few more minutes surveying the area and deciding that no threat still existed, I gave the order to open the gate enough so that two of my men and two of Xuan's men and I could go out and inspect the group. The first body next to the gate that I turned over was an American dressed in black pajamas and carrying an AK-47 rifle. He had a number of bullet holes in him and was now deceased. I assumed he had been the leader who was trying to talk his way into our compound. I had my NCO call Major Elliott and request that an American intelligence representative be sent up here to help evaluate the situation. I next surveyed the bodies in front of the gate and determined that none had been casualties prior to the beginning of the firefight. The story about this group joining the 44th ARVN and having been ambushed was a ruse.

We looked for anyone alive and identification or documents on any of the bodies. I told my men to leave the weapons and gear with each body, as there would be time in the morning to gather them up. As it turned out, there were eighty-one killed in action with two men still alive with multiple gunshot wounds. They were brought into the compound for treatment. The first died within the hour and the second, a black American, died several hours later without regaining consciousness. I had hoped that we could get some information from him, but he had a severe head wound and several abdominal wounds. He did have a wallet with his U.S. military ID card and some other personal information to give a start at tracing his identity.

The only other information found was a crudely drawn map in the web gear of a man who may have been the leader of this Vietcong outfit. Some of the Vietcong may have fled from the action, but with no blood trails leading away, it was impossible to tell. The final count of Vietcong weapons was seventy-four, which added credibility that there might have been more Vietcong involved in this skirmish. With the firefight over, we allowed the majority of our defending force to stand down but remain on alert in case any Vietcong returned to renew their attack.

Shortly after sunrise, Xuan, Con, Blevins, and several of our NCOs joined me at the gate. The guards rolled back the barriers and opened the gate. We went out and began to survey the results of the attempted attack on our compound. The temperature was in the high nineties and the dead bodies were already becoming somewhat bloated as they began decomposition. We each fashioned a type of bandanna to cover our noses, which made breathing easier and helped keep us from vomiting.

A helicopter flew overhead and landed on the chopper pad. Two U.S. Army intelligence representatives had arrived. They needed to investigate the incident because of the presence of two Americans trying to lead the attackers into our compound. The two representatives spent considerable time photographing, fingerprinting, and searching the two dead Americans. They insisted on taking the second man's wallet and military ID with them, as well as the map. They looked briefly at each of the other dead bodies but made no comments and expressed no opinions or conclusions when they had completed their survey. As they headed back to their unmarked chopper, I asked if we would get any further information on these men or their unit that might assist us in evaluating the enemy situation in our region. They left without comment.

Later that day, the CIA case officer drove up to assess the area and casualties. We described our battle and the visit by the American intelligence representatives. The CIA case officer tried to figure the troop's organization and location and did supply us with information about the men. The first American had been a sergeant, E-5, with the First Infantry Division who had run off and defected almost a year earlier during a battle in the III Corps area. He had been listed as MIA since that time. The second American had been assigned to the Twenty-fifth Infantry Division in the III Corps area and had defected about three months before. He had been a Black Muslim draftee out of Los Angles and hated taking orders from his white leaders. He had been listed as AWOL. The members of my team were shocked to discover that some Americans actually defected and were fighting against their own countrymen. This was very hard to comprehend and accept.

Major Xuan assigned a team to gather the Vietcong weapons and equipment. The bodies were put in the back of an old Vietnamese truck and carried to the edge of Phan Ri Cua, where a local man would take charge and bury them in a big hole in the town cemetery.

After the first truckload of bodies had been taken away, three Buddhist monks, with their heads shaved and dressed in bright yellow robes, approached the compound, speaking in a very agitated manner to Xuan. Xuan informed us that we had committed a sin in the Buddhist religion by not allowing these monks to come and conduct their required prayer service for the dead. The Buddhist ritual required the gathering of body parts, which included soil exposed to blood, fluids, or other types of gore. The monks then blended these together as they chanted and rang their small bells as part of this ceremony.

At first the monks accused us of purposely removing the bodies too soon so that the dead men would have to be reincarnated without all of their parts. Speaking through Tony, I told the head monk that we fully respected their beliefs but I had not known about their religious traditions and rites. No one locally had claimed any of these bodies. We had been unable to determine their identities or religion, and thus they were being buried in a mass grave in the local cemetery.

The monk smiled and said that it would be no problem to pour the mixture of soil and body parts over the group of bodies before they were finally covered up. This would ensure that all of the parts would be reunited with the proper bodies. The monks were happy, which made us happy. I realized that we would have to take the local beliefs into consideration as we worked with the Vietnamese.

At our advisors meeting, we recognized the need to start getting the members of the Hoa Da Regional Forces company on patrols with the dual purpose of better training and showing their active presence. I presented this plan to Xuan. He thought it was an excellent idea, especially since the members of this unit had been mainly garrison soldiers prior to his arrival. It was decided that the first patrol, with the combined strength of two platoons, would go from Phan Ri Than to the Hoi Tam hamlets. We planned to hike along a line of sand dunes that paralleled Highway 1. This route would pose no problems with land navigation and allow us to concentrate on teaching patrol formations, flank security, responsibilities of the point men, and rear security. Half of the men on our advisory team were assigned to accompany the patrol to try to demonstrate and teach proper patrolling techniques. Since the entire Hoa Da District was considered hostile, we had to issue a basic load of ammunition to each of the soldiers on the training operation.

We formed the patrol, and I explained its purpose. Tony interpreted to the Vietnamese soldiers. This was only a training operation and no one was to fire their weapons unless we encountered a Vietcong force. If that happened, they were to wait until they were given the command to fire by either Con or me. I ordered the advisors and Vietnamese NCOs to perform an equipment inspection on everyone. The majority of the Vietnamese soldiers were not taking the patrol exercise seriously; more than half failed to bring a canteen of water or other required items with them. Others had their canteens but no water. I ordered them all to go get their canteens, fill them, and be back in formation within fifteen minutes. I asked Con to make sure that his NCOs kept track of the men and encouraged them to hurry in returning to the formation. He seemed a little insulted by this request and abruptly turned and consulted with his sergeants.

When fifteen minutes had gone by, only about one-third of the men had returned. I asked Con to try to hurry the others to the formation. He yelled something in Vietnamese to a couple of his sergeants and they walked slowly in the direction of the barracks where most of the men stayed. After another thirty-minute period, about three-fourths of the men had returned and were standing in ranks.

I took Con aside and told him that this was unacceptable and more emphasis would have to be placed on their proper discipline and response. His attitude now was a mix between anger and embarrassment. The men were making him look bad, and he was losing face. He ran over to the barracks wildly screaming and yanked every soldier he saw, forcing them to run back to their place in ranks. Within three minutes, everyone was in place, standing at rigid attention. I again explained the purpose of the patrol and how it would be conducted.

From our initial march out of the main gate, it again occurred to me that these troops were not taking this training very seriously. They were sloppy about the way they carried their equipment; they wouldn't keep consistent spacing between one another; and they were jabbering away instead of maintaining silence as I had requested. A few of the men serving as right flank security had bunched up and were looking back at our formation instead of searching outward for any threats to our patrol.

After a few minutes they fired a couple shots, which kicked up the sand near me. I ran back to Con and told him to order them to stop firing their weapons and get back into assigned formation. He ran over and apparently relayed my instructions. They slowly complied, laughing and talking loudly as they went. Con returned and stated that they claimed to have been shooting at birds. I reminded him that this was dangerous and irresponsible behavior and should not be tolerated on patrol.

About a half hour later, the same thing happened again: the men began randomly firing their weapons in our direction. This time I ordered Con to bring them back into the main formation and to assign another group of men to serve as flank security. He immediately complied and reprimanded the offenders when they returned to the main formation. I made note of their names and called them to the attention of the advisors. I was beginning to see that not everyone in this unit was fully loyal to the South Vietnamese.

The patrol went around the far side of the hamlet and then began their return route to our compound. About halfway back, scattered rifle fire erupted from the left flank security, kicking up sand near Con's and my feet. This time, Con reacted immedi-

Survival of a New Advisor

ately without being prompted: he dragged two soldiers back into the formation, where he reprimanded them and took away their weapons. They, too, claimed to be shooting at birds. I knew this wasn't true because we had not seen a bird all morning.

As we neared the compound, two more shots were fired from flank security, kicking up sand at my feet. The top Vietnamese NCO ran out, grabbed the weapon from the offending soldier, and twisted his arm behind his back. He kept him that way until he dragged him to POW jail. Finally, there was a quick response to a serious problem.

Through Tony, I told the Vietnamese that it was important to maintain silence, order, alertness, proper formation, and security when on patrol. I stated that the firing of any weapons without being ordered to do so by their patrol leader or section chief was totally unacceptable. I added that the shots fired in the direction of our patrol had come dangerously close to hitting several of the Vietnamese NCOs, American advisors, Lieutenant Con, and me. This action would not be tolerated and those responsible would be considered working for the Vietcong. Consequently I would give orders to shoot the offenders if this ever happened again. I let my comments sink in for a minute, looking at the expressions on the faces of the Vietnamese soldiers. Most appeared to be concerned about this serious matter, while ten others sneered with a defiant stare. I tried to commit their faces and names to my memory.

I asked Con if he had anything that he wanted to tell his men, and with that he launched into a bit of a tirade telling them that they looked sloppy, undisciplined, disinterested, and totally unprofessional on this patrol. He said that, overall, they were an embarrassment to this unit, to him, to the district chief, and to themselves. They needed to pay attention and to listen to the advice the American advisors gave. This training would help them improve and save lives during any future contact with the Vietcong.

The next morning Con ordered another patrol. He trained and retrained until all of them got it right. The Vietnamese sergeants and several American advisors critiqued the soldiers on the morning patrol. They covered the proper preparation for going on patrol, to include acceptable uniform, equipment, food, water, first aid supplies, ammunition, and grenades. The advisors emphasized being ready and in formation on time; maintaining silence; rifle fire discipline; staying alert to your surroundings; reporting anything out of the ordinary; and maintaining the proper formation and interval between you and your fellow soldiers. It was then emphasized that these were all very important considerations that would save their own lives and those of other soldiers.

Most of the men paid attention and responded favorably to the training. A number of them asked some very good questions about various aspects of this type of military operation. This encouraged me; perhaps the main problem with this unit was a lack of recent, meaningful training. The American advisors were here now to take care of this deficiency.

The training exercises appeared to have gone well. I felt the troops were ready to try again. Con called for patrol formation. Only two showed up wearing improper items. The patrol was to leave the compound and head to the village of Phu Ninh on the Phan Ri River. I reminded everyone of the policy of not firing their weapons until Con ordered so. Anyone firing toward the group would be considered Vietcong and would be shot. I was pleased that the patrol exited the compound only fifteen minutes later than our planned departure. Finally, some progress.

We went through the village of Phan Ri Thanh and waded across the Phan Ri River at a fording point, where we made good use of a sandbar. The depth of the water at this place was about waist deep for the Vietnamese and about mid-thigh for the advisors. We Americans spread out and paid particular attention to helping any Vietnamese soldiers who might have a problem crossing deep water given the slight current. Only one young private panicked a little and Cuthbert quickly assisted him.

On the other side, we regained our formation and continued our route across a series of large sand dunes in the direction of Phu Ninh. All appeared to be going well when two men on right flank security fired several shots. One of these kicked up the sand between Con and me. Another passed close to my left ear with a sharp crack. I lifted my M-16 rifle and fired two shots at the offenders, striking one in the left shoulder and the other in the right hip. Both fell down screaming in pain, to the shock and amazement of the rest of the patrol members. My marksmanship training and skills were serving me well.

Through Tony, I reminded the soldiers of my stand on anyone firing at our group. I sent our American and Vietnamese medics over to treat the two men. They had suffered only minor flesh wounds with no bone damage. I was sorry that I had to take this severe step, but knew it would serve as a good lesson for the rest of the troops. Lieutenant Con sent a squad of soldiers along with Bolling to take the two offenders back to our POW jail. We now had a crowd of believers, and there were no further incidents during this patrol.

Halfway to Phu Ninh, I saw a number of signs of recent Vietcong activity and pointed them out to Con and the advisors. This was passed on to the rest of the soldiers. They grew very nervous and became more alert for the rest of the patrol. Our forces were not ready for any kind of firefight outside of our compound. Fortunately that didn't happen. We waded quickly back across the river, and all of the soldiers were visibly relieved to be safely back in the compound.

Lieutenant Con and I reported the shooting incident to Major Xuan. He nodded his head in agreement and said that I had acted properly. I had set a standard for the future conduct of his troops. Although, Xuan added, he would have shot and killed them if they had shot at him. Next, I called Major Elliott and reported the incident to him, along with Xuan's reaction. He said that my action was a little severe but should get the point across to the Vietnamese troopers. The two offenders were later determined to be working with the Vietcong. They were attempting to kill Con, several of the other advisors, and me. We were lucky that these men were poor marksmen. The offenders were sent to the jail in Saigon where the worst Vietnamese criminals were housed.

The sand dune patrols gradually progressed to jungle patrols. When I ordered my advisors to dress for one of these jungle patrols, some team members complained that they were missing some of their socks. I had noticed some socks missing also. I told the team just to wear what socks they had, and I would check with the laundry ladies. We would be passing their home on our way to the jungle.

A local woman and her three daughters washed and pressed our dirty clothes. Twice each week they came to our compound, picked up the dirty clothes, and delivered the neatly folded, clean clothes. We provided them with a steady supply of soap that they used to wash not only our clothes but also their own and anyone else needing laundry services. Our supplying them with soap was in effect enabling them to expand their laundry services at virtually no cost to them other than their time and labor. This was a fine example of pure capitalism. We didn't mind. It helped to stimulate the local economy while building up a greater loyalty to the American advisors and our Vietnamese counterparts.

Tony and I entered the laundry ladies' home. Tony translated that we were very pleased with their service then asked them about the missing socks. The women thanked me for complimenting their service and expressed no knowledge of any missing socks. I passed this information to my disappointed team.

We pressed on with our jungle patrol. Early on our patrol, we encountered a huge reticulated python lying between branches on a large tree. The engorged python had just swallowed a large animal, probably a wild pig. I pointed and warned my patrol about the snake and had Tony translate this.

One Vietnamese soldier did not heed my warning. He took a stick and started jabbing the snake. I shouted at him to leave it alone. I remembered an incident when our medics were called to a small, remote hamlet. There they were shown an extremely large python that had been killed and sliced open, revealing the body of a small, dead child that had disappeared during the night. This incident clearly demonstrated the capabilities of these large constrictors.

Survival of a New Advisor

A short distance through the jungle, I suddenly heard a blood-curdling scream. I ran back and found the same Vietnamese soldier trapped between the big tree and a large rock with the python going after him. I thought about shooting the snake, but decided he was a more valuable commodity than the stupid trooper. I hit the python with my rifle barrel, which diverted its attention as the trooper scrambled away to a safer location. Our Vietnamese troops may have progressed to jungle patrol, but they still lacked some commonsense discipline. I only hoped this snake attack taught the soldier a lesson.

A couple days later, I went with two of our advisors and several of the Vietnamese officers to look at the area around the small local dump. As we walked around, I saw a lump of our socks with their distinctive olive-drab coloring wadded up and thrown on top of a small pile of other trash. I took a stick and poked around the socks. As they unrolled, I could see that each had a fairly heavy deposit of dried blood on it. When Con saw what I had discovered, he laughed and said that this was what local women did when they menstruated each month. I told him that these were our socks, and we had not given them permission to use them for this purpose. He responded that they probably thought that we could easily replace them. I was not amused.

Again I marched myself over to where the laundry ladies lived and told them what I had discovered. We expected all of our clothing to be laundered and returned each time. If any more items disappeared, we would go elsewhere with our soap. The head lady became very remorseful and apologetic and guaranteed that everything would be handled in number one order from now on. After that, we had no problems or disappearing socks. Another lesson in capitalism learned—don't irritate your customers, especially when they are providing free supplies then paying you for your labor.

My new advisory role was taking shape. I had developed a working relationship with Major Xuan and the local people, I had escaped from being shot by Vietcong sympathizers, and patrols were finally improving. It was a relief to have survived this big test as a new advisor.

CHAPTER 10
The Medics

As our advisory team became better organized in our efforts to train and direct the operations of the Hoa Da District military forces, I felt that it was important for us to visit and familiarize ourselves with the towns, villages, and hamlets throughout our area of responsibility. To do this in a non-threatening way, we would conduct a survey through MEDCAP. Through this medical intervention, our surveys would educate us about the people, their lifestyles, the status of their health and environment, and hopefully win their hearts and minds. This survey involved sending American and Vietnamese medics into the villages to conduct medical screenings of the local people. Our medical staff was now complete, had been well trained, and were qualified to treat most common medical conditions, including performing a number of minor surgical procedures. This proved very useful since some individuals suffered gunshot wounds, booby trap and land mine explosion injuries, blast trauma injuries, stabbings, broken bones, burns, animal bites, and a number of other traumatic injuries common to living in a rural tropical area and combat zone. For more serious injuries and diseases, we were told to contact a Taiwanese medical team assigned to this region.

Our medics began the humanitarian service by setting up two portable tables in the center of town, upon which they arranged their medical equipment. The medics invited the people who needed medical care to line up in front of the tables. Some of the villagers in the more remote hamlets were unaccustomed to medical care, but they came out of curiosity to check out the freebies.

After the MEDCAPs were held in the first two villages, word seemed to spread rapidly. Thereafter, a MEDCAP visit resulted in the entire population of a village turning out to take advantage of what was becoming a local social event.

These MEDCAP visits became even more popular when the natives discovered the medics were handing out a treat to each child they saw. Treats were usually lollipops, hard candy, or little wooden figurines. The treats were very well received but almost turned out to be a problem when the adults in one hamlet first asked and then demanded to be given the same treat as the children. This caused me to put in a hurried request to our Binh Thuan Province Headquarters for a resupply of treats. After explaining the reason for the treats, an airdrop delivery accompanied our bright yellow mailbag the next morning. Hoa Da District was the first district in Binh Thuan Province to experience this demand of treats, but it was a necessary step to engage the local people with the "round-eyed strangers."

On several occasions we would try to call in a medevac helicopter to evacuate severely injured civilians to a Vietnamese medical center. These usually were South Vietnamese helicopters flown by Vietnamese Air Force pilots. We didn't realize that by doing this, we apparently had raised the expectations of the locals to have this free evacuation service performed almost every time they brought an injured family member to our compound for treatment. This "free service" caused a running and often loud debate with family members. Between the free treats and air evacuation, who would have known that our medical advisory effort would create trouble?

The medics discovered a number of undernourished children due to the limited amounts and types of food available to some of the villagers. In these cases, the medics would give the parents vitamin tablets or high-nutrient tonics to nourish their children. The medics patiently tried to convince the parents and grandparents that these suggested medicines or vitamins would help their children get better. In many cases it was finally explained that the "powerful spirits" in the medicines would defeat the "bad spirits" inside the child. The Vietnamese could relate to this logic. This showed us a new and more effective approach to communicating with the people in our district.

The medics decided to analyze the natives' diet. Through this knowledge they could better understand what impact their eating habits had on their lives, both from a nutrition and an acquisition standpoint. We had noted the products sold daily in the local markets were locally produced, primarily through farming, fishing, hunting, or foraging from the nearby jungles. The following items were routinely available: noodles, rice, cabbage, bamboo shoots, peanuts, green vegetables, muskmelon, watermelon, white tubers, water chestnuts, eggs, chicken, duck, pigs, dog, monkey, ground squirrel, water buffalo, snake, fish, eel, octopus, squid, crab, clams, mussels, lobster, scallops, bananas, coconuts, plantains, papayas, leaves, salt, pepper, herbs, tea, coffee, Tiger beer, Ba Muoi Ba Beer, Coca-Cola, assorted jungle fruits, *nuoc mam,* French bread, and charcoal for cooking.

Soups were a common dish and provided an easy means of combining a number of these types of foods. Much to our regret, we American advisors discovered that the Vietnamese did not boil their soup, so it served as a wonderful breeding ground for many types of bacteria and microscopic parasites.

Shortly after eating a bowl of the delicious Vietnamese soup at a local village chief's house, I developed a serious case of amoebic dysentery–or what we advisors called "the green apple quick-step" or "the trots." During one of my frequent visits to the outhouse with diarrhea, I heard explosions progressively getting closer to the compound. Realizing that the Vietcong mortar might hit the latrine, I leaped outside without pulling up my trousers or taking the time to wipe. I landed between boxes of supplies and hugged the ground. The next shell hit the outhouse, blowing it to bits. When I looked around, I saw five of my advisors and several Vietnamese troopers laughing hysterically over my bare-assed image. I certainly did not think the incident was funny; however, it provided my men amusement, raising their morale.

Finally, after four days, the bout released its stranglehold on my gut but left me pale with little or no energy and appetite. I learned to just say "NO" to any future offerings of soup unless I could verify that it had been thoroughly boiled for at least five minutes. Oddly enough, the Vietnamese thoroughly cooked all of their other prepared foods and beverages so none of these caused any problems.

I was not the only one with the trots. Most of the Vietnamese people had chronic diarrhea and runny noses. Again the medics felt that this probably was caused by the lack of good sanitation practices and poor nutrition. Steps were taken to try to teach the people to boil their soups, to better clean their cookware, and properly wash their hands, especially after they relieved themselves. No one in any of these villages had latrines of any sort. The people just went outside of their village or to the local cemetery to urinate or defecate on the graves of someone else's ancestors as an insult. It was very hard to convince the people that piles of feces left lying around were a perfect breeding place for the swarming flies. By the time they reached two years of age, children were trained to go where their parents and older siblings went to relieve themselves. This earned the child the right to wear clothes covering their bottoms.

My advisory team constructed a closed outhouse, but this effort failed. The villagers did not understand that one sits on the commode instead of squatting on top of it. The squatting resulted in urination and defecation all over the outhouse, which increased the fly and other vermin population. My advisory team admitted defeat and referred to it as the "hell hole." It just proved that suggestions and changes from us foreigners would be challenged or resisted.

The Medics

Malaria was a frequent problem. As mentioned earlier, two types of malaria were commonly found throughout this region of Vietnam: falciparum and vivax, both caused by the bite of a female anopheles. The medics began issuing two types of pills to the people in each of these villages as a means of trying to control the spread and severe attacks characteristic of this parasitic disease. It soon became apparent that we had many more people than supplies. No matter how emphatic our requests to the province superiors or the regional Taiwanese medical team, we were never sent enough anti-malarial medications. The most severe and advanced cases of falciparum malaria often ended in death, most often of small children. It was rumored that the United Nations had formed a medical team dedicated to teaching third-world countries about the dangers of malaria and dispensing appropriate medications and mosquito nets to these rural people. Unfortunately these services and supplies did not reach our area while I was there.

About a month after our MEDCAP surveys, we received a visitor from the village of Thanh Luong. This man was the assistant village chief and told us that a number of his villagers had gotten very sick. One woman had died that morning after showing large growths on her upper legs going into her groin area. I called our medics over and had them listen to the man's description. They both agreed that this didn't sound like anything they had seen or heard about before, so they drove the man back to his village and took a look at the people who were sick. About an hour and a half later, I received a call on the radio from Bolling saying that it had taken a while to examine these villagers with swollen lymph glands and elevated fevers. After consulting their medical field manual, they had discovered several cases of bubonic plague. Bolling asked me to get in touch with the Taiwanese medical team, inform them that we had encountered a village with cases of bubonic plague, and request assistance. Fortunately we Americans had received a series of vaccinations for the bubonic plague prior to our deployment. We would not be at risk.

I located the team chief, Dr. Wu, on the radio, and relayed the message. After I finished talking, Dr. Wu laughed derisively and said that my medics must be crazy; the bubonic plague had not been reported in over ten years. I told him that my medics were very professional and would not make such a claim unless it had merit. I again requested that he come immediately or send other doctors to help us handle the situation. He replied that his team was currently conducting a complex tropical medicine study around the area of Phan Thiet, and it would not be completed for at least another month. He then left the radio. The conversation was over.

I switched frequencies on the radio and again called the medics in Thanh Luong. I told them we would be getting no help from the Taiwanese medical team. We would have to find a way to handle this on our own. Bolling read the field manual to me. The source of bubonic plague was the bite of an infected flea, usually found on rats. He said that they had seen a large number of rats around the village as they examined the twenty to thirty sick villagers. I asked if the village was isolated. Bolling said that it was very isolated on the edge of a large sand dune with no other villages or people nearby. I told him that I had an idea about how to kill the fleas and rid the village of the bubonic plague. I explained my plan and told him to bring the other medic back to the compound.

I sent Amos to Song Mao Compound to pick up several large drums of powdered insecticide. When the insecticide arrived, I led about half of our advisors and several Vietnamese soldiers from the Regional Forces company to Thanh Luong. There we proceeded to lay down a ring of insecticide about four inches deep around the entire village. The medics and I talked to the village chief and told him to move the villagers and their food out of the village and onto the nearby sand dune. There they would have to stay until all of the rats had left their village.

He seemed very puzzled, but, knowing that we were trying to help save his people, he complied. About a half hour after everyone had moved out, I sent my advisors into the village carrying long sticks to rout the rats. Groups of rats ran through the ring of insecticide. I knew that these pests would get hungry and, finding no food, would exit the village to rejoin the villagers and their food. After two hours of thoroughly scouring the village, we were convinced that all of the pests had vacated and joined the tired people gathered on the sand dune.

We then moved everybody and their food back into the village and into their homes. It took less time for all of the rats to return to the village because there was no food on the sand dune. The rats scampered through the ring of insecticide a second time. We waited at least another hour to give the insecticide time to do its work in killing all the fleas, and then we set up a series of feeding stations for these rats containing a type of sweet bait laced with cyanide that the rats quickly gulped down. At the feeding stations, containers of water were placed for the thirsty rats to drink after downing this deadly food. When they drank, it activated the cyanide in their systems, which killed them quickly. We gathered up all of the dead rodents, placed them in several wooden boxes, and carted them off to be buried in a hole in the side of a nearby sand dune.

By this time, the medics had injected the correct dose of antibiotics into each of the patients who had exhibited signs of bubonic plague. The medics returned to the village each day for the next several days until they had completed the course of antibiotic therapy for each patient. Every patient recovered. We had saved the people of Thanh Luong from a devastating tragedy, and they were very grateful to us. My team had performed merciful kindness with no need for payment or taxes. The villagers' appreciation eventually helped us develop an effective intelligence network, as they hated and feared the Vietcong's harsh treatment.

The Taiwanese medical team did show up about two weeks later and determined that there had in fact been an outbreak of bubonic plague. This unexpected health incident and the method we used to effectively defeat the potential crisis surprised them. The Taiwanese doctors asked where we had learned this technique. They found it hard to accept that we had planned and carried out this approach using "Yankee ingenuity." They were quite surprised at the simplicity and effectiveness of our rat and flea eradication plan. Finally, they reluctantly congratulated us on our originality in handling the crisis. After this incident, the Taiwanese medical team responded quickly to assist us when we had a need for their services.

One day, Thornton, and I were driving toward Phan Ri Cua when a rice snake dropped out from under the dashboard onto my lap. Quietly I told Thornton to hold the steering wheel and keep the truck on the road. I grabbed the snake by its tail and whipped it out of the vehicle. I regained control of the wheel and continued driving. Down the road, I noticed a woman lying in the roadside ditch alone with her belongings scattered on the roadside and in the ditch. She appeared to be in pain.

We stopped the jeep and ran to see what had happened to her. It didn't take long to discover that she was in the process of giving birth. At first she seemed more frightened of us than childbirth. When it became apparent that she was too far along to be moved, I helped her remove her wet black pajama bottoms and placed them under her pelvis to provide a somewhat cleaner area for the baby than the filthy ditch. I could see a little of the top of the baby's head just starting to emerge, accompanied by a lot of bloody fluid. By this time she had latched onto my left arm with both hands and squeezed with all her might as she pushed through three sets of painful contractions. The baby boy emerged quickly into my hands.

She had uttered barely a sound throughout this ordeal, although her face had been very contorted and red from the pain. The mother relaxed a bit and lay back, exhausted and breathing rapidly. Fighting off my own shock from the pain of her tight grip on my arm and the sight of the bloody delivery, I really didn't know what to do next. Here I stood with this slippery, blood-covered newborn, still attached to his mother by the umbilical cord. The military had never trained me in childbirth.

I held the baby upside down by his feet and noted that, as I did this, a lot of fluid drained out of his mouth. He gave one massive shudder, gasped twice, and began crying. Each expelled breath caused more bubbly fluid to drain out of his mouth. I decided to hold him upside down until I no longer saw any fluid coming out, and then I handed him to his mother, who laid him on her chest.

At this point, another jeep carrying one of our medics stopped and came to the rescue of both the mother and me by taking over the treatment. I watched as he took a piece of twine from his medical kit, tied off the umbilical cord, and clipped it. At this point, he handed me the baby and helped the mother get up into his jeep. I gently put the new baby back into the mother's arms while Thornton put her personal items into the back of the medic's jeep. The mother appeared to be very appreciative of our help. The medic drove to the village and found the local midwife who took charge of further treatment.

Two days later, I was shocked to see this same woman out working in a nearby field. This demonstrated how demanding life was on the locals, allowing no time to recover after childbirth. The people in this region didn't seem to realize that the high death rate among new mothers might be attributable to infections and associated problems surrounding the lack of appropriate sanitation and period of rest following a traumatic event like childbirth. The new babies seemed to do fairly well unless they had some type of birth defect or serious infection. In that case, they were usually given very minimal care and allowed to pass away peacefully. If a new mother didn't survive, which often happened, the local midwife would usually have a woman with active breast milk from the same or nearby village nurse the new baby and help it survive.

The MEDCAP program was a great asset in winning the hearts and minds of the local people. The survey was most valuable in evaluating our region's health issues. In the tropics you never quite knew what to expect from a health standpoint. We continually encountered tropical diseases and conditions without names or prescribed methods of treatment. Our medics practiced medicine through trial and error. It was amazing how many of these treatments were successful through the basic and consistent practice of using a bar of soap and proper nutrition. I felt blessed to have Sergeant Bolling and his top-notch crew on my team. These medics educated, performed many unsung deeds, and saved and enriched the lives of the locals. The Vietcong had a stronghold on Hoa Da District. We hoped and prayed that our medical humanitarian efforts would sway the villagers to our side.

CHAPTER 11
Major Dramis

Hair grows much faster in a tropical climate, especially when combined with extreme adrenalin output while serving in a combat zone. The inconvenience of the ride to the barber in Song Mao proved to be impractical. Consequently we found a local barber who operated part-time out of his home only a few buildings down the street from the entrance to the Hoa Da District Compound. Through Tony, we negotiated an agreement and price per advisor to get our hair cut weekly. This agreement provided bottles of rubbing alcohol and hexachlorophene liquid soap to properly sanitize his tools before cutting our hair and/or shaving us. Our medics did a great job of properly educating the barber about this need and the steps to be taken to ensure appropriate sterilization of his tools.

We were unsure of the barber's political loyalties, so we felt uncomfortable with him wielding a very sharp straight razor around our throats and necks. Our first haircuts began with five of our advisors carrying their rifles. I then explained in French, Vietnamese, and English that if the barber slipped with his razor, even in the slightest, drawing blood, the advisors would shoot him dead since he must be Vietcong. The first few times the barber was understandably very nervous and perspired profusely while we were there. When things worked out very well, we no longer felt the need to go to his shop armed. Everyone, and especially the barber, was able to relax during the grooming.

The French military had trained him to cut hair fifteen years earlier. We learned that Vietnamese barbers were accustomed to cutting a patron's hair then shaving the back and sides of his neck below the hairline, a practice we were already used to with American barbers. The Vietnamese, however, went much farther: they shaved the front of the neck and the entire face, including the forehead, nose, upper cheeks, and ears, excluding only the eyebrows and eyelashes. We tried to tell the barber that we did not want this extra shaving, but he never seemed to quite understand, so we just accepted it as a part of the haircut routine.

Some of my team and I were walking back from the barber's house one day when we heard the province senior advisor's helicopter flying overhead. It finally landed on our helipad. It was the end of the second week in August, and we wondered at this unexpected and unannounced visit. We walked toward the helipad. Lt. Colonel Thompson and his operations officer hopped out followed by an army major we had not seen before. Blevins, Wilson, Cuthbert, and I met the chopper and saluted these officers. Thompson returned our salute and introduced Major George Dramis, our new Hoa Da District senior advisor. My days as this team's commander had just come to an end.

I tried to hide my disappointment and wounded pride. The advisory team had made steady progress: the replacement of the district chief; establishing positive relationships with the Hoa Da District people; the MEDCAP program; and the improved training and security of the South Vietnamese forces. We were finally on a roll. I could only hope that the arrival of Major Dramis would enhance our progress and not work against our efforts. We saluted and welcomed him to the Hoa Da District Compound. I introduced myself and the advisors. He shook our hands in a cordial manner and said that he was looking forward to getting to know us and to leading the Hoa Da advisory team.

I led Thompson and Dramis to meet Xuan. I called our interpreter to join us and then knocked on the door of the conference room. Con came to the door. I apologized for the interruption but explained that Lt. Colonel Thompson had just flown in with the new Hoa Da senior advisor, Major Dramis, and I wanted to give Major Xuan a chance to meet with them. Con went back inside and explained the situation to Xuan, who immediately came to the door and welcomed them both.

Xuan looked at me with a puzzled expression when Tony explained that Major Dramis would be serving as the Hoa Da senior advisor. I looked down at the floor. Xuan warmly greeted Dramis. He informed Thompson that he was unaware of this appointment and thought that Captain Haneke was serving in that capacity and was doing a very good job. Thompson stated that the commander at American Military Assistance Command Vietnam/1st Field Force Command-Vietnam (MACV/IFFV) Headquarters, Lt. General Peers, felt that this position required a major, not a captain.

Xuan responded that he didn't care what rank the senior advisor was as long as he was an experienced and effective military leader who was here to help organize, train, and supply the Hoa Da District forces to overcome the Vietcong. Thompson and Dramis then met alone with Xuan for about twenty minutes before Thompson returned to his helicopter. He wished Dramis luck and flew back.

The advisory team assembled outside the back of our quarters. I called the team to attention followed by a salute to Dramis. I led him down the line of advisors introducing each man. Dramis said how glad he was to finally be in Hoa Da District and spoke to us for about fifteen minutes. Blevins, Wilson, and I took Dramis on a tour of the complete Hoa Da District Compound explaining the details of our compound defense features and plans. A number of the Vietnamese troops were talking among themselves about the sudden appearance of this new senior officer.

After our tour, Dramis asked why we Americans had no latrine or buildings of our own. By this time, several of the senior NCOs and Zender had joined us. We all took turns carefully explaining the history and slow development of our advisory team and facilities. After this, Dramis commented that he had heard very little of this during his MACV orientation. He admitted that his civil affairs course had featured very little combat and military operations. He was well trained and qualified to deal with the various aspects of improving and building up the local communities after being pacified from their Vietcong influence and occupation. The province level orientation never mentioned combat or enemy activities so he naturally assumed that the Hoa Da District was mostly pacified.

Blevins and I briefed him on the training, qualifications, and experiences of each of our advisory team members. We emphasized that the Hoa Da District was not pacified. Frequent, almost daily, Vietcong activities occurred throughout the region. His reaction was one of borderline shock, and he asked, "Are you kidding me about this?"

We assured him that this was no joke. He sighed and commented that our advisory effort would be on-the-job training for him as well as the rest of us. We unanimously nodded Dramis stated that he would depend on Blevins and me to plan and direct the military training and combat efforts of the advisory team and the local Vietnamese troops.

During the next several days, Blevins, Zender, and I took Dramis around to meet the district chiefs and senior advisors for the surrounding districts, the command staff and advisors for the 44th ARVN regiment, CIA team, AID staff member, and the U.S. Navy swift boat crew. During these meet and greet briefing sessions, I had difficulty making a personal assessment of Dramis, since he asked very few questions, gave limited responses, and never shared his ideas for the advisory team's objectives.

Toward the end of the first week, Dramis met Bolling, the other medics, and me to receive a briefing on our team medical capabilities and MEDCAP visits. He seemed satisfied that these outreach medical services and visits were a positive presence. However, Dramis was opposed to our combat operations and involvement against people living in these same villages. He felt that this type of activity would cause us to lose the support of the "locals." I interjected that we were only forced to conduct these types of operations in response to hostile Vietcong activities conducted by the same people living in these areas. Dramis stared and bit his lip. He reluctantly agreed to my reason. Inside I knew that, for better or for worse, I would end up being responsible for all military activities—be they successes or failures. I took some comfort in the hope that Dramis would stay out of our way in performing our duties. We definitely did not need an inexperienced—and potentially unwilling—extra body tagging along while conducting our activities against the Vietcong, particularly in the field. My disappointment over the insertion of this new officer may well have strengthened these feelings.

Dramis spent the next few weeks meeting with Xuan and various members of his staff as he attempted to get familiar with the Hoa Da District, its people, and its needs. He used Tony most of the time to assist him in translating his conversations with the Vietnamese both in our compound and the villages. This meant that the rest of the advisors were left with the other two interpreters, who only did a very marginal job of interpretation. It didn't take long before the very crummy interpreting hacked the rest of us off. Finally I approached Dramis and told him about the difficulties that we were forced to contend with when using interpreters other than Tony. He shrugged and said that he was dealing with the more important aspects of our advisory effort and so would continue to use Tony.

At this point I began to work in earnest to find suitable replacements for the other two interpreters. It took a couple weeks, but I was finally able to get a good interpreter from Nha Trang and another from Phan Rang. Upon their arrival, we immediately sent the two bad interpreters to Phan Thiet and, thankfully, never saw them again.

To his credit, Dramis was able to bring some organization and progress to our advisory efforts. He had representatives from key villages and hamlets list and define the projects and factors necessary to improve the quality of life for their residents. It was interesting to note that not every village had the same needs or desires, so it would be impossible to do the cookie-cutter approach for each village. Some needed the basics, such as drinkable water and water storage, while others wanted a marketplace, a school, a place to pen their animals up, or else needed help getting the proper seeds and farming tools and repairing moveable Bailey bridges the Vietcong had blown up. Each bridge would require substantial repairs or replacement to keep them safe and passable by the increasing volume of traffic. At present, there was no money or resources to pay for the necessary repairs. This would present a challenge to Dramis in planning and finding the appropriate resources to handle this project. It would occupy his time. Hoa Da District was at the bottom of everyone's priority list for the allocation of aid.

Vietcong activity increased after Dramis' arrival. This often resulted in the placement of scattered roadblocks, surrounded by a few land mines and/or booby traps along the main roads throughout the Hoa Da District. We routinely dispatched a team of Vietnamese soldiers and an American advisor early each morning to locate, disarm, and dismantle these barricades so that normal civilian traffic could proceed safely.

Most of the people were well aware of the dangers the roadblocks imposed and knew better than to try to get around them until the mines and booby traps were dismantled. Occasionally people would allow their impatience to get the best of them and would then try to circle around the barrier. Most of the time, this resulted in setting off a hidden explosive device and getting themselves and others killed or wounded from shrapnel. Inevitably these casualties would be brought to our compound for medical assistance. Some we were able to help, but many were so severely injured that there was little hope.

I will never forget the first civilian casualty I saw brought to us. The man literally looked like a piece of Swiss cheese, with holes of all sizes where his flesh had been blown away. He had severe head wounds, sucking chest wounds, severe extremity wounds, and many shrapnel wounds, all bleeding profusely, over the majority of his body. The man had so much wrong with him that it was hard to know where to begin treatment. Unfortunately at that time our medics were in another village conducting a MEDCAP.

Amos and I applied several pressure dressings to the man's chest area to try to cut off the air loss and assist his breathing. Systematically we went from wound to wound trying to stem the bleeding and save his life. This was no easy task since we periodically had to ask his family members to back away so that we could continue to treat him. They kept crowding around and kept up a high-pitched chatter as we worked. I thought that they were saying words of encouragement, but was later told they were commenting on how bad he looked, which was a normal practice for the Vietnamese. We continued to work on him for almost an hour, but then determined that he was no longer breathing. This severe casualty had come as an unexpected shock to us and didn't bode well for our tour of duty here.

Our medics returned a short time later and, after taking a quick look at the mangled man, stated that there was nothing we could have done to save his life. They expressed great surprise that we had kept him alive as long as we did. Of all the injured people who were brought to us after that, few were anywhere near as bad off. I guess that God wanted us to handle and to be exposed to the worst type of casualty first so that we would not be so shocked by any future cases.

Nighttime attacks on our compound also increased. When the action became intense and the Regional and Popular Forces troops needed to be directed, Xuan turned to his new American district senior advisor for advice. Xuan expected Dramis to request air and/or artillery support against the attacking Vietcong forces, as I had routinely done. Dramis seemed to be at a loss to quickly and properly request these vital services, in spite of my efforts to instruct him. Frustrated with Dramis's lack of timely combat reaction, Xuan started to come directly to me with his initial request for support, bypassing Dramis in the heat of battle.

This put me in a precarious position, because I never wanted to go over my commander's head. However, when we were in danger of being overrun and massacred, time was of the essence, and it was imperative that appropriate action be taken as soon as possible. Frankly, Dramis seemed relieved that somebody else was handling these details correctly and that Xuan was content to operate in this manner.

It would take some time and on-the-job-training for Major Dramis and the advisory members to understand social and ethnic customs, citizen needs, religious and spiritual beliefs, and politics. At least our advisory team was now fully staffed. We were able to give assigned tasks and responsibilities to those who were trained and qualified to handle specific areas of operation. My hope was that we could now function more effectively in providing assistance to our assigned Vietnamese counterparts.

CHAPTER 12
Learning the Supply Game

By the second week in September, the orders finally arrived for the Hoa Da District advisory team to travel to Cam Ranh Bay to pick up the basic load of assigned equipment. The normal helicopter mail delivery and administrative pouch used to transport classified documents such as planned military aircraft bombings and Security of Intelligence (SOI) forwarded us these orders. SOI information was a list of military radio call signs and coded letters or numbers the security command officer used. This coded information changed at least monthly so that the enemy could not decode our messages.

Major Dramis had picked up the pouch that day and read the orders. He chose Sergeant Amos and me to fly to Cam Ranh Bay Army Base to pick up our advisory kit equipment. It was decided that we should try to catch the Australian Air Force Caribou flight that stopped at Song Mao twice a week. These flights were commonly referred to as "Wallaby Airlines" and were usually more reliable than flights by either the U.S. Air Force or Army in this area.

Dramis, several of our team members, and I prepared a wish list of items that we would try to acquire at Cam Ranh Bay in addition to our advisory team kit to enhance our security and living arrangements. These included a number of weapons, ammunition, explosives, two-way radios, two jeeps, a three-quarter-ton truck, and other "targets of opportunity." The truck was not part of our list of equipment, yet we needed it to travel throughout our assigned area to perform our mission, so it was essential that we obtain one.

The next morning, Amos and I caught a ride with Zender, who was headed to Song Mao to coordinate intelligence information for our area. Major Elliott was glad to see us and to hear that we were finally going to be issued our basic equipment. He cautioned me not to get my hopes up about receiving all of the items listed, as there were often shortages and backorders. I asked how likely that was to occur. He smiled knowingly and asked how good I was at trading for equipment within the military system. I told him I had a little experience with this when I was stationed in Germany.

He said that it worked a little differently here in Vietnam. Case in point: most everybody was looking for war souvenirs that ran the gamut from enemy weapons, flags, and uniform parts to items of local interest, such as Montagnard crossbows or brass wrist bracelets. A reasonable, acceptable substitute was always bottles of booze that were readily obtainable through the Class VI store at any larger military base. Elliott reminded me that every potential trade required some item(s) offered up front as a means of barter. Also, I should expect a negotiating process, particularly for the larger or scarcer items.

The Song Mao supply sergeant presented me with a box that contained a beat-up rifle made of parts from several different weapons, two old, worn French pistols, and two weathered and faded Vietcong battle flags. Major Elliott picked out the rifle and said that in the trading game with war souvenirs, it was essential to have a believable story to sell its legitimacy. He examined the rifle and commented that it could still fire. I should tell the story that it was taken from a Vietcong sniper who was shot dead while trying to kill our district chief.

Next Elliott pulled out the two flags and embellished a story about the Vietcong who were leading attacks on our compound on two different occasions. He pointed to several holes in each flag and a couple blood stains. Then he explained that a local tailor made these flags for them. The flags were then given to the local U.S. Navy swift boat crew to tow behind their boat in the salty water to give them the "weathered look." Finally a live chicken was purchased and shot with a shotgun with several of these faux Vietcong flags behind it. The result was holes in the flags with blood stains to enhance the effect.

The story that went with the two French pistols was probably the closest to the truth: these pistols were taken from two French officers when they were captured during a battle with a Vietminh unit in the Indo-China War. When the owners later joined the Vietcong, they then used these pistols as their armament. The pistols were taken from the bodies of slain Vietcong attackers on an outpost near Song Mao. Elliott instilled in me that the rear echelon types (commonly referred to as REMFS, or "Rear Echelon Mother-Fuckers"), were so hungry for this type of stuff that they would gladly accept it and buy into the stories. In fact, most would enhance the story further to raise their stock in trade to impress someone. I broke down the rifle and stuffed it along with the Vietcong flags into my rucksack while Sergeant Amos put the pistols in his.

We arrived just in time to see the Australian Caribou make its final approach for landing. The plane looked just like those of the U.S. Air Force, with the exception of the side insignia and a large white kangaroo emblem on the plane's raised tail. As the tailgate lowered, we saw the unmistakable Aussie crew chief with his ruddy complexion and red handlebar mustache. He jumped to the ground with a cheerful "G'day, sir." We told him that we were headed to Cam Ranh Bay to pick up equipment for our new advisory team and offered to give him a copy of our orders. He waved them off politely and said, "You Yanks are as good as your word. I won't need any orders."

He paused for a moment and said that he might have a slight problem finding two seats on his already-full aircraft. He then said, "Not to worry, mates. That shouldn't be a problem. I'll arrange for a couple of volunteers to give up their seats for you two gentlemen." He went back inside the plane, and we heard his bellowing voice ask for volunteers to give up their seats. After a minute or two, we heard the sounds of a scuffle, accompanied by loud shouts of protest.

The crew chief and a very large, burly fellow-crewman emerged from the plane, each carrying a person by the shirt collar and the seat of his pants. They deposited the "volunteers" on the ground next to the plane and then reached back inside, grabbed two bags, and threw them next to each of these men. By this time, I saw that each man was wearing a badge with the word "Press" on it. The Aussie crew chief brushed his hands together and with a big smile stated, "I guess we're through with those strap-hangers now."

He politely ushered Sergeant Amos and me to our seats. He commented, "The press have no priority; they pay nothing; they show no appreciation; and they generally try to stir up things by vilifying the hard-working military simply carrying out their orders as they try to fight this godforsaken war."

We could hear the two reporters continuing to yell their protestations as the rear ramp was raised and the plane's engines started. The crew chief looked at me with a smirk on his face and said, "And that's how we deal with that no-priority class of travelers." The news media were a constant irritant for the airlines, as they often demanded to fly on any available aircraft, apparently forgetting that the military were engaged in war and needed top priority.

I looked at the other passengers. They were a mix of Americans, Australians, and New Zealanders along with South Vietnamese military, accompanied by a couple family members. The ejection of the two obnoxious reporters, who had been making a number of demeaning comments about the Aussies and their "puddle-jumping" planes during the flight, did not appear to upset anyone. The aircraft made a quick take-off and proceeded to fly to Cam Ranh Bay. We thanked the Aussie crew chief and offered to buy him a round of drinks. He warmly returned the thanks, but he still had half a day of flying left.

Learning the Supply Game

At the information counter I learned about a bus that routinely made the rounds of all of the military bases at Cam Ranh Bay twenty-four hours a day. Sergeant Amos and I walked out front to the bus stop and boarded the waiting bus along with a number of other passengers. After we all had stowed our gear in the overhead racks above the seats, the bus driver reminded everyone to unload their weapons since Cam Ranh Bay was a secure base and carrying loaded weapons was strictly forbidden. We all immediately complied and removed the loaded magazines and cleared the chambers of our rifles. This was a nice break from being in a combat zone where you could be shot at any time. I leaned over my seat and told the driver to let us off at the Explosive Ordnance Disposal Detachment building. He offered no acknowledgment.

As the bus drove around the large base, I noticed that there were at least two Vietnamese villages located within the base perimeter. The people living in these villages worked during the day for the American military. Their jobs included mess hall cooks and aides, hooch maids, construction workers, stevedores on the docks, vehicle drivers, utility workers on the sewage disposal system, and workers for a number of other jobs. At night some of the younger women earned extra money as bar girls and prostitutes. Having fully isolated villages made the medics' jobs easier in controlling the incidence and spread of venereal diseases. The medics would check the girls at least once a week and, if they were clean with no diseases, they got their card punched and dated, signifying that they were safe for intercourse. If they didn't have a current punch mark and date, they were considered diseased and should be avoided until the medics certified them cured.

Cam Ranh Bay was an extensive complex of American military bases built along an extended peninsula surrounded on the east and south by the South China Sea. On the west side was a naturally deep, sheltered bay that was perfect for docking large ships into the base piers. Piers were designated for general cargo, petroleum products, explosive ordnance, and others for vehicles that ran the gamut from jeeps, trucks, mechanized vehicles, and heavy tanks, to helicopters. In addition to the U.S. Army supply base were U.S. Air Force, Naval, and Navy Seabee bases. This peninsula was easily defensible and had a medical center that had become a central evacuation hospital for the northern half of South Vietnam. It also had some of the best beaches, used mainly by the personnel stationed at Cam Ranh Bay and surrounding areas. These large bases had large PXs, Class VI stores, as well as fast-food restaurants and a number of military clubs. At the air terminal, the USO supplied fresh ice cream and cold milk, which some "round-eyed Doughnut Dollies" (female Red Cross workers) handed out, much to the delight of the troops.

The bus finally arrived at the Explosive Ordnance Disposal Detachment building. We walked into their orderly room and one of the EOD specialists greeted us warmly. He explained that the officers' billets were always jam-packed with higher-ranking officers, so it was extremely hard for a junior officer to find a vacancy there even for a night or two. He recommended several vacant beds in the back of the barracks where all of the EOD personnel stayed when they were at Cam Ranh Bay. That sounded great to us. We were each assigned a locker, provided two sheets, a pillowcase, a pillow, and a poncho liner for our bunks. Much to our delight the billets had hot showers and latrines. To us "boonie rats" this was like going to a fine resort to relax.

Amos and I tossed our rucksacks on the vacant beds. We locked our rifles up in their arms room, which was in keeping with a standard rule at Cam Ranh Bay. By this time, I had become so accustomed to constantly carrying my rifle and being on alert that I felt naked and a little apprehensive without it.

Later that afternoon we met with the EOD commander who explained how we could obtain a three-quarter-ton truck for our use at Cam Ranh Bay. He pulled out a post map and showed us where we needed to claim our advisory kit equipment. After further explanation about the do's and don'ts of living at Cam Ranh Bay, he took us to the ordnance battalion motor pool to get us a vehicle. From there we headed toward the battalion mess area, where they were having an outdoor barbecue with all of the trimmings. This featured pork ribs, beef, and chicken all smothered in a mild sauce that left a very pleasant aftertaste. Amos said that we should kidnap this mess sergeant and take him back to Hoa Da District. It would sure beat having us die from our own bad cooking. After dinner we went back to the EOD billets to get some much-needed sleep. It was comforting to be housed in a secure building on a secure base with screens on the windows and doors to keep out the nightly parade of vermin and insects. For the first time since my arrival in Vietnam, I finally slept soundly.

The next morning Amos and I did our morning ritual without Vietnamese spectators, ate breakfast, and headed toward the battalion motor pool to borrow a three-quarter-ton truck. We were given a map of the entire Cam Ranh Bay complex and directions to the army logistics complex of warehouses, motor pools, and supply yards. Driving through the main base headquarters we passed a large PX and Class VI store and the officers and the NCO clubs, which we noted for our return.

Amos found a parking spot in front of a one-story building. We went inside and were told that the equipment issuance center was two buildings down and to look for the very tall sergeant major. He would take care of our equipment and supply requests.

We strolled down two buildings and entered the main door only to see a never-ending line of soldiers, each representing the forces of coalition allies (i.e., South Korea, Philippines, Thailand, New Zealand, Malaysia, etc.). Each had a lengthy list of equipment requests. They received no less than about 95 percent of what they requested regardless of their priority. An hour later it was our turn. I optimistically handed our approved orders for our advisory basic equipment list to the tall sergeant major. He was about six feet eight, appeared to weigh over three hundred pounds of solid muscle, and looked mean as a snake.

At first he glared at Amos, and then at me. He hastily scanned our lengthy list of equipment, then, without referring to any records or conferring with anyone, stated gruffly that he would issue less than a fourth of the items that day. These items would not include any vehicles, radios, weapons, generators, barbed wire, sandbags, or food. We were issued several pots and pans, cooking utensils, ten five-gallon "Jerry cans" (five for water and five for gasoline), three Coleman lanterns, one small water purification setup, and one small lead safe in which to secure our classified documents.

"The rest of the items," he said, "are on backorder. They should be sent to your compound in about six months or more."

I pleaded that our compound was fully manned with a team of American Army advisors. We were in great need of all of these items for our survival and ability to carry out our assigned operations. His indifferent response indicated it was no concern of his. I asked if I could return later in the week. The giant gave me another glare with a smirk and bellowed not to bother because we were at the bottom of all of the priority lists for equipment and supplies. As a last resort, I attempted to offer him some of our "war souvenirs," but he quickly held up his hand in a dismissive manner and said, "Sir, I either have whatever you are going to offer or I don't need it. This offer will absolutely not influence me to make any of these items of equipment available for you any sooner." My first attempt at negotiating a better deal had been totally rebuffed.

We shrugged our shoulders, gathered up the meager equipment, and stowed it away in the back of the truck. Approaching the long row of warehouses, I had an idea. I told Amos to stop at the warehouse area. He gave me a puzzled look. I told him that we were going to make a house call on the NCO in charge of each of the warehouses to see if any of them would be willing to bargain or trade for some of the items we so desperately needed.

Amos said, "What do we have to lose?" He stopped at the first warehouse.

As it turned out, I was either incredibly lucky or God took pity on me, because the very first NCO we called on turned out to be Sergeant First Class Kanahoe, a native-born Hawaiian who had served as a platoon sergeant in my same company at the First Battalion 54th Infantry in Bamberg. We had left Germany about the same time. Sergeant Kanahoe recognized me immediately. We shook hands and brought each other up-to-date on what we had been doing since leaving Bamberg. This was to be his last assignment before retiring from the army. He planned to move back to Hawaii to be with his family. Amos shook his head in disbelief; he had trouble believing that the two of us had recently been stationed together in Germany for a year.

I informed Kanahoe that I had attended the Special Warfare School to be trained as an advisor and was now starting a new advisory team in the Hoa Da District, Binh Thuan Province. I expressed my concern regarding the lack of equipment we were and the attitude the sergeant major displayed. Kanahoe didn't seem very surprised. He asked if we were setting up a totally new advisory team and compound or just taking over and trying to improve an existing one. I assured him that it was a new team and compound in an area with no American units anywhere nearby. Kanahoe said that this made a difference. We should have been given more support since we were new.

He walked us over to meet the NCOs in charge of the adjoining warehouse, who turned out to be native Hawaiian also. A surprised look crossed my face. Kanahoe laughed and said that all of the NCOs running these warehouses and supply yards were native-born Hawaiians. "We call ourselves the 'Pineapple Brigade.'"

Most of these career military soldiers had grown up together in Hawaii and some were even related to one another. Talk about a close-knit group. He expressed that it would not be necessary to offer any war souvenirs, although a fifth of good scotch or bourbon would always be welcomed. I nodded. He supplied us with four gross (four thousand) poncho liners, which were very popular camouflaged, lightweight silk-covered, all-purpose padded mats that were used for bed covering in the tropics. Kanahoe mentioned that poncho liners were the most sought after and tradable commodities in all Southeast Asia. We should use our supply of poncho liners to negotiate for truck transportation for shipment of the equipment to the airport. If we negotiated the deal properly, these trucks would be available to assist us for the rest of our tour whenever we had business to conduct in the Cam Ranh Bay/Nha Trang area.

He also recommended that we save a supply of poncho liners as negotiating material for the U.S. Air Force, Army, and Australian/New Zealand aviators, as poncho liners worked better than official travel orders. He reminded us that most of the U.S. Air Force transport planes in Vietnam were now piloted by U.S. Air Force Reserve or National Guard crews who were trying to acquire as many war souvenirs as they could during their six-month tour of duty in Vietnam.

I pulled out my wish list and read. We needed radios, preferably four PRC-25s and two VRC-46s; three long-range radio antennas; two electrical generators; four .50-caliber machine guns with tripods; four M-60s or .30-caliber machine guns; eight BARs; two 90mm recoilless rifles; four grenade launchers; three M-151 jeeps; two three-quarter-ton trucks; twelve foldable canvas medical stretchers; three medical aid kits and surgical instruments along with a full range of sterile and non-sterile medical supplies; four field tables; one large foldable table; fifteen metal folding chairs; one large refrigerator (electrical or propane); one stove (electrical or propane); two large rubberized water storage bladders (120-gallon size); two water purification kits with a large supply of iodine tablets and disposable carbon filters; five thousand sandbags; rolls of barbed wire along with a supply of steel posts to string them on; and as much toilet paper as possible. I added that we would also need a large supply of canned and packaged foods and cases of military rations. In short, our advisory team currently had next to nothing and needed everything.

Shaking his head, Kanahoe commented that we had been shortchanged. He said that even the third-country allies were given almost everything they requested. He thought for a second then told us to check back with him in the morning. By then he

Learning the Supply Game

would have had an opportunity to talk to several other key NCOs who could possibly help us out. We expressed our sincere appreciation for any assistance he could arrange as well as for the cases of poncho liners.

The next morning Amos and I returned to see Kanahoe, who took us to meet two other Pineapple Brigade warehouse NCOs. The well-organized supply personnel loaded the items into our truck at various designated locations in the warehouse district. The Pineapple Brigade were able to issue us two PRC-25 radios; one long-range radio antenna; one .50-caliber machine gun; four BARs; two grenade launchers; eight medical stretchers; two medical aid kits with a range of surgical instruments; a variety of sterile and non-sterile medical supplies; two field tables; eight metal folding chairs; one large water storage bladder (one hundred gallon capacity); one water purification kit with a limited supply of charcoal filters and iodine tablets; three cases of toilet paper (three hundred rolls); twenty cases of assorted canned food; four cases of C-rations; five cases of long-range recon patrol rations; three five-gallon-sized Jerry cans for potable water; and three five-gallon-sized Jerry cans filled with mo-gas for our two existing jeeps. Upon completion, we did not sign for anything. We thanked the Pineapple Brigade with a half-gallon of Seagram's Crown Royal bourbon and a half-gallon of Canadian Club Black Label whiskey. Kanahoe's token gift was a half-gallon of his favorite, Chivas Regal scotch. He beamed at receiving the scotch and commented that bartering was a greater motivator than simply doing your routine job. Everybody needed something and everybody had their price. This appeared to be a universal constant throughout the military service.

Kanahoe suggested that we follow him to a going-away reception being held at the air rescue detachment building. He said that he was sure it would be worth our while. Sergeant Amos and I followed him to the air rescue hangar, which had been decorated appropriately for the team's departure party. They had just completed their year's duty, where they developed a great reputation for making a number of heroic rescues and had flown a lot of missions during the recent Tet Offensive. This unit flew mainly Kaman "Huskies" HH-43B helicopters with intermeshing rotors and a twin-tail design. These choppers had initially been designed as fire suppression and rescue aircraft, but had been pressed into service to perform pilot and crew rescues for downed aircraft in South Vietnam.

It didn't take long for the crowd to gather; accolades were given to each of the heroic departing airmen. The toasts continued and a never-ending supply of alcoholic beverages flowed long after the official ceremony. Kanahoe introduced us to several of the air rescue detachment members, who in turn introduced us to their commander and several other officers. We talked at length about our advisory duties and the fact that we were unable to get adequate equipment and supplies the army issued for our security and needs. I laid it on a little thick about having no American support for fifty miles and daily contact with the Vietcong. Yet we couldn't get them to issue us compound defense weapons, sandbags to construct bunkers, barbed wire, or normal food.

After drinking a few more toasts to the brave men from air rescue and the brave men from our advisory outpost, their commander promised me that he would get us two machine guns and ammunition, a VRC-46 radio, several grenade launchers, two crates of sandbags (four thousand), two hundred claymore mines, and two cases of General Westmoreland's private supply of the finest Delmonico steaks. He said that I would have to be there no later than 0800 hours the next morning to make this happen. We shook hands on this offer and drank a couple more rounds. It was obvious that neither of us were feeling any pain when we finally left to return to our quarters.

The next morning I had to battle a severe headache while taking a cold shower to wake up and overcome the excesses of the night before. I managed to fortify my stomach with some toast, scrambled eggs, and several cups of strong coffee before driving over to the air rescue detachment building, arriving at just about 0800 sharp. The officer-in-charge, whom I had met the night before, was very surprised to see me. He offered me a cup of fresh coffee while he summoned his commanding officer, who had not been able to get out of his bed yet.

Half an hour later he showed up, quite hung over. He greeted me warmly and confessed that he had not expected me since I had appeared to be drunk the night before. I assured him that while I was certainly feeling no pain then, I had been well trained by the Special Forces and had a very good memory of his offer and the agreement on which we shook hands. He laughed and told me to return about noon to pick them up. I thanked him and said that these items would really help out our advisory team. I offered the untaken "war souvenirs" of the rifle, two pistols, and two Vietcong flags. He gratefully accepted them along with the stories for each.

I drove back to the EOD detachment, arriving in time to help Sergeant Amos get the equipment and supplies onto the truck for transport to the air field for loading on a Chinook helicopter. Our earlier poncho liner negotiations with the truck battalion sergeant major had gone quite well. He had come through with the proper size truck. The poncho liners were earning big dividends for us. I told Amos that he would have to fly back alone, because I was staying on longer to pick up the additional equipment the air force detachment commander promised. Amos said that he could manage quite well and would get all the help he needed from the Vietnamese when he got back to the Hoa Da District Compound. I assured him that I would be flying in the next day. He saluted, got into the truck, and headed over to the air field.

Noon arrived. When I got to the air rescue detachment building, the equipment was stacked up just inside the hangar. There were .50- and .30-caliber machine guns with about twenty cases of ammunition for each, along with two grenade launchers. All of the other items were there, including two frozen boxes containing twenty prime Delmonico steaks. The air force detachment commander told me to guard these with my life. If anyone asked where I got them, just mention that it was a gift. Several of his men quickly loaded everything onto my truck. I thanked everyone, saluted, and drove back to my billets.

At the EOD detachment building, I begged the NCO in charge to put the steaks in a freezer where they would not be stolen. He assured me the steaks would be secure for my flight the next morning. Unlike the nights before, I didn't sleep very well. I had a sense of impending dread, which I chalked up to having to leave the good life at Cam Ranh Bay and return to the austere conditions at the Hoa Da District Compound. I got up early the morning of September 18, took a leisurely shower, then packed up my gear and grabbed a bite to eat.

The NCO in charge had a couple men help me load up the truck, to which he added my two cases of steaks, and drive me over to the air field. He backed the truck up next to the helicopter where I gave a copy of my orders to the pilot. The crew chief then enlisted the services of his crewmembers to transfer my equipment onto the helicopter. Everything fit easily with the exception of the two large cases of empty sandbags, which took up too much room with the rest of the cargo. At first, they said that I would have to leave them at Cam Ranh Bay, but then they reloaded a couple other items and made room for everything. I boarded the chopper, climbed over several large boxes, and found my assigned seat. Two cases of frozen meat occupied a spot on top of the large box next to me. The engines were cranked up, and we were soon airborne on our way to Hoa Da District. It was another very hot and humid day in Vietnam. The prospect of going back to primitive living conditions that did not include electricity, running water, sit-down latrines, or regular access to American food was not very appealing.

The crew chief came over and said that the pilot wanted me to come up front and help him locate my compound, since he was unfamiliar with the area. I went forward and noted that we were flying just off the coast by the city of Tuy Phong. We soon reached Phan Ri Cua and I told the pilot to follow the road heading southwest. When we reached the area where I was sure the compound was stationed, I could see nothing but a few scattered houses along Route 1 and a couple dirty and cluttered villages nearby. I asked the pilot to circle the area in a wider pattern, but I still could not identify the Hoa Da District Compound. We tried it twice more without success. The pilot said he would fly to Song Mao and drop me and my gear off. This did not bode well.

We flew onto the landing strip on the edge of town. The crew unloaded and piled up all of my gear. Since it appeared that I would be totally alone out there, the pilot said that he would attempt to contact the Song Mao advisory team to inform them of my arrival and request someone come to pick me up. After the departure of the Chinook, it got very quiet, and I soon began to take notice of the oppressive heat. I increased my alertness, rifle at the ready, scanning the surrounding area hoping and praying that no Vietcong outfit would show up and try to capture and/or kill me. But then my concerns shifted to the steaks. I worried that they would spoil in the direct sun.

After spending a very nervous forty-five minutes alone, a truck from the 44th ARVN regiment drove up looking for some supplies that were supposed to have been flown in for them earlier that day. I asked the driver if they would give me a ride to the Song Mao Compound. They agreed and helped me load my equipment in the back. After the ride to the compound, we unloaded everything in front of Major Elliott's office. I thanked the two men and carried the two cases of melting steaks over to the mess hall. As I walked inside, several of the advisory staff rushed up to me and asked if I were all right.

This caught me completely off guard and I responded, "Why shouldn't I be all right?" They looked at one another and stated that a Vietcong regiment had completely overrun the Hoa Da District Compound the night before. Not everyone had been accounted for, and I was listed among the missing. Suddenly I understood why I had been unable to identify my compound from the air.

Elliott came running in and said, "Thank God you're alive!" I told everyone how I had sent Amos back to the compound the day before while I stayed in Cam Ranh Bay one more day to collect some defense weapons and additional equipment. Elliott wiped his eyes and said that my delay most likely saved my life. I asked if he had received the call from the Chinook about my arrival, and he said he had not.

I donated the cases of steaks to the Song Mao team, who gratefully accepted them, and said they would keep one case frozen for the Hoa Da District advisory team. I asked for a lift to Hoa Da District Compound to see what assistance I could render. Major Elliott and his radio operator said that they were just getting ready to go over there. We jumped into the jeep and took off. On the way, Elliott talked about the attack.

CHAPTER 13
Realities of Combat

Major Elliott began by telling me that the compound and advisory team would never be the same as the result of last night's overwhelming attack. Reliable Vietnamese intelligence sources had warned about an all-out attack on the Hoa Da District by a Vietcong Main Force-reinforced regiment two days earlier. The attack began about 2200 hours. The Vietcong approached the compound, following paths through the old French minefield. Two Popular Forces Units platoons, with the responsibility of guarding the north and west sides of the compound, had apparently defected to the Vietcong and aided their entry. The attacking force then quietly walked through the compound into the courtyard. There they blew apart surrounding buildings and bunkers with 57mm recoilless rifle, grenades, and satchel charges before anyone was aware of their presence. The surviving defenders later reported being badly outnumbered: a 35 to 1 ratio. The Song Mao duty officer received the few radio reports that leaked out from the compound. It was reported that all of the buildings in the compound were systematically searched, looted, and blown apart, while the Vietnamese soldiers were massacred. Within a short period of time, the Vietcong had wiped out all resistance and totally occupied the Hoa Da District Compound. Elliott sighed. I was speechless.

He continued talking. At about 0530 hours, he had talked to Dramis. He, Zender, and Xuan had taken refuge in a new and previously unused bunker early in the morning. Dramis had urged Song Mao Compound to call in air support when it was assumed that no more friendly troops were still alive in most areas of the compound. Two U.S. Air Force F-100s had arrived about an hour later and dropped their bombs on the west and north sides of the compound where they could see Vietcong activity as well as the suspected Vietcong route back into the mountains. They made several strafing runs, all with undetermined results, and then returned to their base in Phan Rang. No one at Hoa Da District ever requested any follow-up.

The Vietcong occupiers finally left the compound about 0800 hours that morning. An exact casualty count had yet to be determined since there were so many dead, wounded, and missing. The number of Vietcong casualties was also unknown, although reports of a number of blood trails leading outside the compound would indicate that there were some. A request for medevac helicopters was made about 0830 hours when it was confirmed that the Vietcong forces had totally withdrawn.

I took a deep breath and tried to grasp the reality of the situation. I could not believe that my compound was gone. I stared blankly out the jeep's window. Major Elliott broke into my dazed thoughts and suggested that when we arrived at the compound, we would help any survivors, treat and evacuate the remainder of the wounded, count the dead and missing, and compose an initial assessment on its impact on the Hoa Da District. Majors Dramis and Xuan were pretty well overwhelmed by this attack and could use our help. A team from Binh Thuan Province Headquarters would arrive in the afternoon accompanied by key members of the MACV staff to get a firsthand look. I replied with a soft "Yes, sir."

This whole scenario worried me to death. I felt very guilty for extending my stay in Cam Ranh Bay by a day and not being present to help my comrades handle this attack. When I expressed this feeling to Major Elliott, he assured me that I had acted properly. I shouldn't hold myself accountable for something that I was unable to predict or stop. He explained that this "separation guilt," as the experts have labeled it, is a fairly common thing among combat soldiers, especially when severe losses occur. It shouldn't be taken seriously.

No guards stood at the Hoa Da District Compound gate when we drove into what had been the main courtyard. I did a double take. I was unsure that we were in the right place because the scene was so surreal. None of us spoke. The buildings surrounding the courtyard were badly battered and were missing roofs and walls. Two buildings were totally reduced to nondescript piles of rubble. Some of the wreckage was still emitting smoke along with the putrid smell of death and rotting flesh. Scattered bloody and dismembered bodies, in the grotesque positions they had assumed in death, dotted or mounded around the rubble. Hordes of black flies and beetles had already ascended on this unexpected bounty of rotting flesh. It was becoming impossible to see the pieces of uniforms on most of these bodies to confirm that they were part of our Regional or Popular Forces Units and not Vietcong.

In spite of this gruesome scene, I was struck with the need to try to identify these casualties before they decomposed further, making them unrecognizable. I softly mentioned it to Major Elliott and immediately he assigned two of his sergeants the task of getting with the ranking Vietnamese officer to try and get this process moving.

I became acutely aware of the extreme quiet that had come over this normally active and noisy compound. Major Elliott and I found Master Sergeant Bolling in a cleared back section of the compound, where a few remaining wounded Vietnamese had been gathered for treatment. Several were waiting for another medevac chopper to arrive to take them to a hospital for more extensive diagnosis and treatment. The French hospital was the most intact of all of the buildings, although its roof and large wooden support beams had fallen inward. There Major Xuan, Major Dramis, and a couple of American and South Vietnamese officers and NCOs stood surveying the terrible results from this devastating attack.

The two majors barely acknowledged our arrival. All appeared dirty, with an accumulation of grit, blood, and soot, and were totally dazed Dramis kept repeating, "This is so awful! I just don't know how it happened!" Elliott and I tried to reassure them that we had come with additional support from Song Mao Compound.

I slowly scanned the back half of the compound. The two adjoining Vietnamese troop barracks that had housed over four hundred men from the Regional Forces were now two extensive piles of blackened rubble emitting the smell of burning human flesh. Amos emerged from behind this rubble appearing somewhat less disoriented than the other survivors. I asked him what had happened to these barracks and their occupants. Amos took a breath then replied that four teams of Vietcong sappers had quietly infiltrated the compound, implanting explosive and incendiary charges around both buildings. They blocked the main and only useable doorways for each building. Then the Vietcong set off the explosive charges that simultaneously leveled and set both structures on fire with all of their occupants and equipment still inside.

Those few soldiers who managed to escape ran or crawled out of the building with their clothes on fire, screaming horribly. For over two hours, explosions continued from the ammunition and grenades contained in the barracks. I shook my head. Since my initial arrival at Hoa Da District Compound, I had tried in vain a number of times to get the Vietnamese to unblock another exit or two in each building so they would have other ways out in case an emergency occurred. Now it was too late to reinforce that safety measure. These men had all paid the highest price for not taking this necessary precaution.

I took a deep breath then asked Amos how the other advisory team members had fared through the attack. His eyes dropped. He replied that although none had been killed, six had been wounded and were medevaced out by helicopter early that morning. They included Blevins, Whitehead, Hale, and three others. Wilson was badly shaken-up emotionally and was unable to perform any of his assigned duties. At first, Wilson was very edgy and irritable with everyone, but as the hours progressed he became nervous and finally withdrew into a fetal position. Wilson? I was stunned to think that a twenty-five-year military veteran would suffer from battle fatigue—or as the medical field now called it, post-traumatic stress disorder.

Amos admitted that the advisors became aware of the attack well after the Vietcong had spread throughout the compound. Once alerted, they immediately grabbed their weapons and ran out in one of two directions: back of the building or through the inner building courtyard. Zender, Dramis, Bolling, Xuan, Con, Vo, and later Blevins and Whitehead chose the inner courtyard direction. Amos pointed at the one-time inner courtyard. He explained in length that Blevins and Whitehead apparently had followed the others through the inner building courtyard and into the conference room.

Two Vietcong soldiers fired two 57mm recoilless rifle shells into the front of the conference room building, thereby causing the roof with its support beams to come crashing down, rendering them unable to escape. Whitehead sustained broken legs and an arm plus some degree of head trauma. Although a heavy beam across his chest pinned Blevins in place, he was able to move his legs and an arm somewhat. The Vietcong heard some moaning from Whitehead, as well as detected the movement of Blevins. Since the explosion blocked clear access into the building, they decided to roll a grenade in the vicinity of the detected motion. Several seconds later, it exploded, showering metal fragments into Blevins' legs. Several large beams shielded Whitehead, but his moans continued. The Vietcong tried to move some of the debris, but soon discovered that the massive beams were too heavy, so they fired several shots with their rifles into the area where they thought the enemy soldiers might be. Fortunately, they missed both Whitehead and Blevins.

Moans persisted. The two Vietnamese launched another grenade to eliminate these pesky survivors, and once again it landed between Blevin's legs—he kicked it away. When it detonated, Blevins sustained additional fragments in his lower legs, while Whitehead received wounds in one arm and leg causing his moaning to grow even louder. The annoyed Vietcong, wanting to finish this task, rolled two additional grenades into the building. Both grenades ended up between Blevin's legs again. Once more he was able to quickly kick them away before they detonated. The combined concussion of these grenades rendered Whitehead unconscious while causing Blevins to momentarily lose his hearing, get very dizzy, and see stars. He remained perfectly still and made sure not to make any noise. The two Vietcong soldiers listened carefully and shined their crude flashlights all around the area before deciding that they had finally terminated their stubborn enemy.

Amos wiped the sweat from his brow and stated that the Vietcong forces finally left the compound early the next morning. He personally found Blevins and Whitehead and asked the rest of the surviving Americans to help rescue them. After great difficulty, they were pulled out of the rubble and were medevaced.

Besides Amos, several other advisors had survived by fanning out to several places around the compound. They attempted to link up with the various Regional and Popular Forces platoons that were assigned compound defensive responsibilities. Unfortunately they encountered mass chaos and hysteria among the few defenders. It soon became apparent that the units assigned to the west and south sides of the compound were no longer there. The Vietcong units kept steadily pouring into those sides of the compound sounding their bugle calls, loud whistles, and bloodcurdling cries as they came.

These advisors soon discovered that the other bunkers located at the four corners and midpoints of each wall had also been destroyed, along with their personnel and weapons. They were finally able to locate a couple small groups of soldiers from the Regional Forces Unit. They attempted to bring them together to

Realities of Combat

form a more organized resistance force. This seemed to work for a while; they were able to delay and drive some of the attackers back a little and better establish a defensive perimeter.

Unfortunately they began to run low on ammunition and were forced to send several soldiers out to try to scrounge any additional ammunition they could find. Two came back with no additional ammunition and two others never returned. Everything indicated that the compound was in imminent danger of being totally overrun. The advisors recognized that they were unable to organize and mount any defensive effort, so they decided to split up and find a place to hide out until the attack was over. This seemed the only way that any of them might survive. Amos said that he, Cuthbert, and six Popular Forces Unit soldiers worked their way close to the POW area and hid out in the rubble of a nearby government building that had been destroyed. The other defenders from that original group were hunted down and killed.

I assured Amos that he had responded correctly. There was no other course of action given the large influx of Vietcong. Amos nodded and looked me in the eye. He said there were more terrifying stories. I told him to continue. He walked over to what remained of our advisory space and explained that two of our American advisors had run out the back door of our building when the attack began, only to encounter a hail of Vietcong gunfire and rocket-propelled grenade explosions next to them. They each received multiple metal fragment and gunshot wounds from the explosions, knocking them to the ground. Fearing for their lives, they played dead in the hopes that the Vietcong would pass them. They did not realize that a Vietcong Women's Action Company had led this devastating attack. The Vietcong women took the wounded advisors' rifles, grenades, and bandoliers of ammunition and then turned them over to see if they were still alive. One woman fired an "insurance shot" from her rifle into each of our American advisors to guarantee their deaths. Obviously these women were not intending to take any prisoners.

Hale sustained a wound from this shot in his upper left shoulder and fought hard not to react from the severe pain to indicate that he was still alive. He was sure that he was about to die but was powerless to offer any resistance. The sergeant was wounded on the inside of his upper left arm causing him to flinch and let out a loud moan. His additional penalty came when this Vietcong woman stabbed him with her bayonet in his upper right chest area. Luckily this weak thrust veered off of a rib bone and was only a flesh wound. He fought hard to remain motionless, praying that God would help him survive. Satisfied that she had finished him off, she moved on. Throughout the rest of this attack, our two advisors lay motionless as the attackers repeatedly ran all around them and several times would stop, look them over, search their pockets, and then move on. Both reported, somewhat embarrassed, that they finally had to let go and pee in their pants. They were worried to death that some of the passing Vietcong women would notice the wetness and stop and shoot them again. Fortunately this didn't happen.

Amos had told the advisors that it was a fact that wounded or killed people frequently emptied their bladders and bowels as the result of the trauma. When the attackers had finally departed, both advisors gave signs that they were alive to their passing fellow advisors. They were treated and evacuated along with Lieutenant Blevins and Sergeant Whitehead.

Women were responsible for a large part of this brutal atrocity! I couldn't believe it. After a moment to take in this information, I asked Amos about the others and how they had escaped injury or death. He said that Dramis, Xuan, Con, Vo, Zender, and our radio operator, Thornton, ended up in the newly established command bunker behind the district chief's headquarters building. Although the Vietcong forces won total possession of the Hoa Da District Compound, they did not think to check the new bunker. Probably their most recent intelligence information had not indicated that this bunker was ready for use. Consequently the occupants of the bunker hid there quietly and were not discovered or wounded during the entire attack and occupation.

Dramis was eventually able to reach Song Mao Compound and Elliott by radio and asked him to call in an air strike shortly after daybreak.

While staring at the rubble, Amos and I were met by Dramis, Xuan, Zender, Con, and Cuthbert. I asked them each for their recollections of the attack so I could put together an orderly presentation of the events for the investigators. It took them all a few moments to realize what I was saying as they began trying to recall those horrific events. From what I could piece together, the attack started when the attacking force, comprised of a reinforced Main Force Vietcong regiment, arrived outside the west and south walls of the Hoa Da District Compound. Two of our defending Popular Forces platoons, who we believed defected to the Vietcong, allowed the attacking force to quietly enter the compound without a shot being fired.

The lead element of the force was approximately a hundred women from a Vietcong Women's Action Company. They were seasoned combat veterans who fanned out, blowing up the remaining bunkers and defensive positions, while massacring all of their occupants. In the process of performing this act, they so thoroughly butchered all of the men that there were no survivors among this group of defenders. The women then opened the main gates and let the remaining attackers into the compound, and the destruction Amos had informed me of ensued. Two buildings remained untouched by the Vietcong. One was the small POW enclosure. The attackers did not harm or set free any of the prisoners or their family members. The other building that remained undamaged was the large white agricultural storage building.

I thanked them each for their emotional accounts and assigned several men to pick up all of the weapons, grenades, ammunition, and explosives. They were to stack these up in the back of the compound near the Vietnamese slit-trench latrine. I explained that if any explosives appeared to be Vietcong or set up as booby traps, they should clearly mark them in place. An EOD team would come and dismantle them.

Amos's conclusion appeared to be true. The Vietcong attackers had never intended to take any prisoners. Their goal was to totally annihilate all of the defenders. The dead had bullet wounds to the head or bayonet wounds to the chest. The message was clear—the Vietcong controlled the Hoa Da District so all other forces should take note and stay away. This really enraged the other advisors and me. We were compelled to track down these cold-blooded murders, but first we needed to overcome the results of this devastating attack.

We scoured the compound, tallied the causalities and reported seven American advisors were WIA. The South Vietnamese totals were 498 KIA, 71 WIA, and 105 MIA. It was impossible to determine either KIA or WIA Vietcong totals, because they carried away their casualties. We could not differentiate between Vietcong or friendly casualty blood trails without knowing which Vietnamese were defectors or MIA due to being kidnapped.

As the result of this attack, the Hoa Da District's military forces, with the exception of three Popular Forces Units platoons guarding bridges along Highway 1, ceased to exist. I radioed the province senior advisor and impressed upon him the extreme need for replacement military forces, as it would take entirely too long to recruit and train new military forces from around the province. Besides, our advisory team needed quick protection.

The province senior advisor said that he would look into this situation and get back to us soon. I cautioned him that it wouldn't take long for the Vietcong to realize how defenseless we were and come back to finish us off. I gave him a preliminary report on our causalities and the number and types of missing armament, and requested replacement advisors for those who were medically evacuated. I emphasized that we needed good, qualified replacements in order to complete our assigned mission. He repeated that he would look into the matter. I left this conversation with little confidence that anything would come from my requests. My belief of serving as sacrificial lambs for Binh Thuan Province remained with me.

Among the Vietnamese KIA was our loyal interpreter, Tony Nha, who was cut down in a hail of bullets as he ran out of the back door of our sleeping area. He had been bayoneted multiple times as well. Tony was a true warrior and was extremely loyal to all of our advisors.

Around noon, a flight of about fifteen American Huey helicopters flew over our compound, made a wide right turn, and landed. Commander of MACV/IFFV northern half of South Vietnam, Lieutenant General Peers, his command staff, and several MACV representatives, along with an armed security detail, had come to investigate our situation.

Dramis ordered me to go meet Peers and his staff and to give them a report on the details of this attack. It immediately occurred to me that I was being set up to take the blame for this disaster, even though I had not even been at the Hoa Da District Compound for several days before or during the attack. I decided to be truthful, direct, and candid. In short, I would let the blame fall where it should and not try to be diplomatic or politically correct. I certainly did not intend to take the rap for this disaster.

I went up to Peers, saluted him, identified myself, and asked how he would like to handle things during his visit. He returned my salute, walked a short way from the helicopters, and gathered about a dozen of his staff officers and MACV representatives around in a big circle. In a gruff and forceful manner, he stated, "Captain Haneke, I would advise you to start telling us all about this disaster immediately. We will open it up to questions when you're done."

I replied with a snappy "Yes, sir" and began by explaining that the Hoa Da District advisory team was newly established. We had been trying our best to organize and train the local Regional and Popular Forces Units while at the same time trying to obtain the appropriate arms and equipment necessary to effectively accomplish our assigned mission. I mentioned that the Hoa Da District Compound had previously served as a French hospital prior to the 1954 armistice ending the Indochina War. All of the barbed wire surrounding the compound pre-dated that time and was now so rusted that it didn't present a barrier against an attacking force. Since we had been unable to get any sandbags despite much effort, the bunkers were made out of wooden ammunition boxes, and I explained the dangers these presented.

Peers immediately called his command logistics staff representative over and ordered him to thoroughly survey the compound and arrange for appropriate barbed wire, steel fencing stakes, sandbags, claymore mines, and any other appropriate defensive equipment to be sent to the compound before the end of the week. Turning to me he asked where my commanding officer, Dramis, was and why he wasn't here with us. I told him that Dramis was on the other side of the compound with Xuan, dealing with some of the casualties.

Peers grunted, "I'll deal with him later."

I continued describing the events leading up to the attack as well as what happened during the course of the disastrous action. When I finished, he turned me over to four of his staff officers and a MACV representative to fill in some more details.

Peers, accompanied by several officers, walked off to find Dramis. The first colonel, whom I believe was his operations officer, told me to snap to attention and start showing better military bearing. This definitely caught me off guard and caused my heart to sink as he began inspecting my uniform, belt buckle, boots, and personal appearance. The colonel began screaming, "You had a hell of a nerve reporting to Peers looking so shitty with improperly shined boots, no shine on your belt buckle, as well as dirt and blood on your uniform." In combat units we were issued blackened belt buckles and boots not designed to be shined so I wondered what was wrong. For a moment I had a flashback to my days as a plebe at West Point, where I had to endlessly endure the loud and vicious reprimands from the upperclassmen no matter what I did or didn't do. The colonel just wrangled on. I just knew that my military career was now totally ruined.

He kept up his loud tirade for several minutes until Peers came back and mercifully told him, "Knock off the shit, Colonel!

This is a combat situation and is neither the time nor the place for this kind of Mickey Mouse crap! You are acting like a real Rear Echelon Mother-Fucker! These soldiers are under enough stress already without you adding to it! Kindly stick to your assigned task of finding out pertinent information about what happened here."

The colonel gave a loud "Yes, sir!" and stepped back and allowed the other officers to ask appropriate and pertinent questions about our military forces, the attacking forces, the tactics the Vietcong used, and the outcome of this action. The officers seemed most surprised by my mention of a Women's Action Company leading this attack. They had heard rumors of such units, but had never encountered any evidence of their participation or effectiveness in combat. It was therefore assumed that their main role in the Vietcong structure was one of administering to sexual needs, cooking, and/or nursing the male soldiers. I told them to look around at the carnage and note that the most severely butchered were the handiwork of these women. As I watched them examine the corpses more closely, I could tell that the ferocity that had led to the condition of these casualties amazed and horrified them. They finally concluded that this unit would be taken more seriously and carefully tracked through intelligence sources in the future.

The officers recognized the attack as the efforts of the Eighty-Nine Main Force Vietcong Company. I mentioned that a couple of our American advisors and several surviving members of our Vietnamese units had heard several foreigners, non-Vietnamese, talking in their native Asiatic language, but no one was actually able to identify it. The MACV representatives seemed particularly interested in this information and asked a number of questions, but I was unable to help them further on this detail.

During this session with the staff officers, I decided to add to my list of equipment requests despite my recent supply acquisition, which was safely stored at Song Mao Compound. As I had felt all along, the only time the military would pay attention to the Hoa Da District's needs was when something big and disastrous happened. This was it. Taking advantage of this opportunity, I asked about getting an adequate number of trained replacement troops, both Vietnamese and American, to fill the major void.

One of the officers went and conferred briefly with Peers, and when he returned, he announced that two companies of Cambodian mercenary soldiers would be sent to the Hoa Da District within the next two weeks. This was great news, and a godsend to me! The Cambodians had experienced troops and hated the Vietcong, so we could count on them for their loyalty. We were relatively certain that our previous units had been peppered with Vietcong and Vietcong sympathizers, which had made it very difficult to rely and trust any of them. These troops were all left over from the time when Captain Manh was district chief. The colonel added that Peers would replace the advisors soon from American units already stationed in Vietnam instead of waiting for a new class of advisor-trainees to graduate. This was good, but I asked that these American soldiers be experienced and highly motivated instead of a bunch of screw-ups. I had already had some bad experiences with this latter type. He promised that he would do his best in that regard.

Another staff officer started asking questions about the tactics the attacking force used, including their main axis of attack, weapons used, and tactics utilized to overcome the inside compound defenses. Xuan and Peers had joined us by this time. Xuan explained that the main attack came from the south through what had been the old French minefield. Another officer said that these mines, if any were still there, would certainly not work after all of these years.

As if on cue, Xuan's dog ran out into the area in question chasing a large rat and a large, exploding mine immediately blew him up. The dog's head and part of his front torso landed on the ground immediately in front of the staff officers. Without changing his expression, Peers said, "I guess that ends the question about whether any of those mines still work."

Xuan held in his emotion and continued to explain about the defection of at least two Popular Forces Units platoons that were responsible for the south and west sides of the compound. They had enabled the Vietcong to quietly enter the compound and position their forces to blow up the bunkers and troop barracks before any of the defending forces were aware of their presence. I had assumed all along that there were still some Vietcong sympathizers in the units, but had been unable to seek them out. I certainly had not been aware that there was a concentration of them.

Peers and his staff spent the next two hours touring the compound, asking many very detailed questions about the attack, and taking copious notes. They put together an educated theory about what led up to the attack; what made us vulnerable; better organization and tactics we could use to defend ourselves and the compound; and what steps, both short- and long-term, could be taken to try to prevent further attacks.

Peers emphasized that we needed to learn quickly from this situation and our mistakes because the Main Force Vietcong generally were creatures of habit. Once successful in a particular method of attack, they would routinely rehearse and continue to use those same tactics with the expectation of a victory each time. He suggested that, for starters, we change the outer and inner defenses of the compound somewhat every single week. This might mean dividing the compound internally into several zones and sectioning off each zone with a barbed-wire fence. These zones could be reorganized slightly each week. The Vietcong intelligence sources would report these facts back, which would most likely cause them to delay a future attack until they could revise the compound mock-up in their base camp and practice assaulting it multiple times.

He further advised us to set up a good external defensive system utilizing at least five to seven layers of barbed-wire fencing interlaced with claymore mines. Peers would provide us with the materials, supplies, and equipment needed to carry out this type of plan. Sternly, he reminded us that we must learn from this situation as he didn't expect to ever have to come back here under the same or similar conditions. His staff would put together the details of the Hoa Da District Compound attack. This report would be distributed to every advisory team in South Vietnam as a cautionary example to help keep them from experiencing a similar fate. Finally the officers returned to their choppers and flew off in a noisy and very dusty display of force. I hoped that this military show would keep the Vietcong at bay for at least a few more days or weeks so that we could reinforce, reorganize, and rebuild our compound and advisory effort.

Elliott smiled broadly. He commented that we must have impressed Peers or all of us would have been relieved instantaneously and our military careers ended in disgrace. Apparently he had a reputation of not tolerating any incompetence or bullshit. I was certainly glad and relieved that I had decided to take the direct and truthful approach in dealing with him and his staff. It appeared that I might have saved my army career after all.

Elliott had ordered a truck to retrieve and deliver my recent Cam Ranh Bay acquisitions. He and his men eventually returned to Song Mao Compound. The remaining Hoa Da District advisors were on our own. We got to work finding and setting up a suitable place to sleep, store our remaining and new equipment, and defend it, if necessary. These advisors included Dramis, Zender, Cuthbert, Wilson, Bolling, Amos, and me. We were all extremely nervous and frightened about being in this remote area without a sufficient military force to adequately defend ourselves. None of us slept very well that night in spite of our extreme exhaustion.

CHAPTER 14
Rebuild

The next morning Major Xuan and Con pulled me aside. The major stated that the family members from Binh Thuan Province would come to claim the bodies of their deceased loved ones. Beginning today and over the next several days, there would be Buddhist priests, monks, paid mourners, and family members praying for the spirits of the dead while parading through the compound. I remembered the Buddhist custom of collecting body parts of the deceased. I truly did not want these priests and monks to repeat their painstaking removal of bodies. This looking for fingers, toes, chunks of flesh, teeth, flecks of skin, bones, pieces of missing skull and brain tissue, hair, and pieces of internal organs required considerable time.

I protested. We could not just leave bodies lying around rotting, so I asked Xuan how he would recommend storing them since we had no refrigeration or ways of preserving them. Carefully we inspected the remnants of the two burned and gutted barracks. It became apparent that there were not enough identifiable remains left for the families. We decided to take whatever human remains we could find among the rubble and store them in the large white storage building after covering the floor with a layer of lime, which would greatly neutralize the smell of decomposition and repel unwanted local vermin. All of the ventilation ports in that building were already covered by screens to keep out flies and mosquitoes, so we did not have to worry about those pests.

Xuan asked the Buddhist priests and monks to come pray for these men while we had their remains gathered and moved into the storage area. After looking at the remains and listening to our explanation about this process, the Buddhist priests and monks consulted with one another and finally approved our solution. They didn't openly say it, but we could tell that they really appreciated our consideration of their religious beliefs, and the gathering of the remains would make their job easier.

Xuan, the Vietnamese survivors, and the advisors located and gathered the casualties. This was difficult work with all of the heavy, bulky beams, stone, and masonry walls that needed to be cleared to search the building interiors. Once all the remains were found and placed in the storage unit, the Buddhists priests and monks began to mediate the division of these unrecognizable bodies. To my surprise, they managed to assign a group of body parts, which they claimed to be the entire body, for each family.

Two days later the family members arrived filled with grief but seemingly satisfied that they got what they came for, particularly since the Buddhist priests and monks had supposedly handled all of it. The Buddhist Litany for the Dead involved parading through the areas where the deceased men had ended their lives. The monks, wrapped in their bright yellow garb, continuously chanted in a monotone voice while clanging their little hand cymbals and sometimes carrying a large umbrella to ward off the bright sunlight. The Buddhist priests wore dark-colored shawls and a black type of headgear over their normal clothing as a sign of mourning.

Although the strong, sickeningly sweet smell of the burning incense did a great job of covering up the very noxious smell of burned and decaying human remains, it became overpowering. Most of us wore handkerchiefs scented with aftershave lotion to cover our noses in a crude attempt to block the scent. Despite this attempt, the smell of incense, added to the smell of death and burned flesh, was burned indelibly into my nostrils and memory. Any attraction I formerly had for incense or strong perfumes was long gone.

General Peers kept his promise. A Wallaby Airlines plane landed with shipments of barbed wire, fencing stakes, sandbags, a 4.2-inch mortar, two 81mm mortars, two .50-caliber machine guns, two .30-caliber machine guns, four BARs, four .45-caliber "grease gun" sub-machine guns, ten 12-gauge military shotguns, six M-79 grenade launchers, and six cases of claymore mines. An abundant supply of ammunition accompanied these weapons, but it all seemed to come from older stock from some obscure warehouse. Case in point: several cases of .45-caliber tracer rounds from WWII were given to us as ammunition. Before this, I had never even heard of a .45-caliber tracer round. The .50- and .30-caliber machine gun ammunition dated back to the late 1940s and early 1950s.

I asked our advisors to test fire these weapons with samples of the ammunition to make sure that all were fully functional. All firearms worked fine. This wasn't exactly the protection we were hoping to receive, but we would certainly make good use of it.

A team of U.S. Army combat engineers eventually joined the priests and monks. These men were to help clean up and renovate the compound's buildings damaged during the attack. They toured the compound and made extensive plans for clearing out all of the debris and restoring the remaining buildings to fully useable status. The team arrived with two bulldozers, a front loader, two large dump trucks, and other equipment to get the job done quickly. Their own security team accompanied them, as well as the means to support and defend themselves: food, field sleeping arrangements, and weapons.

That same day, the gate security guards summoned me. A civilian vehicle containing two Americans was waiting to enter the front gate of the compound. They were two news reporters who had heard about our attack. The reporters had managed to get a copy of my after-action report and wanted to tour our compound to get some pictures for a follow-up article. I reluctantly gave my permission, but told them not to interfere with any of the compound activities or Buddhist ceremonies being conducted to honor the dead.

About a half hour later, Xuan, who was extremely upset with the reporters, called me and asked me to handle the situation. I walked over to the reporters only to discover that they were having some of our Vietnamese survivors lie down on the ground and pretend they were dead. I quickly intervened and asked what they were trying to do. Since the reporters were unable to get here after the battle, they were trying to approximate some realistic death scene pictures.

Shocked by the audacity, I told them that in view of the massive losses we had experienced, this would not help local morale. I blocked their effort. They strongly expressed words of protest about being within their rights. The reporters claimed that I had no authority to prevent them from accomplishing their job. I assured them that I had every right to control what went on in my compound. They were no longer welcome to stay. I told the Vietnamese guards to immediately escort them out of the front gate and if they refused to go, to put them under arrest in our POW jail. Wisely, the reporters decided that it was time to leave. The commander of the engineers, who observed the incident, came up to me and congratulated me for not taking any shit from these reporters who seemed to think they could do whatever they wanted.

Every few days, our compound received mail delivery. Helicopters from Phan Thiet Province Headquarters would drop off bright orange, yellow, or red mail bags and pick up outgoing mail. In combat areas, we did not need to use postage. We just wrote "free" in the upper right corner of the envelope. Mail usually reached us within two to three weeks, while our outgoing correspondence averaged a month. It was not unusual to have as many as ten to fifteen letters from home per mail delivery.

It was particularly rewarding to the men to receive family pictures and homemade care packages of candy, dried fruit, brownies, cookies, or other treats. On occasion, the army threw in a copy of *Playboy* and at least one issue of the *Stars and Stripes Asian Edition*. We also received our ration supplement kit, which contained a mix of Lux, Dial, Ivory, and Palmolive soaps; fifty cartons of Winston, Salem, Camel, Pall Mall, Lucky Strike, Marlboro, and Kool cigarettes; twenty packs of pipe and chewing tobacco; Colgate, Crest, and Pepsodent toothpaste; Hershey, Mounds, Chunkies, and Butterfinger candy bars; and our dreaded six cases of Canada Dry quinine water. My men wanted soft drinks.

It was during one of these mail deliveries that I received one of my wife's letters. Enclosed was a clipping from a prominent New York newspaper. The "pseudo-report" mentioned Major Dramis's and my names. It portrayed the American advisors as indiscriminately killing women and children and being the aggressors in the September 18 attack on the Hoa Da District Compound. It left the reader with the impression that we got the beating that was coming to us and made the Vietcong look like a bunch of local heroes who were just trying to protect the poor villagers—so much for truthful reporting. We allowed no more reporters into our compound during my tenure there.

To my amazement, the engineers quickly removed and hauled away the useless building debris. With the bodies removed and the building remnants carted away, I hoped the memories of this tragedy would now begin to fade somewhat and we could get on with the business of rebuilding the compound. My hopes were replaced with a reality check when the engineers reminded us that the old mines would have to be removed before they could safely construct a new defensive perimeter. This meant that somebody would have to do the laborious and very dangerous task of physically probing for and removing all of the mines on their hands and knees. French, Japanese, Vietminh, and South Vietnamese forces had emplaced the mines over a period of many years. We were aware of the mines' potential danger, as Xuan's dog's deadly encounter had demonstrated. Xuan confirmed that there were no existing plans or maps indicating the exact locations, number, and types of mines. We decided to put in a request for an EOD team to be sent to the Hoa Da District Compound to rid us of this hazard.

The next afternoon two EOD NCOs and an explosive engineer drove to our compound. They huddled with the combat engineers for a few minutes then broke the bad news. It seemed that by policy, EOD teams did not remove mines and explosives from a minefield, but would detonate them all after somebody else had removed them. The combat engineer commander stated that combat engineers did perform this type of work. Unfortunately, his detachment didn't have the men or special equipment needed to perform this task. Their earliest availability would be in two months, because they were completing a project to clear an area in Phan Rang.

The message came across loud and clear: we were on our own in removing all of the mines. I asked the engineer if he would at least put our compound on the schedule to come and bulldoze the perimeter when they finished in Phan Rang and after we removed the mines. He agreed. The EOD team ended our meeting by instructing us on the correct techniques to safely probe for and remove the types of mines they had seen around our compound. These included anti-personnel fragmentation mines, concussion mines, and Bouncing Betty mines. The prospect of this frankly scared the hell out of the other advisors and me.

The next morning several advisors and I took our KA-BAR knives and began the lengthy and dangerous process of removing the land mines. We began to the left of the front gate and spread out, each with a ten-foot-wide section, marking our lanes with cloth tape as we went. Each lane was wide enough so that if one of us accidentally set off a mine, it would not wound anyone else. The first several mines were easy to see. They were mostly above ground, rain and wind having weathered them. Even though we could see these mines, it was still necessary to thoroughly probe the ground in our entire sector to make sure that we located all of them. We left nothing to chance.

The morning's progress was very limited. The job's complexity awed us and made us cautious. Late that afternoon, we encountered a number of the more dangerous Bouncing Bettys. Bouncing Bettys were vintage World War II mines that bounced groin high when stepped on, spraying metal ball bearings. These consisted of two parts: the main explosive part and a triggering part located several inches away from the main part.

By the end of day one, we had progressed about seventy-five to a hundred feet and had dug up approximately five hundred mines. Four carriers augmented our group of probers. The carriers placed the extracted mines gently into a wooden box and then carried them carefully to a designated location in the back of our compound, where they were stacked in preparation for the EOD personnel to detonate them.

Day two went much smoother, although we were still very nervous and realized that one mistake could kill us. As we progressed farther through the Bouncing Betty zone, we began to encounter a different and larger type of combined concussion and fragmentation mine that was obviously Japanese from some of the writing. The detonators on these were badly rusted. This made them even more unstable and dangerous to handle, so I told the other probers and carriers to be aware and use greater caution. By the end of what felt like a never-ending workday, we had progressed a third of the way around the compound. We had dug up about 1,800 mines. By this time we probers had developed stiff necks and sore backs and knees from the concentrated and demanding conditions of this task. I decided to give the team a twenty-four-hour break to work the kinks out and give our minds a rest.

When we resumed, we probers had adopted a variety of head coverings and uniform variations to help us work more comfortably. These ranged from a towel inserted under the back of a hat to the wearing of a locally acquired broad bamboo Coolie hat that provided cover over the head, neck, and upper torso. Bandannas covered our foreheads and sides of the head to keep perspiration from dripping into our eyes. This was critically important considering the job's intense concentration.

Although the next day started out calm, the winds soon increased, kicking up the sand and making it very difficult to see.

By noon it had gotten so bad that I called off the project until the winds abated. The probers, carriers, and I tried to spend the rest of the day indoors, avoiding the blistering sun we had endured the past several days. Although we achieved a respite from the sun, we were unable to escape the assault of blowing sand that seemed to invade everywhere. If you were not careful to keep your mouth shut, you paid the price of having grit in your mouth. This presented a problem with eating. Every bit of food became impregnated with a layer of sand.

By the following morning the wind had subsided and we resumed our mine-clearing duties. This day proved very challenging: we encountered an area where a number of old unexploded hand grenades, booby traps, and ammunition had been carelessly tossed and forgotten. We handled all of these items with the same care as the mines. Late that afternoon, we finally completed our circuit around the compound and felt certain that we had removed all of the mines. The team and I surveyed the incredibly large pile of mines and booby traps that we had unearthed. We were all so dazed and numb. It didn't seem possible that we had dug up that many explosives. It was a relief to be finished. Amazingly, there were no explosions and nobody got wounded or killed. We notified the EOD team to come and detonate all of the explosives.

The two EOD sergeants were stunned, when arriving the next day, by the amount of explosives. They couldn't believe we had finished the job in such a short time. They decided that this would be too large an explosion to set off within the compound. Consequently they divided the project into three parts and started loading the first group of mines into the back of their truck. When the loading was complete, they drove the mines to the edge of the large sand dune behind the compound. There they carefully stacked this dangerous cargo and then rigged their own explosive charges to detonate the pile of mines. A large number of curious Vietnamese had gathered to watch this process with great interest. These onlookers were required to retreat to safer grounds. Once everyone was safe, I signaled the

Rebuild

EOD team. Following their loud, repeated shouts of "fire in the hole," they detonated the pile. The loud explosion and concussion shocked the Vietnamese. When the EOD team was set to detonate the second pile of mines, it took no encouragement to have the locals clear out of the danger zone. This blast emitted a greater amount of debris into the air but caused no danger. The last explosion was the smallest of the three. It took a little more time to set. The EOD team then wanted to be sure that there were no remaining mines and booby traps. Their final inspection confirmed that they had left no hazards. It was now safe for the engineers to bulldoze and proceed with the rebuilding of the compound.

The next morning the engineers began rebuilding by putting the roof beams and trusses back in their proper places. They accomplished this with the front loader, several block and tackle devices, and agile roof balancing by the men. It appeared that they had to be part monkey to get up and stay balanced. The men used a number of wooden planks to attach both sides of the weakened beams as support shims, thus making the beams even stronger than they had been originally. They replaced the broken roof tiles with sheets of galvanized metal that they sealed with a quick-setting, caulk-like substance to make the roof watertight. They finished off the inside of the buildings by putting up sheets of plywood to serve as the ceilings. They generally repaired the damaged walls by setting up support forms anchored on existing parts of the walls, followed by placing dislodged stones and bricks back into their approximate former locations. Several layers of cement covered the sides of these renovated wall sections. They painted all these white.

Two new structures were constructed to serve as troop barracks. These buildings were made out of sheets of galvanized metal for both the siding and roof, which were both rain and vermin proof. The engineers provided at least four doorways into each building. We did not want to repeat the recent tragedy of all of the troops, unable to escape, being burned alive during an attack. Our Vietnamese troops were to line the outside and roofs of these barracks with several layers of sandbags for greater protection. The engineers also supplied mosquito nets and frames to mount on each bed. When the renovations were finally completed, these buildings were in much better condition than they had been before the attack.

A group of engineers then took the rolls of barbed wire, with the fencing stakes and concertina barbed wire in between, and strung the five-layer barbed-wire fencing barrier around the entire compound. They set most of the claymore mines in strategic places among the fencing to add a further deterrent. The detonating wires were then run to the location of the nearest bunker. Trip flares and cans with small rocks as noisemakers hung from the barbed wire for additional warning.

The final project was to build two raised platforms about ten feet high, one behind the advisors' quarters and the other behind the new Vietnamese barracks buildings. On each of these platforms they installed a thousand-gallon rubberized bladder to be filled with purified water that we could all use for safe drinking, cooking, and washing our dishes, a major improvement.

Xuan, Dramis, the engineer commander, and I walked through the buildings for the final inspection. The job had been well done. Major Xuan was very pleased and thankful to have his compound fully restored so that the Vietnamese could resume their normal activities. He told me that he had not imagined the task could be accomplished so well and so quickly. I told him that this was the direct result of the visit and efforts of Lt. General Peers and his staff.

We were now able to move back to a suitable building. It was great to no longer have to camp outdoors with only minimum protection from the weather, mosquitoes, flies, rats, or other vermin. We thanked the engineers for their expert, professional, and timely help. Xuan, his officers, and senior staff members held a little awards ceremony to present some tokens of their appreciation to all of the members of this combat engineer team. We bid them farewell as they boarded their vehicles. This show of American military might presented a deterrent and challenge

Rebuild

to the Vietcong. The new compound afforded us some time and relief from the fear of an immediate follow-up attack.

Although conditions in the Hoa Da District Compound were beginning to take a turn for the better, the period of time surrounding the devastating and tragic attack put those of us who had survived on an emotional roller coaster from the realities of combat to extreme fear for our lives. Feelings ranged from extreme grief, fear, and numbness to a period of hope and optimism as the supplies began to arrive. These experiences would be forever etched in our minds as we faced the guilt of not joining our comrades in their ultimate destiny.

For their service during this attack the following were later awarded:

Lieutenant Blevins: Combat Infantry Badge, Silver Star, Purple Heart

Sergeant Whitehead: Combat Infantry Badge, Bronze Star, Purple Heart

Major Dramis: Silver Star

Sergeant Amos: Combat Infantry Badge, Bronze Star

Sergeant Cuthbert: Combat Infantry Badge, Bronze Star

Sergeant Bolling: Combat Medical Badge, Bronze Star

Tony: Posthumously awarded the American Combat Infantry Badge, Bronze Star, Purple Heart

Major Xuan: American Bronze Star Medal

First Lieutenant Con: American Bronze Star Medal

All other American advisors: Combat Infantry Badge, Bronze Star

CHAPTER 15
The Cambodians

Within seven days of their arrival, the team of combat engineers had performed an incredible job of cleaning up the total mess that had been our compound. During reconstruction, we had received shipments of furniture to replace all that had been destroyed on September 18. Major Xuan, his staff, and all of the personnel that worked at the Hoa Da District Compound headquarters had new desks, chairs, filing cabinets, work tables, typewriters, office equipment, a conference room table, map boards, beds or cots, bedside tables, and footlockers in which to store their uniforms and clothing. The American advisors received new beds, portable desks, a safe for securing documents, two small conference tables that could double as eating and meeting areas, sixteen metal folding chairs, a small propane oven and stove combination, a medium-size propane refrigerator, a set of dishes and eating utensils for sixteen people, two large cooking pots, four small pots, two large frying pans, two small frying pans, sufficient cooking utensils, eight Coleman lanterns, lantern fuel, two PRC-25 portable radios, and one VRC-46 radio with a large base antenna to handle our communications with the outside world. The best gift came in the form of a portable wooden hut that was all screened in and would be perfect for our eating and meeting area.

The engineers informed us that MACV Headquarters had approved us to have a new advisory team compound constructed. It was expected to take place before the end of 1968. Pacific Architects and Engineers, the largest civilian contractor in the Far East and where my father's Korean friend worked, would handle construction. This sounded great to us. We would get decent quarters instead of the cramped temporary ones with which we had been dealing since our arrival. As a rule of thumb, field operations run better if you have comfortable quarters to relax and clean up in when returning from an operation. Song Mao Compound was a case in point, with its secure and modern conveniences, facilities, utilities, and kitchen.

On the morning of the tenth day after our attack, a group of South Vietnamese Army trucks came rolling into our main gate and halted in the central courtyard. Xuan, Dramis, Con, and I greeted them. The trucks contained two companies of troops sent to replace those from our old Regional and Popular Forces Units who had been killed or were missing after the attack. As it turned out, they were a company of Cambodian mercenaries and a company of South Vietnamese troops who had been trained by the Vietnamese Special Forces. They had recently served as Civilian Irregular Defense Group (CIDG) forces in the Southern III Corps area. CIDG forces were Southeast Asian troops that American Special Forces highly trained. Their commander approached us and stated that they were to be assigned here temporarily until two Regional Forces companies could be located and sent to take their place. I knew it sounded too good for us to be assigned Cambodian troops on a permanent basis.

Con and I had their commander tell them to dismount and take their gear to the two new barracks buildings, where they would be housed during their stay. The commander and NCOs carried these instructions out and assigned them, by company, to a barracks and specific bunks. After being given some time to stow their gear, they were reassembled in front of the barracks. Xuan, Con, Dramis, both the Vietnamese and American operations NCOs, and I briefed them on the current military situa-

The Cambodians

tion. Con and Vo then led them on a tour of the compound and defensive perimeter.

The Cambodians' commander assigned specific individuals to each of the bunkers and fighting positions along the walls. It was easy to tell that these were combat-experienced troops by the way they thoroughly checked out their positions, visibility, fields of fire, and source of re-supply of ammunition. They also coordinated with each of the nearby positions to their right and left for target responsibilities. One of our NCOs took a group of Cambodian soldiers to three mortar pits. The Cambodians thoroughly checked out the 4.2-inch mortar, the two 81mm mortars, and their supply of mortar ammunition. After close examination, the team of men dug inside each mortar pit to include an area underground to safely store the mortar ammunition for immediate use. They separated the ammunition by HE (high explosive), luminary, smoke, and white phosphorous. They overlooked nothing.

The next day, the Cambodian mortar crews requested permission to fire several mortar shells to aim, register, and scope each weapon. Mortars were capable of firing at high angles up and over barriers to reach a desired target. The Vietcong were considered masters in the effective use of mortars, and the Cambodians were aware of this fact. They wanted to perfect their mortar use skills before contact with the Vietcong. Their request was granted if they would fire the old ammunition first and fire at specific known range targets out in the sand dune so as not to upset some of the nearby villagers. The Cambodians also requested and instituted a nightly fire mission of harassment and interdiction (H&I) mortar fire at varying times on predetermined targets outside our compound. These were changed nightly. Fire missions were between two and four rounds of H&I from the 4.2-inch mortar because we had plenty of ammunition for it.

There was no Vietcong response because these rounds impacted harmlessly out in the sand dunes or other remote areas. They did, however, put the Vietcong on nightly notice. The local villagers duly noted the presence of these new, well-trained

Cambodian soldiers and their activities. I am sure information was quickly passed on to the Vietcong units in their mountain base camp. We were trying to feel them out. If they decided to undertake a mission in our region, they might just find themselves on the receiving end of some big mortar round explosions. This would be a whole new ballgame for the defenders.

About a month later, in October, we struck pay dirt with our H&I rounds when we launched a couple of them in the middle of a large Vietcong force that was preparing to attack the town of Phan Ri Cua. Accompanied by air support, our compound caused the Vietcong to kick off their planned attack before they were properly positioned and ready. In this action, we wiped out the majority of the Women's Action Company and other elements of the Vietcong Attack Force that participated in the devastating September attack on our compound. The "Purple Road" on the sand dune indicated the Vietcong's severe losses. We were elated to get revenge. However, it did result in my $20,000 dead or alive wanted poster since I ordered the raid.

Soon after the Cambodians' arrival, their units sent a couple patrols out each day to various parts of the Hoa Da District. This enabled them to make their presence known, as well as to better familiarize themselves with the district, its villages, and its people. The Cambodians had an appointed purchasing agent who went to the marketplace in a few nearby villages and purchased their food after fair negotiations with the local merchants. This was an important improvement. Under the previously practiced policy, set by former District Chief Captain Manh, the soldiers would go to the local markets or farms and take what they wanted, offering no payment. Consequently there was no respect or liking of the South Vietnamese military in this region. When the American advisors showed up, the villagers assumed that we would be operating the same way as the South Vietnamese soldiers. This move to pay a fair rate for food and supplies was a step forward in winning the hearts and minds of the locals.

One rough spot we encountered with the Cambodian troops was the type of latrine facilities they were forced to use. While the district chief, his officers, and the American advisors were allowed to use the enclosed two-hole latrine facilities in the little shack, the rest of the troops were relegated to using the open slit-trench facilities near the back of the compound. This meant exposing oneself to all types of weather, vermin, and occasional onlookers while taking care of personal needs. In the Special Forces camps, at which they had been recently serving, they had become accustomed to using enclosed multi-hole, burn-out-style latrines that offered greater privacy and shelter. In short, we were just too uncivilized for their liking.

Majors Xuan and Dramis met with them and mentioned that they had requested new enclosed latrines to be built. They expected the team to arrive shortly to carry out this project. They didn't tell the Cambodians the total truth. The latrine project was to be contracted out through the locals. This meant numerous layers of bureaucracy to wade through getting the funds allocated, then selecting a contractor and building materials long before the project could ever begin. This explanation seemed to temporarily calm them down, though, and they got back to taking care of their assigned military matters.

As the Cambodian troops' patrolling became more active, we began to get better local intelligence reports about the Vietcong and their activities. We received our first indication that the Vietcong had sent a "hit squad" in the middle of the night to a small village that our patrol had just visited the day before. The village was located near the edge of the Hoa Da District closest to the mountains. The Vietcong gathered all of the villagers in the center of the hamlet and began interrogating the village chief and several others about supporting the South Vietnamese and their "American Puppets." These men denied that they had given us any information about the Vietcong and had only talked politely with us. The Vietcong then shot the village chief and viciously gang-raped his wife and ten-year-old daughter, both of whom died shortly after from this brutal attack. They kidnapped the chief's eldest son and forced him to go with them to perform hard labor. The Vietcong political cadre member proceeded to give an hour-long lecture to the rest of the locals about getting their minds right and supporting only their hardworking Vietcong brothers and sisters who were there to fight their battles for them.

The Vietcong cadre consisted of highly trained Communist professionals. After the Vietcong had taken charge of a village or hamlet during a nightly raid, the cadre took over. They used terrorizing lectures and indoctrinations about Communist Vietcong principles and fundamentals. They intended these fear tactics to send a strong message out to other local villages and hamlets in the region. Word of this treatment spread quickly. Villagers became less friendly and welcoming to us. However, they always appreciated the medical care that we gave to them and their family members, which the Vietcong never offered.

The horrific news about the village chief and his family hit us hard. We decided that it was time to start setting up some ambushes to welcome these "hit squads." To do this undetected, we would include the ambush force with our regular patrols and drop them off quietly near their assigned sector as we passed through the area. Fortunately this move usually went totally undetected. The ambush squads waited until after dark to get properly set up in their ambush formation. We knew from experience that these local Vietcong used the trails and roads just like everybody else and only rarely cut through the countryside or jungle growth. With that bit of knowledge, it was relatively easy to select and set up our ambush site near a hamlet that was to be a prime Vietcong target.

We had no Vietcong activity the first two nights of this effort, but struck gold on night number three. Our daytime patrols had spent two days at a particular village due to the severe malnourishment and health problems we had encountered there. Our medics spent that time giving care, particularly to the children and elderly. They had severe lesions all over their bodies, high temperatures, and severe diarrhea. The medics never found a name for the condition, but did have success with injections of penicillin, scrubbing with bars of soap, and instructing them to boil their water before ingesting rice and soups.

The Cambodians

After the second day of treatment, the Vietcong decided that it was time to make an example of these villagers. At about 0100 hours, the Cambodian ambush team got a signal from their lookout. A party of about fifteen armed Vietcong was moving down the trail toward the village. When they had moved fully into the ambush kill zone, the team leader gave the signal. The team shot down all of the Vietcong hit squad with little resistance. This was a classic L-shaped ambush formation that allowed the ambushers unhampered view of the trail directly in front of them and back in the direction from which the enemy had come. The primary kill zone was on a section of trail where the embankment on the far side dropped off sharply down a rough, rocky slope to a small stream, giving the Vietcong forces nowhere to escape this sudden fusillade of gunfire except to try to go forward or escape backward.

The Cambodians were armed with M-16s, two M-60 machine guns, and several M-79 grenade launchers. They proved to be very accurate and effective with their fire. Fifteen Vietcong were confirmed killed. Several documents, weapons, and maps were gathered from the bodies. These maps provided information about the exact location of the main Vietcong base camp. The ambush sent a not-so-subtle message back to the Vietcong that they did not own the night. They better look over their shoulders, because we might just be operating out there as well.

We began setting up an average of three ambushes each night near different hamlets and encountering Vietcong teams at least three nights a week. Sometimes we even encountered the Vietcong at more than one hamlet in a night. At first the Vietcong teams had between ten and fifteen members, but when three of those were totally wiped out, they cut back to only five.

The ambushes went on for about two weeks. By then the Vietcong had taken enough casualties and grief from this new Cambodian unit. Reliable intelligence information from several sources informed us that the Vietcong were again going to attack our Hoa Da District Compound and wipe us out for good. On the night before the attack actually came, we had reduced our ambushes to only one. Two listening posts of two men each were situated about three hundred yards outside the walls of our compound. We also alerted the Popular Forces Units platoons guarding the highway bridges to be prepared for an attack.

At about 2230 hours, we received a report from listening post number two outside of the west wall. They heard some soft voices and movement of an undetermined number of people maneuvering into some kind of formation. We told the listening posts to quietly retreat and reenter the front gate. When they were safely inside, Xuan gave the order to fire a couple illumination rounds from the 81mm mortars and follow that up with a couple HE rounds from the 4.2-inch and 81mm mortars to the areas just outside the lines of twenty-foot-high cacti that ringed the compound on two sides. The illumination rounds revealed some movement near the cacti. Immediately after the HE rounds there were several screams of pain, followed by movement, and then silence. After a few minutes another firing of illumination rounds was ordered, only this time no further movement was detected.

Fifteen minutes later, three Vietcong mortars fired near the cacti on the southwest corner of the compound, landing harmlessly behind the troop barracks. They got off another set of rounds before our mortars began firing a counter-battery barrage. The Vietcong's second set of rounds impacted close to the white storage building, causing only a slight amount of damage and no casualties. At this point the rounds from our mortars caused at least one secondary explosion. We hit our target, and fired two more rounds of follow-up shots. All was quiet for the rest of the night.

The next morning we all scoured the area outside the cacti where our mortar rounds had struck. Several pieces of debris from a couple of destroyed 60mm mortars scattered the ground. Nine separate blood trails dotted the sand headed toward the mountains. At least two of these resulted from bodies being dragged some distance where several more people then picked them up and carried them.

The Cambodians

Walking in the same direction, we found a couple pieces of equipment that had been dropped during the Vietcong's hasty retreat. These were two Czech ammunition pouches with a banana clip of AK-47 ammunition in each, four homemade Vietcong grenades, and several Russian bandage wrappers, some covered with blood, indicating that they had made attempts to give first aid to several of the Vietcong casualties. A single Vietcong soldier's body, the back of his head blown off, lay on the ground. He wore the typical Vietnamese peasant black pajamas, a broad-brimmed hat, and a military canvas harness with a couple of homemade grenades on it. Since no sign of any bandages were with him, we assumed that there were other casualties from our defensive actions. We ended our search.

As all this shows, the highly skilled Cambodian troops truly added to the Hoa Da District Compound's defense. It felt great to finally be getting the best of the Vietcong for a change. I just hoped and prayed that these successes would continue.

CHAPTER 16
Chess Game of Life

Two nights later, we heard Vietcong mortars shelling near the Cham village located a little more than a kilometer northwest. This village was located in another district, so we notified the Song Mao military advisors responsible for this district. The American Song Mao advisor said they were unable to contact the Cham militia soldiers to render information, condition, or needs. They did ask if we could possibly fire some mortar rounds along the outside of that village in an attempt to discourage the Vietcong and cause them to end the attack.

The American Song Mao advisor added that the Chams were a different religious and ethnic group than the locals in Hoa Da District, and therefore it would not be appropriate or acceptable for us to send our Vietnamese and Cambodian troops. He guessed that the Cham district chief would not dispatch any troops before midmorning and hoped the villagers could hang on as best they could.

I relayed the conversation to Majors Xuan and Dramis, who were both very surprised and a bit shocked at the lack of support extended to the villagers. Xuan ordered the 81mm mortar crews to fire about five rounds apiece, targeting the area where it appeared the Vietcong mortars were firing. This seemed to cause the Vietcong to reduce their mortar fire a little; however, a lot of rifle and automatic weapon fire from a very determined attacking force replaced that. It sounded very concentrated with a high volume of fire along two sides of the hamlet; we were afraid to fire any closer for fear of hitting some of the defenders.

Just when we thought that the attacking force might overrun the hamlet, a sudden fusillade of concentrated rifle and machine gun fire, punctuated by periodic and numerous grenade blasts, erupted out of the hamlet toward the Vietcong positions. This apparently caught the Vietcong off guard and their incoming fire tailed off considerably. We next heard the Vietcong mortars coming from another side of the village. This concentrated barrage on the hamlet kept up for over thirty minutes, round after round impacting all around the inside of the tiny Cham village. The Vietcong again tried to make a direct assault, firing every weapon with little or no outgoing fire from the Chams.

Again it seemed that the Cham village was about to fall when another concentrated fusillade of rifle fire and grenade explosions came from the Chams. This pattern of heavy Vietcong mortar barrage and assault fire being met with heavy return fire from the Chams occurred twice more. Shortly before dawn, the Vietcong finally broke off their attack and retreated back to their mountain base camp. Detecting no further Vietcong presence or activity after sunrise, I drove with our medics, Cuthbert, Amos, and Zender over to the Cham village to see if they needed any help after a terrible night of continuous attacks.

The Cham village chief and his security detail of several heavily armed men greeted us by the hamlet's front gate. The men were about five feet seven inches tall with very dark brown skin and round eyes. They warmly greeted us and wanted to show us how they had survived the Vietcong attack. We were amazed to find that each militiaman had their families with women, children, and elderly parents living there with them. Although their small houses were very simple, each had a well-prepared bunker system for them to retreat into during this type of attack. There appeared to be a lot of damage and devastation to the houses, but the bunkers remained secure and intact. Only two men had experienced very minor wounds during the savage assault. Each had a small piece of shrapnel or two in an arm or shoulder from the mortar barrages. Our medics quickly patched them up then handed out candy to the eager children and some of the elderly until they ran out.

Zender, Cuthbert, and I followed the Cham village chief as he surveyed the four sides of his embattled hamlet. Used Vietcong shell casings littered the ground on all sides of the village right up to the barbed-wire and heavily sandbagged walls. As the medics were finishing up, three jeeps containing their Cham district chief, his staff of officers, two American advisors, and two medics came driving up. The Cham district chief was very pleasant and thanked us for offering to help out his villagers. He said his people were capable of taking care of their own needs and didn't need Vietnamese support. I reminded him that we advisors represented the American forces, not the Vietnamese, and we were willing to help him and his people any time. We saluted and drove back to our compound.

Later that afternoon we received a visit at our compound from the two American advisors to the Cham district. They reported that the attacking Vietcong were believed to be part of the regiment that had overrun the Hoa Da District Compound recently. They also believed that the Cham villagers had killed at least thirty-five Vietcong and wounded many more. At least forty blood trails led away from the village across the sand dunes toward the mountains. Everyone was very proud that the "hearty little Chams" had held out so well and inflicted a high price in casualties on the Vietcong. We American advisors made notes of the Cham's underground bunker features. These detailed notes were sent on to other advisors, as well as to Xuan, his officers, and staff. In the future, the Hoa Da District Compound fighting positions would be greatly improved with deeper and safer underground defensive features all thanks to the "hearty little Chams."

The morning after the attack on the Cham village, our compound received an unexpected visit from an irregular unit of South Vietnamese troops. I met with their single American advisor, wearing an American Army NCO's fatigues, which identified him as an advisor to the PRU. I remembered our advisor training in both Fort Bragg and Nha Trang, where we learned that the PRUs were a special "Black Ops hit squad." They were recruited, trained, organized, and controlled by the CIA. Their mission was a part of Operation Phoenix, the brainchild of William Colby, the director of the CIA. PRUs had the mission of traveling unannounced to a Vietnamese district, where they would round up the people whose names were on the "Black List" the CIA provided. The list usually consisted of the hardcore Vietcong political cadre, operations specialists, and family members.

Those on the list were rounded up and displayed in front of the local villagers. A brief lecture was given to the people on the evils of the Vietcong and Communism, followed by a reading of the charges against these captured Vietcong agents. Once completed, the PRUs took the Vietcong members to the edge of the village and shot each of them, along with their families. On occasion, a higher-ranking hardcore Vietcong cadre member would be tortured before finally being executed or evacuated for further interrogation. All of this was intended to dissuade the Vietnamese villagers from giving any aid or support to the Vietcong, and to turn in names to the local district chief if they knew of any Vietcong living or operating among them. I felt sorry for the villagers. It was difficult for them to know who to support: troops from both sides were selecting villagers and torturing and executing them and their family members.

On this particular day, five of the PRU soldiers raped and executed three of the women family members of the accused Vietcong. When I heard about this, I was very angry and made a point of telling the PRU advisor that this sort of conduct was totally unacceptable and made our side look no better than the Vietcong in the eyes of the people. The PRU advisor glared at me in disbelief. He spurted that his troops were taken out of the worst jails in Vietnam and could care less about what I thought. These PRUs have been given blanket approval and very wide latitude by MACV and the CIA to do whatever it took to identify and eliminate hardcore Vietcong. He finally admitted that he was a CIA case officer and really didn't have to answer to anyone outside the CIA.

Many of the villagers seemed to know the PRUs. They may have recognized the distinctive black skull and crossbones on their berets, or maybe it was from prior brutal exposure to the group. Whatever it was, the people instantly knew and were deathly afraid of them. The PRUs spent two days operating out of the Hoa Da District Compound, mainly at night, visiting at least five villages during that time. We were not allowed to send an advisor along with them, and they never furnished us with either the identities or number of deaths that they inflicted. The PRUs caused a setback to our advisory team successes, and we did not want to see their return anytime soon. I fully understood what the PRUs were trying to accomplish through their type of operation; however, I felt their overly harsh tactics served no purpose in our area at the present time. This was evident shortly after the PRUs had departed and signs of the Vietcong increased.

That afternoon my radio operator, interpreter, and I were driving down the highway, when we noticed a bus stopping in the middle of nowhere. Two armed men hopped on the bus. We decided to follow and check for anything out of the ordinary. Several miles down the road, the bus came to a stop before it crossed a guarded bridge. The two armed men jumped off and ran into a thicket of palm trees and cacti when they saw us coming up behind them. We leaped out of the jeep and went up to the bus. The driver and a number of the passengers were very nervous and distraught. We questioned them through our interpreter. Most of the passengers were scared and reluctant to talk about the incident.

Two women finally spoke. One woman mentioned that the Vietcong tax collectors boarded buses along the main roads several times a month. The other woman added that before the Americans came, the Vietcong used to set up periodic roadblocks and collect money from all of the travelers, whether they were on buses, Lambrettas, bicycles, trucks, or on foot. The people were going to market, and the Vietcong were aware of their routine. If any of the civilians failed to give them money or something of value, they were subject to being beaten or shot. We assured these frightened Vietnamese that we Americans only wanted to help and would never require them to pay anything. The bus then continued on its way and we returned to our compound.

I called a meeting of the advisors, Xuan, and Con, and briefed them on what we had discovered. We decided to assign a team of four soldiers, two Vietnamese and two Americans, to monitor the Vietnamese daily routine and to detect any Vietcong presence or activities—such as tax collectors or land mine and/or booby trap emplacements—along the two main highways going through the Hoa Da District. The team was to stop and detain the tax collectors as well as notify the duty officer in the Hoa Da District Compound about any dangerous conditions. During the next two weeks, the team found several roadblocks with a couple emplaced mines and booby traps each morning. They organized several of the local police officers to disassemble the mines and booby traps and remove the roadblocks so that the normal daily road traffic could continue.

The third week, our team witnessed two armed men stop and board a bus traveling from Tuy Phong to Phan Ri Cua. They called for backup and a three-quarter-ton truck of Cambodian soldiers met them just across the bridge to Phan Ri Cua. They flagged down the bus and surrounded it. The team saw no Vietcong soldiers among the passengers, so they called for them to surrender or be shot. Two very meek-looking men got off the bus and five Cambodians immediately seized them, eager to do them great harm. Our Cambodian troops were ordered to keep them in custody while the bus was searched. We found two AK-47 rifles they had been carrying, four bags of Vietnamese money, several pendants, religious medallions, watches, and a number of other valuable items. The local people confirmed that these were the Vietcong tax men who had been working this area for over a year. We returned the contents of the bags to the bus riders, although the return of the cash led to a couple of debates for three men. Each claimed more than the total amount of cash available. Eventually, it all turned out well and the Vietnamese passengers were very thankful for our intervention.

The tax men were taken to our compound where Zender, Xuan, and a couple Vietnamese intelligence NCOs interrogated them. Through this process, we learned about the local Vietcong methods and sources of gathering resources to support their needs. These two characters were turned over to the local CIA case officer to extract further information. We later heard that the CIA was successful in breaking them down and extracting more useful information.

Xuan decided to restart the ambush patrols, setting out between two and four separate ambushes nightly. He would use the information gathered from our daily intelligence sources as the basis for placing at least two of these ambushes and then consult with the advisors to decide on the locations of the others. One morning, while trying to assess these intelligence reports and the results of our ambushes, we noticed one prominent trail coming out of the mountains and going down to one of the fishing villages on the South China Sea. This trail was yet to have an ambush. Consequently, we decided to set up one of our larger ambush forces, consisting of four American advisors and a combination of Cambodian and Vietnamese troops, along a narrow strip.

The patrol leader used a large U-shaped ambush formation, consisting of at least two machine guns at the far ends, two along the two midpoints, and one in the bottom center of the U-formation. The troops were also fitted with six Browning automatic rifles, a number of M-16s, four M-79 grenade launchers with canister, HE rounds, and a number of claymore mines that lined the inside perimeter of the formation with overlapping fields of fire. A listening post of two troops stood on top of a higher sand dune off to one side of the trail. Observing strict noise and light discipline, the members of the patrol waited for enemy forces.

Sometime after 0245 hours, a signal from the listening post detected an approach with several large animals that sounded like horses. The troops were told to remain quiet and wait until the enemy was in the kill zone. It appeared to be a Vietcong supply train using horses coming down the trail. Once in the kill zone, the ambush began: first they fired the claymore mines, which was followed by machine guns, automatic weapons, and grenade launchers. The deadly firing continued until there was no return fire or further movement. Several minutes later, a detail of Cambodian soldiers was sent to examine the enemy troops caught in the ambush. There was a lot of excited jabbering among the Cambodians as they shined their flashlights on the enemy column.

Finally one man ran back to the patrol leader and advisors and reported that this was not a Vietcong pack train after all, but instead a pack train from the area drug lord. The pack train was loaded with recently harvested opium and was probably on its way to being shipped out. He stated that there were thirty dead men and eight dead horses fully loaded with the drugs. The patrol leader immediately put in a radio call to both Xuan and Dramis to report what had happened.

Xuan responded quickly. He ordered the patrol leader to take his men and secure the area around the ambush site until the drug lord's men arrived. Xuan warned him that not one grain of drugs should be missing, as the drug lord's men were better armed than the patrol. Fortunately Xuan and the drug lord knew each other and had a rapport. He informed the drug lord of what had occurred and expressed his sincere apologies for this dreadful mistake, as well as offered to make payment for any losses.

As soon as the sun came up, I was ordered to take five men, an interpreter, two jeeps, and a three-quarter-ton truck to the ambush site. We arrived a few minutes after the drug lord's men. Their appearance was very menacing. Their group leader was a large, story book-like character, well muscled, oriental (probably Chinese), about six-feet–five-inches tall, weighing around three hundred pounds, and had a large "Fu Man Chu" mustache. He was carrying a Thompson sub-machine gun with a long double magazine, a sawed-off 12-guage shotgun strung across his back, and two bandoliers of ammunition clips crisscrossing his chest. The giant leader had a group of about fifty large and very well-armed men surrounding our group with automatic weapons at the ready. I tried not to show that I was scared as I led the discussion.

I began by offering our deepest apologies and explained that our ambush was to stop the Vietcong. This incident had been a huge error. We had no intention of going against the drug lord or his men. Our troops had no idea that the drug lord's representatives were passing through this area. We had thought that the pack train was the Vietcong hauling supplies and equipment. After we realized our mistake, we had our men guard the cargo and weapons. I then offered to pay the drug lord fair damages for the men and horses killed in our ambush. The giant leader listened very carefully to our interpreter's translation. He stated that their dead men and horses were of no consequence to them, but the cargo and weapons were all important. Humbly, I asked if we could help in any way. Twisting the end of his mustache, he replied that our trucks could take the cargo down to the fishing village where it was originally headed. I told him we would be happy to transport the cargo the rest of the way.

He barked a few orders to several of his men. They immediately scrambled to take the cargo off the dead horses, loaded it onto the back of the truck, and disposed of their dead. Two of his men climbed in the truck with our driver while the giant leader and four of his men and four of my men went in the two jeeps. The giant ordered me to drive the cargo to the fishing village. I revved up the engine and told our patrol leader and the remaining American advisors, who were pacing nervously, to gather up their gear and head back to the compound. They gratefully obliged.

In the village, we were directed to drive down to the beach where we unloaded all of the cargo next to some small, round boats. These boats would be used to take the cargo to a larger boat when it arrived. We then said good-bye and offered another apology to be given to the drug lord. Very much relieved, we drove back to Hoa Da District Compound.

Several days later we received a radio call from the commander of the U.S. Navy swift boat that was assigned to patrol the South China Sea coast along the Tuy Phong and Hoa Da districts. He asked us to meet him at the fishing dock area in Phan Ri Cua. This was an unusual request, so I took two jeeps with Con, Zender, Amos, the Vietnamese operations NCO, and a small security force of Cambodians. When we pulled up to the dock area, we noticed an unusual-looking sampan boat and twelve large, rough-looking men squatting in a group on the ground with several U.S. Navy men surrounding them with submachine guns pointed in their direction.

The swift boat commander came over to explain the situation. They had just captured this bunch of pirates, who had been targeting various hamlets and villages along the coast for many months. The navy had been looking for them for some time and could probably pin a lot of crimes on them, ranging from murder, rape, theft, arson, kidnapping, and smuggling to selling aid to the Vietcong. Pointing to three dazed teenage boys in another group, he told us that these boys were kidnapped from a village near Tuy Phong during a raid last night. A search of the pirate's sampan had revealed a cache of arms, ammunition, grenades, rice, other food items, processed supplies of opium and hashish, gold, and some precious stones, all in quantities far greater than these men could use for themselves. They were obviously raiding various areas to acquire goods and hostages and then negotiating the sale of these items with groups of Vietcong, bandits, or pirates.

Since the rules under the Status of Forces Agreement with the Vietnamese would not allow the U.S. Navy to handle this matter, the swift boat commander requested that we take charge of the sampan, the cargo (minus a couple of war souvenirs for the "Swiftees"), and the pirates. Then he looked at me for a response. I excused myself and contacted Xuan and Dramis. I informed them of what we had encountered and asked them to send the three-quarter-ton truck loaded with more Cambodian security forces to secure the pirates and escort them to the Hoa Da POW jail. I went back to the swift boat commander and told him about the arrangements. In the meantime, I deployed the small security force I had brought with me to help augment the navy men.

A while later the truck full of Cambodians arrived, followed by an old French flat-bed truck that Xuan had commandeered from some place. The pirates recognized they were Cambodians and passed a couple comments among themselves about not doing anything rash that might get them killed. The team of Cambodians took charge of the pirates. They took each pirate, tied his hands securely behind his back, and looped a noose around each neck. This was then connected to a long rope tether that ran the length of the column of men. The ends were securely tied around the waists of both the first and last man in the column. Holding automatic rifles, the Cambodians supervised the pirates as they shuffled to the Hoa Da District Compound. While this was going on, all of the loot taken from the sampan was loaded onto the trucks for transport back to our compound. I expressed our thanks to the Swiftees for a job well done and offered our help in the future. They asked that we keep an eye out for more war souvenirs. I heartily agreed.

The next day the CIA case officer along with several of his team members interrogated and removed the pirates from our POW jail site. Xuan had taken charge of the confiscated items and attempted to find the rightful owners. After a few weeks, no one claimed ownership. Xuan distributed the food to help those in need in the Hoa Da District. The arms and ammunition were secured in a strong room in our compound, while the valuables had become the property of the Hoa Da District. Shortly afterward, the Binh Thuan province chief contacted Xuan and demanded that he send all these valuables to him for safekeeping and eventual distribution.

Instead of refusing to comply with this request, which would have caused all kinds of problems, Xuan simply told the province chief that all of the valuables had already been spent on essential and unfunded programs, including our security forces. He added that he would be sending the province chief two rare rifles and a pistol taken from the pirates' weapons collection. That made the province chief happy and closed the subject. Major Xuan sure knew how to play politics.

Another threat to the South Vietnamese and their American advisors in northern Binh Thuan Province came in the form of political corruption. Major Elliott had informed me initially about suspected corruption involving the South Vietnamese senator from the Hoa Da District. It came as no surprise to me when our intelligence sources reported the senator was definitely funding and sharing information to the area Main Force Vietcong units. He had inspected our compound via a Vietnamese Air Force helicopter the day before and after each of the three biggest attacks we had suffered.

I offered to "trip" with my rifle firing in his direction on full automatic the next time he came for a visit. After a few scoffs from the other advisors, we reasoned that this would only get me into trouble. The senator would be quickly replaced with another loyal comrade to continue the Vietcong dirty work. Xuan devised a plan to counteract the senator's deception: we would change some portions of the compound's defenses after the senator left on his next visit. This included setting up alternate locations for the mortars, claymore mines, other weapons, and troops, as well as setting up other barbed-wire barriers within the compound. I asked our local CIA case officer to place the senator on the PRU Black List for elimination. We felt these precautions were all we could do to protect ourselves from him.

As American advisors, we were required to improve the living conditions for the Hoa Da District people, stay ahead of enemy threats, achieve some victories, and remain healthy and alive. Nowhere in our advisory training were we given the impression or information that we would be dealing with a host of enemies consisting of a motley mix of bandits, pirates, drug lords, smugglers, and corrupt politicians, in addition to the Vietcong. It was a chore to envision what the next challenge or crisis would be to strike our compound. We were so nervous from being on constant alert that none of us slept more than three hours a night. Those of us who smoked had increased our consumption rate to about three packs of cigarettes per day. This helped to control our nerves and push us forward with very little sleep. I just hoped and prayed to God that we would properly play our part in this chess game of life.

CHAPTER 17
Fighting Victor Charlie

The continual need for our military forces to be involved with "Victor Charlie," or "VC" as we Americans sometimes called the Vietcong, greatly reduced the time we could spend with the villagers working on civic action programs. Our intelligence sources had reported several hardcore Vietcong political cadre members being sent to the Hoa Da District. These cadres were different from the regular Vietcong. The political cadre was well trained in Russia or China and had an easily understood speaking style in the local dialect. They frequently gave examples to illustrate and emphasize their speaking points on proper thinking and behavior for being a loyal Vietcong.

The locals were not stupid and, in their effort to survive this seemingly endless conflict, tended to back whichever group was in town at the time. Over the years, they certainly had enough complaints against both sides to keep them from backing either one. Between the seizure without payment of their rice and crops, the forced recruitment or kidnapping of family members, and the periodic kangaroo courts and executions of whole families, neither side had endeared themselves to the average villagers. When representatives for either side showed up, villagers assumed there were going to be trouble.

To respond to these intelligence reports, Xuan began to send out "Hunter-Killer Teams" to the targeted villages in an attempt to disrupt and, hopefully, capture some or all of these Vietcong political cadre members. After several near-misses, during which our troops seemed to enter one side of a village while the Vietcong were rapidly exiting the other, we decided to change our tactics: we totally surrounded the village to prevent any escape. This tactic worked extremely well. Within a few days, several members of their security teams were killed when they shot at our forces.

We were able to capture, alive, two teams of hardcore Vietcong political cadre members. The first team had four members and the second two. They turned out to be just talkers and not fighters so they surrendered quietly with no resistance. When they failed to offer any information, we turned them over to the local CIA representatives where stricter interrogation techniques could be utilized.

Days later the CIA reported that two members of the first team were high-ranking and had responsibility over the "Hamlet/Village Indoctrination Program" for the northern half of South Vietnam. They provided valuable information about the political cadre's role in the Vietcong mission and plans for the II Corps area. The cadre's presence in the Hoa Da District stressed the level of importance the Vietcong placed on the area. It now appeared that Victor Charlie was prepared to win, at all cost, in our district, so we had better be prepared.

Our patrols to the hamlets and villages continued. We found ourselves traveling farther and farther away from our compound and our mortar fire support. Eventually we were outside of that protective zone all together. Another source of artillery or mortar fire was needed to render assistance when or if our troops came in contact with Victor Charlie or other unfriendly forces. We had already agreed to rule out requesting any fire support from the 44th ARVN because it was always too erratic and inaccurate, both in timing and area of impact. There had been a couple of incidents where we requested their fire support along the outer perimeter of our compound, but their rounds impacted instead in the middle of the nearby Vietnamese village, causing destruction to homes and injuries to the locals.

I decided to contact the locally assigned navy swift boat commander to see if he would be able to handle fire support missions for us. He responded affirmatively that this was one of their coastal responsibilities. His boat was equipped with a permanently mounted heavy-duty 81mm mortar with a gyroscopic firing system that could shoot farther than a regular mortar and drop the rounds very accurately, within inches of the desired target, regardless of the condition of the sea.

This sounded great to me. His mortar reached a wider area than our compound mortars. Unfortunately his swift boat would only be on station until the end of the month, when a navy destroyer would replace it, armed with their far-reaching five-inch guns, for the duration of the following month. After that his boat would return for another month. If available, the destroyer offered very reliable fire support.

A couple nights later, I accompanied an ambush patrol into the middle of the coastal sand dune area. It was labeled a "Free-Fire Zone" since anyone out there was most probably the Vietcong. There were two small hamlets in this area that were reportedly abandoned. Recent intelligence reports believed that Victor Charlie was using these abandoned hamlets to store food and supplies. We decided to set up an ambush along the only trail leading into and out of these hamlets. For once, the weather greatly assisted us with a prevailing breeze just strong enough to keep the mosquitoes away. It was great not to be eaten alive while we were trying to concentrate on the possibility of approaching enemy soldiers.

We had encountered no enemy troops and were beginning to get a little restless when all of a sudden there was a tremendous explosion near the first village, followed quickly by another, then another. I recognized these explosions as part of a U.S. Air Force B-52 arc light raid. I yelled for everyone to quickly follow me. We all got up and ran for our lives as the many bombs continued to fall in a pattern that targeted the two villages and their surrounding areas. Although running through sand and small patches of sea grass would normally be very difficult, as frightened as we all were, we scampered quickly. We all felt that we had never run so far or so fast. When extreme fear is your prime motivator, it can stir up enough adrenalin to perform some incredible actions.

Safely back at our compound, I consulted the weekly security bulletin to check the map's grid coordinates for the areas of which we were supposed to stay clear. I verified that we were a good ten kilometers away from the banned block of map coordinates for that twenty-four-hour period. Somebody in the air force had screwed-up big time and almost cost us our lives. I later reported this error to the U.S. Air Force liaison officer, but I never learned if he had passed my information on to his higher-ups.

The next morning I took a patrol back to the two villages for a bomb damage assessment. We found three badly blown apart dead Vietcong near what appeared to be the remnants of several large bags of rice, dried meat, shattered rocket launchers, and a number of destroyed wooden boxes of B-40 rockets with Czech markings on them. The two villages were totally demolished and there were sizeable bomb craters throughout the area. There were no other signs of Victor Charlie. It appeared that our intelligence had been late or early for a planned build-up. At least we knew that these former hamlets would now be useless to the Vietcong unless they rebuilt them, and that didn't seem likely. We sent our assessment report to the U.S. Air Force, MACV, and Navy. Now we could concentrate our efforts on other areas of the Hoa Da District.

We began to see increasing signs that the Vietcong were resupplying and regrouping their forces in this region. The navy swift boat commander reported a larger number of junks, sampans, and other small vessels used to carry men and materials along the coast. The number had become so great that the Swiftees were no longer able to stop and search more than 50 percent of encountered vessels. They had to scan and randomly select the vessels that looked most suspicious to them, which meant that some men, arms, and materials were getting through their gauntlet. As it was, the navy was finding food, military equipment, and supplies on the searched ships. Some had written proof that they were under orders from the South Vietnamese, while many had no such proof. The commander requested additional U.S. Navy boats be assigned to help better monitor these vessels. He commented that similar Vietnamese Navy surveillance efforts were only marginally effective, since they were paid to look the other way and not intervene with black market smugglers and drug lords' shipments.

Some of our intelligence sources were reporting more small groups of Main Force Vietcong troops coming into the Hoa Da District. These small groups eventually would link up with their mountain base-camp comrades. This had us all very worried. We knew that when Victor Charlie considered the timing right and their training and equipment up to snuff, they would launch another major attack on the Hoa Da District Compound. Simply put, they wanted us out of business permanently.

To better prepare for any future attacks, we took a number of precautions. Among these was trying to render our claymore mines tamperproof to the Vietcong, particularly at night. It was a common Vietcong practice to quietly reverse the direction of the claymore mines so that when the Vietnamese/Americans set them off, the shrapnel would shower the defenders instead of the Vietcong attackers. To prevent this reversal, we emplaced the base supports of the mines in a square block of cement about the size of a large brick. Then we aimed them in the direction away from the compound. Next, under one of the corners of the cement square, we placed a mouse-trap detonator connected to a booby trap—and in some cases, a trip flare as well. As these mines were set, anyone tampering or attempting to move them would set off our surprise booby traps with a large explosion, thus blowing their hand(s) off and, at the same time, alerting us to their presence near the compound. These cement blocks and booby traps proved very effective.

A couple nights later, four large explosions and trip flares going off simultaneously along the west and south sides of our compound alerted us. Loud screams of pain were heard as our tamperproof mines claimed their first victims. The trip flares showed a number of shadowy figures lined up along the wire barriers with long objects in their hands. These were Bangalore torpedoes, used to blow through our wire barriers, while wooden ladders would allow them access to the compound.

All of our troops had quickly gone to their defensive positions. The order was given for the mortar crews to fire a couple illumination rounds each so that we could better determine the nature and direction of the attack. These revealed about seven waves of attackers. Three Vietcong Bangalore torpedoes exploded along our lines of wire fencing on the south side of the compound. At the same time the expert Vietcong mortar crew launched a barrage of concentrated mortar fire, which impacted repeatedly along the inside of our defensive walls about every fifteen seconds. We were all very frightened, but we stood firm. Our mortar crews began firing high explosive rounds along the line of attackers, trying to delay their advance.

Xuan ordered firing of the claymore mines along the outer two south and west lines of fencing. These massive blasts seemed to mow down the better part of the first two waves of attackers. The following waves continued to aggressively push their attack toward our walls. As a Vietcong soldier fell, another soldier from one of the supporting lines of troops immediately took his place.

The pressure of the assault was continuous. Our mortar crews continued to rain down HE rounds, while the Vietcong mortars continued their punishing barrage on the inside of our compound. When one of our 81mm mortars ceased firing after sustaining a direct hit and killing the crew, I grabbed two of our soldiers and ran over to the mortar to activate it again. Several teams of Vietcong breached the outer wall along the south side as we struggled to reset and reposition the mortar. These teams immediately encountered our surprise of the two new internal barbed-wire fence lines, which halted their progress. Some of the Vietcong soldiers attempted to find a way around these barriers, while several others stood there and began to fire B-40 rockets at our mortar pits and other key targets within our compound.

One of our Vietnamese soldiers and I were still adjusting the 81mm when suddenly there was a massive explosion: we had been on the receiving end of a Vietcong B-40 rocket. The explosion knocked me onto my back. I felt dazed and my head pounded. There was a stinging pain in my left shoulder from shrapnel, and I was covered with some kind of goo. The Vietnamese soldier that I had been working with was missing his head and upper torso. The goo was a mixture of his brains, blood, and other body parts. My stomach churned. While I was trying to clear my head, I heard a couple more nearby explosions from the Vietcong B-40 rockets. I located and picked up my M-16 and fired in the direction of Victor Charlie's rocket-propelled grenade launchers. It ended the RPG firing.

Climbing out of the mortar pit, I ran in the direction of the breach, firing my rifle as I ran. As I neared that spot, a couple AK-47 rifle rounds hit and my rifle was shot out of my hands. I immediately picked it up and discovered, to my horror that the rifle barrel was slightly bent and the receiver partially shattered. It was nonfunctional. I had no effective weapon.

Before I could retreat, two Vietcong soldiers suddenly confronted me. The first soldier took a shot at me from very close range and, by the grace of God, missed me. I took my battered rifle and whacked him solidly in the head, knocking him to the ground. He did not get up or move, so I turned my attention to the other soldier, who was fumbling while trying to reload his rifle. I performed a tried-and-true vertical butt stroke series with my damaged rifle on his head, knocking him senseless to the ground. I used the heel of my boot and, with all of my strength, stomped it through his rib cage, puncturing his lungs, heart, and other internal organs. He was dead. Turning my attention back to the first soldier, I noticed that the force from my rifle had bashed the front and right side of his skull. He too was deceased. When fighting a hand-to-hand situation, a rush of adrenalin causes a super-human reaction in an attempt to survive. It was a grim realization.

Xuan sent a group of Cambodian troops to the location of the breach. They fought hard to either kill or repel the remainder of the Vietcong both inside and outside the compound wall. When it became apparent that Victor Charlie's attack was not going as planned, the leaders blew a series of whistles to withdraw. The KIA count was fifty-eight for the Vietcong, eight for the South Vietnamese and none for the Americans. Twenty South Vietnamese and two Americans suffered wounds. Victor Charlie learned that the Hoa Da District forces were no longer an easy target.

CHAPTER 18
Requisition

The next day, Amos and I caught a Wallaby Airlines flight out of Song Mao to Cam Ranh Bay. We had been given a requisition to resupply our ammunition, grenades, rations, food items, and a replacement for my damaged rifle. The Aussie pilots and crew members were their usual cheerful selves. When they heard where we were stationed, they mentioned that word had spread of our recent successes against Victor Charlie. At Cam Ranh Bay, we had better success on our supply acquisitions than our last trip. We better understood how to handle the military supply system and did not mention that we were advisors. The first day we acquired two PRC-25 radios; multiple cases of .50- and .30-cal ammunition for our machine guns; M-16 and .45-cal ammunition; HE, smoke, white phosphorus, and thermite grenades; detonation cord, detonators, C-4 and Flex-X plastic explosives; M-79 grenades; ten cases of long-range recon patrol rations; and large cans of food items, such as peanut butter, dehydrated potatoes, green beans, peas, spinach, fruit cocktail, peaches, pineapple, pork and beans, and a few other items. I was also able to trade-in my messed up M-16 for a brand new one. We were pleased.

I asked the EOD commander for permission to go to their explosives disposal area and fire my M-16. I wanted to get it zeroed in before I had to go back into our combat zone. He mentioned that they would be setting off a couple explosions to get rid of some faulty ammunition, so late in the afternoon would be a great time. Amos and I followed the EOD detachment trucks through the military base to their disposal area next to a beautiful large lagoon. They off-loaded the remainder of the faulty ammunition and rigged the pile with explosives. We all took shelter a safe distance away behind a big sand dune. After they loudly broadcast the required "fire in the hole" announcement three times over their loudspeakers, we covered our ears as they set off the blast. We waited about ten minutes before coming out of our sheltered area to check the results. All of the faulty ammunition had been thoroughly destroyed.

The EOD detachment commander told me to get my rifle and get it zeroed in. We set up a few targets. The EOD men fired their weapons at some of the targets while I tried to carefully sight-in my rifle. That went on for about thirty minutes. It was extremely hot and humid. The EOD detachment commander, noticing our discomfort, suggested we take off our uniforms and take a swim. The idea sounded great until I looked out and saw a shark fin circling the water.

I pointed out the fin, and the EOD detachment commander said, "Not a problem." He grabbed two thermite grenades off his belt, pulled the pins, and tossed them into the lagoon. A seven-foot white tip shark leaped out of the boiling water and swam quickly away. Amos and I stripped. While running down to the beach, I was startled as I came face-to-face with a five-foot sandy-colored ape. I cautiously went around my hairy friend and joined Amos, who found the encounter amusing.

We had only been in the water for about fifteen minutes when a jeep and four two-and-a-half-ton trucks loaded with fully armed army soldiers sped down the beach in our direction. When the jeep reached us, we recognized the ordnance battalion commander fully armed with his steel pot, pistol, and flak jacket armored vest. We came out of the water naked and saluted him. He yelled at us to get the hell out of this area and wait in his office until he returned from this fiasco, whatever that meant. Without getting dressed, Sergeant Amos and I grabbed our clothes and gear and hopped into our jeep. A long line of two-and-a-half-ton trucks loaded with troops dressed in combat gear raced past us heading toward the EOD demolition area.

Back at the ordnance battalion commander's office, Amos and I were told that we had just set off a Cam Ranh Bay-wide Vietcong attack alert with our actions on the demolition range. The ordnance battalion commander checked and found out that the EOD detachment commander and I had indeed filed with the proper authorities at Cam Ranh Bay Army Base for detonating explosives and firing weapons that afternoon. Unfortunately this information had not been disseminated widely. He went on to explain that the demolition area was just down the big hill from the very large ammunition storage depot at Cam Ranh Bay. All the ammunition and explosives shipped to the northern half of South Vietnam were stored there.

A new, nervous detachment of security guards had heard the explosions, followed by the firing of several rifles. These guards let their imaginations get the best of them and reported to their superiors that there had been a landing of sampans filled with Vietcong troops on the beach area below their posts. They claimed the Vietcong were charging up the beach carrying and firing .50-caliber machine guns in an attempt to assault the ammo dump. The ordnance battalion commander had questioned the call based on the fact that the sampans would never have made it past the coral reefs that lined the Cam Ranh Bay coast. However, their superiors, not wanting to ignore this possible threat, had sounded a base-wide alert. The designated alert force quickly donned their combat gear, mounted their trucks, and sped to the area where the assault was alleged to be taking place.

By this time my knees were shaking, and I wondered if my military career was over, but then a broad smile came across the ordnance battalion commander's face. He told me that I should be very proud of myself. I had received a new weapon and proceeded to "trigger" the first base-wide enemy alert that had been called at Cam Ranh Bay in over a year. He added that

I should not feel bad about it, because the very sloppy reaction by several of the units pointed out some glaring deficiencies in both the organizational planning and the actual performance (or lack thereof) of several of these units. Since he was the designated alert force commander, or "leader of the pack," this week, he made Amos and me promise that we would not talk to anyone at Cam Ranh Bay about this incident. So the legend of the "Phantom Regiment Attack on the Cam Ranh Bay Ammo Dump" was born.

That evening in the PX, I overheard several excited conversations among small groups of officers and troops asking if they had been involved in the vicious and bold attack on the ammo dump. In most cases, they replied that they had not, but knew several people who had been there. The story grew. Amos and I struggled to keep from laughing. After all, we came from an area where real combat was going on.

Early the following morning, we went over to the vehicle compound and attempted to requisition a replacement jeep for the jeep destroyed when our compound was overrun. This time we even had orders specifying that we were to be issued a replacement jeep since the original had been declared a combat loss. The NCO in charge looked our orders over several times, then announced that he had none to spare at this time. There were a couple American combat brigades coming in-country before the end of the week and all of the jeeps in his area were designated for them. I asked for a used jeep since we needed one badly in our remote location. He continued to chew on his unlit cigar for a moment, shrugged his shoulders, and said, "No can do, sir. I have my orders."

Amos and I looked at each other and hatched out a plan to "requisition" a suitable jeep that night. We drove over to the air base and dropped in to visit the air evacuation detachment commander, who still owed me a couple favors. I promised the detachment commander and his crew some war souvenirs if they would assist in our "requisition plan." That piqued his interest. He arranged for a C-123 plane to be parked off to one side near

Requisition

the aircraft hangar with the tail ramp down late that night. I explained that we would be secretly loading items at that time and would appreciate the tail ramp closed after we had completed the job. He agreed to close the ramp and find a flight crew whose memories would not retain the list of items transported on their plane. Take-off was set at 0600 hours the next morning. Amos and I thanked the detachment commander for all of his help.

Next, we drove over to the warehouse where Sergeant Kanahoe worked. We asked him if he had located an electrical generator. Kanahoe nodded and told me about a generator in an unmarked box located inside the engineering tools warehouse yard. He gave me its exact location and a good time to pick it up when the NCO in charge and his staff would be at lunch. The generator was there illegally, so its loss would never be reported. This sounded great. We drove into the warehouse yard, where we were relieved to find that nobody was around. The 25 KW electrical generator box in question was difficult to verify. The nomenclature originally stenciled on the box by the manufacturer was sprayed over with black paint in an attempt to hide the true contents. Finally we found it. After loading the incredibly heavy box onto the truck, we drove out of the yard trying to look as innocent as possible.

We were now ready for the third part of our requisition plan—the jeep. I had seen a jeep parked at the officers' club every night. It was in mint condition with two new VRC-47 radios installed in the back along with duel radio antennas and had so many coats of wax that it would hold up well in the boonies. This pristine jeep belonged to the U.S. Army petroleum battalion commander. He loved fraternizing with the American nurses and Red Cross Doughnut Dollies, so we figured he would be well occupied far into the night. We also knew that a man in his command position would have no problem getting a replacement jeep issued. In truth, we had not taken anything we were not authorized to have—with the exception of the specific jeep we chose to acquire. Besides, we had greater need of that vehicle and its radios than the petroleum battalion commander.

Amos and I got into the jeep and were pleased to find a simple ignition mechanism that allowed us to easily start it. We drove it to the air evacuation area and noted that the C-123 plane was parked in the agreed-upon place with its tail ramp down. I quickly jumped out of the jeep and went into the dayroom where I found the detachment commander and the aircrew drinking coffee. I asked them to help load the jeep onto their aircraft. The crew chief drove the jeep up the ramp and commented on what a "cream puff" we had bagged. The rest of the crew then strapped the jeep securely in place for the flight and loaded the generator, ammunition, explosives, and food items that we had acquired. It was decided that Amos and I would spend the night on the plane so we would be ready to go at 0600 hours while guarding our precious cargo. The pilot and crew closed up the plane and went into their billets to spend the night.

I didn't sleep well at all, the fear that the military police would catch up with us haunting me. Fortunately the pilot had filed his flight plan early that afternoon prior to our planned departure, so we were never suspected of the dastardly deed of illegally requisitioning somebody else's jeep or any other equipment. The location of our plane in the air evacuation detachment area also raised no suspicion. It was somewhat comforting to know that once we got it out of Cam Ranh Bay, no one would ever question the jeep, especially after we changed the bumper markings to our own unit.

At 0600 hours, Amos and I were awakened from our fitful sleep as the crew opened the side aircraft door and began their pre-flight check-off process. The air evacuation detachment commander handed us each a fresh cup of coffee and reminded me of my promise of supplying them with some war souvenirs. I told him I fully intended to honor that promise. Smiling, he admitted that he enjoyed aiding and abetting our midnight requisition, because the petroleum battalion commander was a real pompous ass who was constantly throwing his rank around the officers' clubs and monopolizing a couple of the better looking and available nurses. The air evacuation detachment commander hoped that our action would knock him down a peg or two, especially if he never learned the truth of his jeep's disappearance. Shortly the plane was airborne and on its way.

I was happy to see a group of both American advisors and Vietnamese soldiers gathered at our airstrip to help us unload. While Amos directed the unloading, I ran over to the advisors' living quarters and picked up five Montagnard crossbows, four Montagnard blowpipes (made from hollowed-out bamboo), six Czech AK-47 rifles, two Russian SKS rifles that we had captured from the Vietcong, and five "weathered" Vietcong battle flags. I carried the war souvenirs out to the plane and gave them to the pilot. These souvenirs would be their reward for keeping the details of this trip confidential. The plane was soon emptied and took off to resume its planned flight to Phan Thiet.

Xuan was extremely glad for the supply of newer and more reliable ammunition, as well as a generous, complimentary supply of good American pipe tobacco for him to smoke. Dramis couldn't believe the jeep and said that I should report it. After our advisors Elliott and even Xuan asked him if he were "out of his fucking mind," he thought better of that idea, especially after I told him we would not be issued a jeep for at least another year. The advisors were all very happy to see the variety of canned foods, but the highlight was the electric generator. This would provide some comforts of home when the electrical wiring and fixtures were installed in the advisors' newly promised quarters.

Word spread that some of the U.S. Army Special Forces group in Nha Trang were questioned extensively about whether or not they had taken the jeep or knew anything about its disappearance. Several of them responded with, "No, we didn't do it and don't know who did, but our hats are off to whoever pulled it off without a trace because we sure wish we had been the ones." Amos and I were very relieved that our requisition was a success and the identity of the "midnight raiders" was never revealed.

CHAPTER 19
The Police Chief

The next morning Major Xuan held an important meeting in his conference room. The purpose of this meeting was to bring all of the leaders together to better understand the needs in the Hoa Da District. Xuan started the meeting by welcoming everyone and describing the bad state of affairs that he had inherited from his predecessor. He explained how his staff and the American advisors had been trying to help the local people and asked for some suggestions to further improve their lives. A couple of village chiefs said that they would welcome the building of a marketplace in each of their areas. Another asked for a school, while others asked that some kind of water storage facilities be built. Above all, the greatest concern was adequate security to protect the villagers from bandits, pirates, and the Vietcong, although this was not openly stated.

The police chief spoke up, while glaring hatefully at Major Dramis and me, stating that before the American advisors arrived here, there were few, if any, security problems or incidents in the Hoa Da District. He spent ten minutes continually blasting the Americans as "capitalist stooges and puppets" who had brought only trouble and violence to everyone in the entire area. His Marxist rhetoric and diatribe of hate aimed at the Americans clearly marked him as a Vietcong who had infiltrated the local government. This confirmed that we could not count on him or any of his police officers for any support or assistance. When the police chief finished, Xuan disputed the police chief's observation and explained how the Americans had helped the Hoa Da District people. Unfortunately the damage had been done and those in attendance were very intimidated and reluctant to add any comments. They were clearly afraid of the police chief.

After the meeting ended, Xuan told Dramis and me that he had suspected the police chief, a number of his officers, and several other district officials were working for the Vietcong, but he still lacked concrete proof to take any action against them. Our attention was suddenly drawn to a loud scuffle in the area between the troop barracks buildings and where the advisors were billeted. Outside we saw three Cambodian troops and two advisors restraining a Vietnamese woman dressed in the peasant black pajama outfit with the conical straw hat. She was scolding them loudly and struggling to get free of their grasp.

One of our sergeants explained that the Cambodians had observed her walking at a steady pace from the south wall of the compound to the troop barracks buildings and then toward the building where we were housed. When they attempted to question her, she only replied that she had come to Hoa Da District Headquarters to register her new granddaughter and had gotten confused about how to leave the compound. Con checked to see if she had gone to the office where these registrations were handled, only to find that she had not been there.

The woman was a Vietcong "pacer," whose job it was to go into a potential Vietcong target area and pace off the distances from the outer walls to important target areas. When that was done, she would report these measurements to her leader. These would then be given to the Vietcong commander and mortar crews who would be a part of the attacking force. They would then know the exact distance and direction of each target within their objective area. As it turned out, the single large tree in our compound was to be the initial target to determine the distance to the rest of the buildings. We cut the tree down to try to reduce that threat. The woman ended up in our POW jail after being interrogated. We were not able to learn much, since she was a very low-level operative with one specific task to perform.

When the police chief heard about her capture, he demanded to take her to his office for questioning. I blocked him from having any contact with her. The police chief threw a fit and wanted me arrested for preventing him from doing his job. Xuan backed me and told the police chief to go back to his office and forget about the woman. With that, the police chief stormed out of the compound and drove off in a hurry. His irate response alerted us that the Vietcong were gathering information for another attack.

The rest of the day was spent revising our compound's defensive system. The advisors were all getting very nervous again about another attack. We made sure that the mortar pits had a full complement of ammunition available and within easy reach. Several of the other advisors and I ran a check on the placement of the claymore mines, trip flares, new booby traps, and noisemakers along the various layers of our barbed wire fencing system. We even added some new surprises for Victor Charlie from the supply of explosives we brought back from Cam Ranh Bay. Finally we put two listening posts outside of the south and west walls of the compound, where the Vietcong usually tried to gain entrance. General Peers' words kept coming to mind about the Vietcong being creatures of habit and reusing the same tactics that had already been successful. That night, as an added precaution, we doubled the security forces on alert around the entire compound, while the rest attempted to sleep with our rifles, ammunition, bandoliers, and web gear with grenades attached within easy reach.

About 0200 hours, the advisory duty officer came running into our billets reporting that both listening posts were reporting a lot of movement outside of their positions. We grabbed our weapons and equipment and ran to our assigned positions. I found Xuan and Con and asked if it might be a good idea to fire several illumination rounds with the mortars to give us an idea about the size and location of any Vietcong forces gathering outside the compound. They agreed and gave the order for the two 81mm mortars to fire two illumination rounds each. Just as our mortars began their fire mission, we heard the distinctive *whump whump* of several Vietcong mortars being fired at us from two sides. Our illumination rounds went off, revealing a large number of black pajama-clad Vietcong attackers lined up in rows on the south and west sides of the compound. Xuan immediately ordered all of the mortar crews to fire HE rounds.

By this time, the Vietcong mortar rounds began to hit our south, west, and east defensive positions. This alerted us to the possibility that Victor Charlie intended to breach the east side of the compound. The activities on the south and west sides were a distraction to pull our attention away from the area where the main attack effort would be concentrated. I got Xuan to send word to the defenders along the east side to be extra alert and send out a warning if an attack effort was launched. The Vietcong mortar attack kept our defending forces pinned down for a period of time.

Our 4.2-inch mortar crew was given the mission to locate and wipe out these Vietcong mortar crews. Enemy fire did decrease from our mortar response. West wall defenders reported a Vietcong mass moving into the area. When the first two waves were close to the outer layer of fencing, Xuan gave the order to set off the claymore mines there. They all exploded simultaneously with a tremendous blast that cut down almost all of the attackers in the first two waves. Those Vietcong in the next wave appeared hesitant or unwilling to suffer the same fate as their predecessors, so they aborted their attack.

We were hoping this was a sign that the Vietcong were going to end their attack, when suddenly we heard blaring bugles and shouts from the east wall, followed by the explosions of Bangalore torpedoes along the outer barbed-wire fencing. I ran to our mortar crews and had them redirect their fire outside the east wall. Xuan had the defenders fire the claymores mines on the east side too, but the Bangalore torpedo blasts had eliminated many of them so this had little effect. I diverted some of our defenders from the north wall to take up positions to reinforce those along the east wall.

We defenders fired all of our weapons continuously at the attacking forces, hoping that we could stop them before they breached our walls.

At this point, the attackers were throwing their ladders across our fallen barbed-wire fencing. I got on the radio and requested air support. The Song Mao Compound duty officer relayed our request to Phan Thiet, where it was sent through MACV channels to a higher headquarters for approval. It took over an hour and a half before we got the response that our request would be honored, but not before the U.S. Air Force AC-47s completed an air support request for two U.S. Army units in the Pleiku area. This wouldn't help us a bit since our battle would be over by then. Victor Charlie would either have retreated or we would all be dead—so much for timely air support.

It became apparent that Victor Charlie would not be launching any further attacks along the west wall. Xuan diverted west wall defenders to reinforce the east wall. These troops arrived just as some of the Vietcong attackers had finally breached the east wall and were fighting their way inside. These reinforcements let go a blast of coordinated, devastating fire in that area, effectively wiping out all of the attackers who had gained entry. The Vietcong mortars had been wiped out completely or ceased firing, so our mortars were free to concentrate all of their efforts along the east side of the compound. The Vietcong hastily retreated toward their mountain base under the heavy volume of return fire.

Several hours later we received a radio call asking if we still wanted the air support that we had requested earlier. I replied that the battle was now over and Victor Charlie was long gone. I questioned why air support was not approved sooner. He replied that we were low priority behind all of the U.S. and South Vietnamese units. This reinforced my feelings that we were on our own.

Early the next morning, a number of us went outside the compound to survey the results of this attack. The Vietcong had left a number of their dead tangled in the barbed wire around our compound. We found a total of sixty-three Vietcong bodies along with a number of blood trails heading across the sand dunes in the general direction of the mountains. Walking along the east side, we were very surprised to note that one of the Vietcong bodies stuck in the wire was that of our Marxist-spouting Hoa Da District police chief. From his position, it appeared that he had been leading the attack. Near him were three members of his police staff. They would no longer be causing any problems for Xuan or the people of Hoa Da District.

Notification was sent throughout the Hoa Da District about the Vietcong dead in our compound for relatives or friends to come and claim them. Nobody claimed any of them, although there were a number of villagers who looked them over and seemed to smile knowingly with relief when they saw the bodies of the police chief and his three officers. Over the next couple days, five other police officers failed to report for work and nobody could find them anywhere. My guess is that they were also Vietcong. They were either wounded in the attack or defected to the Vietcong full time after the battle. Their family members had also suddenly disappeared. In either case, the local police department was now effectively purged of all of its Vietcong operatives. This helped to finally offer effective police security to the Hoa Da District. Victor Charlie's stranglehold and reign of terror was closer to being over in this region.

We gathered several Vietcong weapons from the police chief's failed attack. I discovered what appeared to be a brand new AK-47 automatic rifle with the Cosmolene preservative still on the stock and barrel of the weapon. Further investigation uncovered ten others along with large amounts of Vietcong ammunition, Bangalore torpedoes, and several satchel charges. A request was issued for an EOD squad to assist us in safely disposing of these weapons. They arrived by chopper early the following morning and looked closely at the acquired weapons. The

The Police Chief

squad recognized the new automatic rifles as AK-50s, dubbed this because of its improved magazine-feed system, which permitted a larger magazine and faster rate of fire. This automatic rifle was supposed to be more durable than the AK-47. The squad leader speculated the AK-50s had just arrived from their suppliers in North Vietnam, and the Vietcong were trying them out under battle conditions for the first time. The EOD were surprised to find that none had jammed, had no mechanical problems, and had been used without removing the Cosmolene protective coating. After the EOD had disposed of the leftover explosives, I gave them two of the AK-50s, much to their delight. These were genuine and very rare war souvenirs.

Later that morning, the CIA case officer came by to examine one of the AK-50 automatic rifles. He seemed to take a great deal of interest in the results of this attack. He confided that the police chief was known to direct Vietcong hit squads and political cadres. The police chief was going to be a hard man for the Vietcong to replace. I was glad to hear all of this, but wondered why we were not notified about the police chief's activity. The CIA case officer had another bit of news. An unconfirmed force had assassinated ex-Hoa Da District Chief Manh.

Wow, I thought. The clan of ex-District Chief Manh and the police chief were now gone. I gave the CIA case officer two AK-50 rifles as a thank you. He too was delighted with his war souvenirs.

That afternoon, an unexpected Army Huey chopper arrived with a MACV intelligence section chief and his deputy. Zender soon came out and explained that these were his commanders. The intelligence chief had received word about some new Vietcong weapons that we had just captured, and he would like to take a look at them. It was amazing how fast this information had traveled. I was relatively certain that it had come from Zender since I knew that the EOD squad would not be spreading this confidential information. The two officers examined the rifles, conferred with each other, and stated that they would have to take all of the AK-50s with them. They explained that the army weapons experts needed to put them through detailed analysis, since this was a first encounter with such a rifle.

I said that we would like to keep a couple of them since we had captured them. The MACV intelligence officers gruffly responded that this was not possible since these were new Vietcong weapons needed for evidence. I reluctantly brought out the six remaining AK-50s and turned them over to him. The intelligence leader gave me a hard look and asked about the others. I told him that we didn't have them anymore. We had turned them over to the local CIA case officer. He shrugged and stated that trying to get them back or even an admission that the CIA had them would be fruitless. They loaded their prizes securely onto their chopper and departed for their headquarters in Nha Trang.

I told our advisors that if we ever encounter any more of this type of Vietcong weapon, we would hang on to them. Unfortunately we never saw or heard of any more in our area. As for me, I found comfort in knowing that the troops and my advisors at Hoa Da District Compound had exterminated the police chief and his cronies. We could stand our ground while fighting Victor Charlie.

CHAPTER 20
The Pale Montagnard Woman

One day a Cham woodcutter's ox cart came to the front gate of our compound and off-loaded a very frail-looking woman. Her skin was very light, almost white. The woodcutter explained through our interpreter that they were coming back from a day of gathering wood in the jungle for their charcoal business when they saw this woman lying by the side of the mountain trail. She was barely alive and needed water, food, and medical care. They said that she was trying to tell them an unbelievable story about being underground for over two and a half years working for the Vietcong.

We rushed the pale woman to our medical dispensary. Our American medics began trying to save her by infusing two bottles of dextrose to feed her badly depleted system. It appeared that she had not bathed in quite a while. The medics cleaned the infected sores that covered her entire body and gave her a couple injections of penicillin. After this treatment, she began to show some signs of improvement and wanted to tell us her story. She did not speak the local Cham dialect, but could speak another dialect that one of the woodcutters understood. He translated her words into Vietnamese that our interpreter understood, who then explained what was being said, in English, to us. This was a painfully slow process.

The pale woman explained that she was a Montagnard who had been captured several years ago, along with her entire family, when a Vietcong raiding party overran and captured her hamlet in the mountains. The men and boys had been taken away to serve as soldiers and load-bearers for the Vietcong in the Central Highlands, never to be seen again. She and the other women and girls were taken to a large Vietcong base camp somewhere along the Ho Chi Minh Trail in Laos. There they were forced to serve as cooks and what she called "pleasure girls" for the Vietcong and North Vietnamese Army troops. The woman had seen the Vietcong take three large men, not Asiatic, north. They were wearing some kind of uniforms, looked very dirty, and appeared badly treated so she assumed they were American prisoners.

Several times she and the other women were moved because of nearby bombings. Her eyes filled with tears as she recalled the time when her sister and two daughters tried to escape during the confusion of one of these bombings but the Vietcong shot them down mercilessly. Some time after that, her only surviving daughter and her other sister died of malaria without being given any help.

The pale Montagnard woman wasn't sure how long she spent in these camps but remembered the brutal Vietcong guards and soldiers frequently raping her. Unlike most of the other women, she never got pregnant from these rapes because she constantly chewed on bitter bark that was abundant in the jungle. Her grandmother had taught her about the bitter bark's medicinal power in aiding birth control and controlling malaria. She took these precautions because she could not bear the thought of giving birth to a baby from one of these brutal Vietcong savages.

The Vietcong eventually took the woman to a place where she joined a large work crew that was being used to excavate a large, elaborate tunnel system where the Vietcong and North Vietnamese Army could better hide their troops and supplies from detection and the increasing bombings. She spent many months underground digging out this extensive system. She was

The Pale Montagnard Woman

not allowed outdoors but preferred this job because she was no longer subjected to the sexual attacks and beatings from the Vietcong men. She was sure that this was also due to the fact that all of this hard work had aged her well beyond her years and turned her into an ugly old woman.

When the tunnel complex project was completed, the workers were marched a long distance, moving only at night, to a new location where they began excavating an underground hospital. This trip was slow and took a number of days due to the weakened condition of this work force of slaves. The pale Montagnard woman said that she really enjoyed being above ground and outdoors breathing fresh air and drinking fresh water. While she worked on this hospital, however, she was underground again.

Her skin had turned from a dark brown to a pale white after many months in no natural light. All of her teeth eventually fell out due to malnutrition, so she could only gum what little food they provided. Her food consisted of poor quality rice with an occasional piece of fish or rat and some type of root vegetable. The water was not very clean to drink. Water for washing was only allowed once a week. To cope with these horrific conditions, she filled her mind with memories of pleasant times with her family. This saved her from going mad like several of the other workers.

She described the underground hospital in detail. She provided information on how the hospital was laid out using exact measurements of length, width, and height. In effect, we now had our own "pacer." The hospital was big enough to house forty patient beds with four rooms where the doctors could treat and operate on the wounded Vietcong soldiers. It had five separate and well-hidden entrances leading into it. She told us where the entrances were located and how they were hidden. The nearest entrance to the hospital was pointed out in relation to where the woodcutter found her.

Next she explained the fairly sophisticated ventilation system that pumped fresh air throughout the hospital, while the filtration exhaust system took the bad air out. It also disguised the sterilization of surgical instruments and any cooking smoke from the large eating area. It sounded like an underground restaurant for the hospital staff and transient troops. She informed us that the hospital complex was undergoing an addition to serve as a storage area for Vietcong supplies and equipment, as well as a stopover lodging place for the Vietcong and North Vietnamese. After working on this hospital for about two years, she had finally gotten so weak that her service was no longer needed. Instead of killing her, they took her out by the side of the trail and left her there to starve and be eaten by the wild animals.

In a meek voice, the woman asked us to please take over that hospital and rescue the "diggers" who had been captive workers for so many years. They had managed to survive under impossible conditions and would like to return home to their families. She weakly grasped my hand and asked that we help her pray to the spirits of her ancestors and the spirits of the mighty trees where she was born and lived before the Vietcong came and took her away. I talked to her gently for a few minutes until her eyes closed. I quietly said a prayer for this brave woman and asked God to forgive her sins and take her to be with him throughout eternity. A short time later, her breathing stopped and her spirit went to join those of her ancestors. She was finally at true peace. The Cham woodcutters agreed to take and bury her according to the Montagnards' customs.

Xuan, his intelligence NCO, and Zender had joined us for the better part of her story. All agreed that the pale Montagnard woman sounded legitimate. Xuan further noted that she would not lie about these things; otherwise, according to her beliefs, the spirits of her ancestors would not forgive her, thereby forcing her spirit to wander throughout eternity. Her account was transcribed with references to exact locations in the Cham and Hoa Da districts.

We all knew that we didn't have much time to plan and carry out our operation. The longer the planning process took, the higher the possibility of detection. It was decided to classify this information as "Secret" in hopes that the Vietcong would not learn our intent to root out and destroy their elaborate hospital complex. It was further agreed to keep this plan as a strictly Northern Province operation. This meant that we would be combining the military forces from the Hoa Da, Hai Ninh-Song Mao, Tuy Phong, Phan Ly Cham, and Luong Son districts. According to Elliott, this had never been attempted before and would set a whole new precedent.

The group decided that the district chief of Hai Ninh-Song Mao would be the overall commander of this task force since he was a lieutenant colonel with the greatest amount of experience and seniority. The military forces would be composed of Tuy Phong Vietnamese troops; Chinese and Cham troops from the Cham and Hai Ninh-Song Mao district; and the Cambodian and the highly American-trained Civilian Irregular Defense Group (CIDG) Vietnamese troops from Hoa Da and Luong Son.

We planned to launch this joint operation in five days. The Chinese and Cham troops would set up a blocking position behind and beside the location of the hospital and all of its entrances. The American advisors, the Cambodians, and CIDG troops would approach from the front side and enter at three points to capture this complex. We expected to encounter enemy resistance at the entrances to the underground complex. The Tuy Phong Vietnamese troops would be held nearby as reserve forces.

The plan was fairly straightforward, but neither these leaders nor military forces had ever worked together before. Major Dufort moved his CIDG troops from Luong Son into the Hoa Da District Compound. When the planned day arrived, we were all nervous and excited as we got up at 0300 hours and donned our weapons and equipment. We kept strict radio silence prior to the assault so as not to alert the Vietcong. A red star cluster flare would shoot overhead as the sign to begin the raid. After a non-eventful march, our troops arrived at the hospital complex area about 0530 hours. We spread out off to one side of the trail to wait for the specified assault time, which was 0615 hours.

At 0605 our troops quietly and nervously spread and squatted into attack position along the front of the underground mountain hospital. Xuan and I sent word down the ranks to quietly check weapons and equipment. At 0615 hours, we looked upward, expecting the signal flare to appear at any second. When that didn't happen, we wondered if some of the troops had not arrived in their appointed positions. We prayed that no one would walk along the trail and detect us as we waited for the assault signal. At 0618 hours, we saw the red star cluster fired overhead. Our unit commander gave the order to begin the assault through the three main entrances to the underground hospital.

The American advisors and the Cambodian and CIDG troops quickly located and entered the somewhat hidden entrances. Two shots were fired: one near the entrance of the far left tunnel and the other in the center tunnel. I was afraid that we had gotten ourselves into an ambush situation. As it turned out, the Vietcong guards fired these as a warning sign then ran farther back into the tunnel system to escape our assault. When we reached the main hospital chamber, we found a large, well-supported area containing forty beds lined up in four rows of ten bunk-beds each. We checked each bed and found five badly wounded patients who were too injured to be moved. In the operating room lay two badly wounded patients, both under anesthesia and being operated on at the time of our entry. The Vietcong doctors and nurses had run out the back of the complex as we entered the front.

We then went and checked the troop sleeping and eating areas and found no one there. It was very eerie to see water boiling on the stove in their small kitchen as well as twenty bowls with hot rice and vegetables sitting on the two tables and chopsticks scattered about. People had been eating breakfast and had made a hasty exit out the back. I heard a scuffle and saw two of our men drag two Vietcong soldiers out from behind one of the patient beds. They apparently were orderlies who were taking care of the severely injured patients. From the looks on their faces, they were absolutely terrorized by our presence and the capture of the hospital complex.

The Pale Montagnard Woman

Our search of the complex took us into a large area behind the hospital where about fifty cots were set up. A few contained Vietcong clothing, military gear, and family pictures. Behind this sleeping chamber was a larger area filled with supplies of medical, military, and food items. While we were checking this area out, we heard several moans and gasps from behind the wall of supplies. Two of our men found their way behind the wall and discovered thirty people trembling together in a squatting position. They appeared old, pale, and overworked. We determined that these were the "diggers" that the pale Montagnard woman had been a part of for so long.

The diggers looked at us with blank stares filled with pain, exhaustion, and nutritional deficiency. They were ready to accept what fate was now dealing them, knowing that life could be no worse than the one the Vietcong forced them to live. Through our interpreter, we were able to make them understand that we had captured this complex. We were now going to feed, treat, and help them get cleaned up to go back to their home villages. At first they didn't seem to comprehend what we were saying, but as they talked among themselves for a few minutes, they began to understand what was happening. They stood up and began to smile and bow to us repeatedly to show their appreciation.

Majors Xuan, Elliott, Dufort, and the Hai Ninh and Tuy Phong district chiefs entered the underground hospital to join the rest of us. They marveled at its size and complexity. Everyone wondered where the Vietcong hid the dirt that was excavated. Both Xuan and Elliott asked the obvious question: how many other underground facilities might there possibly be in this region? We hoped we might get some information from the diggers and any prisoners that we were able to round up from this operation.

Elliott said he had received a radio call from Hai-Ninh Chinese forces. The Chinese forces had intercepted and captured over forty Vietcong who were trying to exit the hospital complex through several back entrances. The Vietcong prisoners were to be sent to the Song Mao Compound for questioning and processing. I showed Elliott the diggers. They were very feeble and would require assistance on their trip to Song Mao Compound for physical care and to be questioned for information regarding the Vietcong. Only one of the five injured Vietcong patients was ambulatory. The other four would have to be carried on litters. We looked around and found about twenty-five American-issue stretchers that would serve nicely for transporting these patients. The two patients in the operating room had died from their wounds during the assault. I wanted to claim them and the other five wounded patients as casualties from the latest attack on our compound, since that was the only recent Vietcong contact reported in our region. However, it was not my position to make this determination.

Our Northern Province troops guided the prisoners, diggers, and those on stretchers back to Song Mao Compound. I looked over the prisoners. Ten of them I assumed were the main medical personnel, since they didn't have that outdoor weathered look like the rest of the Vietcong soldiers. Xuan, a couple Vietnamese intelligence personnel, and I attempted to ask them a few questions but got only looks of extreme hate in response. I impressed on the operation commander the importance of special treatment to the diggers because of the extreme abuse and trauma they had experienced from their brutal Vietcong captors. Before we gathered information from the diggers, we needed to give them time to relax and realize that they were finally free. The operation commander agreed.

This would be our last contact with the people we had rescued or captured, as well as the underground hospital complex. The operation commander posted a detail of his Chinese and Cham soldiers to guard the hospital complex until other South Vietnamese military forces arrived. These other forces would study the facility, ship out the equipment and supplies, and finally destroy it completely.

By the time we arrived in Song Mao, word of our discovery and success had spread widely. Waiting for our captives and us were intelligence teams from the CIA, MACV, ARVN, IFFV, Binh

The Pale Montagnard Woman

Thuan Province, and several others that I had never even heard of before. When the Vietcong saw what was waiting for them, they seemed very shocked and their air of defiance suddenly melted away. All of these representatives from the various agencies seemed to want to take part in the success of the moment. Xuan, Elliott, and I made sure that the diggers were provided good food, water, medical care, and a chance to get cleaned up and put on clean outfits. The diggers were surprised. Their abusive treatment had, at long last, come to an end. They were now being treated almost as celebrities.

The diggers provided excellent information about the Vietcong and their activities, according to our CIA case officer. He felt sorry for them, because the Vietcong had totally wiped out some of their villages. The CIA case officer informed us that all of the Vietcong patients captured, as well as those two who had died on the operating room tables, had been wounded in the latest attack on the Hoa Da District Compound. We were to count them as part of that Vietcong casualty count. I was correct in my assessment and thanked him for the update.

The Hoa Da District advisory team and our troops were not a part of the follow-up process of the capture. We did see a number of U.S. and South Vietnamese helicopters fly into that area over the next couple days bringing teams to study the complex, take out the supplies and equipment, and finally a team of combat engineers to destroy the complex. Although our compound was several miles away from the site, we still heard the loud, muffled explosion and felt the ground shake from that huge blast. The military alliance from the northern districts in Binh Thuan Province had been successful in destroying a critical part of Victor Charlie. I knew that without the deathbed story of the pale Montagnard woman, none of this would ever have been possible.

CHAPTER 21
Life's Cruel Detour

In you, O Lord, I have taken refuge; let me never be put to shame; deliver me in your righteousness. Turn your ear to me, come quickly to my rescue; be my rock of refuge, a strong fortress to save me.

Psalm 31:1-2

As the morning of November 1, 1968, began, we received word from over our team radio that President Lyndon B. Johnson had declared a cease-fire throughout all Vietnam for all military operations against the Vietcong and North Vietnamese Army. These meant that we were not permitted to fire on, arrest, or try to impede the Vietcong forces that we might encounter in any way during this period, unless they first fired on us. The cease-fire stopped the daily bombings over the Ho Chi Minh Trail and North Vietnam, which were intended to interdict the flow of men and supplies from North Vietnam and China to the Vietcong and North Vietnam Army Forces operating throughout South Vietnam, Laos, and Cambodia. This was definitely not the will or the strategy of the field soldiers forced to wage this war and who had been having great success against the Vietcong and North Vietnam Army since the Tet Offensive Communist defeat.

This cease-fire could not have come at a worse time for the northern Binh Thuan Province advisory teams. Xuan and I agreed that the cease-fire allowed the Vietcong time to recruit, train, equip, and deploy their reinforcements. They would undoubtedly attack the Hoa Da Compound again when they were certain they had obtained the advantage. They had already shown that this was their normal pattern after other cease-fires.

Within a few days of the cease-fire, we began to see first small groups and, later, fully armed units of Vietcong walking, in broad daylight, along the line of sand dunes behind our compound. Although I knew that it would be a court martial offense to fire upon them, I just wanted to call in an air strike and finally put an end to this group of thugs once and for all. It was as if they were doing this to dare us to start something with them. These taunting actions did give us the opportunity to get a more accurate idea of the size and numbers of their forces in our area. During this period, I gave binoculars to a couple advisors and their Vietnamese counterparts to track the Vietcong activities. I certainly did not want to take the chance that these Vietcong walks turn into an attack on our compound.

The cease-fire did not stop the Vietcong from putting out roadblocks and booby traps at different places along our local roads every night. It also did not stop the semi-weekly Vietcong visits, forced indoctrinations, and executions at some of the Vietnamese hamlets. Despite their actions, we were not to initiate any fire against the Vietcong until they first fired directly on us. This was another example of how the politicians were using semantics, changing definitions and parameters to limit our abilities and opportunities to take decisive action and win this war against an elusive enemy. If anything, these severe limitations were setting the local villagers up to be victims of Vietcong abuse. All of the advisors were really fed up with the Johnson administration, which had trained and deployed us to fight this war. They figuratively tied our hands behind our backs to keep us from gaining ground against and defeating our enemy. We were thankful about President Johnson's announcement not to seek re-election. The advisors had all sent in our absentee ballots voting for Richard Nixon with the hope that he would give us the support we needed to win or get us the hell out of this godforsaken war.

During the cease-fire, we began to spend our time better training our Vietnamese forces in participating in civic action activities needed around the Hoa Da District. These included guiding the villagers in constructing and setting up appropriate marketplaces as they had requested. Our medics were given the go-ahead to recruit and train a number of local people to receive a basic course in first aid training so they could help provide health care services to the people of their own village. The village health representatives worked with our medics at the periodic MEDCAP visits in their villages. This provided additional assistance for the medics as well as input from the health representatives, a win-win situation. At first we expected that the lack of funds to pay these trainees would present a problem. Instead, the training and title gave these people greater social status and reputation in their villages, which presented them with far greater gains than a salary.

About mid-morning on November 2, two panel trucks and a jeep, all painted white and bearing the company logo of Pacific Architects and Engineers, pulled into our compound. The man in charge asked to see one of the lead American advisors. Both Major Dramis and I went to meet him. I immediately recognized him as the Korean gentleman I met in Nha Trang, who had known my father in Tageu, South Korea, in the 1950s.

He greeted us and said that he had been assigned as the project coordinator in charge of building our new advisory team Hoa Da District Compound. I warmly welcomed him and said how great it was to see him again. He told me that he and his crew of Korean and Vietnamese workers would make sure that we had a first-rate compound. Dramis was quite surprised by this exchange. I later told him how my father had helped out the man and his family by getting them housing and jobs at the American military compound when they lost everything during the Korean War. Dramis found the spirit of Oriental loyalty peculiar. He did not understand the warmth and gratitude the Orientals felt to pay back a great favor.

We needed to meet several requirements to get the new advisory building underway. The first was to move the wooden portable building that we advisors had used as our kitchen, eating, and meeting areas. At first one of my sergeants said that we would have to dismantle the building then re-erect it in a better location away from the construction site. The Korean gentleman politely interrupted and said that would not be necessary. After Xuan's agreement on the appropriate new location, one of the engineering team leaders organized a large work party of one hundred Vietnamese and Cambodians from our military forces. These forces were to be paid an extra fee if they would help us with this moving task. The engineer team leader then had the workers move the stacked sandbags away from the wooden building while we advisors moved all of our items outside.

Next, the workers were split into two squads, one for each of the long sides of the structure. A supervisor was assigned to each squad. An additional twenty-five men were standing by to use if necessary. A man stood in the center of the future building site to direct and mark the exact location. The engineer team leader briefed all of the workers on how, on command, they were to lift and carry this structure to the new site one hundred fifty feet away. The two squads then took their places and, on command, lifted the wooden building off of the ground. When it was determined that everyone was comfortable with their part, the next command started the building moving slowly forward toward the new site.

After the men had taken about fifty steps and were comfortable with this process, somebody started a rhythmic chant that men on both sides of the building quickly picked up. Con explained that this was a good way to get the workers thinking about something other than the strain and the pain involved in the assigned task. About midway, the building began to teeter a bit as some of the men began to tire a little. The engineer team leader immediately assigned an additional fifteen men to lift the back part of the building to end the teetering. This proved successful and the building moved, without further complications, to its new site.

Before putting it down, the men rotated the building a few degrees until it was finally in the proper position. A great cheer then broke out among both the workers and observers. The Korean gentleman and his supervisors then carefully checked the building over and pronounced it very stable and ready for occupancy. He had a team of workers take the sandbags and build a protective barrier around the structure once again. This wooden building would be improved to serve as our kitchen and dining and meeting area. It would be fully wired and hooked into the newly acquired electrical generator, while a propane tank was to be used for the stove and refrigerator. We advisors were happy to finally have some modern conveniences.

Next, the construction crew measured and marked off the outline of the advisory quarters and placed the wooden supports to lay the concrete foundation. The concrete was hand-mixed in large wheelbarrows since there was no large mixer available. This mixture was then poured inside the supports on top of rows of rebar then leveled and smoothed over when the desired depth was reached. Four teams of men mixed and poured the concrete from sunup to sunset. Slowly, over a several-day period, the new structure began to take shape. It would have three bunk rooms: one large room for the enlisted men and interpreters, a smaller room for the junior officers, and one room for the senior and deputy senior advisors. The plans also included an activities/dayroom, an operations/communications center, a five-bed medical dispensary, small arms and ammunition storage room, and a supply/equipment room.

As great as this project was progressing, I would not be in the Hoa Da District to see its completion.

On November 13, 1968, morning brought another oppressively hot and humid day. I awoke about 0600 hours with the sudden disturbance of two advisors entering our barracks following their two-hour shift on radio watch. I opened my mosquito netting and sat up on the edge of the bed, careful to survey the area over which I would be extending my feet and legs to ensure that no undesirable vermin awaited me. Grabbing my trusty shotgun with which I slept, I knocked my boots over onto their side then tapped each hard several times to shake up any visitor that had tried to take up residence during the previous night. I allowed them the usual five-minute crawl time during which only one tarantula emerged. Cautiously I picked each boot up by the heel and at arm's length turned them upside down and again tapped hard on the sole. This resulted in only one small scorpion falling to the floor. After all of this preparation, I knew it was safe to put my boots on to begin a new day.

Perspiration flowed heavily out of my pores. This time it was not caused by the high humidity but my unsettled, restless night. I had experienced an increased awareness of pervasive danger that something terribly bad would happen to me if I remained in or near the Hoa Da District Compound today. Haunted by my dream intuition, I asked Sergeant Cuthbert for a report on the last radio watch tour. He replied that all had been quiet and routine: no radio traffic, calm weather, and no detected enemy activity, either near our compound or at the bridge sites that our Popular Forces Units platoons were guarding. I thanked him and he went to his bunk to grab a couple hours of needed sleep.

I picked up my empty canteen and walked over to our team hut to fill it from the water bladder. I then took a couple salt tablets with several deep swallows of water, topped off the canteen again from the bladder, and went into the hut. There I encountered the new MAT team leader, First Lieutenant Riley, who was meeting with his assistant and Amos. They were planning for the patrol to be run later this morning from Long Ha village through Hoi Tam hamlet and Ha Thuy village, ending at Vinh Long hamlet on the South China Sea later that afternoon. The purpose was to follow up on current intelligence reports of recent Vietcong activity in several of the villages along the coast. This activity appeared to indicate the Vietcong intent to reestablish their presence in that area. We wanted to discover their purpose and block it before they became entrenched in that region again.

I told Riley that I was planning to accompany the patrol, just as an observer. He seemed pleased. At that point Dramis entered the team hut and joined us for a cup of coffee. When he heard what was being planned, he complimented the patrol plans. However, he told me that I would not be going along since he needed me for chores.

I asked him what the chores entailed. Dramis put down his cup of coffee and responded that I was to relocate the two fifty-five-gallon drums of "foo-gas" from outside the barbed-wire barrier of our compound to the implanted ground locations for our defense upgrade. I tried to explain to him that a couple of the POWs in our stockade had moved the drums out there, and I had already given orders yesterday to have these same POWs move them back to their proper locations sometime this morning.

Dramis glared at me and barked that he didn't give a shit about the POWs. He was now giving me a direct order to go out, personally, and move those drums inside the wire before noon today. I pleaded and explained about my restless sleep and premonition about something bad happening to any members of our team who might go out into that area today. He argued that I was full of shit and just trying to find any excuse to keep from obeying his order. I assured him that this was not the case. I was only trying to have the POWs who put the drums in the wrong locations move them back to the right locations.

Dramis grew more agitated and responded that either I personally move them that day or he would bring me up on UCMJ Article 15 Charges of Direct Disobedience of a Verbal Order. Not wanting to see my military career end over such a trivial matter, I replied, "Yes, sir, I will personally move these drums before the end of the day."

Satisfied, he added that I needed to meet with Xuan within the next half hour to finalize plans for several proposed military operations in the Hoa Da District and that he would not be attending this meeting since he had other pending issues. This usual lack of participation in the military operation planning was consistent for Dramis. There was always an excuse. Again I replied with a "Yes, sir."

At 0915 hours, I watched the patrol march out the front gate of our compound. I wished that I were with them. Fear and dread still lurked in my heart. Something bad was going to occur during the early afternoon hours—I knew it. I took a deep breath and tried to erase my dire thoughts as I entered the conference room and saw Xuan, Zender, the CIA case officer, and a couple members of the Hoa Da staff. Over the next two hours we discussed the success of several of the recent operations conducted against the Vietcong using strong intelligence from several of our most reliable agents. It was noted that our agents, Montagnard woodcutters, had spotted several Vietcong patrols coming down from Nui Ga Lang Mountain and entering Thon Dong Tren and Thon Truong Thanh hamlets. These same patrols, minus a few men, were seen a few days later leaving these hamlets and returning up the trails into the mountain. It appeared that the Vietcong were trying to insert themselves into the hamlets again.

One of our agents had reported that he had overheard several of the Vietcong talking about returning to these hamlets the night of November 19. It was decided that an operation would be scheduled to kick off into that area very early the morning of November 20. The objective was to surround the hamlets and conduct a detailed search of the entire area. We would round up everyone who did not normally live there, along with any weapons or equipment. The CIA agent stated that our quick response to this type of potential threat would send a clear message to the Vietcong that they were not welcome in the Hoa Da District and would be eliminated if they attempted to reenter the region. We then drew up plans for the units that would be participating in this operation and everyone was cautioned to treat this information as secret.

When the meeting ended, I returned to the team hut to grab something to eat before I began my assigned project to move the "foo-gas" drums. Dramis was there and decided to join me on the project. I cautioned him that this would not be a good idea since the senior advisor and deputy senior advisor should not be together in any dangerous areas for the simple reason that if both were killed or wounded, the advisory team would be without its main leadership. He brushed this off with some comment about my continuing to try to find a way out of doing this damned job. At this point, I felt that fate had totally taken over and was driving me uncontrollably into being in the area that would expose me to danger that would totally disrupt or end my life.

I stubbed out my after-lunch cigarette. Dramis and I walked to the left side of the compound, through the gap in the barbed-wire fence that was formerly a minefield. Beyond the outer barrier of tangle-foot wire was the first drum. It was lying on its side on top of a small sand hill. I started to turn the heavy drum and push it in the direction from which we had come with the expectation that Dramis would be joining in and doing his share of the work. This was no easy task since the soft sand offered a high degree of resistance. As I struggled to roll the drum first down a small hill and then up the side of the next one, I felt Major Dramis make a half-hearted effort of pushing on my back instead of pushing on the other half of the drum. This was really starting to irritate me; I had the drum well up the next hillside almost at eye-level and knew that without Dramis' full effort we were not going to make it on the first try.

That was the last thing I remember. They say that you never hear the blast nor feel the explosion that gets you, and they are certainly correct.

A massive explosion from a command-detonated mine blew up. A lone Vietcong, who was situated nearby behind a low stand of cactus, set it off. The weapon was a U.S. Navy five-inch artillery shell, to which was attached a number of soft drink or beer cans containing broken glass, razor blades, rusty nails, jagged metal, and other items designed to mutilate a target, and all were coated with a thick crust of human excrement intended to infect those targeted. The explosion blew me about eighty feet through the air, causing me to land on a barbed-wire fence. My left jaw struck a metal stake onto which the barbed wire was strung, leaving my body dangling to the left side. Dramis had been blown thirty feet in another direction and landed in the sand. The concussion rendered us both unconscious.

The blast propelled the intact drum about fifty feet in another direction. Hanging in this web of barbed wire, I thought that our compound had come under attack. As the combat leader of our advisory team, I felt that it was my duty to stand up and point my team in the direction from which the attack was coming, even though I was badly shaken up and disoriented. After a number of efforts to accomplish this failed, I began to go through a mental evaluation of what had just happened to me—how badly injured I was, my chances of survival, and if anyone was nearby.

I remember feeling the intense heat of the sun beating down on me as my body was powerless and motionless in the entanglement. I was really struggling for each breath and was totally blind. A loud-pitched ring, a by-product of the massive explosion, rung in my ears as intense waves of severe pain continued to sweep over me, making me feel faint and nauseous. Faintness turned into annoyance by what seemed like somebody tapping my left shoulder every couple seconds. What was really happening was that every time my heart beat, a stream of blood spurted out of my severed carotid artery and hit my left shoulder. I realized that I was dying.

My emotions turned to my wife; I thought, *What is Mary going to say since she told me to come home safely?* At that moment I uttered what was the most sincere prayer of my life: "Oh God, help me!" Almost immediately, I heard a very soothing and calm voice say, "Remain calm. Turn your head all the way to the left. Have faith and I will see you through all of this." I was not shocked by the presence of the voice and did exactly what it told me to do. Turning my head to the left mainly constricted the carotid artery, greatly reducing the flow of blood, while also allowing the accumulated teeth, flesh, and general gunk to dislodge partially from my throat and slide a little to the left to make breathing a little easier.

The other advisors had heard the thunderous explosion. When they looked in the general direction where Dramis and I should have been, they could only see a black cloud of smoke rising. They naturally assumed that we had stepped on one of our mines. Woolridge ran out to where we were. He screamed for his teammates to bring two stretchers and to call for a medevac chopper. Unfortunately our team senior medic, Bolling, had journeyed to Nha Trang for the day, while the assistant medic was holding a MEDCAP at a couple of the local villages and had taken our supply of stretchers with him. Since Woolridge was new to our team, he did not know that we had no working stretchers available, so several other teammates took down two doors in the old barracks and came running out to help carry us back into the compound.

I was conscious when the other advisors arrived at my side to begin trying to free me from the barbed-wire fence. I was unable to communicate since I was extremely weak and fighting for each breath of air. I was aware that they were trying to work very quickly and kept saying that they hoped the chopper and a medic got there soon or they were going to lose me. As they finally lifted me off the fence, a wave of extreme pain engulfed me and rendered me unconscious again. That probably worked in my favor, since I later heard that the trip back to the main compound was extremely rough and my litter was dropped a couple of times as two of the sergeants alternately vomited along the way because of the ghastly sight of our bloodied and broken bodies.

It was mid-afternoon by the time the advisors got me back inside the compound. A moderate wind had whipped up, causing a lot of dust and sand to be blown around. They were afraid that this dust was causing me breathing problems. Somebody got a towel, dampened it, and lightly draped it across my face without keeping a distance above my nose and mouth. Shortly thereafter, I became conscious. I panicked by the increased difficulty to breathe. At that point the calming voice again spoke to me and told me, "Stay calm, relax, and breathe slowly. Have faith for I will see you through all of this."

I heard the sound of an approaching helicopter, which I hoped and prayed was a medevac chopper. Then I heard a slight scuffle near me with one or more of my advisors telling some Vietnamese to get away from me. Apparently there was a Vietnamese soldier claiming to be a medic who kept trying to inject some purplish-colored fluid into me. Fortunately my fellow advisors didn't recognize the fluid, so they kept him away from me. He might have been legitimate, but he also could have been trying to finish the job started by the command-detonated mine. After all, the desire to collect that $20,000 price tag for my head could motivate some people to resort to some pretty extreme measures to guarantee that I would not survive.

When the chopper finally landed, the advisors quickly carried me over to it and transferred me from the door litter onto one of their stretchers. The medic on the chopper had a very calming voice and told me that he would help me to breathe. I was aware that he was cutting a tracheotomy into my throat and windpipe. There was never any pain as he was making the incision. I immediately felt relief and breathing became easier. He moved on to clamping the carotid artery and jugular vein to slow the bleeding, followed by inserting an IV tube into the artery in the back of my left knee, the only undamaged major blood vessel. Two bottles of blood plasma ran through at maximum flow in an attempt to replenish some of my fluid levels. At this point, still blind, I lost consciousness again.

CHAPTER 22
24th Evacuation Hospital

The chopper flew to the medical aid station at Phan Thiet. I briefly awoke. Major Dramis was holding my left hand tightly and giving me words of encouragement. I figured he was experiencing pangs of guilt over forcing me to retrieve that stupid drum. Both Dramis and I were quickly carried into the treatment area. I was severely injured with over 90 percent of my body wounded, while Dramis had sustained wounds over about 30 percent of his body with the metal fragments having passed through my body before injuring him. The force of the explosion had blown off my right leg above the knee so that it was hanging on only by a connected tendon; the outer half of my left foot and four fingertips on my right hand were blown off; my left eye was blown away; a number of metal fragments had gone through the right eye, rendering it totally blind; all of the frontal sinuses were blown away; the skull in my left forehead and surrounding the left eye socket was shattered; the jaw bone was shattered in three main places; a number of teeth and bone chips from the lower jaw and surrounding flesh were blown out and wedged in the back of my throat; the carotid artery in my neck had been severed with a two-inch section blown away so that each beat of my heart was pumping out blood; the jugular vein in the other side of my neck had been severed; a section of the right side of my nose had been blown away; my whole face had been blown apart; a number of abdominal and chest wounds had caused severe internal bleeding; and extensive shrapnel wounds had caused severe injuries to the genitals, buttocks, right arm, and the remainder of my legs.

Dramis's injuries consisted of a number of leg wounds, including a severed left Achilles tendon, several wounds to his right arm, hand, and shoulder. Looking at us, the Phan Thiet medics immediately determined that our treatment required a better-equipped facility. The medics hooked two new bottles of blood plasma onto me and then carried us back to the waiting chopper for our continued flight to a larger field hospital. Dramis was taken into the emergency room for treatment at the larger field hospital, while I was transferred because of their inability to treat my head and thoracic wounds. They attached two new bottles of whole blood to me in a desperate attempt to replace some of my lost fluids. When I was blown up, my dog tags had been blown off, as had my uniform shirt with the exception of my collar, which showed that I was a U.S. Army infantry captain. My trousers had been shredded and looked like a bloody sieve from all of the shrapnel that had penetrated them. Without the dog tags, my name, religion, and blood type were unknown. Fortunately, when the blood type is unknown, they usually resort to giving O positive blood, which is my blood type. A Roman Catholic chaplain was summoned to give me the Last Rites, since the doctors felt that I would not survive the day. The next stop was at the surgical hospital at Di Anh. Again they were unable to treat my severe head and thoracic wounds, so they too had their Catholic chaplain give me the Last Rites, attached two new bottles of whole blood, and sent me on.

The final stop for the chopper was at the 24th Evacuation Hospital in Long Binh. This was the last resort surgical hospital, where it was hoped they could treat all of my wounds. The chopper delivered me and then left without a trace, literally. There was no record of a medevac helicopter being dispatched to Hoa Da District that day, nor do these choppers usually take the casualties to more than one hospital to seek treatment. This helicopter, which I believe was sent by the Almighty, made the difference between life and death for me.

At the 24th Evacuation Hospital, Captain X, as I was dubbed, was quickly taken into the receiving triage area, where the doctors and nurses were unable to detect any pulse or active signs of respiration. After spending a couple minutes examining me further, they declared me dead, summoned their Catholic chaplain, who in turn administered the Last Rites for a third time that day. They pulled a blanket over my head and upper torso and put my stretcher behind a screen as they prepared the area to receive the next combat casualty who might arrive at any minute. At this point, I again heard the calming voice who said, "Give them a sign that you are still alive. Have faith for I will see you through all of this."

I attempted to call out, but not one word did I utter. The tracheotomy had caused the air I breathed to bypass the vocal cords so I was unable to make any sounds. Realizing my dilemma, I started to thrash around with all my remaining strength, causing the metal IV pole with the glass bottles of whole blood still attached to the tube in my leg to come crashing down on the floor. The loud noise startled one of the nurses. She immediately looked behind the screen, saw me thrashing around, grabbed the nearest doctor, and yelled, "This guy is still alive! Let's get him into surgery and work on him now! There's still a chance we might save him after all!"

I felt them move my stretcher into the operating room, lift me onto the operating table, and begin cutting the remainder of my uniform off. Somewhere in the process, someone gave me the anesthesia that put me out for the rest of that lengthy surgical session. The entire surgical "A Team" worked on my surgical case. This consisted of an anesthesiologist, vascular (thoracic) surgeons, neurosurgeons, an orthopedist, an ENT surgeon, a general surgeon, and an ophthalmologist.

The vascular surgeons first repaired the damaged carotid artery by successfully grafting to the severed section a portion of the largest intact artery harvested from the amputated right leg.

As it turned out, I was only the second patient to survive this new experimental procedure. (This and several similar cases became the basis for all of the vein-graft surgery performed since that time.) They also stitched together the partially severed jugular vein, as well as repairing injuries to several other major blood vessels at various places in my body.

The surgical team next attempted to perform the necessary neurosurgery to clean out and repair the head, sinus, eye, and extensive facial wounds I had sustained. After making an incision from one temple across the top of the forehead just above the hairline to the other temple, opening up my head, they noted that my brain was starting to swell so they quickly closed it up with the intent of trying to repeat the same procedure the following day, if I survived that long. The repairs to my face, neck, and sinuses took a lot longer and ultimately required over one thousand metal wire sutures to reattach and close all of the parts properly. It was generally felt that the sites of the wire sutures would heal much better, leaving fewer scars than the regular catgut sutures.

While this was going on, another doctor was examining my internal wounds and inserting several chest tubes in my right side to drain the blood and excess fluids that had been accumulating in my abdominal cavity since I was wounded. He also cleaned and stitched up the wounds in my genitals, as well as inserting a Foley catheter. An orthopedic surgeon completed the amputation of my right leg and the outer half of my left foot, which would require debridement until any infection was eliminated and a skin graft could be attached. He completed the amputation of two of my fingertips and miraculously reattached the tip of the right ring finger that had been discovered lodged in a hole in my trousers. My thumb-tip miraculously regenerated itself over a period of time. The surgeon cleaned up and removed as much of the foreign bodies that he could detect in the many open wounds throughout my right hand, arm, and entire body.

The surgeons were concerned over other exposed body parts and my oral health. One area was the base of my buttocks, where the flesh and muscle tissue had been totally blown away leaving a couple deep holes extending all the way to the bone and tendons. Another concern was behind my lower left thigh, which had similarly had the flesh and some muscle tissue blown away to the bone, although not as severe as the area in the buttocks. This was fortunate since none of the essential ligaments or tendons had been severed in that area. Both wounded areas would require semi-daily debridement until the muscle tissue and outer flesh could regenerate and cover the bone again. As for my oral health, the surgeons cleaned out all of the broken teeth, bone fragments, and debris lodged in the back of my throat. They decided to postpone the oral surgery for another day until I was a little stronger.

All this surgery required over fifteen hours to perform. I received over a hundred and fifty pints of whole blood during the first forty-eight hours. The surgeons extracted from my body bone fragments; a combination of multi-size metal fragments; broken glass from beer, Coca Cola, and whiskey bottles; rusty razorblades, nails, and wire; pieces of aluminum; blades of grass and other types of green vegetation; small jagged stones; small strips of rubber; several dead insects; and lots of sandy soil. I was hooked up to a ventilator running through my tracheotomy hole and an IV tube in my left arm to which were hooked three bottles of whole blood, dextrose, and another kind of nutrient to help build up my system. Three drainage tubes came out of my chest and abdominal cavity, as well as a drainage tube attached to the stump where my right leg had been amputated. All in all, I was such a mass of bandages, tubes, bags, and leads from several monitoring machines that it was hard to tell there was a living patient under all of this apparatus.

The next morning the neurosurgeon, Dr. Lieutenant Colonel William Hammond, felt that it was essential that they try to perform the head operation again since it was vitally important that they get that area cleaned out and the skull repaired or removed as necessary. This time the brain did not swell and they were successful in cleaning that area out. They found that the covering surrounding the brain had not been seriously penetrated, which added a degree of hope for my ultimate recovery.

Unfortunately the portion of damaged skull in my left forehead had been severely shattered and was removed. This included the portion of the skull that formed the left eye socket. Following that surgery, they routinely gave me high daily dosages of at least two or three different antibiotics intravenously to try to counteract the highly contaminated nature of the weapon. They also gave me the maximum possible daily dosages of the anticonvulsants Phenobarbital and Dylantin in an attempt to keep me quiet and to prevent any seizures, which were a hazard from severe head trauma.

The first two days at the 24th Evacuation Hospital were rough. Three times I had to return to surgery because I had developed severe bleeding. During one of these surgeries they discovered a couple second-degree burns on the lower right side of my back. These burns required semi-daily debridement, followed by saline irrigation and the application of an antibiotic-filled anti-burn ointment that smelled quite bad. Due to the nature, amount, and severity of my wounds, there were generally one or more nurses working on me almost all of the time.

On the morning of the third day, my identity was discovered: Captain X was now listed as Captain William G. Haneke. I went back into surgery for surgical repairs of my jaw, teeth, and mouth. This was performed by Dr. Robert L. Thompson, a renowned oral surgeon, who kept extending his tour in Vietnam because that was where his talents and experience were most needed. He determined that my jaw had been so severely shattered in at least two places that the first preference would be to take a bone graft from another part of the body. In my case, this was not an option due to the large amount of bone lost. The only other option in my case was to try the experimental "bones-in-a-bag technique." This required collecting all of the available jaw bone fragments and splinters together, setting fragments in the approximate shape of the former jaw bone, and covering them with a gauze bag that would eventually disintegrate and be absorbed by the body.

Thompson performed the bones-in-the bag operation, cleaned out the wound sites, closed the surgical site, and wired the jaws closed for an indefinite period to knit the bones together so that they would be strong enough to permit normal activities. If that didn't work then they were fresh out of treatment options. I would most likely be forced to exist on a liquefied diet for the rest of my life. After the oral surgery, I was assigned to the bed closest to the nursing station on Ward 6, the Neurosurgical Intensive Care Unit.

Early the fourth day I regained consciousness. I immediately was aware of an excruciating level of pain, the likes of which I had never even dreamed was possible. The pain radiated throughout my entire body. I heard several people walk past me and speak to one another using some medical terminology that I did not understand. Several times I tried to speak to them, but was unable to make any sounds no matter how hard I tried.

I next tried to move my arms and hands so that I could wave to them and get their attention. After all, I had a lot of questions about what had happened to me; where I was; whether or not I was even alive; how long it would be before I would recover well enough to rejoin my advisory team; could I contact my wife and family; and a hundred other questions. When I was unsuccessful at trying to wave, I tried to relax and begin taking a mental inventory of my body. Both of my legs felt intact and really hurt. The right leg burned badly and felt as if someone were sticking an ice pick in at least a dozen places. Although I could feel all of the parts of both legs, I was unable to move either one. I was unaware that my right leg had been amputated and would later learn that when a limb has experienced a traumatic amputation, the nerves still try to send the message of what they last felt to the brain—in my case it was extreme pain as the leg was being torn apart and blown off. This feeling is called "phantom" or "ghost pains."

I next concentrated on my mid-section and detected severe burning and sharp pain throughout my groin, buttocks, and hip areas. This intense pain extended deep inside my groin and abdomen. My chest, back, and stomach were extremely sore; it felt as if I had been badly beaten and was now one solid, nasty, and very sore bruise that made it hurt to even breathe. I knew I had no option there, so I moved onto my head and neck. Both pounded with a sharp pain so severe that I could hardly concentrate, yet I had no feeling in my mouth, jaw, forehead, or ears. I became aware of the fact that I was unable to see anything and then realized that there were bandages covering both of my eyes.

My mental inventory finally reached my arms. My right arm and hand felt as if they were one massive, raw, and painful sore that had been covered tightly with a piece of burlap. I was unable to move them even the slightest bit. My left arm felt the best of any part of my body. Other than a sharp ache on the outside of my lower arm where the IV needle was inserted, there didn't seem to be any pain at all. I felt that this would be my best body part to try to move first. Concentrating with all my might, I succeeded at moving my fingers slightly one at a time. Next I lifted my hand a little at the wrist, raising and lowering it about an inch. No luck: my arm seemed to be tied to my bed. My mental inventory had revealed that I was in terrible shape and that probably every nerve ending was experiencing maximum severe pain.

I continued to hear voices nearby, but was unable to signal or communicate in any way. I concluded that I had died and was now in Hell. Where else would one be subjected to such an extreme level of pain and not be able to communicate with anyone else? I just couldn't figure out what I had done in my short life that was so bad that I would end up going to Hell for eternity. Maybe serving in war and killing the enemy was a mortal sin after all. But what about all of the stories in the Bible about David, Samson, and others killing the enemies and then being rewarded by God instead of being sent to Hell? What about the calming voice, which I assumed was the voice of Jesus, telling me to have faith for he would see me through all of this? These and a dozen other questions came swirling out of the painful fog that gripped my brain. This all led to an extreme level of frustration that I had no way to resolve and caused me to just let go and start to cry.

I remember feeling the tears stream down the right side of my face, accompanied by an intense burning around the left eye, caused by the salty tears coming in contact with the open gashes in the area. At that point, I heard a male voice ask if I were finally awake. I tried to speak in response, but only managed to make my lips move a little. I felt him poke something into my throat, and he said, "Go ahead and speak now if you are awake."

I was surprised when I was able to speak in a quiet, raspy voice. I told this man that I was awake and wondered if I was still alive or had gone to Hell. He chuckled a little and said that although I had been very badly wounded, I had survived and was still very much alive. I asked where I was, and he replied that I was a patient at the 24th Evacuation Hospital in Long Binh, which was the main surgical center in all of South Vietnam. I then asked him what ward I was on and if he could tell me how bad the wounds were. He said that I was in neurosurgery and that he was only a corpsman and would have to get the head nurse on this ward, Captain Mary Lou Knable, to tell me about my medical condition. Neurosurgery—that confirmed that I had sustained a bad head injury. My head continued to be my Achilles heel: as a young child I fell out of the moving car in Wyoming; six weeks later, on the beach in Port Huron, Michigan, I was hit hard over the head with a steel shovel. This time I knew that it would be a lot more serious. The corpsman said that he had to retrieve some medical supplies and would be back in a few minutes.

Shortly thereafter, I heard a female and a male talking quietly and intently just out of earshot. I was aware that someone had walked up to the side of my bed and was apparently checking my IV line and attached monitors. I again tried to talk but only experienced the rush of air through my tracheotomy tube, although this time it made a slight whistling noise.

I felt someone put their finger over my tracheotomy tube and a nice female voice introduced herself as Knable, the ward head nurse. She said that the corpsman had told her that I had some questions. I said that was true. She asked who I was. I replied that I was Captain William Haneke from Advisory Team Thirty-Seven in Binh Thuan Province. Knable indicated that they had just found that out earlier, but she wanted to hear it from me if possible. She said that I had been brought to the 24th Evacuation Hospital because of the severity of my wounds, especially my head. Most of their patients normally came from units in both the III Corps and IV Corps areas. I told her that my compound was in the II Corps area. I asked her if she would describe my wounds for me.

Knable hesitated a moment and then said that I was a patient on the Neurosurgery Intensive Care Unit and was attached to a couple of monitors, as well as an intravenous feeding tube system. These were helping to replace my lost fluids and monitor my vital signs. She went on to say that from my injuries, it appeared that I had experienced severe blast-induced trauma, probably from a land mine. At that point, I heard a male voice and was told that it was Dr. George Lavenson, the vascular surgeon. He was part of the team that had operated on me. I asked that he explain my condition in layman terms and to be completely honest.

Lavenson said, "Hello," and then proceeded to slowly and plainly describe the extent of my injuries and the surgeries that had already been performed. He started with describing the severed carotid artery and jugular vein then gave a lengthy assessment and treatment for my other injuries. At this point Lavenson paused and asked me how I was doing and if I understood what he was telling me. I told him that I was doing my best to take it all in, but it sounded as if I were very lucky to be alive after suffering these severe wounds. I was very sorry to lose a leg. The right leg was the best one to lose since the surgeons had badly messed that knee up after I had injured it in Ranger School.

I wondered if there was enough of a stump left to be fitted with an artificial leg. He responded that my stump was a little over thirteen inches long, plenty long to be comfortably fitted with a prosthetic leg. When the grafting healed completely, Lavenson assured me that I would be a good candidate for prosthesis and a specialized shoe for my half foot.

I asked Lavenson how long I was expected to be in the hospital for all of my surgery, recovery, and rehabilitation. He paused for a couple minutes, told Knable that he had promised to give me honest answers, and then replied that it would take at least a year or longer to go through all of the rehabilitation process. I sighed and quietly said that I would not be able to rejoin my unit. He said that my assumption was correct and that as soon as they were able to stabilize me, I would be sent along to the U.S. Army Hospital at Camp Drake, Japan, for further treatment, and then back to the United States to a military hospital near my family.

I thanked Lavenson for his explanation and candor. He said that he was very encouraged by how alert and perceptive I was after being so severely wounded. He ended by telling me that if I needed to talk to him further about anything concerning my condition and care, he would try to come over and talk to me.

Lavenson seemed like a very compassionate man. I hoped that he would be able to adequately treat me with all of my problems. I was just very thankful to God that I was still alive and seemed to still have my mental faculties. After I was able to think about it a bit, I was very grateful that I was on the Neurosurgery Ward and not the Psychiatric Ward. I figured that with a set of severe head injuries, I would have my work cut out for me to prove that I was mentally competent to participate in decisions being made concerning my course of treatment and rehabilitation.

I heard a machine being wheeled over to my bedside. Knable told me that she would now have to suction out my tracheotomy tube. It was beginning to fill up with mucus and would soon cause me problems breathing. I heard the suction machine being turned on and soon felt the suction tube being inserted in the tracheotomy tube. The loud gurgling noise told me that the mucus was being removed. I actually felt my breathing get easier as she finished. She told me that this suctioning would be a regular, semi-daily action that would have to be performed as long as I continued to have a tracheotomy tube. This was just one of those inconveniences that I would have to learn to adjust to and live with during my recovery period. All this information totally exhausted me and caused me to lapse into a very deep sleep.

Two sets of hands woke me. They propped me up on my right side and took the dressings off of the area around my left buttocks and upper left thigh. Somehow they could tell that I was awake; the lady told me that she was Lieutenant Cathie Henderson, a nurse who worked on the neurosurgery ward. I was able to nod a little to indicate that I understood. She explained that she and the corpsman were in the process of cleaning my wounds to remove any dead tissue, which I soon discovered meant cutting away with surgical scissors until they hit live tissue. Henderson was very gentle and apologized for any pain or discomfort that she would be causing me.

After this cutting was completed, they put several towels under my leg and buttocks then rinsed that area thoroughly with normal saline solution. Finally they used a long Q-tip swab to apply an antibiotic ointment to these open wounds before applying new dressing. Next they took the dressings off of my burns and said that these were healing well enough that they would no longer require care. This pleased me. I was making good progress in my healing and this gave me initial comfort and hope that I would have a chance eventually to get healed and rehabilitated.

Dr. Donald Brief, the general surgeon, walked up as Henderson was finishing. He told me that he would be removing the extensive packing in my nasal and sinus cavities to evaluate how I was doing. It took a while as he slowly and gingerly removed all of the gauze packing that had been wedged into the cavities that used to be my frontal sinuses.

As the last part came out of the right side, I could suddenly sense a very salty taste, and he immediately requested that the nurse bring a surgical tray, extensive packing materials, a cauterizing instrument, a flashlight, a bottle of sterile normal saline solution, and more towels. He yelled "Stat!"

When they responded with all of the requested implements, he took a long forceps from the surgical tray and reached into my right nostril and grasped something deep in the area where my former frontal sinuses were located. Brief requested that the corpsman change the angle of the flashlight slightly. He retracted the forceps holding onto a small piece of shrapnel that he dropped with a metallic "clink" in the surgical tray. Next he inserted a piece of gauze to absorb some blood then examined the area further and noted that he saw two more small pieces of shrapnel. Again he reinserted the forceps into my nasal cavity to remove the particles, depositing them into the surgical tray to join the first one.

Brief commented that from what he had seen, I was just riddled with shrapnel from the weapon. He was sure that there was probably more in that area, but he was unable to see it at this time. After thoroughly irrigating the area with the saline, he cauterized the area and inserted a swab coated with antibiotic ointment. Slowly and carefully he repacked the entire nasal cavity with the sterile packing material. Brief gave Henderson some instructions on how to carefully check on my status then left the ward.

Henderson came back to my bed and, taking the index finger on my left hand, showed me how to speak by covering the trachea hole. I asked her if my family had been notified of my injuries and where I was located. She said that to the best of her knowledge, the Department of the Army had sent representatives to both my wife in Scarsdale, New York, and to my parents in Richmond, Virginia, to let them know the details of the attack and my current condition. In addition my father would receive a daily telegram from the commander of the 24th Evacuation Hospital updating the details of my status. The vice chief of staff of the army, General Bruce Palmer, who was a West Point classmate of my father, requested this.

It became apparent to me that the more I slept, the less pain I would experience, and the faster I would be able to heal from all of my wounds. I found comfort knowing that I was receiving the best possible treatment and care from a team of dedicated medical professionals. I thanked the nurse for her help and slipped off into a semi-coma.

A procession of casualties was continually being brought to the 24th Evacuation Hospital seeking treatment. The doctors, nurses, and corpsmen put in long hours working on very difficult cases with insufficient staff, space, and medical supplies. They provided the finest available surgical and medical services to both American and Vietnamese military, civilian personnel, and Third Country National Forces (Australians, New Zealanders, Koreans, Canadians, Filipinos, Thais, Cambodian mercenaries, Laotian mercenaries, and diplomats from a host of allied countries). These staff members worked very hard and, I suspected, played just as hard during their limited free time trying to forget about all of the extreme trauma and death they were forced to deal with daily.

On one occasion, I remember hearing Lieutenant Henderson discuss the fancy yellow dress she was planning to wear to a tropical theme party. There was also some discussion about decorating the mess hall and holding a memorial service during the upcoming Thanksgiving period. These days were not referred to as "holidays" in Vietnam since combat operations generally don't take any time off unless a meaningful joint truce had been agreed upon. In spite of their off-duty activities, these staff members were never absent or impaired when their assigned shifts came around. They knew that their services were badly needed and without them a large number of their patients would not have a chance of survival. A number of the staff spent their off-duty time volunteering and helping at a local orphanage or nearby leprosarium. This was a testament to their professionalism and dedication to mankind. They were the true "A Team."

CHAPTER 23

Visitors

When I was awakened some hours later, Captain Knable was again on duty, and there was a flurry of activity nearby on the ward. I could hear several female voices shouting in the sing-song Vietnamese dialect that I actually partially understood. They were shouting that they did not speak English and couldn't understand what the nurses were trying to do to their son/husband. I took that to mean that one of the voices belonged to the mother of the patient in question and the other belonged to his wife. That would be consistent with the normal Vietnamese custom of the entire family staying in the hospital at the bedside of a family member when they were undergoing treatment as an inpatient.

I caught Knable's attention. I told her that I spoke some Vietnamese and French and would try to translate and calm these family members down if possible. She almost begged me to try since they were extremely agitated and creating a problem. After some urging, Knable was able to convince the Vietnamese patient's wife to come over to my bedside. I greeted her and told her that I was an advisor to the Vietnamese and would try to translate so that she and her family could understand what kind of treatment was being given to her husband. Since my voice was very weak, she initially had trouble hearing me. The Vietnamese woman loudly told the rest of her family members that I spoke good Vietnamese and to be quiet so that she could hear what I was trying to tell her.

Proudly, she told me that her husband was a member of the elite Special Forces-trained Civilian Irregular Defense Group Force in the camp at Dak To. I responded that I too had been trained by the Special Forces, which seemed to please her. She said that her husband had been badly wounded in the head during an ambush four days before and that his mother, father, their oldest daughter, and she had come to this hospital on a Vietnamese helicopter. Now they were very concerned about her husband's treatment. Almost as an afterthought, she mentioned that the family had no place to stay in Long Binh except here with her husband. They had no money or anything to trade for food. I repeated all of this in English for Knable. She immediately instructed one of the corpsmen to go find their equivalent of a hospital social worker or civic affairs officer. I asked the woman when they had eaten last, and she replied that it had been at least three days since they had food. Again I translated this for Knable.

The civic affairs officer who dealt with the Vietnamese patients and their family members appeared. Knable told him that these people had not eaten in three days, had no money for food, and had no place to stay in Long Binh since they were from Dak To. The civic affairs officer said that he would be able to take them to the mess hall for a meal and would then try to come up with a solution to handle their lodging, bathing, meals, and cleaning of their clothing while they remained at the 24th Evacuation Hospital.

I translated this into Vietnamese to the wife, who in turn informed her family members. She asked me how they were treating her husband and said that she only wanted him to get better and not die. I relayed this to Knable, who replied that one of the bullets struck the husband's head. It hit the right front of his skull and bounced off without penetrating the bone, leaving a superficial wound. The other bullet had slightly penetrated the skull removing the right eye. The doctors had removed the bullet. Knable said that they were now trying to remove the bandages to rinse out the wound. She reiterated that the medical staff was only trying to help him recover so that he could go home with his family. I slowly translated all of this, and it seemed to calm the family members down a lot and the wife kept thanking me for my help.

The family was obviously very stressed out by being unable to communicate and find help for their personal needs. I suggested to Knable that if they were going to routinely treat Vietnamese patients in this hospital they needed to make provisions for a reliable interpreter to be available at all times. She agreed and said that the hospital administrator had just been authorized to hire a couple interpreters to serve around the clock. They would hopefully be on site in the very near future.

I asked the civic affairs officer if he was ready to take the family to eat. He replied that he was, and I explained to the Vietnamese wife that this officer was now going to take them to the mess hall to eat. She reminded me that they were unable to pay for their meals. I told her that this officer would take care of that for them. The proud Vietnamese people, as a rule, did not like to accept charity if they can avoid it. I explained their pride to the officer and he said that it was part of his job. He then thanked me for helping to defuse this very tense situation.

When the family left, I asked Knable if there were any other Vietnamese patients on the ward. She replied that there were currently two who were unconscious, each with very severe head and abdominal wounds. I asked if their family members were with them. She said they had been here for the better part of two weeks but had returned to their home villages since there was nothing more that could be done for either of their patients.

I asked Captain Knable how many beds were on the ward and was told it was a double ward for neurosurgical patients—Wards Five and Six—with Ward Six serving as the intensive care unit with ten beds normally and the capacity for two more should incoming casualties necessitate, as had been the case during the

Tet Offensive. Ward Five served as the neurosurgical step-down unit for the less severe cases.

I heard very little conversation on the unit, other than the medical staff and the Vietnamese family. I wondered if there were any other patients and if any of them were conscious. Knable said that there were actually two other American patients on the ward. One was a whole different category of patient. Although I was told he gave signs of being fully conscious, the doctors assured the staff that he did not comprehend anything that was going on around him. I asked her to tell me more about his situation. She said that this American had been leading a Vietcong assault force against an American Military Police outpost near Saigon that had killed four of the ten Americans. He was shot twice in the head. The .45-caliber bullets had penetrated the lining of the brain, but the bullets could not be removed without killing him. He spent his time in the back corner of the ward, his head propped up in his bed, with at least one American MP with him at all times. I questioned if the MP was to keep him from escaping.

Knable emphatically replied, "No, it's to keep the hospital staff from finishing him off since he's so hated for what he did to those American soldiers." She believed that he was alert because she said his eyes followed anybody who passed by his bed. When he was stabilized, he would be transferred to the POW ward at the 93rd Evacuation Hospital, located at the other end of the 24th Evacuation Hospital. Knable said that she could not wait for this to happen since she lived in fear that someone would "bump him off."

I asked if the 93rd Evacuation Hospital was part of the military stockade that was referred to as the Long Binh Jail, or LBJ Prison. Knable said that yes, it was. This stockade was reserved for the worst Americans throughout Southeast Asia. She had not heard of any other Americans that had gone over to the Vietcong or North Vietnamese Army to fight against their own people. I told her briefly about the incident at the Hoa Da District Compound—how we gunned down the two Americans with the

Vietcong before they gained access to our compound and how the intelligence people tried to keep this incident secret. These guys didn't live to make it to LBJ Prison so they were part of the secret statistics the intelligence community was keeping on Vietnam. Knable expressed her disbelief that a fellow American could turn on his own country.

Knable sighed and informed me that there was an unconscious American patient in the bed next to mine. She said that it was so strange to look at him and realize that there was nothing wrong with him at all. He had no visible marks and looked so perfect in comparison to those of us who bore such severe wounds. His injury was a small wound at the base of his skull where a sniper had shot him. Knable sighed and thanked me again for all my help and said that she had several patients on Ward 5 to whom she needed to attend.

My injuries were all starting to throb and ache at once, particularly my head, so I mentally withdrew to my special place where my tropical paradise was absolutely beautiful. By doing this self-hypnosis, I was able to effectively wall off my pain and fall off to sleep. It was crude but effective and helped me to avoid asking the nurses for a lot of painkillers. I was deathly afraid of becoming addicted to these painkillers, since I knew that my treatment and recovery were going to extend over a long period of time.

The next time I awoke, I became aware that there were several people at my bedside tending to my wounds. I recognized Knable's voice, but also heard two male voices that were new to me. I stirred and said hello to Knable, and she asked me how I was feeling. I replied that other than hurting all over, I wasn't doing half bad. She asked how my head was feeling. I told her that it was a lot better than when I had gone to sleep. She told me that Lavenson and the neurosurgeon, Hammond, were here and were examining me after the emergency surgery that I had undergone a few hours ago.

Knable asked the doctors to tell me about what they had done during the surgery. Lavenson explained that I had passed out and the monitors had displayed a flat-line. The staff felt that they had invested too much time and effort in my case already to sit back and watch me die, so they wheeled me back into surgery, and X-rays revealed that several larger metal fragments were in the area of the jugular vein, causing an interruption of normal blood flow. Several pieces of bone and other types of matter detected around the injury in my skull were also removed, the procedure requiring the infusion of several more pints of whole blood. Now everything appeared to be working normally again.

Hammond added this shrapnel might have caused my massive headaches. He said that, in all likelihood, my head should feel better. Then he asked me several questions: my name and rank; what service I was in; what country I was in; where I had been stationed; where I was at the moment; the reason for my being at the 24th Evacuation Hospital; was I married; what was my wife's name; what were my parents' names; did I have any children; how old was I; was I a college graduate and, if so, and what college did I attend. I recognized this as an informal evaluation of my mental status. Apparently I answered all of his questions correctly and to his satisfaction. I heard him step away from my bed and talk a little while longer to Lavenson and Knable before leaving the ward. It was comforting to know that I had survived my third neurosurgical procedure without losing my mind. I only wondered how many more of these emergency procedures I would need to keep me alive.

Knable came back to my bed and checked my IV. Suddenly I felt the need for a cigarette and asked her to get me one. She paused and laughed a little, telling me that I was around a lot of bottled oxygen and would set the ward on fire. She asked how much I normally smoked. I told her three packs of cigarettes a day. Knable sighed. There was nothing she could offer. I would have to quit cold turkey. In effect, I would be going through yet another type of withdrawal.

I sensed that someone else had been standing by my bed during my exchange with the doctors. I asked Knable if there was anyone else there. She replied that the Catholic chaplain, Father Pat Flynn, had been standing here praying for me.

I said "Hi" to Father Flynn and asked how he knew about my problems and me. He said that he was mainly assigned to the Long Binh Jail and their 93rd Evacuation Hospital but also came over to the 24th Evacuation Hospital on occasion since he was currently the only Catholic chaplain assigned to the area. He had first learned about me a couple of days before when the ward personnel first summoned him to come and give me the Last Rites because they thought I was slipping away. I asked if that was on the day I was first flown into the hospital. He said that it actually was a couple days later, following some of my very intense surgery. I had apparently required a lot more treatment and surgery than the doctors and nurses had explained.

Flynn went on to explain that over the next few days after that occasion, he had come by the ward to see me and to pray for the other patients and me. He paused for a minute and said that his experiences at LBJ Prison had been extremely discouraging and upsetting since he was dealing mainly with men who were not at all religious and who openly lashed out at clergy, even if they were trying to help them and bring them some comfort. Things had gotten so bad for him that he was beginning to take active steps to resign from the priesthood and the chaplaincy.

Flynn paused and softly asked if I remembered talking to him before this. I had no recollection. He said that he had engaged in several long talks, during which I provided wisdom helping him recommit to his faith in Jesus and the priesthood. I confessed that I believed Jesus had spoken to me several times when I was wounded. The calming voice, which I believed was Jesus, told me to "Have faith for I will see you through all of this." At that moment a revelation filled my soul. I believed that Jesus was speaking through me to have a favorable influence on others like him. I felt truly blessed and honored that Jesus would choose me to help others in need.

There was a moment of silence before a choked-up Father Flynn spoke. He replied that whether it was Jesus or me, the words that I spoke had a profound and positive impact on him, since he had actually been contemplating committing suicide. He was now rejuvenated in his faith. Flynn then placed his hand on my shoulder, said a short prayer, and left the ward. This encounter warmed me, even though I felt unworthy. God's special attention humbled me.

Later that day Chaplain Bert Carmichael, a Methodist minister, came by and thanked me for my comments as it provided him insight. Surprised that we had met before, I asked Carmichael how many times he had visited me. He replied that this would be the fifth time. On two of those occasions, I had been asleep, so he only stayed a short time and said a few prayers. Even though my recognition was a blur, I appreciated his prayers. It was my belief that the more voices raised to God in prayer on one's behalf, the better the chances that they will be heard and acted upon. Carmichael agreed, but God also knew whether or not your prayer was sincere and came from the heart. He believed that God heard even the smallest sincere prayers.

I admitted that this was true, as I had discovered immediately after my short prayer when I found myself hanging on the barbed-wire fence. Carmichael asked me to explain. I told him about the calming voice that had talked to me several times after I was wounded and each time ended with the words, "Have faith for I will see you through all of this." He paused a moment then said that this was truly the voice of Jesus. Henderson interrupted our conversation and stated it was rest time. Carmichael squeezed my left hand reassuringly as he walked away.

When I awoke, an ophthalmologist had come to examine my eyes. He removed the packing from my missing left eye; irrigated the area with normal saline solution; applied antibiotic ointment throughout the eye cavity with a sterile swab; then inserted something into my eye cavity. It felt strange but didn't hurt. He had inserted a custom-made conformer. This would remain until I was fitted with a permanent artificial eye. Its purpose was to hold the eye socket in its present configuration.

The ophthalmologist examined the remaining right eye and asked if I could see anything. I was able to see a little light around the left edge of my eye. He said that during the blast, several small metal fragments had passed all the way through the eye. It had caused extensive bleeding in the center of the eye, a region he called the "vitreous humor." Dense blood particles floated throughout the vitreous humor, blocking my vision. He would be unable to remove the blood, but over time there was a good chance that the eye would absorb the majority of it. His real concern was the status of the retina of the right eye. The blood in the vitreous humor was so thick that he was unable to see through it to make a proper assessment of the retina's condition. This was the kind of injury that only time and prayer would be able to cure

Some of the ophthalmologist's report was encouraging, but the enormity of the whole scenario was just too overwhelming to fully grasp at the moment. Before I nodded off to sleep, I decided to concentrate on the positive aspects of my case, handle the situation only one day at a time, and not look too far ahead. I felt that this approach would help keep me from getting too discouraged.

Later I awoke and became aware that someone was at my bedside examining my groin area. I asked if it was Knable or Henderson and was told, "No, it's Dr. Rohner, the urologist." He was going to take the stitches out of my groin, testicles, and penis. This procedure might be a little uncomfortable but would feel better when he was finished. The urologist wasn't lying: I experienced a series of sharp pains followed by a deep burning sensation. He finally announced that he had completed irrigating the area with saline. I heard him check the urine collection bag and comment to the nurse that my urine appeared nice and clear but still had a slight tinge of old blood. He said that they would continue to keep an eye on it a while longer.

As Dr. Rohner was leaving, I heard Dr. George Lavenson. He was here to check on the healing of the surgical sites for the graft on my carotid artery and the repair of my jugular vein. While removing the dressings on both sides of my neck, he remarked at how well these sites seemed to be healing. This was a pleasant surprise.

Lavenson looked at three other sites, including the stump where I had lost my right leg. He said I was in critical condition when they first saw me, but the presence of the severed leg gave them an intact blood vessel to use for this graft. Lavenson prayed that the graft would heal completely since there were few options available in my case. He ascertained that the repair of the blood vessels had progressed well enough to remove the stitches from all but the carotid artery. The stitches in that arterial graft would have to remain a little longer to guarantee a full recovery. I thanked Lavenson for the miracle procedure that literally saved my life. I drifted off, hoping for no more visitors.

CHAPTER 24

The Purple Heart

I awoke to hear another visitor, but this one had a familiar voice. It was my sister, Captain Margaret Anne Haneke, a U.S. Army WAC officer, who had just arrived from her duty station in Tokyo, Japan. I became aware that she was standing next to my bed and talking to Captain Knable, who was giving her a short briefing on my case and current status. I listened intently for a few minutes and learned several new facts about my treatment. I had been declared dead at least five times within the first thirty-six hours of my arrival at the hospital. Knable admitted that I was a real fighter and they had learned not to count me out.

Tears seeped under my bandaged eyes; with my voice quivering, I welcomed Margaret to Vietnam. She gently raised and kissed my left hand, saying that she was afraid to touch me anywhere else for fear of hurting me. I guessed that looking at my unshaven face adorned with all of the metal sutures and dressings didn't give her a whole lot of uninjured space from which to choose. She admitted that I had been hard to recognize. Margaret chuckled and replied that from what she had heard, I almost met my match with these wounds. I told her that infantry soldiers were tougher than that.

I agreed and asked her how she got here. She had arranged to get compassionate family travel orders since she was stationed fairly close to this region and my wife and parents were unable to come all the way from the States. Margaret had volunteered several times to get assigned to Vietnam, even if it was on a temporary duty basis. Not having been successful in her efforts, she now found a way to justify her visit and could legitimately claim to have been on orders to Vietnam.

I asked Margaret how she and our family were getting information on my condition and treatments. She said that after the initial notification from the Casualty Notification Detail, they had been receiving daily cablegrams from the administrator of the 24th Evacuation Hospital. Margaret added that a family friend, Major General Roderick (Rod) Wetherill, who was serving as commanding general of Defense Intelligence for MACV, had come every other day to check on my status. He had phoned my father with a medical report, which provided my father an opportunity to get answers to specific questions. I was unaware that Wetherill was in Vietnam or had come to see me.

Margaret talked to me for a little while and then suddenly she was silent. I became aware of several other people coming up to my bed. After a couple of minutes, I heard the wife of the Vietnamese soldier, for whom I had translated a couple days earlier, greet me very softly as *Dai Uy* (Captain) Hero, which was an expression of extreme respect. I greeted her in return and asked how her husband was doing. She said that he was much better, and would be able to return home after some more treatment and rest.

The Vietnamese woman patted me on my left hand and thanked me for all of my help and kindness. The American officer had arranged for their meals and two bedrooms. She commented that she would never pay me enough. I did not expect any payment since I was only helping out a fellow soldier and his family who were having difficulties at that moment. I asked that she and her family show the same kindness to somebody else in need—in that way they could repay my kindness. Again she patted my hand, thanking me again and again, and told me that I was very wise for somebody so young.

The Purple Heart

My sister asked me what that was all about. I explained what had happened with the Vietnamese patient and his family. I was just happy to have been a part of helping them out at a difficult time. Margaret expressed that my intervention was sweet; then, lowering her voice, she said that the American soldier with the MP was really starting to give her the creeps. Knable had told her a little bit about him and why he was being guarded.

Margaret stated that, in her opinion, he did not belong on the same ward as the allied troops who had been wounded in combat fighting for our side and were virtual heroes compared to that traitor. Since she first came onto the ward, he had been following her every move with his eyes and appeared to be quite alert in spite of what the doctors and nurses said about him. Coincidently, Knable came over and announced that she had just received the authorization to have the traitor moved to a bed in the 93rd Evacuation Hospital POW ward first thing in the morning. She sounded very relieved and was not sorry to see him leave. Margaret and I agreed.

After Margaret's visit, I began to experience incredibly sharp and rapid pains in my lower right leg. I had to remind myself that the leg was no longer there. It felt as if somebody had an ice pick and was stabbing me hard and often in the area of my calf, ankle, and foot. Knable must have seen that I was having a problem and came over to me. She explained that these were phantom pains caused by the nerve endings that were severed by the explosion. Weather changes, use of my stump muscles, or bumping the stump may cause flare-ups. Phantom pains would decrease as I healed. Unfortunately this type of pain would be a part of my life, and I had to find a way to live with it. I asked if there was any way to make them stop. Knable sorrowfully told me, "Not really, other than by taking a strong painkiller each time." She asked if I wanted a pain shot now. I refused, since I was trying to avoid all painkillers and the danger of becoming addicted. I would try to retreat to my private tropical island where I could forget about my wounds and the pain.

The next morning, I heard a commotion as a number of new voices gathered around my bed. The hospital commander said that we were all being honored with a visit by the famous comedian Joey Bishop and his assistant, Regis Philbin. There was a momentary pause, then Joey Bishop spoke up and thanked me for my service in combat. I thanked him for coming to visit the troops in Vietnam. It was important that people in the United States knew and cared about what we were doing in Vietnam.

Bishop asked me where I was from. I told him that my wife was staying with her parents in Scarsdale, New York, and my parents were living in Richmond, Virginia.

Knable pointed out that I was a West Point graduate. Regis, a New York City boy, spoke up and joked that I had been fully adopted by the state of New York after that experience. Joey Bishop interrupted and said they all would be praying for me to get well soon.

About a half hour after the comedians had left, my sister came in. Margaret expressed her disappointment in missing them. She had taken the time to eat breakfast and talk to Dr. Lavenson about my case. Lavenson told her my survival in just getting to the 24th Evacuation Hospital without bleeding to death and then surviving complex surgical procedures was nothing short of a miracle. He had explained about the arterial graft that he and the other vascular surgeon had successfully performed on my severed carotid artery. Margaret said that he spoke of it with great pride.

A little while later Chaplain Carmichael stopped by and was introduced to my sister. He asked how I was doing and I told him that "every day in every way, I am slowly getting better and better." This phrase became my slogan before long, and I even heard several members of the hospital staff repeat it. Carmichael said that it was great to hear my very positive attitude. I assured him that the Vietcong had blown my body apart, but I was not going to allow them to defeat my spirit. If I allowed that to happen, I would be cheating God, my family, my profession, and myself. He said that this was a healthy way to approach my healing process, and said a short prayer asking God's continual healing grace.

Margaret was talking to me about some of my treatments when I suddenly got a very salty taste in my mouth. I motioned her to quickly find the nurse and tell her that I was starting to bleed badly in my sinuses. Henderson ran and grabbed Dr. Brief. After a cursory examination, Brief ordered Henderson to retrieve the usual instruments and supplies. He asked Margaret to wheel over a light stand. He said, "If you stand around here, someone will put you to work since we're always short staffed."

Margaret brought it over and quickly plugged it in for him. In the meantime, Brief had removed all of the packing from both of my nostrils and open sinus cavity. By this time, Henderson had returned with the needed equipment, instruments, and medical supplies. With a set of long forceps, Brief began probing into my nasal cavity, causing pain. He asked Henderson to apply some gauze then rinse the area with normal saline while he continued to probe. After another minute that seemed like an hour, he announced that he had extracted two pieces of glass, one about the size of a dime and the other about half that size. Brief explained that these had probably been missed during the initial surgery because they were clear glass and hard to distinguish next to the surrounding tissue. He had Henderson rinse the area again and dab it with gauze as he looked further and discovered a few more bone fragments. After he cauterized the area, Henderson gently repacked my sinus cavity and nostrils again. My throat felt very raw from all of the blood drainage, while my head and sinuses pounded so badly that it felt as if a jackhammer were beating against them. I retreated to my little tropical island refuge to try to escape the intense pain.

The next morning Knable awakened me by changing the IV tubing and entry site in my left arm. By this time, the IV needle had already been inserted in several places on the inner arm near the elbow. Unfortunately each of these sites functioned for only limited periods before they shut down and blocked any further passage of fluids. She explained that this time she would try a vein on the back of the left hand near the index finger. Knable warned me that it would be a lot more painful to insert the needle at this location, but this vein site would last a lot longer. She didn't lie about the intense pain, which was tempered only slightly by the knowledge that these life-saving fluids were flowing freely into my body once again.

Knable and a corpsman performed the routine cleaning and cutting of dead tissue from my wounds. No matter how many times this procedure was performed, the intensity of the pain never seemed to decrease in the least. She noted that both drainage sites had been discharge-free for at least forty-eight hours, so it was time to remove the tubes and allow the sites to heal completely. The drainage tube was then removed from the end of my right leg stump, along with the right chest tube. Knable reminded me that I still needed to have a skin graft applied to the end of my leg stump sometime in the near future. I asked her if that would be a very painful process, but she did not answer me directly. Instead she said that the procedure would finally seal the end of my stump so that I could be fitted with a prosthesis and relearn to walk.

Dr. Thompson, the oral surgeon, came by and examined my jaw. He had tightened the wires holding it immobile and told both Knable and me that the site of the mandible or jawbone was less mobile, indicating that good healing was starting to occur. In the middle of Thompson's exam, Margaret returned and met the doctor. He gave her a brief synopsis of my case and outlook for the future, which sounded very serious with limited hope of independent living. When the doctor left, I assured Margaret that I was determined to fight hard to beat all of these negative predictions. She made no comment. I was beginning to notice that my sister was avoiding discussions about my condition, treatment, and potential recovery, which I suspected had become too painful for her. Margaret changed the subject. .She had been meeting with the provost marshal to follow up on an incident that had occurred in the women's billets the night before. There had been a growing number of occurrences where a Peeping

The Purple Heart

Tom had been detected looking in through the upper screened area of the women's barracks. Margaret said that she had seen him at least three times previously so arranged with the military police to set up a trap for him. It apparently worked and they apprehended the "Peeper." I thought about this as I drifted off to sleep again.

When I awoke, Margaret was no longer there, and I heard a lot of activity on the ward near the nurses' station. There were a number of official-sounding voices talking to Knable as she briefed them on my case and condition. I could hear them gathering around my bed. An official-sounding officer said, "Captain William Haneke, General Creighton Abrams, the MACV commander, is here to award you the Purple Heart medal for your wounds received in combat operations." This came as both a surprise and a relief, since I had been continually haunted by doubts about whether my injuries had come from enemy actions or from some stupid mistake caused by either Major Dramis or me. I was pleasantly surprised to hear that the Purple Heart was being presented to me by Abrams, a West Point classmate of my father and the commander of General George Patton's lead unit during World War II that fought its way in to relieve the besieged allied forces in Bastogne during the Battle of the Bulge.

General Abrams came over and said, "Bill, do you remember me?"

I replied, "Yes, sir. You are now the MACV commander, and were a West Point classmate of my father. We last saw each other in the spring of 1966 when you and several other army commanders were conducting a military seminar for the First Class Cadets at West Point."

The general, sounding surprised, said, "That's right. Your memory is very good in spite of the wounds you've suffered." Abrams said that he was very proud of my service as an advisor and was even prouder to be the one to present me with the Purple Heart. He informed me that I would be awarded other combat decorations later. I was extremely honored to be receiving this award from him and was very sorry that my injuries would not permit me to rejoin my men at this point. He told me that he, my family, and the American people were grateful for my service, and my main objective now should be to concentrate on my healing and rehabilitation. I thanked Abrams for honoring me with his visit. He asked me to give his best wishes to my father and family. Knable and the hospital commander thanked Abrams for coming to see me. They told him that this visit and presentation would do me a world of good and encourage me to continue working hard on my recovery. Abrams thanked the 24th Evacuation Hospital staff for their dedicated and professional service and encouraged them to keep up the good work.

About twenty minutes later, Margaret returned from eating lunch and said that she had encountered Abrams as he and his men were heading toward their return flight to MACV Headquarters in Saigon. Abrams told my sister that he had just awarded me my Purple Heart medal. Margaret complained about her bad luck at missing such important visitors. I suggested that she might ask the members of the nursing staff if they knew of any scheduled visitors before she left for her meals. We both laughed.

On November 21, the young, perfect-looking soldier with the bad head wound had a severe seizure and quietly passed away. That same day Margaret had been helping a quadriplegic soldier by writing a letter to his girlfriend. While she was doing that, a nurse informed soldier that he had a phone call from home. The nurse positioned the phone and braced it so that he could easily use it. Margaret and the nurse left his bed area to give him some privacy. After a few minutes, the phone fell to the floor and the man sobbed hysterically. Two nurses calmed him. The soldier tearfully told them that his family, including his girlfriend, said he shouldn't bother coming home, but instead find a nice veterans hospital where he would spend the rest of his life. My sister, the nurses, and the man all wept. How insensitive could this family be to a man who had served his country in combat, survived his wounds, and was now living mainly to see his family and home?

This news was like a dagger in the heart of all of us who had been severely wounded. We were immediately haunted by questions about how we would be accepted or rejected and treated by our families, wives, and friends when they saw how badly disfigured and disabled we had become. What options would we have if our families turned away from us?

There was always a lot of activity and commotion on the ward. I soon learned to ignore it all and sleep most of the time. Margaret came and stayed nearby, mainly during daylight and early evening hours. The members of the nursing staff put her to work. My sister retrieved equipment, instruments, and supplies; she also emptied patient bedpans and urinal bottles, a chore that she really, really hated to do.

On the Saturday before Thanksgiving, it was decided that my condition had been sufficiently stabilized to allow me to be safely transported to the 249th General Hospital at Camp Drake north of Tokyo. This was one of several military medical centers being utilized to render further medical treatment and services to critically ill soldiers. As I considered this next chapter of my life, I reflected: the Purple Road with its $20,000 reward for my life had earned me the Purple Heart medal. I wondered what hurdles still had to be crossed and what God ultimately had in store for my family and me.

CHAPTER 25
Japan

Sunday, November 23, 1968, the day of my departure from South Vietnam, started very early as the ward staff organized and packed up my medical records, X-rays, medications, medical supplies, and personal belongings. Margaret had come to the ward to help with the process. She would accompany me on the trip as far as Japan, where she would return to her duty station at Camp Zama as I underwent additional treatment at the Army 249th General Hospital at Camp Drake, north of Tokyo. Dr. Lavenson would be traveling along to watch over and render necessary medical treatment. I had previously detected that there might be a mild attraction between Lavenson and my sister, so this might have further stimulated his professional interest in the success of my vein graft.

Knable injected my usual three antibiotics into the IV port. At this point, I was still only able to get nourishment through my IV tube. I had taken no food or beverages by mouth because my jaws were wired shut. My weight had dropped from 175 pounds to 75 pounds. Several members of the hospital staff stopped by to pay their respects and to wish me well with my further treatment and rehabilitation. This overwhelmed me. My sister and I expressed our sincere thanks and appreciation to the staff of the 24th Evacuation Hospital for saving my life and their dedicated care.

About midmorning, I felt four men gently pick me up and move me onto the padded stretcher on top of the gurney. As they did that, a couple nurses helped to guide the IV tubing, the catheter apparatus, and the blood pressure monitor. After I was properly situated, someone carefully spread a sheet over me since I was still unable to wear pajamas or any other clothing with my open wounds and wire sutures. A nurse placed a folded blanket in the space where my right leg would have been, saying that this would prove useful later when the temperature cooled during our flight. My head and pillow were gently lifted as someone else inserted my medical records and X-ray folder under the mattress beneath my head. Just before I was wheeled out, Henderson came over and applied a coating of medicated ointment to my entire face and neck to provide a protective layer over the metal sutures. Both she and Knable patted me on the left shoulder and wished me the best.

My gurney rumbled through the cool hospital. Suddenly, we were assaulted by the extreme tropical heat and humidity. Lavenson checked my IV and told Margaret and me that we would not be going to the Bien Hoa Airfield after all. Instead, we would be catching a helicopter that would take us to Tan Son Nhut Airbase in Saigon to be put on a larger U.S. Air Force plane, a C-141 Starlifter, which had extensive medical equipment. This change in flight caused me to squirm. Lavenson asked me if I was all right. I told him about my recurring nightmare in which the departing Vietnam flight would be forced down, and I was to be captured and very slowly and painfully tortured to death. Lavenson assured me that this was all in my imagination and the direct result of the trauma I had suffered in combat. I differed; I felt that these dreams appeared too real and vivid to be simply a figment of my imagination. They were more like a premonition of coming events. Lavenson and Margaret both tried to calm me down. I took a deep breath and said that I was anxious to get the heck out of Vietnam. The ramp was raised and the chopper engines soon cranked up for the thirty-minute flight to Tan Son Nhut. I was praying hard throughout the entire flight asking

Japan

God to let us make it safely to our destination. It was a great relief when we landed.

We had an hour wait before I heard two new voices saying it was time for us to get on the plane. I felt two men, probably orderlies, pick up my stretcher and carry me across the portion of runway to the plane's rear ramp. The orderlies commented on how light I was compared to most of the patients they usually carried. Lavenson informed them about my combat wounds. He added that I was conscious and able to fully understand what they said. They both then thanked me for my service in Vietnam and promised a safe trip to Japan.

Lavenson and Margaret sat down in the seats immediately next to my stretcher. Margaret heard the now familiar gurgle of my partially-blocked tracheotomy tube. She asked the nurse for a sterile suction bulb and a towel. The nurse quickly produced these items and Margaret knelt down to perform this task. I was very thankful to be able to breathe easier afterward. As she was finishing, a patient sitting across from us asked who was so special as to rate a doctor and a nurse traveling with them for their personal care. Without hesitating, Lavenson replied that this was a very critically wounded infantry soldier who would not survive the trip without the extra medical care. Lavenson then asked what was wrong with him. He sheepishly replied that he had pulled his back lifting sandbags at a camp near Saigon. Nothing more was heard from the man during the flight.

I was glad that Dr. Lavenson and Margaret were traveling with me, but this was clearly not the way that I had originally envisioned my departure from Vietnam. Of course, this was better than being carried in a body bag. We waited as a number of other stretcher-bound patients were carried up the ramp and placed in their assigned rungs as directed by the head flight nurse. When everyone was settled, the head nurse welcomed us all on this medical evacuation flight out of Vietnam. That elicited a number of weak cheers from several of the patients. The nurse stated that we would be landing first in Tokyo, where a number of patients would be offloaded for two hospitals there.

The rest would continue on to the United States. Soon I heard the sound of the rear ramp being raised followed by each of the four jet engines being started up, as well as the air conditioning system coming on. The sudden blast of cool air was a welcome change from the sauna-like temperature outside.

This was the first time I had flown on a C-141. I was amazed at how quiet the engines were in comparison to the other air force jet transport planes. When we were off the ground, the pilot announced that we were on route to Japan. A few more cheers went up. Twenty minutes into our flight, the pilot announced that there was a slight change in plans and the plane would be turning around to make a stop at Cam Ranh Bay to pick up some additional patients. A loud, audible groan went up from most of the patients.

This really alarmed me, as I felt that my recurring nightmare would come true. I was powerless and now convinced that fate was continuing to work against me. I was not destined to make it home alive. I prayed for God's mercy and protection. Again I heard the calm voice telling me to relax and have faith that He would see us safely to our destinations without allowing any enemy interference. I knew then that this was the voice of Jesus and was confident that we had His protection.

The plane touched down safely and very smoothly. The engines were shut down and the rear ramp lowered. Those of us on the plane hoped that this loading would not take too long since the oppressive heat was making it hard to breathe. I heard the footsteps of the men carrying the stretchers coming up the ramp of the plane. After twenty minutes a whine came from the ramp being closed. We were told that our flight would be the first off the runway since we had been classified as a "priority cargo."

As we taxied, I thought about the incredible and unspoiled white sand beaches all around the inlets and South China Sea side of this long, tropical peninsula. Few of these beaches were ever used and many were inhabited only by the native creatures like the sandy-colored apes. I remembered the incredibly clear light blue water. You could see down almost a hundred feet and enjoy the colorful coral formations and the numerous tropical fish with all of their vibrant colors. In a time of peace, these beaches would clearly qualify as some of the most beautiful in the world. With these, I would retain at least a few pleasant and beautiful memories of this very hostile region.

The plane paused briefly at the end of the runway as its engines were fully revved-up, and finally we were airborne again headed out over the South China Sea. The pilot informed us that we had encountered no other diversions and our next stop would be Tokyo. That announcement was accompanied by more cheering from the passengers. Most of us still found it hard to comprehend that we were finally leaving the combat zone.

The temperature on the plane had really cooled down fifteen minutes into our flight. I was beginning to shiver a bit, so Lavenson extracted the blanket and covered me completely with both the sheet and blanket. The added warmth felt wonderful and stopped my shaking. I soon drifted off to sleep on this very smooth and quiet flight. I dreamed of walking with my wife on the beaches of Hawaii. Hawaii was the place where we had scheduled to meet for my R&R leave in about four weeks, had I not been wounded. In my dreams, I could allow this pleasant scenario to happen with no interruptions.

I don't know how long I had been sleeping when I heard the pilot announce that the plane had just crossed the "point of no return"—the point at which there was a shorter distance to your final destination than where you'd left. Immediately everyone raised their voices in a loud and enthusiastic cheer. We had finally broken away from Vietnam. Lavenson checked my IV, my temperature, and blood pressure, then turned down the covers and checked my dressings. He called for the flight nurse to assist him in removing a large dressing around the base of my left buttocks.

By the time the nurse arrived, Lavenson and Margaret had propped me on my side and removed the blood-soaked dressings. The nurse handed Margaret a flashlight and asked her to shine it on the site. Lavenson took the forceps and probed the area where he was able to detect the source of the bleeding. He must have noticed that Margaret was getting very queasy, because he told her to relax as this was a fairly routine process and looked a lot worse than it really was. After a couple minutes of probing, he detected two small metal fragments. I felt him pull the first piece out that I judged was about the size of a pencil eraser. He reached back in again but was unsuccessful in pulling out the second piece. Using another instrument out of the tray, Lavenson was able to extract a very jagged piece of metal about two inches long and an inch wide from the wound site. The site was irrigated with saline-soaked gauze pads, followed by several swabs of a strong disinfecting and cauterizing agent. Lavenson put a small amount of sterile packing into the wound site and then covered the whole area with a multi-layered sterile dressing. He again asked how I was doing. I replied that I was much better now that he was finished. Before I drifted off to sleep, I heard another patient across the aisle comment to another one that I had really been "shot up bad." He could now understand why I needed a doctor to accompany me on this trip.

I was awakened again as several of the other patients were saying that we had landed at Tachikawa Air Force Base in Tokyo. Two hospital attendants informed me that they were going to carry my stretcher into the Air Evacuation Office of the 249th General Hospital. Inside the hospital, Lavenson tried to locate the doctor in charge. It took him over a half hour to locate the appropriate physician. Finally the doctor and an administrator appeared and announced that they would admit me since my condition would take longer. Lavenson spoke up, saying that my trip from Vietnam had been very stressful and he would be checking me over again. The local doctor replied that this would be useful. If he needed any supplies, he could walk across the hall to the emergency room and requisition them. This didn't sound as if we were getting off to a very good start.

Lavenson left and returned a little while later with a number of dressings, sterile towels and swabs, a bottle of normal saline, and some medicated ointment. He closed the door to the office to block the strong draft then pulled the covers off me to inspect my wound sites. After removing several of the dressings, he said he was pleased to see no more bleeding. He put me back in a more comfortable position and pulled my covers back up. Shortly thereafter the doctor and administrator came over and asked Lavenson to give them a brief summary. After a few minutes of his presentation, the other doctor cut him off and said that they were very short staffed in the hospital at present. He would not have the time to listen to a lengthy discourse. Lavenson countered that it was very important that someone hear all of the details.

    The doctor then pulled down my covers, looked me over for a few minutes, but did not touch me or really examine me. I heard him very hurriedly leaf through my medical records, note the stack of X-rays, and say that the documentation in my chart would be good enough for the ward staff on the neuropsychiatric ward since they did not have a neurosurgery unit at this time. Lavenson and my sister both said that although I was very weak and didn't communicate a lot, I was mentally competent and didn't need to be on a psychiatric ward. The doctor replied that due to my head injuries this was where I would receive the proper care. He added that I certainly would not be the only patient on the psychiatric ward with head wounds. After a little more discussion, it was apparent that neither Lavenson nor Margaret were going to change my ward assignment, so they thanked the doctor and administrator and asked that they see that I got good care. Before I was wheeled away, I thanked Lavenson for saving my life, and Margaret for coming to Vietnam. I asked her if she would be able to come visit me occasionally. She said that she would be happy to visit, but it probably wouldn't be until Tuesday or Wednesday night since she had a lot of catch-up work. We gave each other our love.

    I heard a buzzer sound and the door opening to the psychiatric ward. The attendants wheeled me over to the nursing station and gave my medical records and X-rays to the nurse-in-charge. She thumbed through them for a couple minutes and ordered the attendants to put me in bed number five. The nurse asked me what had hit me. I told her it was a command-detonated mine covered with human excrement. She commented that the Vietcong had done a number on me and welcomed me back from Vietnam. The nurse noted that I required some cleaning after my trip and informed me that I would be staying at the 249th General Hospital until my condition stabilized enough for safe travel to the closest military medical center to my home.

The nurse left my bedside and about fifteen minutes later returned with a cart that she told me contained some towels, a washcloth, soap, and a basin of warm water. She pulled down the sheet and began gently washing around the areas on my face, head, and neck where the metal sutures were still in place. The nurse noted that these areas seemed to be healing nicely. She said the whiskers from my beard were starting to grow long and were entangling with these sutures in a number of places and that she would leave a request on my chart for one of the corpsmen to shave me in the morning. When the nurse had finished bathing me, she mentioned that the doctors would probably get me off of the IV and try another method of feeding starting tomorrow. I would not be a good candidate for a nasal-gastric tube because of my frontal sinuses being blown away. The nurse commented that I was going to be a real challenge to treat with all of my maladies. I agreed.

It had now been eleven days since I had been wounded, but it felt more like an eternity with all of the pain and problems. I just prayed that the doctors could find some way to feed me. The thought of "real" food sounded appealing. The nurse recommended that I get a good night's rest, because the doctors would be in the first thing in the morning and would examine me thoroughly and decide my course of treatment.

The next morning, I was rudely awakened by somebody poking me hard repeatedly in my right arm and side and yelling to the nurse that I had snuck in during the night and had taken Ralph's bed away from him. I could hear someone running over and leading the agitated man away, explaining that Ralph had left yesterday to fly home to the States, and I had been brought in from Vietnam and assigned to this bed yesterday evening. This corpsman told him not to touch me again since I was very seriously wounded. The corpsman then came back to my bed, apologized for the man, and asked if I was all right. I told him that although the hard poking had hurt, I didn't think that he had touched any of the wounds or caused any serious problems.

The corpsman welcomed me to the neuropsychiatric ward and explained that the majority of the patients were suffering from varying degrees of battle fatigue. Some were very heavily medicated and not at all mobile, while others had varying degrees of freedom depending on their mental and emotional status. He said that the patients were a mixture of officers and enlisted personnel from all branches of the military and that there were no patients that would qualify for the forensic unit. This was a bit reassuring. The corpsman said that I needed to be aware that there would be times when some of these patients would act up a bit. Some would go on crying jags while others would shout out a series of orders, and then there would be those loudly fighting against imaginary enemy soldiers. I listened intently as the corpsman described some of the patients on the ward.

Almost every night at exactly midnight, one patient would turn into "Captain Midnight, the Infantry Commander." Captain Midnight barked a series of orders to the imaginary men he was leading into combat. This would continue for about fifteen minutes then he would assume his foxhole position amid the stacked-up pillows on his bed. He would remain there, silently on alert, for the rest of the night and sleep by day. He had held a supply military occupational specialty. It was not known if he had ever experienced a night attack or had even been on the front lines.

Another patient was a Navy Seabee, the corpsman explained, who spent the better part of each day drawing up building plans then rearranging his bedside table and chair in an attempt to carry them out. He had been severely traumatized when his unit was overrun and was now unable to speak. A helicopter pilot had experienced two choppers in a row being shot out from under him losing all of the men and crew members onboard. He blamed himself for each of these incidents even though it was not his fault. This pilot would lie in bed sobbing uncontrollably for hours each day. Two infantrymen had sustained direct head wounds from AK-47 bullets and were both now living vegetables.

The corpsman sighed and said that there was a senior master sergeant with twenty-seven years of army service who had been serving with the 101st Airborne Division at a base camp somewhere in the II Corps area. He had experienced the North Vietnamese Army overrunning his unit and camp three times in a two-week period. He had witnessed many of his men being blown up by sappers or annihilated in hand-to-hand combat with the enemy. In spite of his experience, he had never seen anything as violent. His mind shut down, rendering him a mental vegetable lying in a fetal position, mumbling and rocking back and forth all day.

After hearing all these horror stories, I asked the corpsman if I had been assigned to the right ward, since I had a lot of physical wounds while the other patients all had mental and emotional wounds. He said that this was the proper unit for me due to my severe head trauma, and I would receive adequate treatment while here for my other wounds as well. The corpsman had a very gentle and reassuring way of talking that immediately put me at ease in spite of the perceived problems surrounding me.

He said that the head nurse had instructed him to shave me before the doctors arrived for their "grand rounds." I asked what that term meant. Several times each week doctors from other services would accompany the neurological doctors as they visited and reevaluated each patient on their ward. He commented that they would probably spend considerable time with me since I had a lot of medical problems and was new to the hospital.

A few minutes later the corpsman returned, telling me that he had brought a basin of hot water, a straight razor, shaving cream, and several clean towels. He explained how he was going to try to shave very carefully around all of the metal sutures. Even though this presented quite a challenge, he had over twenty years experience as a corpsman and had shaved many men with very difficult conditions. I told him that I would be very cooperative.

First he applied a hot towel on my face and neck, which felt wonderful. This, he said, helped the whiskers to stand up better. He next applied a light coating of shaving cream on the whiskers, then took the sharpened straight razor and began shaving around where my right sideburn should have been. He carefully navigated around several sets of wire sutures, stopping frequently to ask if he was hurting me. So far he was only hurting me a little, but I knew that this task had to be done so he should continue on and complete the job. The whole process took about an hour. Some areas hurt, while I felt absolutely no sensation in others.

After he had finished, he applied another warm towel to my face and gently wiped off any remaining shaving cream, extremely careful not to get the towel hung up on any of the wire sutures. The corpsman examined his handiwork and said that it was now easier to see my face and distinguish the wounds. He told me that there were several areas of scar tissue now on my face where no whiskers were able to grow. I thanked him for taking the time to help me with this difficult task. He laughed and said, "That's why I'm paid the big bucks on this ward."

A little while later, I heard a number of male voices coming from the area of the nursing station. They were speaking in medical terminology about several of the patients in the ward. This apparently was the group of physicians beginning their "grand rounds." They visited the beds by order of their number beginning with bed one. It was decided that the patients in beds two and three had progressed as far as possible and were now ordered to be sent back to the States. The patient in bed four was very reactive; I heard him trying to get under his bed to avoid them. With some coaxing from the head nurse, they apparently were finally able to get him to sit on his bed and let one of the doctors examine him. It was decided that they were beginning to make some progress in his case, but he should remain here a while longer.

The doctors finally gathered around my bed. The head nurse pulled down my sheet to expose my wounds and said that I had just arrived from the 24th Evacuation Hospital in Vietnam the evening before. She gave them a short summary of my wounds and treatment to this point. One of the doctors commented that they sure didn't bring much of me back and probably left some of my best parts on the battlefield. The nurse cautioned him that I was conscious and comprehended everything that was being said. His response was, "Do you think I give a shit about that on this nut ward?" These words cut like a knife into my spirit. I could not believe that someone, especially a doctor, could be so insensitive.

The doctors asked the nurse to remove all of my dressings so that they could determine the extent of my injuries. She quickly complied with their request and not only removed the dressings from my leg, foot, and buttocks, but also from my head, neck, and eye. I could feel the hands of a number of different doctors as they turned me to get a better view of my various injuries. One doctor commented that it was a real miracle that I was alive and that I was facing a very long period of treatment, recovery, and rehabilitation. The other doctors quickly agreed with him.

After a few minutes of examination and quiet consultation, one doctor spoke up and informed the nurse that the grand rounds were finished. He ordered her to remove the IV apparatus and see that I was given nourishment by mouth through a straw from now on. I had lost a lot of weight and needed proper nutrition to gain back weight. The doctor explained that utilizing the IV approach would only keep a patient from losing any more weight and would not allow him to start using the stomach, digestive, and intestinal organs. This all made good sense.

Before the doctor left, he asked the nurse to schedule a daily visit from physical therapy so that they could begin exercising my leg, arms, and hands to keep them stretched and limber to prevent atrophy. I asked the doctor a question about the status of my infections and his plan for continuing the antibiotics to treat them, but he ignored me and moved on to the next bed. In their rush to get to the next patient, the doctors left me lying there nude, cold, and uncovered with no thought about my inability to cover myself. I tried without success to get somebody's attention to help me pull up my covers. I could feel part of the sheet touching my lower calf near the ankle, but I was unable to sit up and grab the sheet. Again I tried calling out several times but got no response.

During the exam process, the urine retention bag attached to my Foley catheter had apparently been knocked loose from its holder on my bed and had fallen onto the floor still attached via the tube. As I was lying there trying to think of a way to get someone's attention, one of the doctors left the group and came hurrying past my bed. As he passed by, his foot got tangled in the tube to my catheter. There was a sudden violent jerk to my penis and groin area accompanied by a terrible searing pain and severe nausea; I saw stars. I felt that I was about to pass out as the catheter with its inflated bulb was jerked out of my bladder and penis. I immediately doubled up with pain and was aware that I was bleeding out of the end of my penis.

The doctor gasped and yelled loudly for help. Immediately the pounding of footsteps came running over to the scene. The first people to arrive seemed to have trouble comprehending what had happened, while the doctor who had caused the incident was momentarily in shock and unable to explain exactly what he had done. Finally he explained what had occurred and I felt several people pack some towels around my penis to catch the blood. The urologist in the grand rounds group took charge of the treatment of this new and very painful injury.

Somebody brought a gurney to my bedside and I was quickly lifted onto it. They then wheeled me to a nearby treatment room to evaluate and treat the accidental injury. Somebody pressed down on the area of my lower abdomen and groin and then somebody else inserted some kind of a hard tube into my penis and slowly ran it up to the area of my bladder then withdrew it. During that process, I mercifully lost consciousness and came to after they had completed this process and inserted a new catheter and whatever else they did to resolve the injury.

The urologist later informed me that the internal catheter bulb had slightly torn the lining of my urethra in a couple places, but the bleeding had mostly stopped by the time he had inserted the tube to examine me internally. He decided to insert another Foley catheter to allow the urine to be drained from my body through the catheter tube instead of coming out of the urethra and touching the injured lining, causing me severe pain and direct exposure to the highly alkaline urine. He put me on another antibiotic that would directly target and help quickly heal the injury. The urologist urged me to let the nurses or a doctor know if the levels of pain or pressure in my abdomen or groin worsened.

I was wheeled back and placed in my bed as the doctors who had been treating me left the ward. They tried to figure out how such an unfortunate accident could have happened and how it could be prevented in the future. I heard one doctor express his feelings about how I had been here less than twenty-four hours and had sustained a hospital-related injury that had caused me to be in worse shape than when I had arrived. He wondered how much longer I would be able to survive this kind of care. I never did find out who the doctor was who tripped on my catheter tubing, but I can assure you that I would never forget the incident; it caused me to achieve an all-new level of pain.

A while later, the head nurse and one of her assistants came to my bed and began the process of cleaning my open wounds. She was a lot rougher with this process than the nurses at the 24th Evacuation Hospital. She cut deeper into the live flesh with her scissors as she took away the dead flesh and applied the medicated ointment. If I could have screamed, I would have been heard all over that end of the hospital. Several times I asked her to be gentler with this process, and each time she told me that from her training, this was the only way to do it properly. All I could think was that she must have received her training in the torture chambers of the Middle Ages. When she finally finished, she told me that she would be removing my wire sutures first thing the next morning. I was afraid to find out how much pain she could inflict while performing this task.

I was just getting comfortable again when an overly cheerful lady with a Japanese accent came to my bedside. She announced that she was from the physical therapy department, and she was here to evaluate me and to help set up an exercise program for my leg, arms, and hands. After what I had already been through that day, I would rather have been left alone. But I figured that I should begin this next phase of my recovery, so I reluctantly agreed. She seemed to speak good English, but after she had pulled down my covers and examined me, she quickly lapsed into Japanese as she rapidly talked to herself while trying to move my arms, my left hand, and finally my remaining leg.

Finally she told me in English that I was very badly messed up, and it was hard to know where to start. She had never been asked to treat anybody this severely wounded. I suggested that it would probably be best to take one limb at a time for her evaluation. She agreed that this would help her not to become overwhelmed with my case and treatment. The physical therapist took her time gently lifting and moving my limbs and hands while humming a sweet Japanese song. During this process, she would stop periodically, particularly if I winced. If I mentioned that she was hurting me, she became very apologetic. It was clear that she really wanted to help and not hurt me.

The physical therapist had been treating me for about forty-five minutes when her supervisor, a Japanese man, came in and started scolding her quietly in Japanese. The two exchanged stern comments for several minutes then I heard the man leave. She politely apologized to me. The therapist's supervisor wanted her to hurry up and spend no more than thirty minutes with each of her assigned patients. She said that she had pointed to all of my injuries, telling him that this was a very complex initial evaluation, and asked if he could use good professional judgment in spending only thirty minutes with me. He finally replied that he could not, but then asked her not to waste any time with this case. By this time, I was exhausted and in a lot of pain so I went into my self-hypnosis routine, retreated to my beautiful South Seas island, and was soon asleep.

Another lady whose accent told me she, too, was Japanese woke me. She introduced herself as a dietitian. She was going to figure out a way to feed me with a liquid diet. She noted that my nostrils and sinuses were fully packed and my jaws were firmly wired together. Opening my mouth with her fingers, she discovered one missing lower tooth on the right side. It left a gap not filled with the material that had been inserted between the other teeth and gums when I was wired together. She asked me if I could suck liquid through a straw if she were to insert one into the gap. I told her that I didn't know but was certainly willing to give it a try.

The dietician asked what kind of liquids I liked best. I replied, "Milkshakes and apple juice." Pleased with my answer, she returned with a container of apple juice. She inserted the straw into the gap and asked me to close my lips and try to suck. I did as she instructed and was able to suck the cool liquid into my mouth. At first it felt great, but then I had a problem swallowing it.

I heard the head nurse come over. She calmly told me that I needed to concentrate on swallowing the liquid and not to choke, gag, or throw-up if at all possible. She reminded me that my jaws were wired together and if any of these things that she mentioned actually happened to me, someone would have to take the pair of scissors that were taped to the wall by my bed and cut my wires. This would ensure that I could partially open my mouth wider, allowing the liquid to drain out and prevent me from choking to death. Of course this would mean an oral surgeon would have to rewire the jaws. This gave me something extra to worry about that I had been totally oblivious about before, but it also motivated me to keep from vomiting. I retrained my mouth and throat and discovered that each swallow of juice was easier.

The dietitian then gave me a milk shake. After a couple sips, I felt nauseated and asked her what I was drinking. She said that I was drinking a chocolate milk shake with some high nutrients added to build up my system. I told her that I could tell that my stomach was not going to tolerate these high nutrients, whatever they were, and asked if she could get me a plain chocolate or strawberry milk shake. She said that she would, but didn't think that these additives were really the cause of my feelings of nausea. A few minutes later, the dietitian returned and gave me a plain strawberry milk shake. It tasted fantastic! I was able to drink the entire thing without getting sick to my stomach. The nurse directed the dietitian to prepare my future meals without any of the high nutrients.

After I finished drinking my first meal, the nurse gave me a cup of some nasty-tasting mouthwash. She told me to take it in, swish it around, and then drain it into a basin that she would be holding next to me. I did this with some difficulty since I was unable to move my mouth enough to swish the liquid around, so I twisted my head from side to side. Expelling it was no problem. The nurse explained that it would be important for me to do that at least twice a day from now on to keep my teeth from decaying.

I fell into a very fitful sleep and had several bad dreams. I dreamt about being under attack in hand-to-hand combat with the Vietcong, who were trying to attack my compound and that I was not able to stand up or use one of my arms. I finally woke up covered in sweat and heard the sounds of the infamous "Captain Midnight" issuing orders loudly in several parts of the ward. Someone gently talked to him as he led him back to his bed. At first it didn't sound as if Captain Midnight was going to give up without a fight, but eventually things quieted down and the good "Captain" returned to his bed where he spent the rest of the night in silence.

I tried to relax and go back to sleep but noted that my stomach and urinary tract areas were both burning and aching intensely from the aftermath of the catheter being pulled out. The night nurse came to my bed and began the debridement of my open wounds. I noted that she was a lot gentler than the day nurse. I thanked her for being gentle after I had experienced a bad day and the roughness of the day nurse. The night nurse scoffed and referred to her as "Captain Do-It-By-The-Book." She felt sorry for the patients because this nurse wouldn't know how to be gentle or compassionate even if her life depended on it. I asked what position "Captain Do-It-By-The-Book" held, and she replied that she was the acting head nurse for this ward until the replacement major would arrive sometime in early December. I replied, "God help us all until that time." The nurse said, "Amen to that."

The night nurse read my chart about the catheter incident and was very sorry for the painful experience. She examined me for a couple minutes and said that she saw no signs of blood or discharge, which was a good sign. I described my discomfort and she said the pain would disappear in the next two to three days. The nurse made a note on my chart to check for signs of problems or lack of healing from the catheter incident. She then left to treat the other patients.

The sound of a rolling cart and banging of pans of water jolted me awake. At each bed the corpsman tried briefly to wake the patient by telling him it was time to "wake up and wash up" before our breakfast was delivered. When the corpsman stopped at my bed, he said someone else would bathe me. About forty-five minutes later another corpsman came to my bed loudly complaining that he didn't have time for this with all his other assigned duties. He yanked the covers off me and plunged the washcloth into the cool pan of water. Roughly he scrubbed my arms, armpits, and chest area. After a couple minutes of this chilling wash, I complained that he was really hurting me. His response was, "All you crazies on this unit don't deserve any better."

Realizing that his treatment was not going to get any better, I asked him to stop and do his other assigned tasks. The corpsman immediately threw the washcloth back into the pan with such force that some of it splashed all over me, stating that that would serve as my rinse job. He then threw the towel so that it partially draped my groin area and stump then angrily stomped off to do something else. This splash of cold water caused me to shiver all over.

I lay exposed and uncovered for almost a half hour until the day nurse, Captain Do-It-By-The Book, noticed me shivering.

Japan

She immediately covered me up and loudly demanded that one of the nearby corpsmen tell her who had been assigned to bathe me. He responded that it had been one of the corpsmen from the ward across the hall because of staffing shortages on the psychiatric ward.

Captain Do-It-By-The-Book asked me how I was treated. I told her what had happened. As soon as she was sure that I was thoroughly covered, she told the corpsman to keep an eye on me, because she was going to the next ward to take care of the visiting corpsman. She returned to the ward a few minutes later announcing that she had "fixed his little red wagon" so that he would never again treat another patient the way he had treated me regardless of the ward. I was tempted to ask what she had done to him, but thought better of the idea. I just kept silent with the knowledge that Captain Do-It-By-The-Book had taken the appropriate action to protect her patients.

Later that morning, I heard a cart wheel up to my bed. Captain Do-It-By-The-Book asked a corpsman to wash his hands thoroughly and come over to help her remove my wire sutures. I told her that I was praying for her and hoped that all would go well. She thanked me and said that she could always use the Almighty's extra help and guidance, particularly in a very complex case like mine.

Fortunately the corpsman had shaved off most of my whiskers the day before, which made the task a lot easier and less painful. The nurse began by spreading what she told me were a couple of sterilized towels. She opened a sterilized suture removal kit that she said contained a collection basin, several sets of forceps, scalpel, small wire cutters, and a couple surgical probes. Next, she gently swabbed my entire face and neck with a sterile solution and began snipping the wire sutures over my jugular vein. I must confess that I was extremely nervous. I prayed that all of the wounds had healed sufficiently so that there would be no problem with bleeding when the sutures were removed. I felt her use the forceps to pull the wire away from the skin. I heard the distinct *snip* of her cutting away a part of this suture line. She then gently pulled the freed suture out of my neck and dropped it in the basin with a metallic *clink*. Proudly she announced that there was one site successfully handled and many more to go. Her assurance encouraged me. This time she was actually trying to be as gentle as possible. I guess she understood this sensitive procedure.

As Captain Do-It-By-The-Book finished, the corpsman dabbed an alcohol swab on the site of the former suture line to again sterilize the area. She then proceeded to the site of the carotid artery. I heard another male voice, which turned out to be the vascular surgeon. He had come over to help supervise the handling of this important site. The two of them then proceeded to work very slowly and carefully to remove all of these sutures. I was thankful that I didn't hear any gasps or indications that the arterial graft had not taken or was causing any concerns. The surgeon commented that Dr. Lavenson had done an inspired job, and he hoped that Lavenson would publish something about his work after the mess in Vietnam was over. He said that he had never seen or heard of anything like this before and also agreed that without this successful graft, I would not have had any chance of survival. The nurse thanked the surgeon for his help.

The process of removing the sutures continued around the rest of my face, neck, upper right arm, and shoulder. During this lengthy period of time, I had partially retreated again into my little peaceful and pain-free tropical island cocoon in hopes of avoiding the pain involved with this procedure as well as any bad news. Captain Do-It-By-The-Book squeezed my left arm and told me she was finished. She was extremely happy with the way all of my suture sites had turned out and asked if I wanted to save any of the wire sutures. I shook my head and told her that I was very glad to finally be rid of them. She chuckled and said that it was surprising what some combat vets try to hang on to as souvenirs of their wounds. I told her that I would like to save any metal fragments, other than sutures, and of course my Purple Heart. Captain Do-It-By-The-Book agreed.

CHAPTER 26
The Scheme

Some time later, I heard a male voice address me as "Bill" and say a couple things about our cadet company at West Point. I knew that the voice sounded very familiar, but I couldn't immediately place it. He then said that he was Bob from "good old F-1," who had really enjoyed being a part of my wedding party. Suddenly I remembered that he was First Lieutenant Robert (Bob) D. Murrill, Jr., class of 1967, who had been in a room next to mine in Company F-1 during my senior year and had served as an usher in my wedding party.

I asked Bob what he was doing here and how he had found out that I was a patient at the 249th General Hospital. Bob said that he had suffered several wounds to his right arm and shoulder in combat several weeks ago and was at the 249th General for follow-up surgery, recovery, and rehabilitation. He expected to rejoin his unit in Vietnam sometime before Christmas. Bob had heard rumors about a West Pointer from the class of 1966 being admitted to this hospital two days ago. He discovered my name on the hospital's patient list and asked to get special clearance to come visit me.

I thanked Bob for making the special effort. I assured him I was assigned to this unit only because of my head wounds and not because I was a "psycho." Bob understood. He had heard that I had been serving as an advisor in Vietnam but didn't know where. I recanted my story starting up a new district advisory team in II Corps, which had finally started progressing well during the last month—and then I got blown up by a command-detonated mine on November 13. Bob expressed his regrets.

I explained my wounds and injuries to Bob, the surgeries and treatment at the 24th Evacuation Hospital, and being transferred to Japan for additional treatment before my final recovery at Walter Reed Army Medical Center. I quietly confessed that I was afraid that the severity of my wounds would lead to my retirement from the army. I was not prepared to give up without a fight. Bob asked if Mary had been told about my wounds. It was my understanding that she had been notified initially. She was being supplied with a daily cablegram and also phone calls to my parents from Weatherill. Bob said that he would try to call her. I thanked him and asked that he cushion his description of my condition so that I didn't sound hopeless.

I mentioned that my sister Margaret was a WAC officer stationed at Camp Zama here in Japan, and that she should be visiting later this evening. Bob hoped he would run into her since he was housed on the orthopedic ward just down the hall. Bob stated that he would try to visit me periodically over the next couple weeks. I replied that that would be great and asked if he were married yet. Chuckling, he said no since he had been concentrating on his army career before getting serious about any one young lady. He added that this didn't prevent him from enjoying the favors of a number of very attractive women.

While we were talking, apparently several doctors had walked over to my bed. They asked Bob to leave the ward for a few minutes. The doctors identified themselves as orthopedic surgeons and said they would be evaluating me. They stripped off all of my dressings and talked among themselves as if I was not even there. This worried me. Their conversation led me to believe that my left leg was in very poor condition with its open wounds and might well have to be amputated above the knee. Another surgeon commented that, in his opinion, my right arm and shoulder looked pretty bad as well and should have shown better signs of healing by this time. It looked like a piece of raw, rotten hamburger and had to "come off." As they appeared to be finishing up the exam, I asked for their evaluation and projected treatment. They told me that they would be conferring later that afternoon and would let me know in the morning when they finished their scheduled surgery. I heard them leave the ward, still discussing my case.

Bob returned and whispered that from what he had heard, the orthopedic surgeons were planning to do some butchering on me. He said they were the same surgeons who had performed minor surgery on his wounds. I asked if they were all experienced and board-certified in their field. He laughed derisively and said that none of these "young docs" were board-certified or very experienced; they were all either doing their internship or residency right after graduating from medical school. He believed they were just barely doctors, having little or no experience.

Alarm bells started going off as I realized I may have another limb or limbs amputated. I asked Bob if he had signed a form giving approval prior to his surgery. He said that he had signed. This gave me hope that no one would be operating on me unless I gave permission to do so. Somehow I would have to verify that further surgery on either my left leg or right arm was not necessary. I wasn't exactly sure how I was going to arrange for this, but I began praying silently and intently asking for God's help and guidance in keeping my remaining limbs.

I talked to Bob at length about my concerns about the surgeons' intentions and the strong possibility that they might try to amputate my other leg and right arm. I could think of myself as an amputee missing a single limb, but would have difficulties facing life as a multiple-limb amputee. Bob didn't think the doctors would amputate any further limbs without my permission unless it was necessary to save my life. He added that he would be happy to help me out in any way possible in my potential showdown with the doctors.

Suddenly Bob stopped talking and listened closely. He said that I had developed a serious gurgle in my breathing. I told him that a nurse would have to suction my tracheotomy tube followed by rest. Bob called one of the nurses. I asked him to stop by that evening so that he could meet Margaret, and we could all discuss several courses of action to block further amputations. He agreed wholeheartedly.

The friendly night nurse had just come on duty and came over to help me. Expertly she suctioned all of the mucus build-up from my tracheotomy and asked if I was able to breathe any easier. She noted that all of my wound dressings had been removed and asked if I knew why this had happened. I explained that earlier this afternoon, several orthopedic surgeons had come by and performed what they called a "thorough evaluation" of my status. The nurse gave an acknowledging moan and began the debridement of my wounds. I asked her if she thought it might be necessary to amputate either my left leg or right arm. The surgeons had stated that there were problems with the healing of these two limbs and that amputation of each would be a strong possibility.

The friendly nurse examined my wounds. In her professional opinion as a former orthopedic nurse, amputation of either of these limbs would not be necessary or desirable in my case. She asked if the doctors had given me a firm evaluation during this exam. I told her no, that they would come by in the morning to give me an evaluation and treatment plan. She whispered that these "orthopods" were not being supervised by any board-certified or experienced orthopedic surgeons. They had a usual modus operandi of operating on all of the "fresh meat," meaning newly arrived casualties. I asked her if I could block their efforts by not signing the surgical release form. After a very noticeable pause, she said softly that this would be true for patients on normal units, but this would not apply to patients on a psychiatric ward since a competency argument could be made. This meant that these new doctors could get away with performing radical surgery without my permission or that of any family member. She confirmed that this was true. I asked if I could be transferred immediately to a non-psychiatric ward. She responded that this

The Scheme

would not be possible because of my severe head injuries. I thanked her for this information, and told her that I was expecting a visit from my sister. I asked that she help her find her way back to my bed as I fell asleep from exhaustion.

Sometime later, I felt someone gently touch my left arm and heard a voice say, "Hi, Billy. How are you feeling?" It was my sister. I expressed my thankfulness for her visit. Slowly I went through the process of describing what had happened to me since I arrived at the 249th General Hospital. When I finished, Margaret seemed incredulous about my predicament, particularly the possibility of the surgeons amputating two more limbs. I asked her to help me get me out of this hospital before any surgery. I mentioned that my usher and fellow West Pointer, Bob Murrill, would also be stopping by to see me this evening. I suggested that between the two of them, maybe they could devise a plan for my departure from this torture chamber. I asked Margaret to give our dad a call and let him know the situation and ask for his advice too.

A few minutes later, I heard Bob's voice as he made his presence known to Margaret and me. My sister updated him about the evaluation and the subsequent conversation with my evening nurse. He agreed that this didn't sound good at all. Margaret told Bob that she was going to call our dad when she left tonight. She asked Bob for his advice. Bob agreed that this was a good idea since our dad's long career and contacts in the military would probably be invaluable. I don't remember much more about that evening since I fell into a deep sleep shortly thereafter. Apparently Margaret and Bob talked for a while about my situation and discussed a couple possible options including asking my father to use some "command emphasis" on getting orders to transfer me out of the 249th before any surgery.

Wednesday morning, the orthopedic surgeons returned to my bed. One of the doctors said that after discussing their evaluation of me, they had decided it was essential that they immediately amputate my left leg around the hip and my right arm around the shoulder. I told them that I had heard my wounds were making good progress, which I felt didn't indicate amputation. One doctor countered that I was wrong and could not make such a decision. I replied that I would not sign a surgical release form. The doctor began laughing derisively. They needed no authorization from the patients on this ward since we were all mentally incompetent. I countered that my competency had never been assessed since I was wounded. He had better check with the main hospital Judge Advocate General (JAG) lawyer before doing any surgery on me or they might well find themselves being tried before a general court-martial, which could put a quick end to their medical careers. I was only bluffing and throwing them a curve ball to gain some more time before the surgery.

I heard the doctors retreat to the other side of the ward to confer before returning to my bed. They agreed to track down the hospital JAG this afternoon to get his opinion, but would definitely schedule my surgery for first thing Friday morning. Another surgeon stated that he was also going to track down the psychiatrists and schedule a competency evaluation. It didn't sound to me as if I was going to receive an unbiased assessment from anyone in this hospital. I had, however, bought another day's delay in this exchange. Thursday was the Thanksgiving holiday for all American personnel at Camp Drake.

Captain Do-It-By-The-Book came over to suction my tracheotomy and perform the debridement. I asked her if the orthopedic surgeons' plans for additional amputations were medically necessary in my case. This was not her decision to make, and the surgeons were within their rights to make this determination. I pointed out that if surgery were to take place then debridement was unnecessary on these limbs. She replied that there was always an outside chance that the amputations would not take place, so she owed it to me to continue to treat my wounds as originally prescribed. She admitted that the wounds were improving and amputation of these limbs were not needed. I thanked her for her candor, and then asked her advice in helping me delay or head off the amputations. I felt absolutely powerless to keep this terrible, unnecessary, life-changing surgery from taking place.

The Scheme

She said that she would think it over. It had become very clear to me that a number of the medical staff members did not approve of these amputations, but they had no say.

That afternoon Bob came to see me again and asked how I was doing. After my conference with the orthopedic surgeons, I was not doing very well. The surgeons had decided to amputate my left leg around the hip and my right arm around the shoulder, but I had raised enough questions about the legalities of their actions to postpone the surgeries until Friday morning. In the meantime, the surgeons were trying to track down the hospital JAG to get his opinion about my rights and get a psychiatrist to perform a competency evaluation. I told Bob that I didn't have any confidence about an outcome in my favor. I guessed that it would end up being a matter of "professional courtesy" between physicians to make sure that their butts were covered in this situation.

Bob was impressed with my quick thinking to stall the surgery and agreed that my prospects sounded very grim. He asked what he could do to help. I told him to give my father a call and ask him to call one of his top rank West Point classmates to see if they could block the surgery and transport me immediately to Walter Reed Army Medical Center. Impress upon my father that if I was left here at the 249th General Hospital any longer, these surgeons were going to carve me up, which would ultimately result in my death. Bob believed that my analysis of this situation was correct and not overstated. He would be glad to help me out. He asked if this would conflict with what my sister was doing. I said that if my father heard this from two credible sources, he would be more inclined to act quickly and decisively. Bob said that he would get back to me tomorrow and went off to phone my father.

That evening Margaret came in to visit me. I told her everything. I told Margaret that the psychiatrist had not shown up yet, and it was my hope that he had already departed on Thanksgiving leave. Margaret gasped at the turn of events. After a pause to gather her thoughts, she said that she had talked to our father the night before, explained about my current situation, and asked for his advice. She said that his daily call from an administrator at the hospital had said nothing about amputating any other limbs. Margaret reiterated the urgency and made known to him that the administrator probably would not get the information until after the two additional limbs had been amputated. My father told Margaret that he would make a few calls.

I thanked Margaret for calling and then recounted my conversation with Bob that afternoon and my request for him to call our father as well. She agreed that this was the right thing, because it would lead our dad to act more quickly. I asked her to please pray for me. She replied that she was already praying and had enlisted the aid of the Camp Zama base chaplain and a number of her friends and coworkers to raise their prayers to God on my behalf. I thanked her. We talked a while longer then Margaret left, saying she would be back to see me on Thanksgiving Day. A short time later I fell into a deep sleep.

Thanksgiving Day, November 28, 1968, came and had a relaxed holiday feel to it, with reduced staffing. I had been awake for a short time when it became apparent that I needed to have my tracheotomy tube suctioned. It felt as if a large glob of stuff was blocking it, allowing little air to pass through. I was finally able to get the attention Captain Do-It-By-The-Book. She detected a large blockage that required the removal of the entire tracheotomy apparatus. After cleaning it out, she retied the tracheotomy tube so that it would stay in place. I softly asked if she had any advice about my pending amputations. She whispered that she had heard a rumor that there was an inquiry about my situation from some high-ranking army officer in the Pentagon. She didn't know anything more about, but it was definitely a good sign. I certainly hoped and prayed that this was the result of my father's efforts to get me out of here.

A little after noon, I heard the dietary cart being wheeled onto the ward with the Thanksgiving dinner for the patients. I heard appreciative comments about the servings of turkey, mashed potatoes, gravy, cranberry sauce, green beans, and pumpkin pie.

It was a traditional American Thanksgiving Day dinner. When everyone else had been served, the dietary aide brought me my liquid meal. This time they showed a little more flexibility: a cup of cream of turkey soup, apple juice, and my requested root beer shake. I was able to drink it all and felt very thankful to have survived to be here that Thanksgiving Day.

Shortly after I finished, Bob came in and wished me a Happy Thanksgiving. I wished him the same and asked if he had been able to get in contact with my father. He said that he had reached him on the first try and spent almost an hour filling him in on the details regarding surgery and the doctors at the 249th General Hospital.

After Bob's conversation, my father immediately contacted his West Point classmate General Bruce Palmer, Jr., vice chief of staff for the U.S. Army. He asked for his immediate assistance in getting my surgery blocked and then having me transported to Walter Reed Army Medical Center. Bob said that from the way my father talked, he had already talked to General Palmer about my situation and had only to call him again to enact a plan. This news was the best possible Thanksgiving present he could ever give me. He was glad to help. We talked for a few minutes more before he excused himself to eat his Thanksgiving dinner.

Despite this promising news, I drifted in and out of a fitful nap. I had nightmares about a team of very uncaring surgeons carving my limbs off. In my mind, I was now struggling to see the real difference between the Vietcong, who wanted to blow me up, and these surgeons, who wanted to carve me up to gain a little more experience. Again it felt like fate was pushing me against my will toward the same outcome. At this point, I was praying with all of my might asking for God's mercy in preventing these unnecessary amputations. I was afraid to relax and place any credibility on General Palmer's efforts to block the self-motivated actions of the orthopedic surgeons.

Late that afternoon Margaret came to see me and apologized, saying that she had slept late. I told her not to apologize, that I had promising news to report. I recounted my earlier conversation and Margaret was very encouraged by Bob's news. She would call our parents to wish them a Happy Thanksgiving and find out the latest information from General Palmer. I asked her to give them my love and to give my wife, Mary, a call and my love. Margaret kissed my hand and said that she would be happy to make the calls. The dreaded Friday morning came. I had been awake for some time when I heard the corpsmen distribute the patient washbasins. I had not slept well and spent the better part of the time praying. Suddenly the loud and very angry voices of several men entered our ward. They came immediately to my bed and, without identifying themselves, began cussing at me and saying that they didn't know who in the Hell I thought I was; I was nobody special, and they were not going to take the shit I was passing out without taking steps to counteract it. At this point, two of them picked the foot of my bed up off of the floor a couple inches and then slammed it down hard with a loud *bang*. They did it twice more.

They shouted, "We're really pissed off and don't give a shit about what happens to you!" They would try to find a way to preserve their careers and also get even with me. I wasn't exactly sure what had happened, but felt it was time to remain silent given their highly agitated state. After making a few more obscene comments to me, they stormed out of the ward, still spouting their venom as they went.

Captain Do-It-By-The-Book rushed over to my bed and asked me if I understood what had happened. I said that I didn't, but I figured that they would not be operating on me this morning. She laughed and said that not only would they not be operating on me today; they would never get a chance to operate on me at all! She held my left hand and stated that when the orthopedic doctors arrived at the hospital that morning, they were ordered to go to the hospital commander's office. There they were informed that a direct order from Vice Chief of Staff of the Army, General Bruce Palmer, Jr. had arrived late yesterday stating that no surgery was to be performed on Captain William Haneke unless it was an absolute emergency and necessary to save his life. The general further stated that all courses of treatment on Captain Haneke would be thoroughly reviewed by Surgeon General of the Army Lieutenant General Leonard Heaton, and appropriate action would be taken if any neglect or maltreatment was uncovered. These orders further directed that on November 30, 1968, a surgeon was to accompany Captain Haneke while a U.S. Air Force med flight transported him from Japan to Walter Reed Army Medical Center.

After a big sigh, Captain Do-It-By-The-Book said that she didn't know how I had pulled this off since I was in critical condition on a psychiatric ward and didn't have access to a phone. I told her that I had just prayed very hard that I would be saved from any unnecessary surgery or medical treatment. This was God's way of rescuing me from those inexperienced surgeons. She said that however I had arranged for this to happen, it had been exactly the right move at the right time. The doctors were furious that their little game of operating on all of the battlefield casualties had been discovered.

Captain Do-It-By-The-Book whispered that the surgeons were scared to death that their medical careers might now be in jeopardy. I told her that whatever came out of all of this, they had brought it on themselves. It was my hope and prayer that those of us who had been seriously wounded would now have a better chance to get professional, proper, and fair medical treatment. She said a loud "Amen" and quietly confessed to me that she had been afraid to challenge this group of doctors on numerous cases. It was general knowledge that many of these surgical procedures were totally unnecessary. I shuddered to think about all of the unnecessary amputations, permanently altering the course of those patients' lives.

Around noon, Bob came in and congratulated me for avoiding the surgeries and retaining my limbs. Bob whispered that the word was all over the hospital about some patient on the psychiatric ward getting word to the vice chief of staff of the army to rescue him from the orthopedic surgery "butchers." He also observed that all of the doctors and nurses were treating their assigned patients better. They had realized this incident would most likely result in an investigation of several doctors. I commented that the results would speak for themselves. I took comfort in the fact that those cocky bastards were now shaking in their boots and wondering about their medical careers, but most of all I hoped that all patients would have a chance of receiving better care in the future. Bob overwhelmingly agreed. I thanked him for acting as my loyal messenger to smuggle out the awful truth about this torture chamber. He said that he was more comfortable playing that role than the guinea pig that I found myself forced to play. I reassured him that I had said nothing to anyone about how I received help. Bob patted me on the shoulder and said that it was nice to be on the winning side as he headed back to his ward.

Early that evening, Margaret came in and excitedly informed me that she had heard about the ruckus going on at the 249th General Hospital when she arrived at her office at Camp Zama early that morning. She exclaimed that news sure traveled fast, particularly when the vice chief of staff of the army had gotten involved. I asked her if she had told anybody that it was she, her brother, her father, and Bob who had caused this response. She replied that she had said nothing to anybody except Bob, Dad, and me. I told her that neither Bob nor I had talked to anybody either, so there was a lot of wild speculation about how a critically ill, blind, immobile patient on the psychiatric ward was able to sneak out and place a phone call to the Pentagon without being detected. We both laughed and said that most of the staff members were probably suspecting one another of aiding and abetting me in this effort.

I told Margaret that other than the surgeons, who pitched a real tantrum first thing this morning, all of the staff members had been extremely polite and helpful to me all day long. She asked if any of the surgeons had been back to see me. I said, "Absolutely not!" They had probably slunk off somewhere to present a very low profile and to lick their wounds. I added that if they were smart, they would start preparing their responses for

The Scheme

the investigating officer who was sure to come soon to follow up on this incident.

I informed Margaret that I would be transported to Walter Reed Hospital, leaving sometime Saturday afternoon. To this Margaret replied, "Thank God!" My sister packed up my few possessions from my bedside table into a pillowcase, which she said could easily be put on my stretcher for the trip back to the States. She didn't have a whole lot to pack up since I had no clothing, personal memorabilia, or toiletries, but I did have my Purple Heart medal and the dependable Timex watch. Margaret picked it up and joked that this watch, which I had been wearing during the explosion, would make a great commercial for the Timex slogan "takes a licking and keeps on ticking," especially since it was still intact and working perfectly well. (This watch, which I had purchased for $29.95 at Fort Bragg just before going to Vietnam, continued working perfectly for another eighteen years after I was wounded. It only required a replacement watchband due to the blood that had permeated the original band.)

While admiring my Timex, Margaret and I overheard two nurses discussing the fact that the orthopedic surgeons had cancelled several other patient procedures scheduled for that day and Monday. I whispered to Margaret that it sounded like those surgeries may have been unnecessary just like mine. One of the nurses ended the discussion by stating loudly that, after this incident, it looked as if the patients would have a chance of getting better medical care, and from her point of view this was long overdue. The other nurse responded that she certainly hoped that this would be the case. "At least my fate made a difference for others," I told my sister. Margaret agreed and then realized the time. She said that she would have to leave in order to catch the last bus back to Camp Zama. She would be back tomorrow in time to see me off on my journey back to the States.

A short time later, I heard the night nurse come over. She said that she would be cleaning my wounds for the last time before I left the 249th. She wanted to give me a heads-up on who the surgeon would be accompanying me during my trip home.

He was a member of the orthopedic surgery staff, but was not part of the team that had engaged in the tantrum at my bedside this morning. I asked her if that would present any type of concern for my safety. She didn't think so. After she had finished my debridement, I silently thanked God for this favorable outcome and asked for his protection and guidance as I embarked on the next phase of my treatment and rehabilitation process. I asked that he be with me, protect me, and take me safely to Walter Reed Army Hospital. I again heard the very calming voice tell me to have faith; he would be with me through all this. His Word helped me to relax and drift off to the first restful sleep I had in several days.

My stay at the 249th General Hospital ended up having a great impact on the patient care procedures and operations of this facility. When the investigation was completed, a number of disciplinary measures were handed out to the offending physicians and staff members. This included transferring all of the orthopedic surgeons to another assignment elsewhere, and not together. Army Surgeon General Lieutenant General Heaton ordered an investigation of all U.S. Army hospitals in Japan, the Philippines, Guam, Hawaii, and the United States to make sure that the patients, particularly the combat-wounded, were getting the best possible care and not being subjected to unnecessary procedures. It had been a difficult journey home for me, but I found solace in knowing that good had transpired for my injured comrades.

CHAPTER 27

Homecoming

Saturday morning came and with it the normal ward sounds of the pans of water being placed on the patients' bedside tables so they could wash up and face the new day. The head corpsman mentioned that they would be transferring me to the stretcher. As if on cue, I heard the arrival of the other corpsmen and a nurse with the stretcher. The corpsman then lifted up the covers and stuck in another folded blanket in the space where my right leg was missing, explaining that this would help when we landed in Alaska. He then added the pillowcase with my meager possessions that Margaret had packed.

I heard Bob's voice and felt him squeeze my left shoulder. He said that it looked like I would be traveling in style with my stretcher and custom-made mattress. I thanked him again for all of his friendship and help. He said that he would not have been able to live with himself if he had not done something to help me out. Bob wished me a safe trip along with a successful recovery.

About a half hour later, Margaret arrived. She commented that I looked prepared for my long trip. I asked if my medical records and X-ray folder were with me. She looked and said that they had not been put there yet. I heard someone walk up and felt my records and X-rays placed neatly under the portion of the mattress beneath my head. A female voice said that the corpsmen would be there in the next ten minutes to wheel me out to the helicopter pad to catch my ride to the U.S. Air Force Base. Margaret said that she had gotten here just in the nick of time. I asked Margaret if the doctor who would be accompanying me had appeared yet. She felt that he was probably around but wanted to have as little contact as possible after what had happened yesterday. I commented that it was ironic that I was being treated as the bad guy after steps were taken to rescue me from radical, totally unnecessary surgery. I wondered when these doctors would get the blame placed squarely on them, where it clearly belonged.

Several people wished me well and a complete recovery. Margaret thanked them for all of their help. I sensed that somebody else was standing there and Margaret asked him if he was the doctor who would be traveling with me. He said that he was and gave her his name. As I was wheeled through the hallways, Margaret asked the doctor to sit near me throughout the trip and carefully monitor me for breathing difficulties or any other problems. She reminded him that I was still in critical condition, which was why I was assigned a doctor for this long trip. The doctor responded in an arrogant manner that he was fully aware, and he was professionally trained. He then asked if she were my wife or girlfriend. Margaret responded coolly, "No, I am his sister and you need to take good care of him after all of the combat he has been through." The doctor said no more.

I heard Margaret say good-bye and then the door was shut. The engine started. It had only been a week since I left Vietnam, but it seemed like an eternity. I was not sorry to be leaving the 249th General Hospital. I was just glad that I had progressed to a stage where it was no longer necessary to send a lot of medical equipment and supplies along with me.

The nurse directed the doctor to sit directly across the aisle from my stretcher, which was placed on the middle tier with another patient above and below me. She told both these patients that I was in very critical condition and asked them to call if I was having a problem. They said that they were glad to help a fellow combat soldier.

The patient on the top bunk leaned over and asked me what branch I was in and where I had been serving in Vietnam. I told him that I was infantry all the way and had been serving as an advisor in southern II Corps in Binh Thuan Province. He said that he also was infantry before he caught several AK-47 rounds in his backside.

The patient on the lower bunk chimed in that he had been with the First Air Cavalry Division somewhere near Danang and had picked up a number of shrapnel wounds during a bombardment of his base camp by several North Vietnamese Army 122mm rockets. He asked what I had been hit by. I said a command-detonated mine during a Vietcong ambush just outside my compound. He was sorry to hear that but now knew that all three of us had earned our Purple Hearts legitimately. I replied that I was sure of that. The pilot welcomed us onto this express flight back to the "Good Ole USA." I faintly heard someone say that this would be a smooth flight as I drifted off to sleep.

The guy I overheard was correct. After what seemed like only a few minutes, the pilot announced that we were making our final approach into Elmendorf Air Force Base in Anchorage, Alaska, and would be touching down in the good ole USA again. The temperature on the ground was minus twenty-five degrees with light snow falling. A few muffled cheers greeted this statement. The pilot informed us that we would be on the ground only long enough to refuel the aircraft. He advised all those who were ambulatory to go inside the terminal building where it was warmer since the rear ramp of the plane must remain down while we were on the ground. Those on stretchers were to notify one of the flight nurses for additional blankets and a hot beverage.

When the engines had been completely shut off, the rear ramp was lowered and the blast of subfreezing air immediately invaded our warm little world. It was such a contrast to the tropical weather that we had grown used to in Vietnam. In the course of my trip from Southeast Asia, I had gone from a temperature nearing 130 degrees the day I was wounded to a sub-zero temperature around minus 25 degrees, a difference of 155 degrees. No wonder I was shivering badly when a nurse came to check on me. She immediately noted that I was unable to wear pajamas so she brought me three more blankets and tucked them in well to keep any chill from invading my little cocoon.

About five minutes later I began to experience a very weird sensation: I got very light-headed and began to have increasing difficulty breathing. This was totally unlike any difficulties that I had previously experienced with my tracheotomy. I was able to get the attention of the upper bunkmate and asked him to call the nurse quickly, because I was having problems catching my breath. He immediately yelled very loud and got the attention of several nurses who came running to my stretcher. By this time I was fighting very hard for each breath.

The head nurse immediately removed the entire tracheotomy from my neck, thinking that I probably had a blockage of mucus. But when it was out and I suddenly was unable to breathe at all, she told one of the other nurses to get a suture removal tray and a flashlight. The nurse returned in a matter of moments and the light was shined down the tracheotomy hole. The head nurse suddenly exclaimed that she saw a large piece of shrapnel totally occluding my airway. Another nurse handed her a set of long forceps, which she took and immediately began the process of probing to dislodge the shrapnel from my windpipe. What seemed like a long time to me, given my inability to breathe, was probably only a matter of a few seconds.

This Angel of Mercy deftly twisted the metal fragment and maneuvered it very carefully out through the tracheotomy hole. She must have displayed the quarter-sized piece of shrapnel for all nearby to see because I heard a few accompanying whistles and expressions of relief from the gathered nurses and crew members. My ability to breathe was immediately restored. It took several minutes of hard breathing before I was finally able to fully relax again.

By this time, one of the other nurses had come back with a straw and a cup of coffee. I don't remember how it tasted, but I sure remember the warmth and how it helped relieve my shivering. While I was sipping the coffee, she asked what had happened to the doctor who was supposed to be looking out for me on this trip. My bunkmate spoke up. He said that the doctor had been the first one to leave the plane, without checking on his patient. He added that as bad off as I was, the doctor should never have left my side. The nurse acknowledged his comment and thanked him.

When the refueling was completed, those that were ambulatory were asked to return to the plane. The irritated nurse dropped a piece of shrapnel into something metal causing a loud *clink*. Sarcastically, she asked the doctor if he could do his assigned job for the rest of the trip. The doctor apologized to her and said that he had to make a very important long-distance call to Washington, DC. She said that he should at least have told her that he was leaving the plane and made arrangements for one of the nurses to keep a closer watch on me while he was gone. Then she added, "That would be the truly professional thing to do." The doctor finally checked me over a couple times during the next phase of the trip after we took off from Alaska. I was very thankful that I experienced no further problems.

I slept peacefully until the pilot announced that we were making our approach into the Washington area and would be landing at Andrews Air Force Base in about twenty minutes. That gave the nurses time to make sure that the appropriate patients were prepared to be off-loaded for Bethesda Naval Hospital and Walter Reed Army Medical Center. The pilot announced that it was partly cloudy and the temperature at Andrews Air Force Base was a balmy thirty degrees, a fifty-five-degree rise from what we encountered in Alaska. We touched down and taxied to a halt near the end of the terminal building where I was told a number of ambulances and buses were waiting to transport those disembarking to our respective hospital destinations.

The engines were shut off and the rear ramp was lowered, allowing the ambulatory patients, staff, and passengers to off-load first. I waited patiently, expecting my assigned doctor to signal the ground crew that I was to be taken to Walter Reed.

The parade of outgoing stretchers finally came to an end and the crew chief began to raise the plane's rear ramp again. I got very worried that I had been forgotten and finally was able to get my bunkmate's attention. I told him that I was supposed to get off and go to Walter Reed. My doctor apparently was not looking out for me again. My bunkmate called over the head nurse and told her that I was supposed to go to Walter Reed and that he had seen my doctor get off the plane with the ambulatory patients and not return.

The nurse signaled the crew chief to lower the ramp again; two crew members came and carried my stretcher to an ambulance that, thankfully, was still waiting for me

It took almost an hour to drive to Walter Reed. Then, I was wheeled into the hospital and moved to the hallway outside of what I was told was the air evacuation office. I was one of four stretchered patients from our flight that were lined up. I soon heard the voices of family members who had been anxiously waiting for our plane to arrive bringing us home from Vietnam. After a few minutes, I heard the familiar voices of my parents and my wife, Mary. I became so choked-up with emotion and happiness at finally being home that I was unable to speak up and let them know where I was. I heard Mary walk by twice and comment after looking at all four stretchers that she didn't see me anywhere. It never dawned on me that I looked so bad that I would be unrecognizable to my own wife and family.

Later I learned that my father finally walked up to each stretcher and checked the name on the attached medical record. After checking the other three, he stopped at mine, looked carefully at the name, then looked carefully at me having no hair, having lost over one hundred pounds, missing my left eye, having my jaws wired together, and my head and neck covered with a lot of fresh scars.

He sighed and softly said, "This is him. It's Billy." With that, tears of joy began streaming down my face, which he immediately recognized and grasped my left hand. When Mary came over she said, "It can't be him; he's a little old man!" My father assured her that it was, and my mother immediately joined them as they all welcomed me home.

I placed my finger in my tracheotomy and expressed how glad I was to be back with them. They had been waiting for over four hours, as a snowstorm encountered in Alaska had delayed the flight. My family took turns holding my left hand, telling me how much they loved and missed me and how extremely glad that I was finally back. Mary and my father each said that it had been very frustrating trying to decipher the telegrams from both hospitals. My father commented that the daily reports from General Wetherill had been a godsend and helped them to better understand what had happened, as well as what surgeries and treatments I had undergone since November 13.

Mary tearfully spoke up and added that they had all helped form a massive prayer chain on my behalf that extended throughout New York, New England, New Jersey, Virginia, Maryland, Ohio, and numerous other states. I thanked them for all of their prayers and support and told them that God had spoken to me several times and said that I should have faith and he would bring me through all of this. I wished Mary a happy second wedding anniversary and told her that I was glad to get home on that exact date. She paused for a moment and said that today was actually December 4, the day after our anniversary. I responded that I had forgotten that we gained a day when we crossed the International Date Line.

At last a doctor walked up and, without introducing himself, started asking me a series of questions. He started by saying, "They certainly didn't bring much of you back." My answer to him was that this might be true, but they brought the best parts back. He asked what parts those were. I quickly added that the Vietcong might have messed up my body, but I wouldn't let them get my mind or my spirit. He proceeded to ask me several more very provocative questions. I could tell that my wife was getting very annoyed at this line of interrogation, so I asked her to please let me finish answering all of his questions.

Finally the doctor asked me who he was. I heard my mother whisper, "How is he going to know this since he is blind?" I quickly answered that he was the hospital psychiatrist and was here to conduct a mental competency evaluation so they could make a determination about to which ward I should be admitted. I added that I would do much better on the orthopedic ward with all of my bone, muscle, and joint injuries. The doctor's tone suddenly softened, and he commented on how perceptive I was in spite of my severe wounds.

He left to confer with the other physicians about my status. After a few minutes I heard them emerge and announce that I was being admitted to Ward One, the officers' orthopedic ward. When they told me the bed number, I commented that I would be in the big room known as the "Snake Pit." This really surprised them, and they asked how I knew it was called that. I answered that this was the same number bed in which I had been a patient back in July 1965 when I had had a knee operation. It was during that time the room was given that name. They both commented that there was nothing wrong with my memory. (I later found out that Max Cleland, a triple amputee who later became the secretary of Veterans Affairs during President Jimmy Carter's administration and then a U.S. Senator from Georgia, had been a patient in that same bed and had been discharged earlier that same day.)

My father asked me what had become of the doctor who had been assigned to accompany me from the 249th General Hospital. I told him that I didn't really know. He had made a habit of disappearing as soon as the plane touched down. My father asked if the doctor had ridden with me in the ambulance to this hospital and I told him, "No." My father then asked if I had experienced any problems during the flight that he should have been there to handle but wasn't. I told him, yes and explained the incident. This sounded like an emergency commented my father. He would be talking to General Palmer about the "Disappearing Doctor" and his conduct on this flight. I had a feeling that the "Disappearing Doctor" had some explaining to do.

Homecoming

My father did talk to General Palmer, who ordered a detail of military policemen to scour the Washington, DC, area to locate the "Disappearing Doctor," then bring him immediately in to meet with General Palmer. The "important" long-distance phone calls were to his girlfriend. It didn't take very long before they found him in bed with her. He was made to dress quickly and was taken to Palmer's office in the Pentagon. There Palmer asked him several questions, having already obtained some meaningful input from the head flight nurse. Calmly he told the doctor that he was disappointed and very displeased with his motivation, performance, and virtual neglect of his one assigned, critically ill patient, who literally almost died in Alaska. He went on to say that as a means of correcting this and providing him with adequate time to carefully consider his misdeeds, he would not be returning to the 249th General Hospital in Japan. Instead, he would be immediately dispatched to the northernmost army field hospital in the most dangerous area in South Vietnam, where he would serve for at least a year without being eligible to take leave.

To ensure that he would not disappear again en route to this assignment, Palmer ordered that a military policeman immediately accompany him the entire way from his office to the assigned field hospital in Vietnam. Palmer finally said that he would be checking up on the doctor from time to time, and if his attitude and performance did not improve dramatically, his next home would be the Long Binh Jail in South Vietnam for an extended period of time.

Palmer then asked if he wanted to accept this assignment or face a general court-martial for direct disobedience of a general order. By this time, it was said that the doctor had grown very pale and told Palmer that he would accept this assignment and hoped that it would not be the end of his medical career. Palmer responded that the choice was in the doctor's hands. He would be judged by how well he treated the patients brought to him. It was reported that this doctor was quite shaken and departed very meekly from General Palmer's office. The assigned hospital was the receiving point for frequent American and South

Vietnamese combat casualties and enemy attacks occasionally overran it. I was pleased to hear that justice had been dispensed. I am sure the "Disappearing Doctor" is still wondering how all this happened.

Two corpsmen took me to Ward One to begin my stay at Walter Reed Army Medical Center, commonly called "Walter Wonderful." My parents and wife accompanied me. The head nurse, Major Baker, welcomed me back from Vietnam,. She took the medical records and X-ray folder from my stretcher and assigned me a bed in the right rear corner of the "Snake Pit." This room, I was told, contained a total of fifteen patient beds and all were occupied by army officers who had been wounded in combat in Vietnam. More than half of these patients were amputees and a number were in traction. These beds were arranged in a U-shaped configuration with enough room in between to allow a bedside table, a chair, and a wheelchair.

Baker introduced my family members and me to the other patients in the room and told them that I was an infantry officer who had just arrived from Vietnam. Several calls of "Yeah, Infantry" and "All the way" went up from several of the other patients. Though I couldn't see any of them, I raised my left arm to acknowledge the cheers of support. My stretcher was moved next to my bed and the corpsmen picked me up and transferred me onto the bed. It felt great to be on clean sheets again after my long journey that had covered over twelve thousand miles.

My parents had elected to wait outside the room while I was being transferred and situated in my bed, but Mary was right there to make sure that everything was done properly. While we were talking, the evening nurse, Mrs. Lewis, a civilian contract nurse, said that she would be washing and changing my dressings after my long trip. She asked Mary to wait in the ward waiting room until she was finished. Mary went reluctantly, saying that she needed to learn about all of my injuries and respective treatments. Lewis assured her that the next day, the head orthopedic surgery resident, Dr. Major John Eberhard and Baker would give a full explanation and prescribed course of treatment.

Lewis carefully washed me very thoroughly after removing all of my wound dressings with the exception of those on my head and eyes. It really felt great and, for the first time since I left the 24th Evacuation Hospital, I actually felt clean again. While Lewis was washing me, she noted that I had skin problems that ranged from a small blemishes to a number of larger, boil-looking red and purplish welts. I had developed these within a few days of being wounded and had been running a constant fever that kept me very thirsty most of the time. The nurse noticed that I was having phantom pains and asked if I was on pain killer. I told her I was trying to avoid taking any painkillers because I did not want to become addicted to them. She fully understood the logic and offered me an APC, a standard army cure-all that would help mask the nerve trauma responses pain. The APC came in powder form and would be given to me with liquid.

In a few minutes, I heard approaching footsteps and chairs being pulled up next to my bed. My mother squeezed my arm and said, "Billy, we are so happy and relieved to have you back with us again. It feels as if you've been gone forever." My father echoed her feelings and said that it had been a real battle to get me out of Japan. He was glad to have that behind us. What went unsaid was that they were happy and very thankful that I was back alive. Shortly after, Mary walked over and said that Lewis had given her a cup of ice water and a cup of apple juice with two straws and asked her to help me drink and to keep track of how much fluid I consumed. This would be a part of the routine recording of my fluid and food intake and output of bodily waste.

Mary asked which I wanted first. I chose the apple juice and explained how we usually inserted the straw through a gap in my teeth. She said that this sounded simple enough and much easier than how the nurse explained. I told Mary that she would have to learn to ask the nurses, doctors, therapists, and other members of the medical staff a lot of questions to understand my complex medical case. I then tried to joke a little by telling her that since we had first met and married, she had to learn military lingo, then German lingo, and now she would be required to learn the medical lingo. This was my way of getting her to become multilingual. Mary didn't find this at all amusing.

My mother changed the topic of conversation to something safe—the weather. We all talked a little while longer, then the phantom pains grew so intense that I was not easily able to participate in the conversation. Mary tracked down the nurse. She asked me to describe what I was experiencing. When I told her about the severe pains in the leg and foot that had been amputated, the nurse decided to give me a couple ground-up APC tablets and suggested that Mary and my parents give me a good night's rest. My family told me that they were going to go to the Walter Reed Guest House and would be back in the morning.

The patient in the bed to my left welcomed me to the "Snake Pit" and introduced himself as a captain who had commanded an infantry company with the First Infantry Division in the Central Highlands of Vietnam. He said that his company had been badly ambushed, and he had taken four AK-47 rounds in his left leg, which nearly shattered the bone in two places. His leg was in traction with a pin through his ankle. I shared my story. At that point, the patient in the bed to my right introduced himself as a major who had been riding in a jeep in III Corps in Vietnam when it hit a landmine that blew him out of the vehicle, badly injuring his back. The major had undergone a spinal-fusion procedure, which had him in a full-body cast for at least four months while his spine healed properly. I thanked them for welcoming me and said how good it was to be back in the States again. I drifted off to the sounds of several TV sets tuned to familiar American programs. It felt great to be back in familiar surroundings.

I was awakened to the sounds of a male voice loudly scolding me for having the nerve to "take a shit in my bed and not bother to call for help." I could feel him roughly pull the covers off of me and push me over to one side of the bed as he surveyed the extent of what had happened. I weakly responded that I had been in a deep sleep and hadn't realized what was happening, and that this was the first bowel movement I had had since I was wounded on November 13. He said he didn't give a crap about that, then asked who I thought was going to clean this mess up.

The captain to my left finally said, "Mr. McCants, it's the middle of the night, and this poor guy has been very badly wounded and just got back from Vietnam late this afternoon. Why don't you give him a break and just do your job and clean up the mess. He obviously didn't do it on purpose."

McCants then added, "If he's that bad off, he sure doesn't belong on this ward." The captain responded that he knew full well that there was no better place at Walter Reed for me to be assigned. McCants snapped back that he shouldn't be expected to clean up what he called this "yard-long line of smelly shit."

Muttering loudly the whole way, he went out and I heard him bring back a cart that turned out to contain clean sheets, a roll of toilet paper, some washcloths, a towel, some soap, and a pan of warm water. He obviously knew what had to be done but was not at all happy. As he began the clean-up process, several other patients joined the first patient and urged McCants to lighten up on me and just do his job. He rolled me over on my right side again, removed the sheet from under me, wrapping the hard lump of feces, then cleaned me and put on fresh sheets and blankets. Sheepishly I thanked him and apologized again.

McCants took my left hand and showed me where he had attached my nurse-call button to the left side of my pillow and said that if I felt I needed to go to the bathroom again at any time, I was to ring that call button immediately. As he left the room, several of the patients reassure me that I had not committed a sin and added that McCants was a little on the lazy side, and that was why he liked working the graveyard shift. They told me not to worry about it. I was soon asleep again.

Morning came and I heard the authoritative-sounding voice of a doctor who introduced himself as Dr. John Eberhard, the head orthopedic surgery resident. He introduced three other doctors who were also orthopedic residents or interns. They all examined me and discussed their observations with one another. This was the norm in a medical teaching center like Walter Reed.

From what I could understand, they all felt that I should have a skin graft as soon as possible to cover the end of my stump, the outside of my remaining half a foot, and the remaining ends of all of the fingers on my right hand. It would be the only way for me to avoid further infections and being rehabilitated. He said that they would try to schedule my skin graft surgery during the next day or two. Diagnostic tests would determine the cause of my fever. When the orthopedic surgeons had finished their exam, they walked back down to the nurse's station and met with Baker about my recommended course of treatment.

Shortly after they left my bed, someone came over and introduced himself as Dave, my assigned corpsman. He welcomed me home from Vietnam and said that he was going to bathe and shave me. Dave conversed with me that he too had recently returned from Vietnam where he had served as a combat medic. He never said any more about his medical qualifications. I later learned that Dave was a Specialist Sixth Class who was drafted into the army and, as a conscientious objector, refused to carry a weapon in combat. He had extensive medical training and had served as a combat medic during two full tours in Vietnam, where he repeatedly treated wounded U.S. Army soldiers on the front lines under heavy enemy fire. He had been awarded the Distinguished Service Cross, a medal awarded for conspicuous gallantry, two Silver Stars, three Bronze Star Medals with V device for Valor, a Purple Heart, and the Expert Medical Badge, which is awarded only to those medics who serve for an extended period of time in direct combat operations with the enemy. He could have sought a deferment from the army because of his status as a conscientious objector; instead, he chose to serve the military and his country by treating those men wounded in combat.

After Dave completed bathing me, my wife and parents arrived and asked how my first night back in the States had gone. I deliberately neglected telling them about my incident with McCants. Instead I told them that I was finally able to relax and not worry about being shot or overrun while I was trying to sleep. We talked for a few minutes then Baker came and asked them to join Dr. Eberhard and the general doctor in the patient day room for a complete evaluation and proposed plan of treatment. They excused themselves and said that they would be back.

About an hour later, Mary came back acting very concerned. She explained that I was being moved to a private room across from the nurse's station where I could receive closer supervision because of my upcoming surgery. Dave then joined her and together they wheeled my bed down the hall to my new room. As we exited the "Snake Pit," a number of the patients wished me luck and said that they would visit me.

Mary told me that my new room was fairly small with a bed, a bedside table, a small chest of drawers for storing extra sheets, pillows, and medical supplies, and a small sink for the medical staff to wash their hands. My parents joined us. My father told me that Dr. Eberhard had scheduled my skin graft procedure early the following morning. They were not very talkative at this point. I figured that this was due to their trying to absorb the details the doctors had just given them of my complex case.

My mother again tried to change the gloomy mood with a safe subject—Walter Reed Guest House. They had been lucky enough to get two rooms there, which was in very high demand from family members of all the newly arrived men from Vietnam. She said that it was an old brick military building and the only decent accommodations anywhere near Walter Reed. It was certainly nothing very fancy, but an adequate and safe place to get some rest after visiting a family member in the hospital. The main drawback was the lack of eating accommodations there; my mother disgustedly commented that one had to visit either the hospital cafeteria or the Red Cross lounge in order to get something to eat, and both of these facilities had a limited menu and operating hours.

All this talk about food made me realize that I had yet to receive anything to eat. I asked Mary if she would ask Baker to request a visit from a dietician because I hadn't eaten. Mary immediately left and tracked down the head nurse, who put a call in to the dietary department. In the meantime, Baker gave

Mary a couple half-pint containers, one containing apple juice and the other apricot nectar, to feed me. They sure tasted good and helped relieve my parched throat. While I was slowly sipping my drinks, my parents and wife began updating me on the many details about my family that had transpired since my departure for Vietnam. Although it had been great to get letters from home during my absence, it was far better hearing all of this in person and knowing that I would not be interrupted to react to a crisis or an unexpected enemy attack.

I knew that it would take time for me to adjust and fully realize that I was finally home from the combat zone and out of harm's way. I wasn't sure whether or not the nightmares that had haunted me at the other two hospitals would continue. I hoped and prayed that they would go away and never return. I had often heard my parents and some of their friends discuss a number of their fellow army officers for whom recurring nightmares of their time in combat during WWII and Korea continually afflicted them. Some of them tried to rid their minds by increased bouts of drinking that impaired and interfered with their work and assigned duties. These men had excellent military and combat credentials but met an untimely end to their promising careers when they were unable to adequately handle their emotions and drinking. I prayed that my life would not end like theirs.

A while later Baker came by to change my dressings again, as well as give me my assigned medications. She cautioned my wife and parents that I was very weak and in constant need of rest. Their visits might cause me to fall asleep. She wanted them to realize that this was not a reflection of my lack of interest, but a matter of my being exhausted. Baker's words were soothing. I felt very safe and secure in my new surroundings and being with my family. It was not the homecoming I had imagined, but I was finally home.

CHAPTER 28
Walter Wonderful

The next morning was the day for my skin graft procedure. Major Baker had come to my room early to ensure that I had not had anything to eat or drink since midnight. I was then moved into my assigned operating room where several assistants transferred me onto the operating table. The anesthesiologist came over and told me that he would be injecting Sodium Pentothal into my IV tube and I should begin counting backwards starting from one hundred. I think I got to ninety-eight or ninety-seven when the lights went out and I became totally unconscious.

I awoke several hours later and was aware of intense burning pain all over my left thigh. A nurse came over to my bed to confirm that I was awake. She explained that I had come through the procedure in good shape and was now in the recovery room. I asked the nurse about the burning sensation on my left thigh. She said the burning pain was the skin donor site. My surgeon would explain the results to my family and me, so I should save my questions for him.

A special lamp was trained on my donor site to assist in the healing. The warmth of that light on my leg actually felt good and helped me stop shivering. Dr. Eberhard was pleasantly surprised with the seeming success of the grafts. The extreme challenge was my left foot. The surgeons had to place the graft on my left foot over an extensive amount of bone with very little flesh to which to attach it. This meant that there might be difficulty in getting consistent blood flow through this skin graft. We were cautioned that although everything looked great initially, only time and healing would determine whether or not these grafts would actually take and be successful. Mary asked what would happen if the grafts failed and was told, "We will face that if and when it might happen."

Mary noticed that I was in extreme pain and requested that I be given something for the pain. Baker went to the nurse's station and returned with a syringe. She injected it into my right hip, saying that I should be feeling some relief within about ten to fifteen minutes. The way I was feeling, that couldn't come soon enough. I was eligible to receive my pain medications every four hours, but soon found that it rapidly wore off after about two hours. While trying to weather the excruciating pain, I resorted to all of the West Point tricks I had used to avoid upperclassmen hazing like self-hypnosis and several other mind-control techniques. None of these techniques were successful in lessening or masking this extreme pain level. I was beginning to relate to how drug addicts felt while arranging for their next "fix." On a number of occasions, my wife begged the nurse on duty to give me my next injection sooner. Each time they tried to console her and refused her request, saying that this prescribed medication was a very powerful painkiller and to give it more often in my weakened condition most probably would cause my liver to fail.

At the end of the second day following the surgery, Baker again examined my graft and donor sites. Although she was very pleased with the healing progress in each of the graft locations, she said that she had discovered a slight break in a couple of the scabs on the donor sites with slight puss drainage. She paged Eberhard and requested that he come take a look at these sites. In the meantime she took a swab of the drainage and sent it to the lab for a culture. Eberhard was glad that Baker had discovered these changes and had sent the swabs to be cultured in the lab; however, he did not want to wait for the cultures to grow.

He suspected that I had developed an infection from something that I had been exposed to in the operating room. We needed to act quickly and treat the condition before it grew worse, as he did not believe that I would survive a infection.

Following the exam, he consulted with other orthopedists. They all concluded that the only course of action was to use the "Wet-Dry Soak Technique" on my donor sites. They would wrap several layers of gauze soaked in normal saline around the infected donor sites and let them stay in place for a period of four hours, during which they would dry and become intermeshed with the scabs and tissue underneath. Then these bandages were to be quickly ripped off, thereby removing the gauze dressings, the attached layer of skin, and the adhering attacking bacteria. The whole process was to be immediately repeated every four hours. Eberhard gave the order for this procedure to be continued indefinitely until he saw signs of the disappearance of the infection.

Just before the changeover of nursing shifts, the outgoing head nurse and the incoming head nurse came to my room and began the process of taking off the dried dressings from my donor sites. I was totally unaware of how intense and painful this process would turn out to be. Mary was there holding my left hand as the nurses gently peeled off the outer layers of the dried gauze. Both nurses apologized as they forcibly ripped off the final layer that was dried and adhering to my wound sites and surrounding skin. The wave of pain suddenly overwhelmed me. All I was able to do was emit a loud gasp of air as tears streamed down my cheeks. I am sure that I hurt Mary's hand as I squeezed it. One of the nurses gave me my next pain medicine injection and then both nurses rewrapped my thigh with fresh, wet dressings to begin the gruesome process all over again.

It was a while before the level of pain subsided enough to ask the nurses a couple questions. I first asked if it would be possible to modify this process some to reduce the shock to my system. Their reply was that this was exactly how Eberhard directed it, with no deviation. They added that he felt this technique would eventually clear up all of the infection. Mary asked if I could be given my shot of pain medications at least fifteen minutes prior to the dressing removal to possibly reduce the intensity of the pain. They agreed and she told me they made a note in my medical chart. After the nurses left my room, Mary stayed a while longer and talked gently to try to calm me down and distract my attention from my pain. I finally drifted off to sleep.

In the middle of the night, I was rudely and painfully awakened as the night nurse and a corpsman began the process of removing the dried dressings. I heard them comment that the majority of the remaining scab material was now gone with the removal of this dressing. The nurse agreed that we were down to raw flesh where they could get direct access to the infectious bacteria. The corpsman asked how long it would be before all of the infectious material was removed and the regular healing process could resume. The nurse's response was that this would be hard to say, but it would normally take at least five days or longer to successfully accomplish the process, depending on how resistant the bacteria was.

It was apparent to me that I would be in for a very long and pain-filled ordeal. At this point, the thought of just letting go and succumbing to my wounds was beginning to seem better and better to me. At least I would no longer be experiencing this terrible pain and lack of certainty about what my future held. This option would also allow me to stop being a burden to my family. I toyed with that idea and possibility for several minutes then the new injection of pain medication kicked in and I was able to drift off to sleep again. As I slept, I had several bad nightmares in which I had been severely wounded in combat and was captured by the Vietcong, who were slowly and painfully torturing me to gain useful information. These dreams played into my actual level of pain. When I awoke, it took me some time to realize that this had just been a bad dream.

The following afternoon, the level of pain had grown so intense that the injections were making little or no difference. Tears streamed down my cheeks long after the dressings had been yanked off at the four-hour mark. The corpsmen who were assisting the nurses felt compassion for me. Finally, late that afternoon, the two corpsmen came in a few minutes prior to the time for removal of my dressings and poured a little normal saline on the dressings. This softened them up just enough so that the skin wasn't sticking to the gauze dressings. Consequently, when the nurse came into my room to redo the dressings, one of these two corpsmen then removed the old dressings and quickly discarded them before the nurse could closely examine them. The nurse then reapplied the proper antibiotic ointment followed by the gauze dressings soaked in normal saline. This process was still very painful, but not as bad. The corpsmen verbally passed on to succeeding shifts of corpsmen that wetting my dressings prior to removal would make the process much easier on me in my gravely weakened condition. This recommended process continued that night and the following morning, making it much easier for me to tolerate and less stressful for the ward staff to witness.

At noon, Eberhard came onto the ward and wanted to examine the most recent dressings taken off me. Everyone on Ward One heard his loud, angry reaction when he discovered that these dressings were quite moist. He called Baker, another nurse, and all of the on-duty corpsmen into my room and emphatically stated that he was very serious about this wet-dry dressing process being handled properly and added that as painful and unpleasant as it turned out to be, it was the only way that they would be able to successfully overcome this infection and save my life. He added that for the duration of this process, he would be the one to come in and change my dressings. If he found that anything out of the ordinary was going on, he would press legal charges for direct disobedience of an order. Eberhard said that he wanted this written down in my chart and asked each staff member if they fully understood what he had ordered. They each responded affirmatively then filed out of the room, with the exception of Baker.

Eberhard reminded Baker that she had the overall responsibility of ensuring that the ward staff members were performing properly, so if she had to make herself available for every shift to make sure of it, then so be it. With that he washed his hands, removed my dressings, and closely examined the donor sites. After a few minutes, he said that he could see that some small progress was beginning to be made, but not as much as would had been accomplished if the process had been done correctly. He then stated that he felt that this breach of proper protocol would probably add another week. The remaining afternoon, evening, and night Eberhard dutifully came to my room and accompanied the nurses in the removal of my dressing to make sure they did it properly.

The therapy did last a week, and each time the pain continued unabated as tears cascaded down my face. My wound sites showed signs of healing, so Dr. Eberhard took new culture swabs and sent them to the lab. Forty-eight hours later, the report came back that the cultures showed no signs of infections, and with that he ended the wet-dry soak torture therapy. The scabs quickly formed over all of the skin donor sites and continued healing without showing any more signs of drainage. I was then freed from protective isolation and allowed to schedule appointments with other doctors and therapists.

One of my first appointments was with the ophthalmologists to determine a course of treatment to help me either partially or fully regain the sight in my remaining eye. When the slit lamp was properly positioned, the chief of service examined my right eye while one of the assisting doctors kept it open and held my head still. I could feel the heat of the bright light and could partially see it as the examination proceeded. After some time the head doctor sighed and stated, "This is going to be a challenging case." He invited the other doctors to take a look and think about what approach each would consider to begin my course of treatment. As the extensive examination dragged on, my eye became very sore and began to tear quite heavily. In spite of that, the doctors continued.

Finally they were finished. The head doctor invited them all to accompany him into the next room. I could vaguely hear a lively discussion going on. After some time, they all returned. The head doctor said they had discovered a lot of damage to the eye. There were signs of entry from several small metal fragments and the presence of blood particles floating in the vitreous. The blood was so thick that they were unable to see through to the retina. The head doctor decided to do what he called "some watchful waiting" in the hope that the eye would soon absorb a lot of the blood particles, so that they could get a better view of the retina to determine the extent of damage and course of treatment.

The head doctor next described his examination of the ocular cavity where my left eye had been blown out, which revealed that it had suffered extensive traumatic injuries with the loss of most supporting bone framework. The eye socket needed to be reformed at the same time as a cranial plastic plate was inserted to fill in the skull defect. He added that the initial treatment of these wounds had been excellent. The tendons that supported the left eye had been tied together with a device described as an "acorn." This would give me the chance to be fitted with an artificial eye. In the meantime, they were going to insert a clear conformer to protect the eye socket from outside debris and impurities and hopefully hold down the chance of developing an externally caused infection.

It was very hard for me to take all of this in and fully understand the implications. My wife finally got to the bottom line and asked the head doctor if I would ever regain any of my eyesight. He paused a second then said that it was very difficult to say at this point, but with a conservative approach to my treatment there was a good possibility that the blood would be absorbed in time and a degree of vision would be restored. The head doctor stated that he would be assigning Dr. Major John Walker to coordinate my case while I was at Walter Reed.

At first the name meant nothing to me, but before I was wheeled to my next appointment, Dr. Walker came over and told us that he was Johnny Walker, whose parents had been stationed at Fort Benjamin Harrison at the same time as mine. We had first met at a party during the summer of 1961 before I had reported to West Point. He assured me that I would receive the best care for my eyes. I did remember him and his parents and really appreciated him taking a great interest in my care.

From the eye clinic, I was taken down the hall to the otolaryngology, or ENT, clinic. There I was again examined and evaluated by the department chief and his staff of physicians. They first removed all of the gauze packing from my nasal cavities. Carefully the physicians poked and probed as far as they could reach with their long, pointed instruments. I heard several comments such as, "I've honestly never seen one this bad before. Most men wouldn't have survived half of what he's been through." Like the eye clinic, when the doctors had all finished their exams, they went into the next room and conferred on their observations.

A short time later, they returned to my exam room and the chief doctor explained that all of my frontal sinuses had been blown out. He said that these areas had all been surgically repaired successfully at the 24th Evacuation Hospital. The doctor said that he could see a couple places where additional cauterization had been performed to stop some bleeding. I replied that I had a couple of instances where metal fragments had to be removed. The doctor said that the surgeon had performed first-class work. The healing process for my sinuses was still going on, but he felt that there was no longer a need to keep the packing in my nasal cavities. This came as great news to me, since breathing through my mouth gave me a sore throat—at last, progress.

About mid-afternoon, Dave came to my room and said that he was to take me to the neurosurgery clinic. Several doctors were waiting and they each took turns closely examining my head; the skull defect that was still present over my left eye socket and the surgical sites of the three neurosurgical procedures. They each spoke with great appreciation and admiration for the high-quality work of Dr. Bill Hammond and his team at the 24th Evacuation Hospital. They further noted the extensive surgical work that had been performed on both the carotid artery and the jugular vein.

The chief doctor finally told Mary and me that the head and neck areas appeared to be healing very nicely, but complete healing was expected to take several more months. He said that I needed to continue to take my anticonvulsant medications indefinitely. The doctor was pleased that I had not experienced any seizures thus far. He explained that I would not be able to undergo my next neurosurgical operation—to implant a cranial-plastic plate in the skull defect in my forehead and eye socket—for at least a year to a year and a half. This was a precaution to ensure that a patient had recovered completely from the previous operation.

The head neurosurgeon invited Mary to join him in the hall. He told her that she should not be hopeful about my ultimate possibility of recovery, because most patients who had experienced traumatic injuries seldom lived to recover; those that did never returned to fully independent or productive status again. He went on to say that, in my case, he felt that I would never be able to walk again and probably would have great difficulty even sitting up by myself.

Mary was totally stunned with the weight of this totally negative prognosis on my condition and chances of recovery. She said that this information was like a mule kicking her in the stomach. At first she struggled to fight back the tears then felt her face get red as anger toward this doctor boiled to the surface. Mary managed to control her rage as she told him, through clenched teeth, that the "real doctors" at the 24th Evacuation Hospital in Vietnam had given their very best to save me and help me return to Walter Reed to undergo my long-term rehabilitation. She expected them to stop playing and start being "real doctors," to step up to the plate and actively help her husband find ways to recover from his injuries.

She added, "He has come too far and fought too hard for you and your staff to give up on him. I will not allow that!"

The head doctor apologized and said that he generally told severely wounded patients' families the worst so they wouldn't get their hopes of recovery up too high. Mary loudly responded that his prognosis had only made her angry, and she would prove the medical staff wrong.

The following morning Mary came to my room and announced that Baker had received orders for my evaluation and treatment with the physical therapy department from Eberhard. He ordered treatment on my leg, foot, stump, hands, and arms several times a day, which would help me to regain better muscle tone, strength, and range of motion. I was to attend physical therapy at least twice a day, beginning that day.

First Lieutenant Smith, the physical therapist, greeted Mary and me at the door. Mary described this sector to me as containing three broad treatment tables with padded mats on top. Five other patients were in the room doing their assigned exercises under the close scrutiny of two physical therapists and three physical therapy aides. Four of the five patients were amputees: two missing a leg above the knee; another missing an arm and a leg below the knee; another missing two legs above the knee and a hand; and the final patient missing four limbs, his eyes, and his nose. In spite of their wounds, each of these men seemed to be very upbeat and positive about their status as they welcomed me.

Smith explained that, in view of my extensive injuries, my first week of treatment would require an extensive period of evaluation, partially through established exercise modalities and partially through a process of trial and error to better determine my actual capabilities. She cautioned that, in my case, this would be a very long and laborious process, possibly extending a year or more. It was still difficult for me to accept that my rehabilitation would take so long. I was used to being able to totally recover from my injuries in a couple of weeks and had expected this process to be no different.

Physical therapy began with me sitting up without assistance, which was arduous after being immobile for several weeks. She next helped me move each of my limbs while trying to determine the extent of atrophy. While doing this, she made notations in my treatment records that helped her to tailor specific exercises to meet my needs. Next she provided resistance to each of my limbs in turn as a means of determining the level of strength that I possessed at this point. Smith was impressed and guessed that I had been in great physical condition at the time of my injury or I would have regressed into a state of almost total atrophy after all that I had been through. She added that I was not there yet, and we were beginning these physical therapy treatments just in time to prevent that from happening.

Smith decided to fashion several sandbag weights for me, weighing a half pound, one pound, two pounds, and five pounds. I would use these weights every day in the physical therapy clinic as well as on my ward. She instructed my wife in this process so she could help me set up my exercise routine in my room. Smith said that when she finished her treatment periods with me each morning, I would be transferred to a hand specialist therapist, who would work with me to regain normal movement, strength, and functioning of my right hand. This was a lot for me to comprehend, so I was very glad that Mary was with me to take note.

I next met Captain Wallace, the hand specialist, who introduced herself and then carefully removed the complicated bracing system of wires, pads, and rubber bands from my right hand. She examined each of my fingers and said the good news was that the skin bandages were actually healing very well. The bad news was that this process would take longer to allow complete healing at each of these sites, so we would have to wait a while longer before we could begin the actual process of bending and stretching each of my fingers on that hand. Wallace said that this wonderful brace had effectively done its job and could now be safely removed to allow my fingers and hand to heal more naturally. She took my right hand and proceeded to bend and stretch each of the fingers and the entire hand to help it regain its full range of motion and flexibility. She then performed resistive measures to determine the strength in each part of my hand. These would be the same types of exercises that she would perform daily, to which were later added gripping and turning exercises to gain greater strength and range of motion.

My physical therapy training progressed from range of motion, weight lifting, and resistive exercises to the point where I was put on a treatment table that would progressively be tilted from a horizontal to a more vertical position. Although this process was intended to evaluate how well my lower extremities would react to the greater weight bearing and increased blood flow, it was slow torture; the degree of pain and discomfort increased proportionally with the increasing vertical angle. As I explained to Smith, I just wanted to be helped to stand up and be allowed to try to ambulate in the parallel bars. She said that, in my case, this process was not as simple as that due to concerns about my circulatory system and the effects of the extensive scar tissue in my lower extremities. Fortunately neither of these turned out to be a problem.

Dr. Eberhard decided that my skin grafts were completely healed and stabilized for physical therapy. Smith was given the order to go ahead and have me fitted with a very specialized shoe that would eventually help me to walk again while protecting and supporting my remaining partial foot. This shoe was high-topped, with support extending above the ankle, completely lined with lambs-wool, and laced up the top and back. The unique lacing made it easier to insert my foot and allowed the proper adjustment to minimize the stress placed on the skin graft along the outside of my foot.

I was now fully aware that I was going through the process of completely reprogramming my body to perform normal daily activities. After spending a couple days of physical therapy appointments wearing this wonderful shoe, Smith and Eberhard felt that I was ready to try to stand up with assistance and hopefully advance enough to begin ambulating on the parallel bars. I was helped into the standing position with a belt around my waist and a physical therapist aide on either side of me, each holding onto an arm and the belt.

Standing on half a foot was painful unsteady. After a wobbly start, I steadied myself and announced that it sure felt great to be standing again. Mary told me later that several bystanders and Smith were shocked by my six-foot-plus height. They had not recognized my true height since I had only been seen lying on a mat or sitting in a wheelchair. I stood for ten minutes before being helped down on the mat for a fifteen-minute rest. I was helped up again for another ten-minute session then into my wheelchair where the shoe was removed. This had been a very exhilarating day with my advance to standing again, but the process wore me out. I was more than ready to sleep.

The next day I started my physical therapy session with great personal resolve: I donned my wonderful shoe with the help of only Smith. I pulled myself up to a standing position inside the parallel bars. Smith intended for me to only stand in place for a longer period than the day before. After some begging, I was allowed to take a few steps. She prepared me for this process by fitting my right arm with a wooden crutch and a supportive belt around my waist. An assistant supported me on the other side. Putting full weight on the metal fragments in my palms was quite painful, but I ignored this as a temporary inconvenience. My goal was to become ambulatory again.

Despite the pain, I used my full weight on my left hand and right arm crutch and swung my leg through, taking my first unsteady step. While the therapists stood amazed at the success of this effort, I again negotiated my second step, quickly followed by a third, and then I rested for a few moments. I followed with three additional steps in quicker succession then added assistance for my return steps to the wheelchair. I was totally exhausted but very happy.

During the next three days, I added more distance to my ambulation on each therapy visit and worked harder on the ward at lifting my sandbag weights to further build up my overall strength. On the fourth day of ambulation, I was taken to a clear place to the side of the clinic, helped to stand with two wooden crutches, then guided to ambulate successfully back and forth in that area. I was now free of the parallel bars and on a mission to overcome the obstacles that my injuries had thrust in my path. I had exceeded Smith's plans and hopes for my progress by a very wide margin.

Several days before the hospital wound down for Christmas, the medical staff decided that they should take steps to remove the majority of the metal fragments causing me problems in my right hand. Early the morning of the scheduled procedure, Dr. Faggott, the general intern, had me wheeled into a treatment room on Ward One, where he started scrubbing my right hand and wrist. He then numbed my entire hand and wrist while assuring me that I would feel little more than a pinprick. When the desired numbness had set in, he began by cutting out a number of pieces of shrapnel from the palm of my hand and placing them in a procedure bowl. Up to this point, I had felt no pain, although I was aware of some pressure being applied as he attempted to extract several of the larger metallic pieces. Finally he removed several pieces of shrapnel from the back of the hand, including a larger piece from the back of the knuckle on my little finger. Although only a small point of metal was visible sticking out of the joint, X-rays had shown that this fragment was actually about the size of a dime.

As Faggott cut through the skin and into the knuckle bone, I flinched from the pain. He stopped what he was doing and made several more injections to try to numb the area further. Unfortunately this never completely worked as they resumed the extraction process in an attempt to quickly remove the offending metal fragment. It was necessary to cut down into the bone of the knuckle to fully remove the metal. The pain was so intense that I gripped the edge of the table tightly. Faggott was a very compassionate man and continued to apologize for my discomfort. He finally stitched up the area and applied a dressing to that finger and the entire hand. The extensive procedure had been successful; Faggott presented me with a large capped test-tube containing all of the metal fragments he had removed. These and my scars were my trophies, in a way, of my injuries. Over the next several years, many more pieces of metal and glass shrapnel were removed or worked their way out of other areas of my body and were added to my test-tube collection.

My next challenge came from the dental clinic. Dr. Colonel Guernsey was the head of the dental service and, as we discovered, a distant relative from my mother's family in Ohio. Guernsey was also an oral surgeon, so he initially took charge of that aspect of my evaluation and treatment. He and two other oral surgeons seemed very impressed with the excellent treatment that Dr. Thompson had given me in Vietnam. Guernsey told me that Thompson was a legend in his own time. The oral surgery team felt that it was necessary to undo the wires immobilizing my jaws to better evaluate the status of healing in my entire mouth and jaw area. Guernsey assigned his most experienced oral surgeon to my case and scheduled the procedure to be handled the day before Christmas break.

This dentist had been a college football player who had gone on to get a dental degree and then joined the army. He had big fingers and was not particularly gentle in the way he treated his patients. Mary had serious misgivings about letting him handle me but was reassured that he would do a very good job. I was helped into the dental chair and Mary was asked to wait in the waiting room.

The dentist performed the procedure with no assistant in the room, saying that all of the assistants had already started their Christmas holidays. He then turned my head at an odd angle and held it securely in place under one arm with the top of my head in his armpit. He began by using a small wire-cutter to quickly clip the wires holding my jaw in place. Using forceps, he roughly removed these wire remnants from between my teeth on the top and out of the gum tissue on the bottom. As he continued, my mouth and jaw were really hurting and blood began to drip out of both sides of my mouth. The dentist put another towel under my chin to catch the blood and continued working. When he had completed this task, he told me to open my mouth.

I was unable to do this, so after a minute or two, he grew impatient and forced my mouth open wide enough to allow one of his fat fingers to go between my upper and lower jaws. He then inserted two other fingers and twisted them quickly from a flat position to an up-and-down position. The jaw responded with a loud cracking noise that my wife heard out in the waiting area. This caused a severe wave of pain, dizziness, and nausea and caused me to pass out.

Smelling salts were being waved under my nose, which caused me to wake to a sea of pain and nausea. The dentist told me to work on getting my jaw open wide enough for two of his fat fingers' width after New Year's. He then wiped my face with the towels to clean off the blood, helped me back into my wheelchair, and wheeled me out to the waiting area to my wife. Mary took one look at me with fresh blood still dripping out of my mouth. She shrieked, "What have you done to my husband? Are you trying to kill him?"

Mary demanded to talk to Dr. Guernsey and told him to look at what this "animal" had done to her severely wounded husband. By this time, the blood had run out of both sides of my mouth and now was slowly dripping down onto the blanket covering me, as if for dramatic emphasis. Guernsey then wheeled me into a treatment room where he examined me further and applied several medicated gauze pads to try and stop the oozing from several places in my gums.

When "Dr. Fat Fingers" tried to come into the room, Dr. Guernsey saw the severe anger on my wife's face and told him to wait for him in his office. He suggested that I allow the jaw to rest during the Christmas holidays and try to gently do the recommended exercises to gain greater opening. They would confer and try to find a better and more appropriate way to proceed.

During the Christmas holidays, different people volunteered to visit the patients who had to remain on the wards at Walter Reed Hospital. Some groups sang carols or popular songs; some shared gifts of candy and other sweet treats; some prayed for our recovery; and some came just to talk and give us encouragement. I particularly remember one little seven-year-old girl, her older brother, and her mother. The little girl quietly tiptoed into my room and gently touched my left arm. She thanked me for my service in Vietnam and wished me a very Merry Christmas. As I turned to thank her, she offered me her little tightly wrapped gift of a stuffed Rudolph the Red-nosed Reindeer surrounded with three packs of Life Savers. She told me that she hoped I would get well soon. The little girl was so sweet and sincere that I could tell that this was not rehearsed, but came straight from her heart. Her mother and brother then chimed in to wish me a Merry Christmas. Mary later described to me the girl's little red, green, and white Christmas outfit with matching hat. She said this visit was totally the little girl's idea. The little girl had used her savings to buy the gifts that she was giving to the wounded soldiers. Tears streamed from my eyes. This caring little girl displayed the true meaning of Christmas.

There were also visits from several ladies from the Daughters of the American Revolution. In the Red Cross lounge, these ladies served refreshments and played Bingo and other games with the patients. Many of the ladies had ties to the military and fully appreciated what we were undergoing as the result of our service and the wounds we had suffered in combat.

One of the best things that happened during this period was my discovery of delicious, flavored milk shakes in the Red Cross lounge, which was open most of the day and night seven days a week. I seemed to have an endless craving for these. Consequently one of my family members would be detailed a couple times each day to bring me either a root beer shake or strawberry milk shake. These shakes were always very thick with good ice cream, never watered down. I can assure you that I finished each one and enjoyed every last drop. Several years later, Mary admitted that they had added eggs and other nutrients to these in an attempt to build me up faster. It was also discovered that my efforts to suck these thick shakes through a straw were very good therapy to exercise my jaw and throat muscles. Who would have thought that drinking my favorite beverage could be so beneficial?

The daily presence of my sister Carolyn, in addition to my wife and parents, was a real blessing during the holidays. Since there was a moratorium on patient appointments during the period of December 24 to December 30, we had plenty of time to relax and concentrate on pleasant memories. The only unpleasantness centered on the fact that we had to stay around the hospital since my condition was still very guarded. I had to remain in bed on the ward. I tried to perform some of the exercises that both the dental service and physical therapists prescribed, as I lay there listening to the conversation among the members of my family. Carolyn and my mother always had an abundant supply of crossword puzzles, which they either clipped out of the daily newspaper or from puzzle books. My mother would sometimes ask for my input to help stimulate my thinking. When she wasn't working one of the puzzles, she would be knitting socks, lap robes, or comforters for the McGuire Veterans Administration Hospital in Richmond, Virginia, where she volunteered her time. Mary too would either work on a puzzle book or on knitting a section of a blanket she was preparing for when I finally got out of Walter Reed Hospital. My mother was ever ready with advice on how to correct any problem that Mary might encounter with her knitting efforts. My father usually had several professional journals he would read, trying to keep up with current conditions in the military or business fields.

On Christmas morning, Mary, Carolyn, and my parents brought a few small packages into my room for an exchange of gifts. I had experienced a very bad night so I was not totally aware of what was going on. The gifts included several new pairs of civilian pajamas. It was a nice change from the heavy, stiffly starched cotton military ones. During the day we received phone calls from Mary's parents, her sister Kathy Ford and husband, John, my Grandfather Haneke, my sister Margaret in Japan, and several other family members. It was great to hear their voices again, cheerfully wishing us a Merry Christmas.

I had been looking forward to the promise of a big Christmas meal and could smell the turkey, sweet potatoes, cranberry sauce, pumpkin pie, etc., as the dietary carts brought the patient trays onto the ward around noon. As the trays reached some of the other patients, I could hear their comments on how good it was to be treated to this wonderful Christmas banquet. This raised my hopes even further. When my tray was finally delivered, Mary and my father uncovered the containers to discover that I had been sent two large containers of split pea soup. In my dietary chart, it stated that I was severely allergic to peas. My father tracked down the dietary aide, exchanged words, and asked her to get a replacement selection that I could tolerate instead of one that would make me violently ill. She said that there was no one left in the kitchen on this holiday, so I would either have to eat what was served or just do without. With that, my father grabbed my tray and immediately went to the dietary department where he was successful in tracking down the head dietitian. He explained the situation. Twenty minutes later, two large, warm containers of the best-tasting turkey soup and a large strawberry milk shake arrived for my Christmas meal.

During the Christmas week, I had a number of incidents that made it necessary for a doctor to remove one or several pieces of shrapnel or debris from several sites in my body. As I became more active with physical therapy exercises, the doctors began to notice through frequent X-rays that a number of fragments were moving slowly from one part of the body to another. My increased muscle usage was causing the pieces of shrapnel to work their way around my body between the layers of muscle fibers without causing damage. The X-rays demonstrated that over a period of months, several larger fragments had moved from my right hip area to my right shoulder. It was further discovered that some of these fragments eventually found a weak place in the skin and worked their way out of my body, while others stayed in one place and my body would encapsulate them in a protective cocoon so they would not further impact it.

Such was the case for a couple larger fragments that are still located in my lungs and left thigh. Several years later, my wife laughingly told some friends that she thought of our bed as "the gravel pit" due to the frequent appearance of sand particles, small pebbles, and small metal fragments that my body seemed to frequently expel.

When I had my next dental appointment after New Year's, Mary stayed with me the whole time. Both doctors Guernsey and Fat Fingers rendered the treatment. Mary noticed that Dr. Fat Fingers had a brace on the little finger of his right hand and asked what had happened to him. Over the holidays, he had been moving a TV set and had accidentally dropped it on his finger, breaking it. This was the first time he had ever suffered severe pain. He now understood my pain. He apologized for his rough treatment and promised to be gentler in the future. Although Mary and I were very skeptical, based on the previous incident, his words proved to be true as he rewired my jaws into an immobile and stable position again. My other appointments with him were gentle and compassionate. I can only conclude that the good Lord sure does work in strange and wonderful ways when getting somebody's full attention.

I had been at Walter Reed Army Hospital for a month. Last time Mary and I celebrated New Year's Eve was on the balcony in Germany right before I was deployed to Vietnam. As we had held onto each other that night, we had wondered silently about our fate. A year had passed. It was 1969, and here we were facing fate at "Walter Wonderful." Mary grasped my left hand and once again we silently wondered about the future.

CHAPTER 29
My Purple Moment

We have troubles all around us, but we are not defeated. We do not know what to do, but we do not give up the hope of living. We are persecuted, but God does not leave us. We are hurt sometimes, but we are not destroyed.... So we do not give up. Our physical body is becoming older and weaker, but our spirit inside us is made new every day. We have small troubles for a while now, but they are helping us gain an eternal glory that is much greater than the troubles. We set our eyes not on what we see but what we cannot see...

2 Corinthians 4:8-9, 16-18

As the end of January 1969 neared, Major Baker came into my room one morning and announced that the hospital commander had given her instructions to clear as many beds as possible since they were anticipating another Tet Offensive in Vietnam and thus a mass influx of severely wounded casualties at Walter Reed. Baker informed me that I would be transported to the McGuire Veterans Affairs Medical Center in Richmond, Virginia, because it offered a more complete and comprehensive array of medical services than any other veterans' hospital in the United States. This worked out great for me since I would need fifteen different services, all of which were either available at McGuire or at its companion institution, Medical College of

Virginia Hospitals. An added benefit was that my parents lived in Richmond.

When I arrived at McGuire Veterans Medical Center via ambulance, I carried with me a thick envelope containing a summary diagnosis, two feet of medical records, X-rays, and other assorted treatment plans that were stacked and bound together. A group of doctors touring my ward my first day there must have noticed the mile-high stack of records because one young-sounding doctor commented, "It looks like we have a real train wreck with this one." An older-sounding man told him that he had just volunteered to study and compose a write-up on my records. This summary was to be presented the next morning during medical rounds. There were several chuckles from other members of the group. The older doctor then introduced himself to me as the head of the department of orthopedic surgery and explained that the others with him were medical interns, residents, and medical students doing their service rotation.

The head doctor performed a brief examination. He was both concerned by the serious nature of my condition yet complimentary of the great care that I had already received. When he finished his exam, he proclaimed that I should not have survived. He directed the head nurse to set up consultations with numerous specialists. The nurse must have complied with his instructions, because the rest of the week was a seemingly endless succession of doctors, nurses, and therapists coming to my bedside to evaluate my status and needs. Fortunately the majority determined that my recovery status had progressed to the point where I would no longer need their service. The doctors in my case took a more conservative approach, which relieved me. One of my prime goals had been to delay aggressive treatment where possible. I hoped and prayed that the medical technology and expertise would evolve to better treat my specific need in the future. This proved very true.

I continued to work very hard in my rehabilitation process to rebuild my strength and coordination. My doctors, nurses, and therapists were so impressed that I was finally allowed to

My Purple Moment

go home on convalescent leave in early April, just after Easter. As I was preparing to leave the hospital, my attending doctor came in and quickly took the entire tracheotomy apparatus out of my throat and covered the remaining hole with a bandage. I thought that the hole would have to be sewn shut. He assured me that it would quickly close on its own. It did.

On April 17, 1969, I put on my green U.S. Army uniform with the help of my father and wife and traveled with my family to attend my army retirement ceremony at McGuire Veterans Medical Center. My father had arranged with his friend Brigadier General John Hines, who was commander of the Defense General Supply Center at Bellwood in Chesterfield County, to conduct my retirement. This was a big event for me, since I was going to do this on crutches, standing for the first time since being wounded. My wife gently guided me, due to my blindness. The aide read the retirement orders, which were classified as a temporary disability retirement. This meant that I would have all of the benefits of a full army retirement but would have up to two years to continue my healing and rehabilitation, within which time I could petition the army to return to active duty. If that petition was not granted, my temporary retirement would become a permanent disability retirement.

I was standing at attention as much as crutches and a missing leg would allow while the orders of retirement were read. General Hines and his aide stood in front of me and pinned on my Combat Infantry Badge, the Bronze Star Medal with V for Valor, a second Bronze Star Medal, the Vietnamese Cross of Gallantry with a Bronze Star, the Vietnamese Service Medal, and the Vietnamese Campaign Medal with Campaign Star. He congratulated me for all of my service and sacrifices. I was then presented a wooden shadowbox with infantry blue background and copies of all of my medals neatly displayed in order. I was absolutely overwhelmed. It was comforting and reassuring to finally be recognized for my combat tour in Vietnam. With my army retirement, I qualified for lifetime health care for my dependents and me, as well as a monthly pension and privileges for the commissary and PX at every American military post in the world. We were pleased.

Army retirement ceremony: Mary (wife), Cpt. William G. Haneke, Marion (mother), Major General William C. Haneke (father)

For the rest of April and into early May 1969, I continued to stay at my parents' home and was taken daily to appointments at McGuire Veterans Medical Center. One day in the second week of May, I had an appointment with Dr. Steve Smilek in oral surgery. After a few minutes, I sensed that Smilek was looking me over more extensively than usual. He then asked me a few questions about how I had been feeling lately, my appetite, and the color of my bowel movements. I found these queries sort of strange. I mentioned that I had had no appetite for the past several days, and my wife had told me that my stools had gone from gray to white in color. Smilek dismissed himself. I heard him talking quietly with my wife. About fifteen minutes later, he returned and asked me to get back into my wheelchair.

Mary came in and calmly explained that I was being admitted to the gastrointestinal unit, where I would be treated for hepatitis. I suddenly remembered what I was told at Walter Reed. They told me that I had received massive amounts of blood, and if I could get past the six-month timeline, I probably would not develop hepatitis. I realized that the six-month date would be in three days. My stomach churned.

Smilek tried to comfort me and explained that I had classic signs of hepatitis—jaundice, white stools, a yellow-tinted cornea, and a very poor appetite. He said I was going to be quarantined to a special room and bathroom due to my infectious condition. When the admitting physician came to examine me, he told my wife that they would try to keep me stable and comfortable until I passed away. The doctor clearly stated this in my presence, as if I were not there or incapable of making decisions. I asked him what I needed to do to convince them that I would survive and be discharged from the hospital in one week.

A little surprised, he gave a sarcastic laugh as if to say, "You don't have a clue about what you are facing." He responded that I must eat high-protein food, and if I began to lose the jaundice and white stools, I would be allowed to leave the hospital. Again the medical system was trying to write me off and pronounce my demise. This really made me mad. I told Mary to please make sure that I ate all of the food they brought me plus any food provided for after-hours snacks.

My high-protein meals consisted of two large containers of liquid liver accompanied by two straws. The concoction smelled god-awful and was nearly impossible to choke down. Mary said that it looked even worse and caused her to wretch when she first saw and smelled it. Despite its grossness, I was determined to down this mess, because I knew it was very high protein and just might help me in some way. As a captive patient, I literally had no other options. I soon developed a technique where I would hold my breath, suck down the scum, take another breath, and then quickly take a sip of apple juice in an attempt to partially neutralize the noxious and chalky taste. I then needed to spend several minutes recuperating before repeating the process all over again.

On the fourth morning, Mary tracked down the ward dietitian to tell her of the terrible food and request a different menu. The dietitian responded that I had been served a high-protein, liquefied selection at every meal, which fulfilled the hospital's nutritional requirements. By this time, my wife was furious. She grabbed a spoon from my tray, filled it with the liquid liver, and shoved it into the dietitian's mouth. She yelled, "How do you like the taste of that crap?" The dietitian started gagging badly and ran to the nearest bathroom, from which we heard her vomit for several minutes. Mary later told me that when she emerged from the bathroom she was wiping her face with a towel while agreeing that it was the worst-tasting slime. The dietician apologized profusely. She marched my tray directly to the kitchen, and twenty minutes later she returned with two containers of hot chicken soup and two cups of vanilla ice cream. The dietician again apologized and stated that their dietary plan policy would change to involve patient input. I never got liver again, thankfully.

On the eighth day after my admission, I was no longer infectious with hepatitis and the doctor approved my discharge from the hospital. He said it was nothing short of a miracle.

Two years later my skull defect in the left eye socket and surrounding skull area was finally resolved with the surgical insertion of a cranial plastic plate by the neurosurgeons back at Walter Reed Army Medical Center. Dr. Hammond, the same surgeon that performed my two initial neurosurgery procedures at the 24th Evacuation Hospital in Vietnam, led the team of physicians. A strong metal mesh grid to rebuild the eye socket filled the area where the skull had been blown away. On top of this grid, they added a layer of strong, quick-setting plastic that they molded symmetrically to closely approximate the shape of the normal eye socket and skull.

Dr. Smilek's exam revealed that some good healing of my wired jaw had begun, so there was hope. Over a period of three years, the jaw did heal. There were a number of surgeries and the installation of a gold crown bridge on all of my remaining bottom teeth. These crowns were all soldered together, which stabilized the bottom jaw after all wires had been removed. Anchored to this bridge were seven artificial teeth to complete the full set necessary to be able to eat normally. After five years of dental procedures, I was finally able to eat normal food again.

Treatment and rehabilitation with the orthopedic and physical medicine and rehabilitation services involved regaining strength and a full range of motion in my limbs. This eventually evolved to ambulatory training beginning with under-arm crutches then advancing to Canadian forearm crutches for better balance and mobility. Finally I was fitted with a temporary prosthesis for my right leg. The initial prosthesis had a thick plaster suction socket, a hydraulic knee joint to more closely approximate a natural knee, and a rubberized and flexible foot. The rest of the leg was made out of wood with a cloth waist belt for greater stability. The total weight of the finished limb was about seventy pounds. At the time I was fitted with my first leg, I only weighed about ninety pounds, so it was a real chore to lift it, put it on, and walk. On the plus side, using it helped me build up my strength and conditioning at a faster rate. In a short time, I was able to progress to the point where I no longer needed my crutches.

Over the years, I utilized my engineering training to assist the medical system by testing newer and more advanced limb concepts to determine their feasibility and ease of operation from a user's standpoint. Some of these turned out to be very good and others were not at all feasible. My current prosthesis has evolved over a thirty-eight-year period from the heavy and uncomfortable limb to one that weighs less than five pounds. It has no wood but extra strong space-age metals, a flexible vinyl socket, an adjustable hydraulic knee joint, and a flexible foot that returns energy to the leg, making it much easier to operate.

My total loss of eyesight posed the biggest hurdle to my rehabilitation. When I arrived at McGuire Veterans Medical Center, Dr. Walter Gearetts, Dr. Dupont Guerry, and Dr. Davis Wyatt, three prominent ophthalmologists, took over my eye treatment. In the spring of 1972, these ophthalmologists decided I was ready to have a cataract removed from my right eye. Dr. Gearetts gave me a general anesthetic, and when I regained consciousness after the operation, I heard Gearetts' voice. He removed my bandages and asked if I could see any light. I allowed my eye to adjust for a moment and told him that not only could I see light, but I could see what appeared to be someone in a white coat standing in front of me with a dark green background behind him.

Gearetts got very excited. He told me not to move and that he would be back in a minute. When he returned, he had a metal frame with adjustable lenses. Carefully, he put them on me, made some adjustments, and again asked me to tell him what I saw. I told him that everything was a bit fuzzy, but I could see him in his white coat with a dark green wall behind him, and someone in a light blue outfit standing off to his left. He then made a couple further adjustments, stood back, and asked me to describe what I saw. I told him that he had gray hair and was in a white coat and his red-colored nametag indicated that he was Gearetts. The walls of the room were painted dark green and the lovely lady in the blue outfit was my wife, Mary. I also noticed that there was a nurse standing in the doorway. Gearetts was so excited that he had tears streaming down his face, as did with my wife.

Gearetts took a few minutes to compose himself. He admitted that neither he nor Guerry had given me much of a chance to regain my sight. During the surgery there were a couple things that happened that made him feel as if God were guiding his hands and mind through the procedure. For example, they had only been able to locate two points of adhesion on the cataract and knew that there had to be at least one other. The surgeons had to locate all of the points to prevent pulling the cataract off with all the "strings" still attached to the retina. If that happened, the retina would be ripped off, and I would become permanently blind. As they were clipping the second point, the whole cataract curled back slightly, revealing two other points. He said that he had never seen this happen before, but it allowed him to safely and successfully complete the cataract removal. Gearetts couldn't be happier with the result. My vision would be correctible to 20-30 through bifocals. These glasses were my key to gaining complete independence and learning how to drive a car again.

My pursuit of being granted full disability benefits with the Veterans Administration took a lot of twists and turns before being permanently granted. Since their administration wouldn't automatically accept the evaluations and decisions the Department of the Army renders, I was required to have each of my group of physicians submit their evaluations of my health. After three months, I received a letter from the Department of Veterans Affairs confirming the fact that I had been granted full benefits with the veterans system as a 100-percent service-connected disabled veteran. This included a monthly pension with lifetime medical care for my dependents and me. The package also included vocational rehabilitation education, housing assistance to accommodate my physical needs, assistance to adapt my automobile needs, provision of any needed medical appliances (artificial limbs, crutches, canes, wheelchairs, special shoes, braces, etc.), and an annual clothing allowance to provide for needed repairs of clothing worn and/or torn by exposure to my prosthesis. Shortly thereafter, I also received a letter from the Department of Health and Human Services verifying that I had been approved for a Social Security disability grant. This was accompanied by a check for that monthly amount plus a six-month retroactive payment to the actual date of application for the benefit. The monthly pension would continue until

I was able to return to full-time employment. It appeared that our needs were finally being taken care of from these grants and associated benefits.

That euphoria was short-lived. Exactly thirteen months after the date I was wounded, I received a letter from the Veterans Administration stating that all of my benefits had been overturned. I was no longer eligible for any assistance through the veterans system. This came as a shock. Since we had waived my army retired pay to receive full veterans' benefits, we now were unsure where we would get enough money on which to live. Mary immediately called the veterans help line and was told that I would have to attend a meeting with the Veterans Medical Review Board. To prepare for this meeting, I again contacted all of my physicians to write a health status review and recommendation. They all stated that my disabilities were highly debilitating, and consequently my full disability benefits should be permanently restored.

A Disabled American Veterans (DAV) representative joined me as my veteran assistance representative, while my father had agreed to drive me to the meeting in Roanoke. When we arrived at the Veterans Administration regional office, we were led into a large conference room where my father, the DAV representative, and I were put at one end of a large conference table. At the other end were a general physician, a social welfare worker, and a VA administrative expert. I arrived in a wheelchair without my prosthesis, hoping that this would call greater attention to my disabilities. I explained why I was there and invited these three men to review the stack of physician letters of recommendation. I could hear the men leafing through the papers in front of them and, after a few minutes, their spokesman, the administrative expert, stated that from what they could see, they found no reason to reverse their decision to rescind my benefits.

I had a suspicion that the physician had not examined a patient in twenty years, and that his only performance was to review medicals and applications for benefits. Relying on my sixth sense, I asked the panel to pick out two of my doctors' letters and read them aloud. After they had done this, I asked them to explain, in layman's terms, what exactly these words meant. None of them were able to decipher the letters, indicating that they were unable to comprehend the bulk of the technical medical information they routinely processed. I tried to explain the content of these letters in detail. They soon cut me off, stating that these would have no influence on the proceedings.

As a last resort, I took off my shoe and sock and placed my severely mangled half foot on the conference table. I then removed my trousers, revealing a pair of shorts and the thirteen-inch stump where my right leg had been blown off. The finale was the removal of the plastic conformer from the socket where my eye had been blown out. I then asked if any of these "gentlemen" would entrust me with their car and see how far I could drive down Campbell Avenue outside the regional office. I got no takers and the meeting ended without the committee reversing their decision or the DAV representative making any statement on my behalf.

On the trip home, my father and I agreed that we had done everything reasonable within the system to appeal this unreasonable decision. The next step would be to contact my congressman and request an investigation into my case and ask that my veterans' benefits be fully and permanently restored. Otherwise I would have no means of income or surviving. To my advantage, Mary and I still had her parents' home in Scarsdale, New York, as our legal address. This meant that Representative Ogden Reid, one of the most liberal members of the House of Representatives, was our congressman.

Mary and my father wrote Mr. Reid a letter requesting his assistance. A day later we received a call from his top administrative assistant asking for the details of my case and the situation with the Veterans Administration. Three days later we got a letter from the secretary of Veterans Affairs apologizing for the mistake. They fully restored my disability benefits, permanently, with the Veterans Administration. We also received a nice letter from Representative Ogden Reid explaining that his inquiry had resulted in the decision to restore the benefits. He added that the loss of these benefits had been started by a VA GS-2 file clerk, who was tired of lugging around my thick file of medical records. The clerk told her boss that all of my disabilities had become "permanently corrected." Needless to say, the clerk was fired from the Veterans Administration.

My next debate with the Veterans Administration was taking advantage of the VA disabled benefits. I began with my request for vocational training in the health care field. Following the submission of my education application, I was assigned a vocational counselor to interview and test me. He made note of my earned bachelor of science from West Point and additional courses from the army. Next he had me take a vocational interest test followed by an intelligence test. After grading my interest test, he stated that it indicated I was interested and qualified for a career in either military or business management. This came as no surprise since that was the field I had been working in since my admission to West Point in July 1961.

I told the counselor that I would no longer be allowed to work in the military because of my severe combat wounds. I would prefer to enroll in a college graduate study program as a health care administrator. He would not approve my enrollment, because I had received marginal grades at the U.S. Military Academy. I tried to point out that, as a cadet, I had been carrying a heavy academic load, military training, and physical aptitude training. He said that this didn't matter because I had not demonstrated ability to do graduate-level work. The session ended with the counselor stating that he would look into vocational training for a public service job that he thought would be true to my abilities.

My wife wrote a letter of appeal to the regional office administrator requesting that a new vocational counselor handle my case. After a brief conversation, Mary and I agreed that I should enroll in a graduate-level course at a local college to prove my ability to handle this level of work. By the end of the week, I was enrolled in a master's degree-level management accounting course at the University of Richmond night college. I paid the tuition and all costs out of my own pocket.

Before my first scheduled class, Mary and I were able to meet with the professor. As a blind student, I would be allowed to tape every class and have any illustrations presented on the blackboard or exhibited in class carefully explained so that I could understand them on the tape. This worked out great. The entire class was very supportive of my needs, and of me. I ended the first semester with an "A." When the new vocational counselor heard about this grade, she granted me permission and support to enroll in a program to get a master's degree in health care administration. After completing two required undergraduate business courses, I enrolled in graduate school at the Medical College of Virginia School of Health Care Administration.

The first year of graduate school was primarily classroom education, while I spent the second year in an administrative residency. I was selected to spend my residency at Medical College of Virginia Hospital (MCVH), a 1,058-bed medical-teaching hospital. By the start of the second semester, one of the MCVH assistant administrators had accepted a new job, so I was offered the chance to serve in his position for the rest of my residency. The administrative job put me in charge of many departments that employed a combined staff of 750 professional and non-professional employees with a total budget of $15 million. This residency turned out to be a great learning experience and allowed me to visit every department and ward in the hospital. I talked about patient care and hospital activities with every staff member, and listened to their stories. I also shared my ideas for patient care from a patient's perspective with many of these health care professionals. They all mentioned that they appreciated this new perspective on care.

In May 1975, I was awarded my master's degree in health care administration at the Virginia Commonwealth University and Medical College of Virginia. I returned to MCVH, where I assumed my new job as an assistant hospital administrator responsible for the same and additional departments as my residency.

My severe injuries from Vietnam had rendered me a permanent casualty. Walking into my office, I took pride in having overcome the odds. I was finally home from the war.

When I first arrived in Vietnam, I was told to "trust not a soul." I did, however, trust God. After all the suffering and sacrifices I had undergone since that fateful explosion in November 1968, I often wondered why God spared me from death. I was always sure that I was being saved and prepared for some greater purpose. In early 2005, this purpose began to unfold and present a unique opportunity. In Christian churches, Epiphany, the revealing of Jesus as the Christ to the gentiles, is represented by the color purple. Epiphany can also refer to insight or an experience to bring something about. My "purple moment" happened one Saturday morning at Bob Evan's Restaurant in Richmond, Virginia.

It started, seemingly, by accident. A small group of military veterans meet at Bob Evan's for breakfast several Saturday mornings each month. This is a great opportunity to have fellowship and swap "war stories" from our years of military service. One particular Saturday, two bedraggled looking young women came into the restaurant, each carrying a baby. One woman had tears streaming down her face and appeared on the verge of becoming hysterical. Two of the veterans went over to them to see if they could help out in any way. The tearful woman explained that she had just driven two days straight from Texas to visit her husband, a U.S. Marine, who had been wounded in combat operations in Iraq. He had just arrived at McGuire Veterans Medical Center in Richmond for treatment. Her car had run out of gas in the parking lot at the hospital, plus she had run out of money. The young woman had not eaten since she left Texas, but she was more concerned about being unable to buy formula and diapers for her baby.

The second woman had driven to Richmond from Massachusetts to see her husband, a U.S. Army Specialist who had been wounded in Afghanistan and was now at McGuire

Veterans Medical Center, too. Her story was similar to that of the tearful woman except she had half a tank of gas in her car and five dollars left in her pocket. She was also concerned for her baby and mentioned that neither of them had any place to stay and the McGuire staff was unable to give them assistance.

By this time, the rest of the veterans had come over and were filled in on the situation. They all pitched in and bought breakfast for the women, took them to buy baby supplies, paid for a motel room for a week, and handed them plenty of cash for food and other expenses. The two women were most appreciative and felt blessed to have stumbled on some veterans who understood their predicament.

Later that day, I got a call from Pat O'Hare and Cal Esleeck, two members of the "Breakfast Bunch." That particular morning I had not been present, so they told me the story about the two young women. They asked me to check with McGuire Veterans Medical Center to see if there was any way to get housing and financial support for the family caregivers of these wounded soldiers. Pat and Cal knew that I had spent time in that same hospital helping patients and family members as well as receiving periodic treatment in several clinics. I was McGuire's "poster boy" for successful rehabilitation. I told them that I would look into it. I remembered and reflected on the importance of family support during my recovery and rehab some years ago.

In February of 2005, I reached the appropriate staff members at McGuire Veterans Medical Center and explained the housing, food, and financial situation for family members of the wounded soldiers from Iraq and Afghanistan. The staff agreed that there was a need but that they could not provide support because these wounded soldiers were all still on military active duty. Talking to family members at the hospital, I soon discovered that almost all of them had given up a job back home to care for their spouse or family member. Roughly half of the normal family income was gone. Seeing their situation from a former patient's view, I understood the importance of family during the recovery process. Something needed to be done immediately.

I called Cal Esleeck and relayed my grim findings. We got together and made a few calls to other veterans in the area to try to muster support for these families. We soon had U.S. Navy Pilot Paul Galanti, Gunnery Sergeant Bill Lylle, Cal Esleeck, Jim DeMent, Chip Houston, and me. We all agreed to go to McGuire to help these families.

It quickly became apparent that we didn't have the funds or organization to adequately handle the growing groups of families. We recruited some additional people and formed a board of directors, registered with the Virginia State Corporation Commission, and were granted our 501(C) 3 charitable tax status for what we called the "Families of the Wounded, Inc." Our donations to these family caregivers started at twenty-five dollars and a free pizza or a batch of cookies, to gradually providing financial help of $6,000 per family.

Each time I watch them tearfully accept our gifts, I am reminded of my path. God spared my life to serve and extend a helping hand to others like myself.

Epilogue

News trickled back to me during my recovery. I learned that Major Dramis was treated and quickly rehabilitated from his injuries in the military medical system. He was able to remain on active duty in the U.S. Army until his retirement. The "foo-gas" drum that Major Dramis and I were attempting to move had remained intact. The drum was emplaced in the defensive perimeter at the left rear corner of the Hoa Da District Compound. One night, Vietcong attackers breached the outer lines of barbed-wire fencing. The American advisors detonated the "foo-gas" drums, killing at least twenty-five Vietcong. This demoralized the rest of the attackers, causing them to break off their assault. This was the payback for our wounds.

The Hoa Da District advisory team was without a commander after Major Dramis and I were wounded. The MACV Headquarters decided to close the compound at Luong Son. The advisors and CIDG companies moved to Hoa Da District Compound to replace the Cambodian mercenaries, who were transferred elsewhere. Major Dufort then became the district senior advisor at the newly constructed Hoa Da District Advisory Compound. We founders of the Hoa Da District advisory team had performed all of the hard work of getting this advisory effort established, organized, and effectively working. Consequently Major Dufort and his team did not have to start from scratch.

The Pacific Architects and Engineers team who built the new facility was led by my father's Korean friend, whom I had met in Nha Trang. The advisory compound remained in operation until the United States evacuated Vietnam in 1973.

Major Xuan was not as fortunate. He had remained as the Hoa Da District chief until the North Vietnamese troops occupied all of South Vietnam in 1973. He and his staff were captured and placed in one of the North Vietnamese "re-education camps," where they all died. Major Xuan was a true Vietnamese patriot and soldier who dearly loved his country. He served his homeland well in his long military career, resisting the Japanese and the French before succumbing to the Vietnamese Communist Forces.

In January 1991, I attended a Vietnam Veterans Tet '68 Victory Celebration and Reunion in Richmond. As I was looking at several displays, I came across a lady asking for donations to the proposed Vietnam Women Veterans Memorial. She mentioned that she was a nurse assigned to the 24th Evacuation Hospital in Long Binh, Vietnam, from 1968 to 1969.

I then asked the million-dollar question. "What service were you assigned to?" She responded, "Neurosurgery."

Tears fell from my eyes. I cleared my throat and said, "Oh, my God! You were my nurse." I quickly told her a few details about my case and the arterial graft for my carotid artery. She gasped and asked if my sister was a WAC officer who came from Japan to visit me. I nodded. The lady gave me a big hug and said that she was Lt. Cathie Henderson Solomonson, the nurse who took care of me. We exchanged phone numbers and addresses.

Several weeks later, I received a call from Cathie inviting me to the first reunion for the 24th Evacuation Hospital staff. It was held at the Mayflower Hotel in Washington, DC, in July 1991. I was very excited and honored to be reunited with these fine health professionals. Present were Cathie Henderson Solomonson, Mary Lou Knable Brown, Dr. William Hammond, Dr. George Lavenson, Dr. Donald Brief, Dr. Calvin W. Thompson, Dr. Paul Harkins, and Chaplain Bert Carmichael, and other nurses. It was

Epilogue

the first time I had been able to *literally* see them. I had the privilege of expressing my sincere thanks and appreciation for all the dedication and professional expertise the medical staff gave me. There was not a dry eye in the entire group after I finished my tribute to them. I just wanted to thank God and them for saving my life.

Cathie Henderson Solomonson, Cpt. Tom Barnett, and 24th EVAC nurses.

Cpt. William G. Haneke (wheelchair) with the 24th Evacuation team at reunion.

After receiving my master's degree in health care administration, I worked in several hospitals as a health care administrator and served for over twenty-five years on boards of directors for a variety of organizations responsible for the health services and welfare of patients and disabled clients. My marriage to Mary lasted thirty-one years, and I am eternally grateful for all her love, support, and intercession on my behalf with the medical professionals throughout my lengthy period of treatment and rehabilitation. Without her, I would not have survived this complex process. Together we raised four children: William, Kathleen, Jean, and Brian. Eventually, Mary and I went our separate ways. In October 1998, I married Karen Sue Miller who has provided me constant love, spiritual support, and direction in writing my memoirs.

On July 4, 2008, at the 117th DAR Continental Congress held at DAR Constitution Hall in Washington, DC, Daughters of the American Revolution President General Linda Gist Calvin presented the DAR National Outstanding Veteran Award to Cpt. William G. Haneke for the creation of Families of the Wounded Fund, Inc, and for his compassion in helping recently wounded soldiers and their families. In August 2010, Cpt. Haneke was appointed by Virginia Governor Robert McDonnell to serve a four-year term on the Virginia Board of Veterans Services as vice-chairman.

DAR President General Linda Gist Calvin presents Cpt. William G. Haneke the D.A.R. National Outstanding Veteran Award from the 117th Daughters of American Revolution Congressional Congress.

Epilogue

Members of the West Point Class of 1966: Secretary of Veterans Affairs, Dr. James B. Peake; Cpt. William G. Haneke; Dr. John P. Wheeler, III; and Secretary of the Air Force, The Honorable Michael W. Wynne, surround DAR President General Linda Gist Calvin.

Trust in the Lord with all your heart; and lean not unto your own understanding. In all your ways acknowledge Him, and He shall direct your path. Proverbs 3:5-6

List of Abbreviations

AID	Agency for International Development
ARVN	Army of the Republic of Vietnam (South Vietnamese RegularArmy)
AWOL	Absent Without Official Leave
BAR	Browning Automatic Rifle
CIA	Central Intelligence Agency
DAV	Disabled American Veterans
EOD	Explosive Ordnance Disposal
ENT	Ear, Nose, and Throat
IFFV	1st Field Force Command-Vietnam (combined I Corps and II Corps)
HE	High Explosive
H & I	Harassment and Interdiction
MAT	Mobile Advisory Team
MACV	Military Assistance Command Vietnam
MEDCAP	Medical Civil Action Program
NCO	Non-Commissioned Officer
POW	Prisoner of War
PRU	Provincial Reconnaissance Unit
ROTC	Reserved Officer Training Corps

CPSIA information can be obtained
at www.ICGtesting.com
Printed in the USA
BVHW041807150121
597965BV00019B/478